OWL

# WOMEN, WRITING,
## AND THE
## INDUSTRIAL REVOLUTION

# SUSAN ZLOTNICK

# Women, Writing, and the Industrial Revolution

The Johns Hopkins University Press

Baltimore and London

© 1998 The Johns Hopkins University Press
All rights reserved. Published 1998
Printed in the United States of America on acid-free paper
9  8  7  6  5  4  3  2  1

The Johns Hopkins University Press
2715 North Charles Street, Baltimore, Maryland 21218-4319
The Johns Hopkins Press Ltd., London
www.press.jhu.edu

Library of Congress Cataloging-in-Publication Data will be found
at the end of this book.
A catalog record for this book is available from the British Library.

ISBN 0-8018-5829-1

# CONTENTS

# ACKNOWLEDGMENTS

THIS BOOK began as a dissertation at the University of Pennsylvania, under the direction of Elaine Scarry, whose gentle but scrupulous guidance helped shape the manuscript and whose remarkable faith in the project sustained my own enthusiasm for it. It also benefited enormously from the readings given it by David J. DeLaura, whose thinking on Victorian prose writers has influenced me since my undergraduate days. In addition, I am grateful to Penn for the travel fellowship that enabled me to spend a year researching in Great Britain and for the writing fellowship that enabled me to complete the dissertation on my return.

At Penn and at Vassar I have been lucky in my friends, who have made the lonely business of researching and writing considerably less so. Over the years, they have become my intellectual community, and the book bears their imprint. Kim Hall, Alison Byerly, and Steve Jensen were as integral to my graduate school education as fifty-book exams and field lists; nevertheless, they were (and remain) notably more fun. Leslie Dunn, Peter Antelyes, Donna Heiland, Ellen Martin, and Margaret Fusco transformed Poughkeepsie from a seeming blank into an unlikely home. Two of my senior colleagues at Vassar, Beth Darlington and Lynn Bartlett, deserved special thanks for their kind, unobtrusive mentoring and for reminding me that a life worth living has both love and work in it. To Uma Narayan I owe debts both intellectual and personal, as I have uniquely profited from her gifts for theory making and matchmaking; for her friendship, as well as Jim Hill's Yankee hospitality, I am deeply grateful. John Stouter's careful review of the final draft was invaluable for the clean logic it brought to some muddy patches. More vitally, however, he has transformed my life into something rich and sweet, and everyday he surprises me with the love I did not even know I needed.

I would like to acknowledge Vassar College for its support of this project and particularly for the generous leave policy that allowed me to complete it. Vassar also made possible the student assistants who provided crucial and much-appreciated help at various stages in the book's evolution.

Many thanks go to Willis Regier, of the Johns Hopkins University Press, for shepherding both the manuscript and me through the publication process with great compassion and humor, and to the manuscript's reader, Anna Clark, for her timely, enthusiastic response and for challenging me to think more historically.

Finally, this book could not have been written without the reassuring affection of my parents, Elaine and Jerry, my brother Robert and sister-in-law Suzanne, and my nephews David and Joshua. In particular, my parents have been bedrocks of support during the long years it took to complete this project, and through it all they nourished me with their undaunted optimism that everything would work out fine in the end. For these reasons and others, I dedicate this book to them as well as to the memory of my grandparents, Samuel and Rose Starin, who always encouraged me to read, to think, and to argue.

Portions of my second chapter appeared, in a somewhat different form, under the title "Luddism, Medievalism, and Women's History in *Shirley:* Charlotte Brontë's Revisionist Tactics," in *Novel: A Forum on Fiction* 24.3 (1991). Copyright NOVEL Corp. 1991. Reprinted with permission. Sections of my fourth chapter appeared, also in a somewhat different form, under the title " 'A Thousand Times I'd be a Factory Girl': Dialect, Domesticity, and Working-Class Women's Poetry," in *Victorian Studies* 35 (1991). Reprinted by permission of the Trustees of Indiana University.

# WOMEN, WRITING,

## AND THE

# INDUSTRIAL REVOLUTION

# INTRODUCTION

THE INDUSTRIAL revolution was a fiction, one of the main discursive events of the nineteenth century. Such a statement is not intended as a denial of the profound social and material transformations that occurred in Britain over the past two centuries, but as a reminder that those transformations were not given a local habitation and a name until the 1880s.[1] For British men and women living in the first half of the nineteenth century, what came to be called the industrial revolution was not a self-explanatory development, but one that required and generated many explanations in the form of treatises, pamphlets, inquiries, essays, articles, poems, plays, and novels. If the industrialization of Great Britain occurred in factories and mines, the industrial revolution took place on paper. When Thomas Carlyle asked in *Past and Present*, "This English nation, will it get to know the meaning of *its* strange new Today?" (7), he merely gave the most precise formulation to a question raised by all the writers who reflected on the significance of infant industrialism. Carlyle's own analyses of England's "strange new Today" proved enormously authoritative, but as each writer reimagined the industrial revolution in light of his or her own experience within Britain's class and gender formations, there arose a variety of competing and contradictory answers.

This book's main contention is that the female and male literary response to the industrial revolution was Janus-faced: while women writers were more likely to look to the future with hope, male writers frequently longed for an idealized (and often medievalized) past. Of course, this book does not argue that all Victorian men who wrote about the industrial revolution disowned it. Surely many nineteenth-century British men embraced what Harold Perkin calls the "entrepreneurial ideal," with its emphasis on self-help, competition, and social and technological progress. But the male critics of industrial modernity who have entered the literary canon—Carlyle, Ruskin, Disraeli, Dickens, and Arnold—repudiated its core values; and their repudiation is matched by that found in the working-class male canon of Chartist and dialect writings. Nor does this book argue that all Victorian women applauded the startling transformations taking place around them. But it does argue that the middle-class women novelists who took Victorian industrialism as their subject did not renounce it after the male fashion. Certainly the two most celebrated women writers who addressed Carlyle's condition-of-England question to puzzle out the meaning of the strange new today, Elizabeth Gaskell and Charlotte Brontë, more readily welcomed the factory world, with all its concomitant social dislocations, than did their male counterparts. And even the female critics of the manufacturing districts who wrote the earliest factory novels, Frances Trollope and Charlotte Elizabeth Tonna, accepted industrial modernity as a prelude to repairing it.

Thus, the antimodern stance that historians have come to identify as one of the defining elements of contemporary Britain has its roots in a distinctly male repudiation of modernity. In the middle decades of the nineteenth century, British national culture embraced an image of itself that exalted the rural and conservative values of the preindustrial world. Put simply, the first industrialized nation embarked upon a course that ultimately led to the rejection of the modernity it spawned. The entrepreneurial ideal never achieved hegemonic status, and Britain emerged in the twentieth century as a nation renowned for revering traditions—as a country seemingly dedicated to the pursuit of quaintness—because its middle classes failed to establish the industrial spirit as the centerpiece of the national culture.[2]

In contemporary Britain, this antimodernism takes the form of what Robert Hewison designates the "heritage industry," where proliferating historical sites, preservation trusts, and museums crowd the social landscape. Writing in the late 1980s, Hewison judged his nation to be "obsessed with its past, and unable to face its future" (9). Hewison's sense of a national crisis of nostalgia is reinforced by Patrick Wright, who noted on returning to England in 1979 after a long absence that he felt as if he had "stumbled inadvertently into some sort of anthropological museum" (1). Perhaps the final irony of the heritage industry is that even Britain's industrial inheritance has become grist for nostalgia's mill. Hewison describes a visit to the Wigan Pier Heritage Centre, where visitors can stroll through a (simulated) mine and then pay a condolence visit to a bereaved miner's family, played by actors inhabiting historical roles: "Kitty [the miner's daughter] opens the back door to her father's cottage, shrugs up her shawl, and in assumed Wigan accents asks if we have come to pay our respects. She brings us in, and explains that her father was crushed in a roof fall a month before, but died out of the pit, 'so there's no compensation.' The coffin is closed because he didn't look too good when he died. The gas mantle is burning above the coffin and the atmosphere is oppressive" (18). As visitors to the Wigan Pier Heritage Centre head off to the Orwell Pub after their interactions with Kitty, they can ponder the fact that the only thing being produced these days in Wigan—where the relics of Britain's industrial age, its mills and mines, stand empty and idle—is the past itself.

Nostalgic appreciations of the national past are so deeply embedded in the British consciousness that, up until only a few decades ago, even academic historians had to remind their readers that the old days were not necessarily the good days. Peter Laslett prefaces his influential study of early modern English society with the following disclaimer: "The world we have lost . . . was no paradise or golden age of equality, tolerance or loving kindness. It is so important that I should not be misunderstood on this point that I will say at once that the coming of industry cannot be shown to have brought economic oppression and exploitation along with it. It was there already" (3). Despite its seeming banality, Laslett's assertion that the world predating the industrial revolution was not a utopia of contented peasants is a telling one: the fact that he felt obliged to disavow, in such emphatic terms, the mythology of Merry Old England underscores the degree to which nostalgia has become fossilized in the bedrock of British culture. But then, given that Laslett's reading audience might have included men such as Harold Macmillan, the former Tory prime minister, who was still insisting as late as 1981 that "the Victorian age was simply an interruption in Britain's history" (qtd. in Briggs, "Victorian Values" 11), Laslett's preface no doubt performed a great public service.

While Macmillan repudiated the nineteenth century and the modernity it heralded, his conservative successor, Margaret Thatcher, was famous for her nostalgic invocations of Victorian values, by which she meant the industrial spirit that Britain had to a large extent rejected. The values Thatcher upheld had "more in common with the values of mid-Victorian liberalism of a radical persuasion," Asa Briggs observes, than with those of " 'traditional' toryism—or of Disraeli's toryism" ("Victorian Values" 12). Indeed, Thatcher's critics were quick to associate the Iron Lady with the worst excesses of nineteenth-century capitalism, as this gloriously splenetic attack by Jeffrey Richards makes evident:

> Thatcherite post-industrial Britain has become the mirror-image of early Industrialisation when, unrestrained by conscience or regulation, there was an upsurge of snobbery, self-interest, rampant individualism, philistinism and social divisiveness. It was against these unpleasant realities of 19th-century life that the great Victorians, the sages and prophets, the statesmen and reformers, the idealists and men of letters, set themselves, castigating, satirising, and seeking to eradicate them. Whether it was Gladstone or Disraeli, Dickens or Shaftsbury, Ruskin or Carlyle, Tennyson or Arnold, General Gordon or General Booth, their theme was (with individual and characteristic variations) a rejection of and an attack upon all those aspects of life to which Thatcherism conduces. (76)

While I do not wish to simplify Thatcher's legacy, I find it suggestive that Britain's first female prime minister repudiated the (male) repudiation of modernity, beautifully captured here in Richards's all-male list of "great Victorians." And in this regard, Thatcher finds herself the ideological bedfellow of women like Elizabeth Gaskell and Charlotte Brontë. To be sure, Gaskell and Brontë never advocated the sins of nineteenth-century life that Richards associates with Thatcherism, but all three women embraced the abstract mechanisms of the marketplace for their liberating possibilities.[3]

The recent revolutions of Thatcherism notwithstanding, England's industrial heritage has not been embraced with the same fervor as its more picturesque, preindustrial past. It is Macmillan's dismissal of Victorian values rather than Thatcher's celebration of them that best exemplifies England's response to its industrial past throughout most of this century. Indeed, Macmillan's scripting of industrialism as an "interruption" in British history belongs to a tradition reaching back to the mid-nineteenth century, when industrial capitalism came to be represented as essentially foreign to British culture (Wiener). Certainly Thomas Carlyle's *Past and Present* connects industrialism, or at least its most severe abuses, with an alien barbarism: Carlyle even figures England's unregenerate mill owners as "Chactaw Indians" and scathingly compares the industrialists' "hundred thousand-pound bills" to the "hundred scalps hung-up" in an Indian wigwam (272). Taking the alien aspect of industrialism one step further, Charles Dickens imaginatively transforms Coketown, his paradigmatic mill town, into a colonial possession dominated by savages, serpents, and elephants and thus represents the industrial city as a place that would benefit from the civilizing mission of the British empire.

The male literary tradition, exemplified above by Carlyle and Dickens, envisions the industrial world as another country, a place overrun with satanic mills, Manchester slums, and Dickensian waifs. But it is important to remember that the industrial revolution—on paper—occurred not only in places like Coketown but also in factory towns like Elizabeth Gaskell's Milton-Northern, a mill town that is Miltonic because it embodies Gaskell's vision of the fall into modernity as a fortunate one. Only by being attuned to each factory town as an imaginary landscape can we begin to apprehend and appreciate the vital differences between them.

Assuredly, this book never aims to show that either the male or the female literary response to emergent industrialism more closely approximates the elusive, unobtainable historical "truth" of Britain's industrial revolution. Instead, it aims for the more modest and attainable goal of tracing out how the industrial revolution—and the modernity it heralded—was imagined and reimagined over the course of the century. It privileges imaginative literature as an object of study because the literary texts of the industrial revolution performed important ideological work for the Victorians, and they continue to perform it by representing the world of nineteenth-century industrialism to contemporary readers. When Carlyle asked the meaning of the "strange new Today," he was essentially asking his fellow writers to participate in the discursive shaping of a new Victorian reality by inventing an interpretive framework through which the indeterminacy of early industrialism could be allayed. So to take up industrial texts as if they were blue books with plots is to misread them because neither blue books nor novels provide transparent accounts of an undisputed industrial reality. What all the writings of the industrial revolution—from essays and poems to parliamentary debates—offer are competing representations of an emerging, contested reality that was in the process of being constructed through their agency.

Of course, the traffic between a literary text and its historical context runs on a two-way street, and the literary response to the industrial revolution was itself shaped by larger discourses about politics, economics, religion, and other social matters. Recent critical studies by Catherine Gallagher and Rosemarie Bodenheimer have asked readers to approach the relationship between industrial texts and their Victorian contexts with renewed sophistication.[4] But whereas these investigations trace out the connections between literary form and social discourses, my work eschews formal analysis for a more straightforward cultural one. It takes up the novel, the poem, the essay as a cultural artifact and uses it to anatomize one of the most important inventions of the nineteenth century—not the power loom or the railroad, but the Victorian "invention" of the industrial revolution.

Mary Poovey observes in her most recent work, *Making a Social Body*, that "it makes a difference to treat history-writing and textual analysis as facets of a single enterprise" (1). That "single enterprise" is the study of culture, and the difference it particularly makes for this project is enormous. For when we place the traditional materials of the historian (parliamentary reports, Chartist newspapers) next to those of the literary critic, the centrality of gender to the literature of the industrial revolution suddenly appears to be incontrovertible. The significance of gender was without doubt incontrovertible to Victorian observers of the factories. Because the early textile mills employed large numbers of young women, industrial labor became associated with a radical reversal of "natural" gender roles, a brave new world characterized by female employment and male unemployment. The first citizen of this new world was the independent, wage-earning factory girl, who emerged as a blank screen on which the Victorians projected their own fears and hopes for modernity. As a result, the social chaos that many Victorians attributed to the factory system throughout the 1830s and 1840s was frequently scripted as sexual anarchy, and this fact can get obscured by a narrow focus on the "great" novels and essays written by the towering figures of the literary canon. Insisting on the gendered nature of the early industrial discourse can shed light on shadowy corners of familiar texts and make new interpretations possible.

This book does not unfold in a strictly chronological fashion, so I will briefly sketch out its organization. The first two chapters are pendant portraits of the canonical male and female response to industrialism, and juxtaposing these two chapters at the beginning highlights the striking gender discontinuities found in the texts of the industrial revolution's most famous writers. The third chapter moves back in time to the early factory fictions written by Frances Trollope and Charlotte Elizabeth Tonna in order to complicate our understanding of the women novelists' acceptance of industrialism. But just as important, the works of Trollope and Tonna reconfirm the discursive nature of the industrial revolution by presenting readers with an estranged picture of it; and the impact of this estrangement can best be felt if Trollope's and Tonna's novels are approached through the familiar, canonical texts of the first two chapters. The fourth chapter, which turns to the literary traditions of the Victorian working class, moves chronologically from the 1830s to the 1870s. Since the working-class response to the industrial revolution is dominated by the male traditions of Chartist and dialect writings, this chapter is aligned with the first both structurally and thematically.

Chapter 1 contends that the response to industrialism articulated in the works of Disraeli, Dickens, Carlyle, Ruskin, and Arnold was rooted in a sense of endangered male privilege that arose out of the sexual anarchy associated with early industrialism. To right a world turned upside down, the male critics tried to ground authority on a transcendent plane located in the paternalistic world of the past. They initially looked to an idealized medieval past, but they increasingly turned to the ideology of that past because, after midcentury, it was understood that the past could be resurrected only through its ideology, which came to be known as culture. Unquestionably, this move towards transcendence has been noted before, but what remains unexplored, and what will occupy this chapter, are the practical consequences of this move. In essence, this transcendence destabilizes the male critics' critique of industrialism. If one contends, as Thomas Carlyle does, that "society, it is understood, does not in any age prevent a man from being what he *can be*" ("Chartism" 164), then the material conditions of life become inconsequential. This dematerialization, whereby the consequential nature of the material realm is denied, characterizes the male discourse of industrialism, which devalues the world it aims to critique.

This chapter takes up Thomas Carlyle, whose early dematerializations and condemnations of the industrial realm were immensely influential, and it traces his influence to Dickens's *Hard Times*, a book enmeshed in Carlyle's dematerializing strategies. After establishing the importance of this dematerialization to the male critical tradition, this chapter proceeds to forge the connections between early Victorian medievalism and midcentury cultural criticism. These two manifestations of the male flight from the present necessarily engage in the same dematerializing tactics: what licenses the male critics' retreat into the past is that the industrial world never presents itself to them as either permanent or consequential.

While the canonical male writers seek a transcendental ground for authority in the historical past, Charlotte Brontë and Elizabeth Gaskell repudiate the past in favor of the present. The second chapter explores their qualified acceptance of the changes taking place throughout Victorian society. If we are to apprehend the industrial novels both women produced, we must accept that for them industrial capitalism seemed to indicate a brighter future for English women. Like all witnesses of the industrial revolution, Gaskell and Brontë refract it through the lens of their own subjectivity, where the reality of middle-class women's unemployment remained perpetually in focus. So while the male critics read the mill girl as a figure of disorder, the embodiment of the subversive potential of industrialism, for Gaskell and Brontë the factory girl functions as an attractive symbol of modernity, which seemed to hold out the promise of female employment to the endemically unemployed Victorian lady. *Mary Barton, Shirley*, and *North and South* all connect women's liberation to the liberating effects of industrial capitalism. They even transform their upper-class heroines into captains of industry, so that both Shirley Keeldar and Margaret Hale can briefly enjoy commercial power before succumbing to conventional marriages. In the end, patriarchal structures resist being swept away by the rising tide of industrial capitalism, and this resistance undermines the two novelists' attempts to yoke female emancipation to the burgeoning factory world. Both women overestimate the liberating potential of industrialism by underestimating the reactionary force of patriarchy because they never fully recognize how imbricated the two remain. Nor do they recognize their own complicity with patriarchal structures, which becomes apparent when they try to balance a desire for feminine autonomy against a need to assert their heroines' middle-class respectability. Thoroughly enmeshed in the contradictions generated by entangled class and gender loyalties, both Gaskell and Brontë are forced to acknowledge at each novel's end that they may have overrated the revolutionary possibilities of industrialism.

The third chapter focuses on the works of the women who first charted the terra incognita of the factory world, and thus it allows us to divide the middle-class female response to the factories into the celebration carried out by Charlotte Brontë and Elizabeth Gaskell and the critique undertaken by Frances Trollope and Charlotte Elizabeth Tonna. Yet what unites all these women novelists (both the well-known and the unknown) and sets them apart from the male critics of the factories is their willingness to seize upon the material world of Victorian industrialism in order to embrace, confront, and repair it. No matter how much Charlotte Elizabeth Tonna and Frances Trollope may dislike industrialism, they accept it as a material fact because accepting the material world is a necessary prologue to reform.

Empowered by the domestic ideology, these pioneering novelists wrote with the goal of awakening in their female readers a moral obligation toward the inhabitants of the factory districts. Specifically, they used the instabilities within domesticity to redraw the boundaries between the public and private realms: Trollope's *Michael Armstrong* and Tonna's *Helen Fleetwood* and *The Wrongs of Women* reveal how the public sphere forms a part of the domestic arena. To arouse their female readers' interest in the manufacturing districts, the first factory novelists highlight the factory's presence in the home by creating a domestic interior crowded with objects manufactured in the public world. In this way, their texts expose the unacknowledged affiliations between the sites of production and consumption, and they call attention to the fact that what they represent—the world of the factory and the process of material creation—often gets repressed and goes unrepresented in the culture at large. So what begins as a domestic critique of the factories quickly becomes a materialist critique of domesticity, one that reveals and reverses the fetishizing strategies underpinning both capitalism and domesticity.

In other words, the fictions of Trollope and Tonna rematerialize the dematerialized world of Victorian industrialism. They expose the conditions of industrial production that have been culturally suppressed and reveal the mechanism that licenses that suppression: the eroticization of industrial production. Rather shockingly, the process of industrial production represented in *Michael Armstrong* and *Helen Fleetwood* resembles human reproduction. On the one hand, this conflation of production and reproduction allows both novelists to condemn the factory system for harming English workers, who are dangerously sexualized through their intimacy with the machines. But on the other hand, it undermines Trollope's and Tonna's reformist agenda and engenders a contradiction as destabilizing as that found in the canonical male tradition. Even though Trollope's and Tonna's early factory fictions were written in support of a specific legislative effort to limit the working hours of women and children, they must abandon the reforms they advocate because the hopelessly eroticized world of industrial production is beyond parliament's help. In the end, both novelists turn to the domesticated middle-class woman (and not a parliament of men) to alleviate a factory crisis framed in terms of moral filth and sexual squalor.

The fourth chapter shifts to the relatively unknown territory of working-class literature but also returns us to the ground covered in the first chapter. Despite the general unfamiliarity of Chartist novelists like Ernest Jones or dialect poets like Samuel Laycock and Edwin Waugh, their replay of the male repudiation of modernity strangely throws readers back into the world of the canonical male critics. The most surprising aspect of the male working-class literary response to the industrial revolution is the resemblance it bears to that of the Victorian medievalists and cultural critics. Whether it be the agrarian dreams of the Chartists or the domestic idylls of the dialect poets, working-class literature looks longingly to a mythic past of preindustrial stability and patriarchal harmony.

Because of the dearth of Victorian working women's texts, this chapter cannot oppose the male working-class rejection of industrial society with a female countertradition accepting and celebrating modernity. Instead, it explores one possible explanation for the absence of a working-class women's tradition: the silencing of working women within the domestic ideology adopted by the working class in the 1830s and 1840s. For Victorian working men, domesticity promised to restore working-class patriarchy and reestablish "traditional" gender arrangements by recasting the independent factory girl in the mold of the homebound middle-class lady. But for the Victorian working woman, it led to an intolerable situation where being both a worker and a woman increasingly became an ideological contradiction while remaining a practical reality. For in spite of the hegemony of the working class's domestic ideal, economic necessity forced Victorian working women to stay active in the workplace throughout the century.

Chapter 4 concludes by exploring the poetry of two Victorian mill girls, the objects of fantasy, fascination, or paternalistic regard in middle-class texts. By the mid-1870s, the confluence of woman and worker proved self-defeating for the pseudonymous Fanny Forrester, a young female operative from Manchester whose poetry reveals the paralyzing contradictions a working-class woman faced in the golden age of domesticity. Unable to inhabit the domestic ideal, Forrester can only see herself (and women like her) as tragic heroines. In contrast, the author of *Autobiography—Poems and Songs of Ellen Johnston, 'the Factory Girl'* glories in her status as a fallen woman and an outcast from the world of Victorian domesticity, singing the praises of mills and machinery in tones reminiscent of Gaskell's and Brontë's celebrations of modernity. Whether they oppose or embrace it, Forrester and Johnston embed their responses to industrialism in the cultural script of domesticity, and thus through their texts we can gauge the pressures domesticity exerted on working-class women's writings, pressures that left most working-class women without a suitable discourse to articulate their own experiences.

By foregrounding the significance of gender to the formation of nineteenth-century culture as a whole, this book reveals the ways in which gender is as indispensable a category as class when analyzing the texts of the industrial revolution. The characters and concepts that populate the literature of industrialism have a prehistory, and that prehistory includes a culture's obsession with the new gender dispensation evolving in the factory districts. So in order to read the cultural thematics of Victorian industrialism through the literary response to it, one must acknowledge that for the men and women living in nineteenth-century Britain, nascent industrialism seemed to herald both a social and sexual revolution. It is the possibility of a sexual revolution—and the impact of that possibility on the writing of the industrial revolution—that this book takes as its subject.

# CHAPTER ONE

# A "World Turned Upside Downwards"
## Men, Dematerialization, and the Disposition-of-England Question

Even his bedroom was lit by gas. Wonderful city! That, however, could be got rid of. He opened the window.

Benjamin Disraeli, *Coningsby*

WHEN THE eponymous hero of Benjamin Disraeli's *Coningsby* visits Manchester, a required stop on the domestic grand tour, he opens a window. At that moment in history, opening a window is not the most world-transforming activity occurring in Manchester, characterized by Stephen Marcus as "the principle site of what was rapidly coming to be thought of as the Industrial Revolution . . . the urscene, concentrated specimen, and paradigm of what such a revolution was portending both for good and bad" (*Manchester* 3). But the opening of a window is, nonetheless, an incident the narrator sees fit to record. It seems that the stuffy commercial hotel room Coningsby has checked himself into has been made unbearable by the introduction of gaslighting, which would have been at the time both a recent innovation and an unperfected one, producing unpleasant fumes that induced drowsiness. That Coningsby encounters this technological innovation in a quasi-domestic setting (a hotel bedroom) in Manchester is not surprising: *Coningsby*'s readers would have associated gaslighting with the new modes of production, since it was first used in factories and then moved into public spaces like hotels before slowly progressing into the candlelit sanctum of the Victorian home.[1] Still, in spite of the bald logic behind Coningsby's actions—his need for fresh air to counteract the noxious gas fumes—it is a strange detail for the narrator's eye to seize upon; or it would be if gaslighting did not function in this passage as a metonym for what Disraeli regards as the whole dubious industrial enterprise, which (like gaslighting) might also prove unbearable. In the end, one cannot but suspect that it is the "wonderful city" itself that Disraeli wishes "could be got rid of," a desire that arises not from a mere grammatical laxity on the author's part but from a pervasive distaste for industrialism, one he shares with the great male critics of the period: Carlyle, Ruskin, Dickens, Arnold as well as Disraeli evince, to the man, an antipathy to infant industrialism.[2]

But, and here lies the great irony, this quintessentially modern posture—this aversion to modernity that forms one of the keystones of the modern—has its foundations in a politically conservative reaction against industrialism. Carried out in the voice of the past, the massive Victorian critique of the industrial revolution that is familiar to readers of "Chartism" (1839), *Past and Present* (1843), *Coningsby* (1844), *Sybil* (1845), *The Stones of Venice* (1851–53), *Hard Times* (1854), and *Culture and Anarchy* (1869) was driven as much by a disapproval of the social leveling it threatened as by the smoke it produced. This is not to dismiss or diminish the profound outrage expressed by these critics at the exploitation, degradation, and poverty pandemic in Victorian society. Historians still debate whether human suffering was exacerbated by the process of industrialization, or whether that suffering was alleviated by it but merely seemed more extreme to a generation that found itself systematically scrutinizing, perhaps for the first time in history, the primitive conditions under which a majority of the population lived. Yet whether one chooses the pessimistic or the optimistic reading of nineteenth-century industrialism, the fact still remains that these Victorian critics, when confronted with serious social injuries, did not (like Arnold's Philistines) blindly glory in the "unrivaled happiness" of modern man. Indeed, it does not detract from the moral impulse animating their texts to acknowledge that coloring their objections to industrialism was a set of political concerns.

The industrial revolution was never politically innocent, and it never entailed merely a change in the material conditions of life. When Thomas Arnold saw the first train pass by Rugby, he is said to have remarked that "feudality is gone for ever" (qtd. in Houghton,

4); and thus he linked a technological revolution with a concomitant social one. Echoing Dr. Arnold, one of the insufferable aristocrats in Disraeli's second Young England novel, *Sybil,* remarks that the railroad has "a dangerous tendency to equality" (101), and thereby makes it clear that the anticipated social revolution was to be democratic in nature. Of course, it is highly suspect history that binds the corpse of feudalism to a railroad track and then blames an oncoming train for running over it. But as Walter Houghton notes, the Victorians tended to ignore the intervening four hundred years between Britain's feudal past and its industrial present, believing that "it was the medieval tradition from which they had irrevocably broken" (1–2). As the last, mostly symbolic remnants of England's frayed feudal ties gave way under the twin pressures of industrialization and urbanization, Victorian critics witnessed what they believed to be a social unbonding given official sanction by laissez-faire ideology.

Born into an age of change, and perceiving that change to be of a cataclysmic nature, the great Victorian male critics struggled to set right a world they felt had gone wrong; or, as one of Disraeli's proletarian pundits laments in *Sybil,* "I think the world is turned upside downwards in these parts. A brat like Mick Radley to live in a two-pair, with a wife and family, or as good, as he says; and this girl asks me to take a dish of tea with her and keeps house! Fathers and mothers goes for nothing . . . 'Tis the children gets the wages" (89–90). This fear of a world "turned upside downwards" is a fear of ending up on the bottom this time around: imperiled class and gender authority forms the subtext of the male industrial discourse. And while the conservative class element found in much Victorian criticism of the industrial revolution has not escaped notice, one of its most salient features has—its overwhelmingly masculine hue.[3]

To grasp the degree to which the male critics' response to industrialism was rooted in a sense of endangered class and gender power, one must first understand that the anarchy associated with infant industrialism was itself gendered. Taking into account the centrality of gender to the material and discursive formations of nineteenth-century Britain, feminist historians have argued for the wrongheadedness of ignoring gender when assessing the conflicts and compromises that constitute Britain's industrial history.[4] Economic historian Maxine Berg even suggests that the industrial revolution was built upon female labor. "It was the female not the male workforce which counted in the new high-productivity industries," Berg notes ("What Difference" 26), and this is certainly true in cotton textile production, the take-off industry of Britain's economic miracle.[5] "Only a little more than a quarter of the [cotton] factory workers, perhaps 50,000 or so in 1830," were adult males according to F. M. L. Thompson's estimates (24).

Not surprisingly, then, contemporary observers associated industrialism with female employment and male unemployment— a world "turned upside downwards" indeed. At the center of this upside-down world stood the Victorian mill girl, the "prototype of the wage-earning woman" who was believed to have been set free from centuries of dependency by a pay packet (Tilly and Scott 63). In her classic account of women and the industrial revolution, Ivy Pinchbeck argues that a woman's ability to earn a wage and retain those earnings was one of the most important transformations wrought by the new machinery:

> In the case of the single working woman, the most striking effect of the industrial revolution was her distinct gain in social and economic independence. . . . Under the new régime every woman received her own earnings as a matter of course. The significance of this change was at once seen in the new sense of freedom which prompted so many young women to retain control of their wages, and even to leave home at an early age in order to 'become their own mistresses.' Though the individual wage was at first bitterly resented by the heads of families, it led ultimately to a new attitude towards the whole question of economic independence for women. (313)

While Pinchbeck embraces the Victorian mill girl as an exemplar of emancipated womanhood, an indication of good things to come, recent feminist historians have been less celebratory about industrialism's liberating potential. They identify a resurgence of patriarchy in the male workers' demands to be paid a family wage, and question just how much control of their wages mill women retained in the face of family pressures and obligations.[6] In addition, they point out that the overwhelming majority of nineteenth-century working women never entered the factories but sought their livings as servants, seamstresses, and casual laborers throughout the period. Yet in spite of her minority status, the female factory worker emerged in the 1830s and 1840s as the future face of the workforce. At that moment, the mill girl became the Victorian cover girl, a culture's icon of what modernity portended and a cover over the economic realities of most working women, who remained in traditional, low-paying occupations and never established the same advantages in other industries that they held in textile manufacturing. It was to the cotton mills, and the disturbingly egalitarian gender arrangements developing there, that early critics of the factories repeatedly turned for proof of industrialism's harms.

Anecdotes testifying to the "perverse" gender relations among the operatives proliferated in the first half of the nineteenth century. To galvanize MPs into taking action on the Ten Hours legislation, framed to restrict women's working hours in the mills, the father of factory regulation, Lord Ashley, fanned the fears of his fellow parliamentarians with this tale of an "unnatural change" occurring in the manufacturing districts:

> Here is a dialogue which occurred in one of these clubs, from an ear witness:—"A man came into one of these club-rooms, with a child in his arms; 'Come lass,' said he, addressing one of the women, 'Come home, for I cannot keep this bairn quiet, and the other I have left crying at home.' 'I won't go home, idle devil,' she replied, 'I have thee to keep, and the bairns too, and if I can't get a pint of ale quietly, it is tiresome. This is the only second pint that Bess and me have had between us; thou may sup if thou likes, and sit thee down, but I won't go home yet.' " Whence is it that this singular and unnatural change is taking place? Because that on women are imposed the duty and burthen of supporting their husbands and families, a perversion as it were of nature, which has the inevitable effect of introducing into families disorder, insubordination and conflict. What is the ground on which the woman says she will pay no attention to her domestic duties, nor give the

obedience which is owing to her husband? Because on her devolves the labour which ought to fall to his share, and she throws out the taunt, "If I have the labour, I will also have the amusement." (*Hansard* 1096)

In Ashley's opinion, by offering waged employment to women rather than men, the factories distort the "natural" gender patterns of British society, a distortion that generates "disorder, insubordination and conflict." And Ashley was scarcely alone in his belief that the factories led to perverse social relations. Miles apart politically from the Evangelical Tory, a young Frederick Engels presents a strikingly similar moment in *The Condition of the Working Class in England,* when he too protests the "reversal of all relations within the family" in the factory towns (173). Letting a member of the working class attest to his own degradation, Engels records the following complaint by an unemployed working man: "I don't know what is to become of us, for it's a good bit that she has been the man in the house and I the woman; it is bad work . . . the world is upside down. Mary has to work and I have to stop at home[,] mind the childer, sweep and wash, bake and mend" (173–74). Echoing Lord Ashley's sentiments, Engels concludes that the factory system "unsexes the man and takes from the woman all womanliness . . . degrades, in the most shameful way, both sexes, and, through them, Humanity" (174). This fear of women working in factories perhaps reaches its apogee in the rhetoric of the Reverend Joseph Rayner Stephens, a defrocked Methodist minister and Ten Hours agitator who frequently spoke before large crowds of working men: "Before I would allow my wife to go to a mill and be worked there," Stephens declares, "that wife should die in her chair, or on the floor, and the verdict should be 'Died by the visitation of God'—she should not die by the visitation of the factory demon" (qtd. in *The Factory Lad* 26).

Tapping into this cultural configuration of the mill girl as a potent, frightening symbol of modernity, the great male critics of the nineteenth century deploy her to represent the social disorder of the present. In her perceived liberation from a patriarchal domestic economy, they saw a shadow of the larger breakdown of the paternalistic structures within Britain. From the first, the vexed question of authority crossed both class and gender lines, so that improper authority, which translated into any power in the hands of women or workers, often got configured simply as female authority. Robert Southey, the conservative poet laureate, imagined the industrial Midlands in the grip of a powerful and evil woman, a Circe who was enchanted but not the least bit enchanting: "Here Commerce is the queen witch, and I have no talisman strong enough to disenchant those who are daily drinking of the golden cup of her dreams" (419).

While Dickens, Carlyle, and Arnold do not stage as dramatically as Southey this crisis of female ascendancy, in all three writers the disorder of industrial society takes on a female form: *Past and Present, Hard Times,* and "The Function of Criticism at the Present Time," whose very titles betray their anxiety about the "strange new Today," represent modernity as a female destroyer, a silent, terrifying figure who contains death and blight within her. There is a strong affinity between the "masculine" mill women populating Lord Ashley's and Engels's texts and Carlyle's Irish widow, Dickens's besotted working-class wife and Arnold's infanticidal mother. Unable to secure help from an indifferent society, Carlyle's widow, lifted from the pages of Dr. Alison's *Observations on the Management of the Poor in Scotland,* contracts typhus and infects her entire neighborhood. This figure, who literally embodies the contagion and corruption of the present and stands in contrast to the revered, life-affirming male corpse of the medieval St. Edmund,[7] gives way to later avatars of ruination—to the drunken, dissolute Mrs. Blackpool, who spoils her husband's life and prevents him from marrying the salutary and salvational Rachel, and finally to Elizabeth Wragg. "Wragg is in custody" serves as Arnold's mnemonic for the poverty, ignorance, and desperation just beneath the prosperous surface of middle-class life; it is his response to the pabulum of those supremely self-satisfied Englishmen Roebuck and Adderly, who believe that they live in the best of all possible worlds. Like Carlyle's Irish widow and Stephen Blackpool's unwomanly wife, Elizabeth Wragg, whose sex is "lost in the confusion of our unrivalled happiness" ("Function of Criticism" 249), symbolizes everything wrong and unnatural in modern life: she is a runaway from a Nottinghamshire workhouse who kills her child in an appropriately industrial setting of gloom, smoke, and cold. For the male critics, modernity is, at best, a diseased woman who carries seeds of destruction within her and, at worst, a madwoman who has escaped the attic.

In response to a feminized modernity, the male critics fashion a new upper-class male identity to counteract and correct it. This identity receives its most influential articulation in *Past and Present,* where Carlyle brilliantly mixes together the traditional paternalism of the aristocracy with the work ethic of the middle classes to fabricate the captain of industry, a man who does not compete in the marketplace or exercise the privilege of a noble birth, but who leads through personal merit and charisma—what Carlyle labels heroism in another context.[8] Moreover, Carlyle goes to great lengths to underscore the manliness of this new leader. He adopts the ideals of paternalism and social obligation most strongly associated by the middle classes with an effeminate, degenerate aristocracy and thoroughly masculinizes them through the martial tropes of chivalry. "Captains of Industry are the true Fighters," Carlyle declares, and one "cannot lead a Fighting World without having it regimented, chivalried" (273–74). Throughout the century, the Victorians used the visual and verbal language of chivalry to define the ideal gentleman, but Carlyle's version emphasized an exaggerated masculinity by reconceptualizing civil life as warfare in which men are "warriors in one true war" (275), and from which women are excluded. Rejecting a new world that seems dangerously and chaotically feminized, Carlyle turns back to the certainties of gender's binary oppositions found in the old world of knights-in-armor and damsels-in-distress, and out of it he creates a modern hero who can restore patriarchal order through manly leadership.[9]

This anxiety about illegitimate female authority and the relief found in the restoration of a truly masculine rule is perhaps nowhere more fully played out than in Benjamin Disraeli's *Sybil.* Presiding over *Sybil*'s upside-down world is a young Queen Victoria, whose coronation forms a prologue to the novel. The death of the old king and the "misplacing" of authority into the hands of a girl queen symbolize for Disraeli both the vacuum at the top of the social hierarchy and the chaos that ensues when a ferocious combination of women, children, and workers try to usurp adult male authority. When Mrs. Carey, one of the novel's working-class characters, is informed—wrongly, to be sure—that the revolution has finally begun and that, with the queen's blessing, Her Majesty's soldiers will "stick their bayonets into the Capitalists," she replies, "I always thought some good would come of having a woman on the throne" (355). While Disraeli shows no particular affection for most of his novel's capitalists, it is nevertheless just this sort of good that he fears. In *Sybil,* female power signifies improper authority, and powerfully ascendant females—variations on the queen—become the mark of social disintegration: in fashionable London drawing rooms, aristocratic ladies select candidates for Parliament and think they "can govern the world by . . . social influences" (215), while in unfashionable manufacturing districts, young factory girls set up in rooms of their own, leaving their often unemployable parents to shift as best they can.

Sybil is the most important of these variations on the queen, and the one explicitly linked to Victoria. But if the novel begins with one woman ascending to the throne and ends with another, the regal Sybil, restored to her rightful patrimony as the heir to the Mowbray estate, it does not so much embrace queenly authority as empty it out by turning queens into figureheads. In fact, what sets Sybil above all the other women in the novel is that she never has a mind of her own. If, as Gary Handwerk argues, *Sybil*'s "domestic plot revolves around a contest between Egremont and Morley for Sybil's mind" (330), then we can read Sybil as a vessel containing Morley's radical commitment to class warfare which must be emptied out and refilled with Egremont's Tory paternalism. Unlike the ladies of the London drawing rooms, Sybil does not try to influence the political actions of Egremont but instead is influenced by him and then, in turn, uses her influence over the people to defend Egremont's aristocratic interests against an attack by the working classes on Mowbray Castle. The marriage at the end of the novel, which Robert O'Kell rightly reads as a religious allegory, "the wedding of a sensitive but secular leadership to the spirit of piety and devotion that provides a divine sanction for the political settlement of true Toryism" (214), must also be read as a political allegory, in which the female monarch becomes an important but empty symbol who takes her meaning (and her cues) from clever politicians like Egremont. Just as Disraeli marries off the novel's independent, energetic factory girls to former working-class radicals transformed into budding capitalists, so does he safely secure Sybil in the embrace of the wealthy Egremont after her dangerous flirtation with proletarian politics. Through both the factory girls and Sybil herself, Disraeli associates working-class radicalism and social disorder with improper female authority: *Sybil*'s upside-down world is righted when masculine authority, embodied in the chivalric Egremont, is reasserted. Egremont may be an aristocrat, but he is an untitled younger son whose moral claim to leadership depends on his enlightened paternalism and manly actions, most notably his dramatic, swashbuckling rescue of Sybil from a drunken mob at the novel's climax.

Although gender has usually been left out of the analysis, the Victorian anxiety about fragmenting cultural authority has been amply detailed by critics, beginning most memorably with Raymond Williams in *Culture and Society*,[10] where he establishes culture as a transcendent solution to the problems posed by emergent industrialism and democracy. He writes that culture "in a very complex way, merges two general responses—first, the recognition of the practical separation of certain moral and intellectual activities from the driven impetus of a new kind of society; second, the emphasis of these activities, as a court of human appeal, to be set over the processes of practical social judgement and yet to offer itself as a mitigating and rallying alternative" (xviii). The tradition of thought that Williams sketches out—stretching from Burke to Carlyle, Arnold, Ruskin, and Dickens—turns to a transcendent realm (culture) to escape the contingencies of history because, as Chris Vanden Bossche observes, for these critics, "the absence of transcendental authority meant the absence of *any* kind of authority or social order, that neither belief nor law, neither order nor justice could exist if social institutions were only self-enclosed systems" (8–9). But despite their attempts to evade the contingencies of history and "the sociohistorical processes of cultural formation" (Vanden Bossche viii), they ironically turn to history itself, or more precisely to the past, to engage this transcendence. What Richard Terdiman terms the "memory crisis" in nineteenth-century Europe can be usefully evoked here: "I argue two theses concerning the century that precedes and still informs our own: first, that one of its most powerful perceptions was of a massive disruption of traditional forms of memory, and, second, that within the atmosphere of such disruption, the functioning of memory itself, the institution of memory and thereby of history, became critical preoccupations in the effort to think through what intellectuals were coming to call the 'modern' " (5). Feeling cut off from their past, as if a sword had sliced through the cord binding the past to the present, the Victorians began to perceive the past as a foreign country, inaccessible to anyone who could not speak the language. But this inaccessibility, its self-enclosed and increasingly autonomous status, made it the perfect "court of human appeal, to be set over the processes of practical social judgement" as well as a "mitigating and rallying alternative" to the present. Thus, it is no surprise that the great male social critics, looking to ground authority on a transcendent plane, located that authority in the paternalistic world of the past, first in an idealized medieval past and then, after 1850, in the ideology of that past, which became known popularly as culture. As the priestly intercessor, not between God and man but between past and present, the critic emerged in the nineteenth century as an upscale tour guide through parts and pasts unknown, the obliging historian of art, literature, and the nation state who neatly directed readers' attention to the cultural monuments encompassing their heritage. And if this quest for transcendence has been rehearsed before, so has its final ironic twist. In spite of the Victorian critics' attempt to establish a transcendent authority outside and beyond the individual, the new figure of authority was nonetheless an individual—the artist himself—whether he was the heroic man of letters in Carlyle's *On Heroes, Hero Worship, and the Heroic in History,* the exegete in Ruskin's *Unto This Last,* or the magisterial Arnoldian critic in *Culture and Anarchy.*[11]

The interplay between culture and anarchy, between transcendence and fragmentation, has been reworked and refined over the years. But the practical consequence of the move toward transcendence—its effect on the male critique of the factories—has been largely ignored. And that effect is a powerful one: for just as the male critics abstract culture from the social and material contingencies that produce it, so do they abstract the individual from those same social and material contingencies by insisting that, in the words of Carlyle, "society, it is understood, does not in any age prevent a man from being what he *can be.*" Carlyle's dictum, when applied to an exploration of the Victorian brave new world, leads to a complicated denial of the materiality of the industrial realm. This dematerialization, in which the consequences of the industrial realm are suppressed, constitutes the cornerstone of the male critics' discourse of industrialization, a discourse that rests upon a problematic devaluation of the world it critiques. The most important figure in this history of dematerialization remains Thomas Carlyle. His early condemnations of industrialism in "Chartism" and *Past and Present* set out the terms for the discussion that followed, and his influence can be directly traced to what is still the most celebrated factory novel, Dickens's *Hard Times,* a text dedicated to Thomas Carlyle and indebted to Carlyle's dematerializing strategies. After detailing this dematerialization in Carlyle and Dickens, this chapter moves on and explores the links between early Victorian medievalism and midcentury cultural criticism; these twin manifestations of the male flight from the industrial present are aligned to this same dematerializing strain, for what makes the male critics' retreat into the past possible is that the industrial world never presents itself to them as either a permanent or a consequential reality.

## Carlyle and the Disposition-of-England Question

At the center of John Ruskin's "The Nature of Gothic" stands his famous comparison of the modern and premodern workman. In it, Ruskin argues that the factory operative condemned to mind-numbing mechanical labor is significantly worse off than the poor serf slogging through the medieval mud:

> Men may be beaten, chained, tormented, yoked like cattle, slaughtered like summer flies, and yet remain in one sense, and the best sense, free. But to smother their souls with them, to blight and hew into rotting pollards the suckling branches of their human intelligence, to make the flesh and skin which, after the worm's work on it, is to see God, into leathern thongs to yoke machinery with,—this is to be slave-masters indeed; and there might be more freedom in England, though her feudal lords' lightest words were

worth men's lives, and though the blood of the vexed husbandman
dropped in the furrows of her fields, than there is while the ani-
mation of her multitudes is sent like fuel to feed the factory smoke,
and the strength of them is given daily to be wasted into the fineness
of a web, or racked into the exactness of a line. (85)

It is a paragraph remarkable for the intensity with which Ruskin
evokes the physical suffering of a laborer—beaten, chained, and tormented—but equally remarkable for Ruskin's ability to discount that
suffering. Devaluing the claims of the material, Ruskin affirms that
the physical enslavement of the peasant pales in comparison with the
mental enslavement of the modern worker; and this logic leads him
to conclude that modern workers riot and protest not because they
are ill-fed but because "they have no pleasure in the work by which
they make their bread" (86) and "feel their souls withering within
them" (87). For the industrial laborer, the material conditions of
production (the alienating particularities of machine work) give rise
to his spiritual inanition. For the medieval laborer, however, the
relationship between the material and the spiritual is suspended: the
material conditions of production (his blood watering England's
fields) have no bearing on his spiritual health (he remains in "the best
sense, free"). In his analysis of the medieval workman, Ruskin mystifies the causal relationship between the material and the spiritual
and dematerializes the medieval workman's material conditions, so
that the "vexed husbandman" of the fourteenth century can emerge
as the model of a freeborn Englishman, in comparison to his modern
counterpart. Through his architectural writings, Ruskin drew a nation's attention to its physical surroundings. To discover an instance
of dematerialization in so material a critic as Ruskin testifies to its
pervasiveness. Ruskin, and the conservative tradition to which he
belongs, inherit from Carlyle a way of seeing the industrial world
that is also a way of knowing, an epistemology, that demands such
abstractions and frequently results in similar contradictions.

Writing in 1855, George Eliot observed that "there is hardly
a superior or active mind of this generation that has not been modified
by Carlyle's writings; there has hardly been an English book written
for the last ten or twelve years that would not have been different if
Carlyle had not lived" (*Essays* 213–14). When Carlyle spoke, Victorian

intellectuals listened. Even when they stopped listening (sometime after 1850), they remained awash in Carlylean thought, particularly his thinking about the condition-of-England question. Carlyle first raised the question in "Chartism," but in his attempt to elucidate the discontent of the Chartists by asking the condition-of-England question, he also posed its complement, the disposition-of-England question: "Is the condition of the English working people so wrong; so wrong that rational working men cannot, will not, and even should not rest quiet under it? . . . Or is the discontent itself mad, like the shape it took? Not the condition of the working people that is wrong; but their disposition, their own thoughts, beliefs and feelings that are wrong?" (120). Here Carlyle sets up the opposition between free will and social determinism which Catherine Gallagher places at the center of the industrial discourse. Although Carlyle questions in "Chartism" the connection between the workers' disposition and their living and working conditions, his fundamental antimaterialism seems to win out when he insists a few chapters later, in a line that firmly aligns him with the believers in an unshackled free will, that "society . . . does not in any age prevent a man from being what he *can be*" and assails the disposition of the workers, the "feeling of *injustice*" (145) that sends them marching in the street. But this victory over the material that he scripts—this transcendence—is largely rhetorical. What propels "Chartism" as well as *Past and Present* is the struggle Carlyle stages between the worker's body and soul in order to decide the nature of the relationship between the material conditions of industrialism and the spiritual disposition of England's workers. This unresolved, galvanizing tension animates Carlyle's two most significant industrial texts, accounting for much of the power and energy of both. Its resolution, which occurs at the end of the 1840s, ushers in the hardening of Carlyle's social thinking characteristic of the post-1850 period.

Despite Carlyle's intense idealist faith—forthrightly asserted in *On Heroes* as "the spiritual always determines the material" (216)— "Chartism" cannot fully sustain its profound antimaterialism because the hungry belly of Sanspotato, Carlyle's archetypal worker and would-be Chartist, rumbles loudly and insistently throughout the text. Even though Carlyle contends that "it is not what a man outwardly has or wants that constitutes the happiness or misery of him" (144), he cannot easily dismiss those outward wants because they constitute a counterdiscourse in "Chartism" that reconnects belly rumbling with political grumbling. When Carlyle foregrounds the "inward things" (143) the discontented worker lacks, he inadvertently reveals how these "inward things" are predicated on outer wants, in this case the uncertain social conditions engendered by the economic instability of the late 1830s: "Economy does not exist among [the workers]; their trade now in plethoric prosperity, anon extenuated into inanition and 'short-time,' is of the nature of gambling; they live by it like gamblers, now in luxurious superfluity, now in starvation. . . . English Commerce with its world-wide convulsive fluctuations, with its immeasurable Proteus Steam-demon, makes all paths uncertain for them; all life a bewilderment; sobriety, steadfastness, peaceable continuance, the first blessings of man, are not theirs" (143). One begins to suspect that Carlyle must overstate his idealism to counteract the evidence he marshals against it. For despite his many statements to the contrary, Carlyle here acknowledges the primacy of the material conditions of the working class by calling upon the boom/bust cycle of early Victorian industrialism, in which periods of high employment and prosperity alternated with times of high unemployment and wracking poverty, to account for the "bewilderment" of the workers. But then, any explanatory model he deploys to diagnose the disposition of the working class in the late 1830s leads him back to where he does not wish to be: the material conditions that are too extreme and insistent for Carlyle, in a supreme gesture of intellectual honesty, to avoid.

A few years later, in *Past and Present,* Carlyle again returns to the body—the human body and the body politic—when he brings the dynamics of body and soul, material and spiritual, condition and disposition, to the foreground in an attempt to resolve—by collapsing—the dualisms he invokes in "Chartism." To free himself from the persistent, seemingly inescapable materialism of the earlier text, Carlyle fashions what Katherine Bond Stockton labels a spiritual materialism.[12] In averring that "the Highest God dwells visible in that mystic unfathomable Visibility, which calls itself 'I' on the Earth" (124), Carlyle embeds the ideal in the flesh of the material because he believes the ideal can exist only in a materialized, embodied form. "The Ideal always has to grow in the Real, and to seek out its bed and board there" (57), Carlyle declares in *Past and Present,* and he then literalizes his ideal in the real bodies of St. Edmund and the Irish widow, which, John Rosenberg observes, function as the "embodied symbols" of Carlyle's belief "that we are indissoluably bound together for good or ill" (123). By transforming the body into a symbol—the real which (literally) embodies the ideal—Carlyle turns to a spiritual materialism in order to evade the dead end of binary oppositions that confronted him in "Chartism."

It is not surprising that Carlyle would interrupt his work on Cromwell in the early 1840s to seize upon the Camden Society's recently published chronicle of Jocelin of Brakelond and place it at the center of his most finely conceived response to early Victorian industrialism. Vital to the medieval world Jocelin represents is a dynamic relationship between material and spirit, a relationship underscored by the important position St. Edmund's shrine occupies in Jocelin's text: wholly material and genuinely holy, St. Edmund's bodily relics stand at the heart of St. Edmundsbury and are a focal point in Jocelin's narrative, which reaches its dramatic climax during the shrine's rededication. Raised within the confines of Scottish Calvinism, Carlyle must turn back to pre-Reformation England to locate a living example of his spiritual materialism. Although he might hesitate to acknowledge it, the fluid relationship between the material and the spiritual that flourishes in the Catholic world of St. Edmundsbury is missing from the Protestant culture out of which he emerged. So, for example, while the Catholic interpretation of the act of communion insists on the idea of transubstantiation, which allows the wine and wafer to become the actual flesh and blood of Christ through the intervention of the priest, Protestant denominations claim Catholic communion to be cannibalistic and reinscribe the event as a purely symbolic one, thereby short-circuiting the interchange between the material and spiritual central to the Catholic rite.[13] Jocelin's chronicle of life in the twelfth-century monastery offers Carlyle that fluidity in St. Edmund, who—like the communion wafer and wine—can breech simple dualisms and be both body and soul, real and ideal, material and spiritual together: "In one word, St.

Edmund's Body has raised a Monastery round it. To such length, in such manner, has the spirit of Time visibly taken body, and crystallised itself here" (56). As both body and spirit, St. Edmund ideally embodies the spirit of the organic social arrangements of the Middle Ages that *Past and Present* aims to recapture. When the severed head of Edmund is "reverently reunite[d]" (55) by his loyal bondsmen, the gesture not only signifies the medieval community's hero-worship of a strong leader but also reinforces, through a literal deployment of the metaphor, his status as the head of an organic body politic. The invading Danes may have been able to sever the physical head of St. Edmund, but the English, who understand him to be their spiritual head, can make the body—the physical body of St. Edmund and the body politic of St. Edmundsbury—whole again by this act of reverence. Moreover, the fact that St. Edmund's body, like the ideal it embodies, is indestructible allows the medieval social arrangements to stand as a viable antidote to the emerging democracy of Victorian England. The dangers inherent in ideals seeking bed and board in the real—they grow "like diseased corpulent bodies fallen idiotic, which merely eat and sleep" (58)—allow Carlyle to account for the corruption of the monastic system, where the ideal took up its lodgings, while holding that the ideal remains uncorrupted. The monastery may have fallen on hard times, and St. Edmund's ideal may have been neglected by the diseased, corpulent bodies of the monks who initially make Abbot Samson's life so difficult. But when St. Edmund's tomb is opened, the monks discover a body like that of a man "dead yesterday" (122), and this signifies that the ideal of St. Edmund has not decayed since the monastery arose around him, even if the monastic institution needs reformation, or more precisely, the Reformation.

While it flourishes in the medieval world Carlyle beautifully invokes, spiritual materialism, which locates the spiritual ideal in a material reality, proves less successful when applied to the live bodies of the nineteenth century. If St. Edmund's perfectly preserved body stands as the embodied ideal of the medieval social order, Carlyle calls upon the declining body of the Victorian working class to symbolize the industrial present. *Past and Present* invokes the starving body of the British worker, which it then enlarges into the body politic: "You have to admit," Carlyle proclaims, "that the working body of this rich English Nation has sunk or is fast sinking into a state, to which, all sides of it considered, there was literally never any parallel" (3–4). Here Carlyle abstracts the failing physical body of the worker into a metaphor, or symbol, for the failed state of the nation. But as they had in "Chartism," the real bodies of British men and women crowd Carlyle's narrative, whether it be the "bare backs" (22) of the workers in Carlyle's critique of an industrial system that produces vast amounts of consumer goods but fails to clothe the naked; or the corpses of Stockport children, done in by their desperate parents for the burial money, an elaborated form of cannibalism that attests to the barbarism of the industrial system; or most dramatically, the poor Irish widow who dies of typhus in an Edinburgh lane but not before sharing her deadly infection with seventeen neighbors. Constituting some of the most powerful moments in the text, as incontrovertible proof that there is something dreadfully wrong with "this rich English nation," these ailing bodies also function metonymically, as part of the "real" world of Victorian England that Carlyle alludes to at the beginning of *Past and Present,* the "scenes of woe and destitution and desolation, such as, one may hope, the Sun never saw before in the most barbarous regions where men dwelt" (3).

A problem arises, however, when Carlyle tries to elude the suffering of these material bodies, which he does somewhat suddenly in chapter 4, "Morrison's Pills." Continuing the metaphor of England's sick body politic, Carlyle declares that the nation cannot be cured by any mere "pharmacopoeia" (23) because England needs to be spiritually regenerated. And this national regeneration will come about only when Englishmen enact the same dynamic between the spiritual and the material that animates the medieval section of *Past and Present*: "Thou shalt descend into thy inner man, and see if there be any traces of a *soul* there; till then there can be nothing done! O brother, we must if possible resuscitate some soul and conscience in us, exchange our dilettantisms for sincerities, our dead hearts of stone for living hearts of flesh" (26). Carlyle calls for a secular communion, in which dead matter is resurrected as living flesh, but this modern act of transubstantiation still cannot transcend the spiritual-material divide in the way the medieval worship of St. Edmund's holy relics can: the real bodies of England's industrial workers may be able to function metaphorically, but unlike St. Edmund's corpse, they are also insistently metonymic and, as such, resist Carlyle's complete abstraction. In the end, this act of communion that Carlyle proposes will do nothing for the real wounded bodies of England's workers, whose material plight cries out for some physical relief, some truly analgesic Morrison's pill, to relieve their suffering.

Since Carlyle's spiritual materialism proves unsuccessful in helping him circumvent the material existence of Britain's workers, he must, like Ruskin, ultimately resort to a double standard in his comparison of the medieval and modern worker. His model medieval workman, Gurth the Saxon swineherd, is not "what I call an exemplar of human felicity," Carlyle informs the reader, but Gurth nevertheless "seems happy, in comparison with many a Lancashire and Buckinghamshire man of these days, not born thrall of anybody" (212). The explanation for the Saxon's seeming happiness rests in his relationship with his master Cedric: "Gurth's brass collar did not gall him: Cedric *deserved* to be his master. The pigs were Cedric's, but Gurth too would get his parings of them. Gurth had the inexpressible satisfaction of feeling himself related indissolubly, though in a rude brass-collar way, to his fellow mortals in this Earth" (212). According to Carlyle's human calculus, even though Gurth may live like a pig, he remains a far more contented specimen of humanity than the Lancashire mill worker, who possesses the freedom that Gurth lacks, but whose freedom is illusory, the "liberty to die by starvation" (212). Carlyle makes a valid point: what kind of freedom is there if one's basic material needs cannot be met? Nevertheless, at this point in his discussion of the modern worker, Carlyle gives more weight to the material (food) than to the spiritual (liberty), whereas the reverse remains true for Gurth, who can survive on crumbs from the rich man's table because the spiritual value of belonging to Cedric and the hierarchy he heads outweighs all material considerations.

The contradictions evident in *Past and Present* and "Chartism," which arise out of Carlyle's engagement with both the disposition and the condition of the English working classes, are preferable to what results when the conflict between the two ceases to animate his writings. By the time Carlyle published his notorious defense of slavery, "The Nigger Question" (1849), the struggle between the spiritual and the material had been decided, and when Carlyle loses touch with the material, his social criticism loses much of its dynamism and its pertinence. If "The Nigger Question" testifies to Carlyle's increasingly strident authoritarianism, his faith that workers have "the divine right of being compelled . . . to do what work they are appointed for" (357), it also demonstrates a resolution of the tensions that enliven his earlier works. In it, Carlyle disdainfully introduces the "idle Black gentleman" (356), the New World counterpart to Sanspotato, the starving Irish worker in "Chartism." But unlike the emaciated Sanspotato wasting away in his Manchester cellar, the recently emancipated West Indian slave suffers not from a scarcity of food but from its excess, "pumpkin at discretion" (356), and no need to toil for it. To be sure, the ex-slaves of the West Indies are not part of the English body politic in the way that even the Irish Sanspotato is, and Carlyle's real quarrel with them is that they refuse to submit to the rule of the white plantation owners. Nevertheless, in spite of the glaring racism of one and the compassionate condescension of the other, both essays share a common concern for the state of the worker's body and its relationship to the worker's soul. So it is astonishing to discover that in "The Nigger Question" Carlyle presents his "idle Black gentleman" enjoying the fruits of a bountiful land not as an example of prelapsarian contentment but as a zombie, possessing "the dead soul of a man" (356), because he does not engage in backbreaking, soul-making labor.[14] By 1849, the well-being of the soul stands so incontestably paramount in Carlyle's mind that a healthy, well-fed body can come to signify death, not life.

This stunning, monumental disregard for the material in "The Nigger Question" signals a calcification of Carlyle's thinking and a departure from his industrial texts, in which the body's needs could not be so lightly dismissed. The struggle between the condition and the disposition of the working class, carried out over the workers' bodies in both "Chartism" and *Past and Present,* invigorates and enriches Carlyle's social criticism because the power of individual will and the potency of material conditions exist in an intimate, if fraught, relationship. It is this highly charged intimacy that Carlyle's best work negotiates.

## Dickens, *Hard Times,* and Dematerialization

When Dickens requested permission to dedicate *Hard Times* to the Sage of Chelsea, the novelist declared that "it contains nothing in which you do not think with me, for no man knows your books better than I" (*Letters* 367). *Hard Times* often strikes readers as strangely un-Dickensian, but then, as a text both inscribed to Thomas Carlyle and inscribed in Carlylean thought, it is Carlylean—a disposition-of-England novel that dramatically enacts the dematerialization of the industrial revolution by working through (with modifications) Carlyle's tenet that society does not "prevent a man from being what he *can be*." The unsettled relationship between the condition and disposition of the working class that marks Carlyle's most vital social criticism also penetrates Dickens's novel, although Dickens remains even more tied to the material world because the novel's realistic assumptions demand it. But in the end, his allegiances to Carlyle force him to depreciate the value of the material realm he wishes to critique and to dismiss as inconsequential the perilous industrial world he labors to create. By devaluing the material world, *Hard Times* depletes the world it aims to condemn; as a result, the industrial milieu, first evoked as an inhumane, life-threatening environment, is reduced to the status of local color.

Dickens expends much narrative energy painting the savage face of Coketown, and accordingly, much of the novel's power dwells in its rendering of the industrial landscape. In addition to striking his famous "Keynote"—"it was a town of red brick, or of brick that would have been red if the smoke and ashes had allowed it" (30)—Dickens describes and redescribes Coketown to an extraordinary degree, and he never permits the dominant visual image of Coketown, the legion of chimneys and the clouds of smoke, to slip far from the reader's mind. Dickens wishes to establish Coketown's status as a perversion of nature, a murderous and merciless environment where even the life-giving sun engenders "more death than life" (117). And because the "attributes of Coketown were in the main inseparable from the work by which it was sustained" (31), at the center of Coketown we find lurking, like the Minotaur in the labyrinth, the soulless machine. Everything and everyone in Coketown is manufactured, from its rows of terraced houses to its mass-produced masses, so that in the final perversion, the only thing left alive is the factory— the melancholy elephants and interminable serpents of production.

Yet despite this nightmare vision of futurity that Dickens conjures up, the savage face of Coketown proves to be no more than a Halloween mask: the text cannot sustain its own organizing metaphor because Coketown neither resembles nor functions as a huge, malevolent factory, churning out an identical and interchangeable citizenry to live identical and interchangeable lives. In the end, the characters retain (however barely) their individuality. Stephen Spector justly argues that in the failure of the "Keynote" to remain true to its own premise—because Coketowners do not act "equally like one another" (*Hard Times* 31)—we see a crack in Dickens's realistic assumptions about "the link between environment and character" (237). In Spector's terms, *Hard Times* fails to represent the industrial scene "realistically" because it runs up against the limitations of metonymy, on which realism depends: "In *Hard Times,* as in realism generally, a person's character is 'read' by contiguous exteriors such as his action, his environment, his clothing, and—in the novelist's formula—his face and figure. To identify an invisible quality—character—by a visible exterior is realism's fundamental metonymy" (231). Neither loud and disorderly like the machines amidst which they work, nor interchangeable like the houses in which they live, the Coketown hands are not contiguous with the "visible exterior" of Coketown; and through this lack of contiguity, Dickens lays bare Coketown's inability to "produce" its inhabitants, or more generally, to determine their existence. Therefore, and somewhat ironically, *Hard Times* is perhaps the least realistic novel in the Dickens canon.

*Hard Times* accentuates the serious inadequacies of realism, the nineteenth century's dominant mode, and for this it is generally applauded by critics. Spector reads Dickens's inability to forge a permanent link between environment and character as an act of "unusual humility" (244) through which Dickens acknowledges the difficulties (and even impossibility) of knowing the working class through simple metonymies, while Katherine Kearns contends that "the real and the surreal coexist because they are interdependent" (877), in that the repressive realism of industrialism inevitably leads to a return of the repressed. Both assert that there is a mystery—whether it be the mystery of the individual's soul enshrined by Spector, or the mystery of the individual's desires celebrated by Kearns—which realism's metonymies, coarsely deterministic as they tend to be, cannot ultimately apprehend. But while Dickens may be actively confronting the limitations of realism, as Spector and Kearns suggest, he is at the same time confronting his own limited ability to envision Coketown realistically. If realism fails so spectacularly in this novel, it is in part because the straightforward metonymies of Dickens's realism are ill-suited to a modern industrial landscape, one dominated by paradoxes and ironies.

The industrial world was not conventionally realistic, in that a simple one-to-one correspondence between the environment and character did not exist. But it is a correspondence on which Dickens nevertheless relies. When he looks at Stephen Blackpool at work in the factory, he observes only "a special contrast" (76) between the quiet, orderly Stephen and the riotous machinery on the factory floor. In this, he reproduces the same "special contrast" that caught his attention when he reported on the Preston strike, which served as his immediate inspiration for the novel. What Dickens cannot grasp, however, is the essential but complex affiliation between the disorder of industrial production and the orderliness of industrial workers, just as he cannot connect the persistent individuality of the workers with the monotony of Coketown's public spaces. Incapable of recognizing the paradoxes that lie at the heart of industrialism, Dickens cannot see that the workers' collected—and collective—manner is a product of the machines. The self-possession so evident in Stephen Blackpool and the Preston strikers resulted from what historians refer to as factory discipline, which roughly translates as the self-discipline that the British worker acquired in order to be an effective industrial operative, one attuned to the rhythms of the time clock and the steam engine. Moreover, Dickens cannot see the paradox apparent to Marx and Engels when they posited that the experience of industrialism did not necessarily reduce workers to automatons but, rather, could awaken them to a higher level of self-consciousness, where "man is at last compelled to face, with sober senses his real conditions of life, and his relations with his kind" (*The Communist Manifesto* 7). Of course, as Steven Marcus has shown, Dickens was not alone in his confused response to the emerging industrial world. Like many other visitors to the industrial Midlands in the nineteenth century, Dickens had no conceptual framework through which he could make sense of it all; and if one keeps in mind Lukacs's observation that description is a sign of alienation, one might even be inclined to read Dickens's excessive description of Coketown as a sign of his own alienation from it as well as his inability to capture and control it imaginatively.[15]

*Hard Times*'s well-established difficulties with the realist mode may be exacerbated by Dickens's inability to see the industrial milieu realistically (i.e., to grasp the ironic relationship between character and environment), but whatever the complicated genealogy that causes it, the metonymic fracture remains; and this inability to sustain any kind of link between character and environment destabilizes Dickens's critique of Coketown. To be sure, there are genuine dangers in an unrelievedly metonymic imagination. In its most exacting forms, it can function as a disassembly line, reducing whole entities to their constituent parts without reassembling them, a state of affairs evident throughout *Hard Times,* where the use of the metonym "Hands" to denote the workers becomes a dehumanizing gesture on the masters' part. For all the dangers of realism's metonymic approach, however, it remains vital to any critique of the industrial realm because if one fully and finally unhitches character and environment, then environment, originally the object of one's critical gaze and the target of one's reforming impulses, fades into insignificance. Caught between a crude determinism and an equally crude idealism, Dickens invokes the material world of Coketown only to dismiss it. Dickens may sketch a terrifying portrait of industrialism, but he does so only to expose its insignificance to the lives of Coketown's workers.

Dickens knew full well the real dangers of factory work. When, only a few years after the writing of *Hard Times,* he quarreled with Harriet Martineau over the need to erect protective fences around machinery, he labeled the antifencing lobby "The National Association for the Protection of the Right to Mangle Operatives." But there are, notably, no mangled operatives in *Hard Times.* In the final draft, Dickens extricated the novel's one industrial victim, Rachel's sister; and only her shadow, in the shape of two passing references, remains (Butwin 177–79). Moreover, in the place where one might expect a thorough condemnation of factory labor, one finds, oddly enough, a paean to the indomitability of the human spirit that pays tribute to the text's Carlylean origins:

> Stephen bent over the loom, quiet, watchful, and steady. A special contrast, as every man was in the forest of looms where Stephen worked, to the crashing, smashing and tearing piece of mechanism at which he laboured. Never fear, good people of an anxious turn of mind, that Art will consign Nature to oblivion. Set anywhere, side by side, the work of God and the work of man; and the former, even though it be a troop of Hands of very small account, will gain in dignity from the comparison. (76)

Despite the crashing, the smashing, and the tearing taking place all around him, Stephen remains immune and isolated from his surroundings, a "special contrast" indeed but one that clearly loses its specialness when Dickens applies it to "every man." Nevertheless, Dickens asserts a noble sentiment—the triumph of man over the machine—although it is a contradictory, self-defeating one in a novel that otherwise insists on the evils, both mental and physical, of factory life and factory work.

Ironically, if one embarked on a study of hazardous occupations in mid-Victorian England based on the evidence presented in *Hard Times,* one would quickly become convinced that the energies of the factory reformers were misplaced. In Coketown, circus performers rather than mill hands stand in need of legislative protection. When Sissy's father plans his flight, he sends his daughter out for a bottle of nine oils, a substance frequently resorted to by the circus people because, as Sissy acknowledges, "It's what our people always use, when they gets any hurts in the ring. . . . They bruise themselves very bad sometimes" (35). Years of such "hurts in the ring" have apparently "used up" Mr. Jupe (40), and no longer able to amuse the customers, he runs away. Of course, one could reasonably argue that the satisfactions and dissatisfactions of a job cannot be reckoned solely by how dangerous it is and that, consequently, the familial organization of the circus, a stark contrast to the purely contractual relationships that prevail in the Coketown mills, outweighs the actual dangers inherent in performing. But the kind-hearted circus folk can no more ensure the happiness and intactness of the Jupe family than Bounderby can reconcile the irreconcilable differences of the Blackpools.

At the level of representation, the inconsequentiality of Coketown's factories, their curiously benign status in the novel, manifests itself as a simultaneous recognition of and refusal to recognize raw production as the determining and sustaining force of Coketown. Although *Hard Times* underscores the culture's effacement of production, production itself still goes unrepresented, and ironically, only the text's refusal to represent gets represented. In acknowledging that fine London ladies "could scarcely bear to hear [Coketown] mentioned" (31), Dickens reveals an intuitive understanding that in a capitalist system, "commodities are seen in their finished form among other commodities and not in the context of the factories in which they were made" (Belsey 126). But while the narrator mocks passengers on the midnight express who dream of fairy palaces when they speed past Coketown's factories, the reader of *Hard Times* is not any better informed about the goings-on in Coketown's mills. Like that other infrequent visitor to Coketown, Mrs. Pegler, the reader can merely gaze up in wonder and mystification at the imposing facades of Coketown's mills: "[Stephen] had been at his loom full half an hour, thinking about this old woman, when, having occasion to move round the loom for its adjustment, he glanced through a window which was in his corner and saw her still looking up at the pile of building, lost in admiration. Heedless of the smoke and mud and wet, and of her two long journeys, she was gazing at it, as if the heavy thrum that issued from its many stories were proud music to her" (86). Both Mrs. Pegler and the reader see only the mill's brick face, although the reader sees the outside from the inside—through Stephen's eyes. By a trick of perspective, Dickens avoids revealing the hidden sources of capitalist wealth, and in its stead he gives us the illusion of such a revelation. Since Dickens constantly averts his eye (and the reader's) from Coketown's productive energies, production in *Hard Times* makes itself noticeable only by its absence. Even Dickens's earlier account of Stephen lost in the "forest of looms" discloses inactivity rather than productivity. Bent over his loom, frozen in a contemplative state, Stephen does not seem (or is not seen) to be doing anything. Unable to resolve the text's basic contradiction—that Coketown both produces and does not produce its inhabitants—Dickens finds an unlikely compromise: he replaces production in Coketown with a reproduction of Coketown. While he leaves one with a palpable sense of Coketown's surface texture—the red-black brick, the smoke, the tramp of the clogs on the streets—taken as a whole, it is a Potemkin village in prose, a series of false fronts behind which there exists nothing.

In the end, the failed metonymy of *Hard Times* is replaced by an extraordinary metaphoricity, which tries to cover over the fundamental absence of the novel's determining link. Spector argues that the "metaphorical transformations" of the "Keynote" thematize "the process of change (or exchange) itself" (232–33), but these metaphorical transformations, in which the sober red brick towns of England's Midlands become a colonial landscape full of savages, serpents, and elephants run wild, also exchange a metonymic realism for a metaphoric one. Dickens compensates for the connection between character and environment that otherwise eludes him through the medium of his imagination and the force of his rhetoric. Ultimately, the only person who truly resembles Coketown, with its savage face, is poor Tom Gradgrind, reduced to a "comic blackamoor" (239) in a circus before he flees England. The savagery of Gradgrindery has reduced Tom to a lawless young barbarian, with no respect for property, propriety, or family; but this does not evidence the deterministic nature of Dickens's realism so much as the deterministic nature of Dickens's metaphoric universe. The metonymic, realistic world of Coketown's factories and red brick churches cannot manufacture its inhabitants, but Dickens's metaphoric world of serpents and savages can, so in *Hard Times* the metaphoric universe replaces the metonymic one that fails.

But while one can argue for a certain metaphoric (if not metonymic) consequentiality at work in the lives of the Gradgrind children, even that evaporates as one climbs down the social ladder, where Coketown becomes incidental to the plot. It is not the machine-made horrors that blight the existence of Coketown's representative worker, Stephen Blackpool, but his unfortunate marriage. In Stephen's fall down an abandoned mine shaft, Dickens wishes us to read a certain poetic injustice, in that the accident makes concrete and literalizes Stephen's status as a victim of industrialism. But Stephen's death cannot carry such symbolic weight. Dickens anchors Stephen's miseries in an unhappy private life; and appropriately, his unexplained promise to Rachel (rather than anything Bounderby or Slackbridge do) sets in motion the chain of events that leads to Old Hell Shaft. Dickens neutralizes any potential menace the industrial environment might pose and thus renders Coketown disturbingly innocuous. As a backdrop to the action rather than in any real sense a determinant of it, Coketown witnesses Stephen's death but does not cause it.

Dickens makes one last attempt to resolve the problem of determinism in the novel. It is Stephen's enslavement to his wife, a dissolute former factory worker, that the narrator finally offers as the determinant of Stephen's fate; and thus, like many other nineteenth-century observers of the factories, Dickens ultimately lays the blame for modernity's dissatisfactions on the Victorian mill girl. If we keep in mind Gallagher's insistence on the importance of the rhetoric of freedom, borrowed from the abolitionist movement, to the early industrial debates about free will and determinism, we can see how Dickens shifts consequentiality in the novel from the public to the private sphere: the language of slavery and emancipation is invoked to explain Stephen's relationship to his wife, not his loom. Mrs. Sparsit notes that he "wishes to be free" (80) from his wife, and in his liberation from the shackles of an unfortunate marriage the narrator places Stephen's redemption:

> [Stephen] thought of the home he might at that moment have been seeking with pleasure and pride; of the different man he might have been that night; of the lightness then in his now heavy-laden breast; of the then restored honour, self-respect, and tranquillity all torn to pieces. He thought of the waste of the best part of his life, of the change it made in his character for the worse every day, of the dreadful nature of his existence, bound hand and foot, to a dead woman, and tormented by a demon in her shape. (87)

In this passage, Dickens transfers the consequentiality of the factory to the working-class family, but then he is left to account for the dysfunctions of Mrs. Blackpool. Because Dickens creates an industrial world extraneous to the lives of its inhabitants, he can offer no explanation (other than inherited traits) for Mrs. Blackpool's vices. Lacking any evidence to the contrary, the reader must assume that Mrs. Blackpool is disposed to get drunk, live in filth, and engage in wanton behavior. In sum, the narrative represents Mrs. Blackpool as a genuine "self-made outcast" (90), an ironic counterpart to the disingenuously self-made Bounderby, and in doing so it falls back on the working-class woman's character to explain the misery of Coketown's workers.

With the material conditions of Coketown transformed into background scenery, the novel emerges as a highly gendered, Carlylean examination of the spiritual disposition of England's workers. In fact, *Hard Times* is as much a moral allegory as a moral fable, with Stephen cast as latter-day everyman caught between two working women, one representing middle-class virtue and the other working-class vice. With no undue haste, vice makes its appearance on Dickens's stage in the form of Stephen's drunken wife, who rapidly descended into debauchery after marriage. Of course, the Victorian reader would have been able to identify her immediately, for she is the middle-class stereotype of the debased mill girl, the perversely independent female who inhabits the texts of Ashley, Engels, and Stephens, parliamentary blue books, newspaper accounts and the reports of social investigators. Certainly Bounderby accepts the dissolute Mrs. Blackpool as a common and commonly known figure. When he tells Stephen he has "heard all this before," he is not claiming to have heard Stephen's particular tale of woe; rather, Stephen recounts a story wearily familiar to him from other tellings, so much so that he can fill in from his own experience the details Stephen does not give: "She took to drinking, left off working, sold the furniture, pawned the clothes, and played old Gooseberry" (78).

If Dickens turns Mrs. Blackpool into one of his culture's most persistent stereotypes, it is to provide the answer to a question he posed a decade earlier when introduced to the piano-playing, poetry-writing women who worked in Massachusetts's Lowell Mills: "Are we quite sure that we in England have not formed our ideas of the 'station' of working people from accustoming ourselves to contemplation of that class as they are, and not as they might be?" (*American Notes* 68). Dickens's experience with American industri-

alism is as important an antecedent to *Hard Times* as his flying visit
to Preston: Stephen's desire for divorce contains the kernel of this
"might be" articulated years before in *American Notes.* While Mrs.
Blackpool embodies working-class women "as they are"—disorderly,
uncontrollable, irrational—Rachel represents the "might be." As a
factory worker who worries about the improprieties of her relationship
with Stephen, Rachel would easily be recognized as the ideal bourgeois
woman even if Stephen did not repeatedly address her as his "angel."
By wishing to divorce himself from his licentious working-class wife
and take in her stead the womanly Rachel, who spends much of the
novel in the suitably domestic activity of nursing Mrs. Blackpool,
Stephen enacts Dickens's strategy for social redemption. Futurity will
be assured when working men separate themselves from their prodigal
working-class ways (and wives) and aspire to bourgeois values. Joining
a long line of middle-class Victorians who blamed the degraded state
of the working man on the domestic inadequacies of his wife, Dickens
scripts the working man's redemption as the transformation of the
notorious factory girl into a model of femininity. In other words, the
disposition of working-class women "as they are" is wrong, and only
their domestication, with a little help from the masters, can right it.

Dickens never exposes Bounderby's expectations about Mrs.
Blackpool as false (after all, his portrait of Mrs. Blackpool is a marvel
of verisimilitude), but the novelist does blame him for failing to see
the "might be" and for refusing to help Stephen escape from the
source of all his sufferings, the bad disposition of his undomesticated
wife. For all his devotion to fact, Bounderby remains a great fiction-
maker, particularly when it comes to his autobiography; in the end,
however, Bounderby's fictional extravagances prove less harmful than
his fitful commitment to fact—to the working class "as they are"—
because it prevents him (and Coketown's other captains of industry)
from imagining an alternate, better possibility for the workers, such
as the one Dickens believed he encountered in New England. If we
read *Hard Times* as a moral allegory, then it reads very much as one
about the failure of the ruling classes to help laboring men divorce
themselves from the "what is" of working-class immorality, embodied
in the working-class woman, and strive for the "might be" of domesticity. By contending that Britain's industrialists lack vision,

Dickens is neither the first nor the last individual to blast a nation's business leaders for their imaginative shortcomings, but in doing so he not only appropriates the Carlylean desire to elude the material but he also thematizes it: in *Hard Times* the ability to overleap the material becomes a mark of vision and true leadership.[16] The text's mild paternalism only vaguely resembles the forceful, autocratic leadership Carlyle proposes in *Past and Present,* but *Hard Times*'s ultimate tribute to Carlyle may be in its willingness to take Carlyle's anti-materialism as the basis for heroic behavior in Coketown.

## Medievalism and Culture

In his scathing attack on the Pre-Raphaelites, "Old Lamps for New Ones," Dickens envisages the emergence of a pre-Newtonian and pre-Chaucerian society in the Pre-Raphaelite Brotherhood's wake, denominating its love for all things medieval as a "young England hallucination" (245). Despite his contemptuous regard for Victorian medievalism, one of the startling things about *Hard Times* is its odd and momentary resemblances to the Young England movement Dickens denounces as hallucinatory. In perhaps the quintessential Young England text, *A Plea for National Holy-Days* (1843), Lord John Manners notes that "utilitarian selfishness has well nigh banished all such unproductive amusements from the land: has it not also banished contentment, and good humour, and loyalty from thousands of English cottage homes?" (5). Manners's text admirably argues for more holidays for working folk, although he unfortunately links these holidays to medieval holy-days and imagines much maypole dancing on the village green. But pared down to its essential elements, his anti-utilitarian argument merely demands leisure time and amusement, and this is, when you get right down to it, Dickens's basic anti-utilitarian plea in *Hard Times*: "People must be amuthed" (49), as the circus manager is fond of saying. Manners wishes to entertain them through the revival of village sports, and Dickens wishes to do it through the cultivation of the imagination, but the principle remains the same: Dickens's circus and Lord John Manners holy-days both offer relief for Britain's overworked workers.[17]

In a rudimentary way, Dickens's Fancy, embodied by the circus folk in *Hard Times* and offered up as the life-affirming alternative to dreary utilitarian Fact, is also a precursor of Arnold's culture, although Fancy remains distinctly lowbrow by comparison. Like culture, it opposes industrialism and cultivates what we could identify as a Dickensian best self—loving, joyful, compassionate, and caring. This is not to offer up Dickens as a closet medievalist or as an unacknowledged man of culture, but to indicate a profound, if unexpected, affiliation between the Victorian medievalists, Dickens and Arnold. They are linked through their repudiation of industrialism in favor of the values embodied in the Middle Ages, Fancy and culture respectively; and they are linked through the complicated dematerialization that underwrites their evasions of modernity and licenses (in the cases of medievalism and culture) a retreat into the past. By dematerializing the industrial world, the medievalists are released from tying the material changes in the productive organization of life to concomitant ones in its social organization. Thus, they can reaffirm an older, hierarchical order that seems to be in its moment of final dissolution, since in their eyes the emergence of the factories requires no radical reconfiguration of the social structure. Even in the decades after midcentury, when Victorian intellectuals lost their faith in the possible resurrection of a feudal order, they still believed in the possibility of reestablishing the ideology that underpinned it, and this ideology became that deracinated entity known as culture, abstracted out of the sociohistorical processes that formed it to emerge as the transcendent authority, untethered to the material world, that the male critics quested for all along.

The first moment of the male retreat into the past, Victorian medievalism, is a well-documented phenomenon, but while so much of Victorian culture was permeated by the feudal ideal—from the taste for Gothic town halls to the rage for Morris wallpaper—medievalism was not a Victorian invention. The Romantics had dreamed of an organic, richly emotional medieval past to contrast with the overly rational and overwhelmingly commercial present. Influenced by the Romantic poets, and perhaps even more significantly by Sir Walter Scott, early Victorian England found solace in a cult of chivalry, which entailed, among other things, restaged medieval tournaments and fancy dress balls. In general, as A. Dwight Culler keenly observes, the Victorians' deep ignorance about the Middle Ages allowed them to re-create the period in their own image, according to their own needs and desires:

> The most intense period of Victorian medievalism ran from the late 1820s to the 1850s, and, given the fact that its practitioners had so little in common—they included Tories and radicals, Roman Catholics and Dissenters, aristocrats and commoners—it can only be explained as a reaction against the forces dominating English life at this time: Whigs, Utilitarians and liberal reformers. Disliking intensely what they saw taking place in England, they took refuge in another age, and that age was large enough, various enough, sufficiently unknown and even mythical, that each person could find there what he wanted—a hierarchy, a community, a code of conduct, a form of hero-worship, a system of ritual, a charitable establishment, a style of architecture, a resplendent wardrobe. (159–60)[18]

In the hands of its two most important early Victorian practitioners, Thomas Carlyle and Benjamin Disraeli, medievalism proved the ideal (and idealized) counterpoint to what came to be regarded as an increasingly democratic present. In turning to the Middle Ages, the two men discovered what Alice Chandler identifies as a "metaphor . . . for a specific social order" (1); and one does not need to belabor the inherently conservative nature of that social order, with its fundamental hierarchies of class and gender. Both men yoke medievalism to a critique of incipient industrialism and conjure up a feudalized factory world that resurrects the social order (and not just the costumery) of the past as an anodyne to what they diagnose as the social disorder besetting the industrial present.

Underwriting the medievalists' vision of history turning back on itself is a refusal to accept industrialism, in all its unmanageable solidity, as a permanent feature of the English landscape. If the industrial world exuded an unreal quality for the medievalists, it is because they hesitated to embrace the world-transforming nature of industrialism. Not sharing Marx's belief in the intractable relationship between social organization and material practices, a belief that

would, according to Althusser and Balibar, "constitute an epistemological break with respect to the whole tradition of philosophy of
history" and revolutionize "the whole problematic of society and
history" (210), the antimaterialist British critics had no reason to
assume that the material organization of life determined the social,
political, or intellectual formations of the nation.

To be fair, while Marx and Engels may have condemned
Victorian medievalism in *The Communist Manifesto* as "half lamentation, half lampoon . . . always ludicrous in its effects, through total
incapacity to comprehend the march of modern history" (42–3), that
march seemed less assured in the decades before 1850. "There was
no belief in the inevitability of industrial capitalism in the 1830s
and early 1840s," Gareth Stedman Jones notes (59). Nineteenth-
century Britain's much-publicized faith in progress, from Tennyson's
vision of "moving upward / Working out the beast" to Darwin's
evolutionary manifestos, corresponds to the period after midcentury:
"The Great Exhibition of 1851 may be interpreted, as indeed it was
by many Victorians, as marking the border between two ages: the
past one bleak, hostile, rent with class warfare and political vituper-
ation, and the future one hopeful, golden, ever-advancing on well-
oiled wheels down 'the ringing grooves of change' " (Brantlinger,
*Spirit of Reform* 3). Historical boundary-making may be treacherous,
but this is one boundary historians generally agree upon. Thus, it is
important to localize Victorian medievalism, as a vital social critique,
in the turbulent years of the Hungry Forties, when widespread unrest
in the manufacturing districts, intensified by depressed trade and
high unemployment, exacerbated what Eric Hobsbawm describes as
a "sense of imminent social explosion" (94), which had plagued British
society since the Napoleonic Wars. Even if the summons to the bar-
ricades was never heard in the slums around St. Giles, and England
remained free of the violent revolutionary uprisings that occurred
with some frequency in France, Chartist agitations and industrial
disputes kept the Victorian fear of revolution well-stoked throughout
the late 1830s and 1840s. "These Chartisms, Radicalisms, Reform
Bill, Tithe Bill . . . are *our* French Revolution," Carlyle thunderously
declaimed in "Chartism" (149–50); and in this supercharged atmo-

sphere, redolent of revolution, the possibility of historical regression existed alongside the probability of historical progression.

No novel better captures this mood of uncertainty about the future than Charles Kingsley's *Yeast* (1848), a Christian Socialist condition-of-England novel that details the hardscrabble lives of rural laborers. Indeed, the title itself refers to an inchoateness of thought that Kingsley identifies as the dominant characteristic of the age:

> Readers will probably complain of the fragmentary and unconnected form of the book. Let them first be sure that that is not an integral feature of the subject itself, and therefore, the very form the book should take. Do not young men think, speak, act, just now, in this very incoherent, fragmentary way; without methodic education or habits of thought; with the various stereotyped systems which they have received by tradition, breaking up under them like ice in a thaw; with a thousand facts and notions, which they know not how to classify, pouring in on them like a flood?—a very Yeasty state of mind altogether. (364–65)

In a line not destined for such an afterlife as Arnold's "wandering between two worlds, one dead / The other powerless to be born," Kingsley describes England in "a transition between feudalism and ———" (271). Perhaps a blank never spoke more eloquently. For Kingsley in 1848, the future was a blank, and anything from a Chartist republic to a feudalized factory world could fill it. While the early Victorians knew they were living in an age of transition, what they were making a transition to remained elusive.

Given this widespread perception of English culture as existing in a yeasty, inchoate state, there was no good reason why the monumental technological transformations could not just as plausibly lead one back to a world of monasteries and feudal overlords as toward a modern, industrialized democracy. It is this unbounded uncertainty that Disraeli captures in the following conversation in *Sybil*:

> "Now, tell me, Stephen," said the Religious, turning her head and looking round with a smile, "think you not it would be a fairer lot to hide this night at some kind monastery, then to be

hastening now to that least picturesque of all creations, the railway station?" . . .

"Had it not been for the railway, we should never have made our visit to Marney Abbey," said the elder of the travellers.

"Nor seen its last abbot's tomb," said the Religious. (82)

While the elderly traveller, the earnest Walter Gerard, envisions the railroad as a kind of midnight express to the Middle Ages, his daughter Sybil, here referred to as "the Religious," offers a more double-edged response. The reader cannot be sure whether Sybil's remark signals consent with her father or whether, by holding the railway responsible for there being a "last" abbot, her reply—like Thomas Arnold's lament uttered as the first train thundered past Rugby—associates the death of the feudal past with the advent of the railroads. Perhaps of paramount importance, however, is the ambiguity of the passage, characteristic of the 1840s, when going back to the future and forward down "the ringing grooves of change" seemed equally likely.[19]

It took something on the scale of the 1848 revolutions, when all of Europe rose up in an effort to snatch democracy from the jaws of reaction, to awaken many Victorians to the fact that the new world of factories and electoral reform was here to stay. Pondering the Paris insurrections from the safety of a London vantage point, a young Matthew Arnold wrote to his mother: "It will be *rioting* here, only; still the hour of the hereditary peerage and eldest sonship and immense properties has, I am convinced, as Lamartine would say, struck" (*Letters* 5). Three days later he informed his sister, "What agitates me is this, if the new state of things succeeds in France, social changes are inevitable here and elsewhere, for no one looks on seeing his neighbour mending without asking himself if he cannot mend in the same way" (6). The Continental revolutions forced Arnold to see social change in the cold light of the inevitable. In contrast, they led Carlyle in *Latter-Day Pamphlets* to attack democracy with a vituperativeness that shocked even his most ardent followers. Carlyle was still imagining a return to the social arrangements of the past when he asked John Stuart Mill in 1840: "And now when will you write of the *New Aristocracy* we have to look for? That seems to me the question; all Democracy is a mere transitory preparation for that" (*Letters* 172–73). But as Engels observed in a note to the 1892 German edition of *The Condition of the Working Class in England,* "The February Revolution made [Carlyle] an out-and-out reactionary. His righteous wrath against the Philistines turned into sullen Philistine grumbling at the tide of history that cast him ashore" (318). Carlyle's realization in *Latter-Day Pamphlets* that democracy was the "huge inevitable Product of Destinies" (427) provoked his sudden, vehement objections, which had been unnecessary in the days when democracy did not wear the face of the inexorable.

One cannot help but be struck by how impermanent industrialism appears to be in the texts Disraeli and Carlyle wrote before midcentury. In a metaphor that recalls *Sartor Resartus,* Carlyle compares the factories to clothing that can be pulled off and tossed aside at will, distinguishing the "noisome wrappage" of "Manchester, with its cotton-fuzz, its smoke and dust, its tumult and contentious squalor" from the pure, undressed creative power of production, "sublime as a Niagara," that he wishes to salvage ("Chartism" 181–82). The sublimity and power of nature represents a transcendent reality to Carlyle, while Manchester represents a mere physical reality—the filthy clothes—in which the other, greater reality is unhappily garbed. Awed and inspired by the might of technology, Carlyle translates cotton spinning into "the triumph of man over matter" ("Chartism" 182), and this leads Herbert Sussman to contend that Carlyle transforms machinery into "an emblem of transcendental power" (15), the factory floor equivalent of the Carlylean dictum that "society . . . does not in any age prevent a man from being what he *can be.*" Once again we see Carlyle's spiritual materialism in action: the ideal of transcendence has sought its bed and board in the flawed reality of industrial production.

And just as Carlyle wishes to deny industrialism the specific material form of Manchester cotton mills, so he also wishes to deny it a specific social form. To be sure, Carlyle's captains of industry are an attempt to mandate strong new leadership to combat the noninterventionist dictates of laissez-faire policy, which Carlyle saw as tending towards sexual and class anarchy. But they are also an attempt to negate the social and political consequences of the industrial revolution by replacing an idle, do-nothing aristocracy with a working, industrial aristocracy and thereby resecuring—at least in theory—

the hierarchical framework of British society. Carlyle's captains of industry are an attempt to disarm, domesticate, and absorb the shocks of early industrialism. By detaching the industrial revolution first from its given material shape (cities, factories, smoke) and then from its developing political shape (democracy), Carlyle tries to rescue its transformational energies while at the same time disallowing it the power to transform British society.

Even more so than Carlyle, Disraeli remains wholly unconvinced of industrialism's power to restructure English culture. The day Carlyle looks forward to—when that "noisome wrappage" of Manchester would disappear—had in Disraeli's opinion already arrived, and he envisions a factory world in the process of ruination. After a commercial traveller (carrying the embarrassing moniker of "G.O.A. Head") tells Coningsby that Manchester, the ur-city of the industrial revolution, is "a dead letter" and "behind the times" (138–39), the improbable Sidonia's famous dictum, "The Age of Ruins is past. Have you seen Manchester?" (101), glows with new meaning: Manchester is a ruin. Everywhere he looks, the narrator of *Coningsby* sees radical instability, a world unraveling at the edges rather than one weaving itself into existence through the ceaseless transformations of raw cotton into finished cloth. In fact, the only brave new world *Coningsby* envisages is rather long in the tooth. The commercial traveller who writes Manchester's obituary advises Coningsby to visit up-to-date Millbank, a mill town on the cutting edge of cotton technology. But with its rural seclusion, Gothic church, and noble-hearted (if not noble) owner, Millbank turns out to be quite old-fashioned, one of the many medievalized factory villages that populate the early Victorian imagination, even though its owner, a pattern paternalist, fancies it the "New World" (144). For Disraeli as well as Carlyle, the factories remain a minor aberration in the long march of English history. If they picture a medievalized nineteenth century, what gives this vision its clarity and its palpability is their unshakable conviction in the *uninevitability* of social change and the instability of industrial modernity.

Not only do Carlyle and Disraeli retain throughout the 1840s a remarkably skeptical attitude toward industrialism, but by insisting on the factual rather than fanciful nature of their medieval idylls, they hold out the possibility of resurrecting the feudal past as a genuine alternative to the industrial present, a possibility made all the more viable because they set a solidly real medieval world against an ephemeral industrial one.[20] Generically, Victorian medievalism belongs to the category of romance, characterized by "its extraordinarily persistent nostalgia, its search for some kind of imaginative golden age in time or space" (Frye 186). Yet the medievalism practiced by Carlyle and Disraeli refuses to acknowledge its roots in romance because it insists on being judged for its historical veracity. Both men offer up their medievalism neither as romance nor fiction but as history, delineated in the nineteenth century as a purely factual discourse. Thus, Carlyle in *Past and Present* can claim to distinguish "the poorest historical Fact from all Fiction whatsoever" (44) because, as Hayden White notes:

> In the early nineteenth century . . . it became conventional, at least among historians, to identify truth with fact and to regard fiction as the opposite of truth, hence as a hindrance to the understanding of reality rather than as a way of apprehending it. History came to be set over against fiction, and especially the novel, as the representation of the "actual" to the representation of the "possible" or only "imaginable." And thus was born the dream of a historical discourse that would consist of nothing but factually accurate statements about a realm of events which were (or had been) observable in principle. (123)

Moreover, not only was history set against fiction but also against myth. In fact, myth and fiction were conflated so that, according to White, "the distinction between myth and fiction which is a commonplace in the thought of our century was hardly grasped at all by the foremost ideologues of the early nineteenth century" (124). Victorian medievalism remains romantic myth delivered in the guise of historical fact, for the Victorians disassociated fiction and history, declining to see them as two forms of verbal representation that share the same mythmaking potential. Nevertheless, these romances which profess to offer realistic representations of the past derive strength from their own paradoxical nature: by presenting an appealingly nostalgic and romantic vision of the world as realistic, and hence attainable, the medieval idylls found in *Past and Present* and *Sybil* tempt readers with the possibility of realizing the romance.

To create this illusion of historical realism, both Disraeli and Carlyle try to save the Middle Ages from its more picturesque incarnations by drawing a distinction between the fashionable medievalism of mock tournaments and their own insistence on the era as a truly—not mythically—superior time. In *Past and Present,* one of the fullest expressions of Victorian medievalism, Carlyle reanimates the twelfth-century abbey of St. Edmundsbury in order to dismiss the notion of the Middle Ages as a golden age. His Bury St. Edmunds is "no chimerical vacuity or dreamland, peopled with mere vaporous Fantasms" (44), and to his credit, he does dispense with the chivalrous knights and pre-Raphaelite ladies that embroider so much of the genre. Moreover, under the reign of Abbot Hugo, all is not perfect in the abbey. Having discovered the joys of deficit spending, the monastery finds itself on the verge of bankruptcy. Worse yet, the monks are "given to idle gossip" (67), and their loose talk hints at a precipitous decline in religious feeling. Such overt debunking, however, licenses Carlyle to gild his portrait of the Middle Ages even more. So, for example, while acknowledging that Gurth the Saxon swineherd (who, ironically, is a fictional character, having found his way into Carlyle's text from Scott's novels) may have been less than enthusiastic about a social system that condemned him and his progeny to pig parings, Carlyle can nonetheless hold him up as an example of the feudal past's humane treatment of the poor and as a striking contrast to their inhumane treatment under the poor laws of the nineteenth century. Carlyle subtly idealizes an age he considers less shabby than his own, but he does so under the cover of writing history, a position supported by the fact that the medieval portions of *Past and Present* were inspired by a real historical document, Jocelin of Brakelond's firsthand account of life in medieval St. Edmundsbury. Ultimately, it is as a historian's truth and not as a poet's dream that Carlyle wants his reader to approach the medieval world in *Past and Present.*

Disraeli's desire to salvage medievalism from its romantic trappings is allied to his need to rescue his own reputation from its Byronic associations. Tied to his political failures, Disraeli's medievalism is a sustained plea by the author for credibility. As one of Disraeli's biographer relates, accusations of insincerity and opportunism were still plaguing the future prime minister on the eve of writing *Sybil*: "He had been in Parliament for seven years, and he had done nothing of real importance. It is true that people listened to him with attention, and sometimes took what he said seriously. But they found many of his ideas eccentric and incomprehensible. Above all, they did not trust him personally. And no wonder. Here was an insolvent, mysterious, half-foreign adventurer with a libertine past and a load of debt, who had married a rich widow for money" (Blake 183). Even Lord John Manners, Disraeli's fellow Young Englander, questioned Disraeli's dedication to the cause, noting in his journal, "Could I only satisfy myself that Disraeli really believed all that he said, I should be more happy: his historical views are quite mine, but then does he believe them?" (qtd. in S. Smith vii). Manners's doubts about Disraeli's sincere attachment to the Young England movement have come down to modern critics, who see Disraeli slyly laughing at the alms-giving, maypole-dancing aristocrats who inhabit his Young England trilogy. No doubt he is. The aristocrats who suffer the stings of Disraeli's satiric barbs are figures like *Coningsby*'s petty tyrant Lord Monmouth, who wishes his grandson to enter Parliament for the sole reason, he informs him, of turning "our coronet into a ducal one" (360), and *Sybil*'s fatuous Sir Vavasour Firebrace, who spends most of the novel scheming to restore to the baronets their "long-withheld rights" (49) to parade around in fancy dress. While these do-nothing aristocrats greedily snatch up all the trappings and privileges of their class—the mummery and flummery of their patrimonies—they refuse the responsibilities. This constitutes a debased medievalism that Disraeli ridicules so that he can resurrect a purified version of it through the character of Sybil.

Like Carlyle, Disraeli deromanticizes medievalism by claiming it as history and not romance. Perhaps more than any other Victorian novelist, Disraeli is obsessed with history, and to grasp his brand of medievalism, one must first grapple with his view of history. Disraeli fills the pages of both *Sybil* and *Coningsby* with huge, undigested swatches of history, painstakingly detailing two irreconcilable world views, the Whig "misreading" of history and the Young

England correction of that misreading. This Whig misreading, the textbook version of English history, tells the familiar tale of constitutional monarchs and commercial interests triumphing over bad kings besotted with notions of divinity and feudal barons simply besotted. Rejecting the optimism, the faith in historical progress implicit in Whig history, Disraeli counters it with a tale of decline, both of the rights of the people and the power of the crown, beginning in the regicidal days of the seventeenth century. In rendering the Whig and Young England variants of history as competing interpretations, and doing so in works of fiction, Disraeli would seem to be suggesting that all history aspires to the condition of fiction, thus leaving himself open to accusations of privileging Tory history over Whig history for reasons of political expediency. But the novelist, well aware of the whispered doubts surrounding him, anticipates the charge and challenges it by creating Baptist Hatton, the antiquarian in *Sybil* who, like Disraeli himself, profits from the plasticity of history. In fact, in Hatton's somewhat shadowy, slightly disreputable figure, we find a self-mocking portrait of the author.[21] By plying a trade in noble patents and forging counterfeit ancestries for newly minted aristocrats, Hatton too molds the past to suit his immediate purposes. But Hatton's sham lords, the equivalent of Young England's maypole fancies, are merely the dross that inevitably gets mixed in with the gold. For Disraeli, neither spurious titles nor specious folk traditions should devalue the feudal past. While Young England's romantic reconstructions of the medieval past and Hatton's individual reconstructions of the aristocratic past may contain much prefabricated nonsense, the ideal itself—incarnated in Sybil—remains intact. Less flesh and blood than symbol of the medieval religious spirit and the medieval social contract, Sybil is paradoxically the real thing, the true heir both to the Mowbray estate and the medieval ideal. When faced with this genuine article, Hatton, who had "a respect only for what was authentic" (252), cannot rest until he effects the reversion of Sybil's ancient rights, thereby becoming one of the novel's heroes. Through Hatton, the supersubtle antiquarian, Disraeli acknowledges the superior historical skills and exegetical talents that enable him to discern the real thing, the legitimate medieval ideal, that can be lost amidst the riot of Young England's chivalric frippery.

Both Disraeli and Carlyle can use their medieval romances to carry out a serious critique of industrial society because they deploy them as historical and hence factual models of what "actually" was as well as what should be; and in this way, both men attempted to, as Jeffrey Spear puts it, "impose the pattern of romance on the process of history, to change England" (6). But this imposition could often lead to—and did in both *Past and Present* and *Sybil*—an impasse. For it is only through the fictional devices of romance that one can move from the past to the present, so that these texts, despite their claims for historical accuracy, lack a certain internal coherence when not read as romance. Carlyle's heroic leader is not an evasion of the very real problems of industrial England, as readers looking for concrete political answers may think, but an answer to them in the "mythical Messiah" common to Frye's romance archetype (187). Just as the heroic Abbot Samson returns the abbey to fiscal and moral solvency, so could a modern hero save a nation likewise plagued.

Similarly, the fairy-tale finish of *Sybil* can seem inappropriate in a novel that bravely, even encyclopedically, catalogues social injustices. Ills ranging from urban blight to rural depression magically disappear at the novel's close, leaving a puzzled reader curious as to just how the marriage of Charles Egremont and Sybil Gerard might keep a handloom weaver from starvation. But Disraeli's happy ending is no novelistic sleight of hand, a typical turn to the private when an intractable public world threatens to upset the novel's closure. Rather, a mythic structure underpins *Sybil* as well as *Past and Present*. The novel takes the form of a quest romance, where "a land ruled by a helpless old king is laid waste by a sea-monster . . . the hero arrives, kills the dragon, marries the daughter, and succeeds to the kingdom" (Frye 189). Disraeli merely updates the myth by substituting a smoke-belching factory for a fire-breathing dragon. Only after the Young Englandish Egremont replaces the impotent old king (who, in this Tory version of the myth, takes the shape of a Whig landlord), marries Sybil, and inherits the two estates does the industrial wasteland revert to its original green and pleasant condition. By restoring manly, paternalistic leadership and thus proper authority, Egremont "solves" all of the troubled land's problems. Victorian medievalism belongs in the enchanted wood of romance and not, as Disraeli would have one believe, in the halls of Parliament. The romance structure of the medievalist texts belies any claim to realism, although so potent is the claim itself that readers expect (and are often disappointed not to find) pragmatic solutions on offer.

Historicizing the genre of romance, Frederic Jameson argues that romance belongs to moments of transition where "two distinct modes of production, or moments of socioeconomic development, coexist. . . . the great art-romances of the early nineteenth century take their variously reactive stances against the new and unglamorous social institutions emerging from the political triumph of the bourgeoisie and the setting in place of the market system" (148). Whether or not two distinct modes of production existed in the early nineteenth century, the Victorian medievalists felt themselves to be uncomfortably straddling two discrete cultural formations, as if the Middle Ages existed just on the other side of modernity, tantalizingly close and eminently accessible. Before modernity came to be seen as the inevitable (if unenviable) condition of being, medievalism could function both as a blueprint for the future and as a remembrance of things past. By 1850, however, the hour of Arnold's hereditary peerages, eldest sonships, and immense properties had indeed struck; and although Victorian medievalism continued through to the end of the century, it increasingly became a fashion for all things medieval. It was only given new life when, in the last few decades of the century, William Morris hitched Ruskin to Marx to produce his powerfully attractive vision of arts and crafts socialism, which uses Marx's historical dialectic to project a postindustrial medieval world, one brought about by a genuine working-class revolution. Early Victorian medievalism lost much of its intellectual energy, as well as its cultural and political power, when modernity began to appear as a *fait accompli.*

The possibility of reestablishing a feudal order faded after midcentury. By the 1860s, when Matthew Arnold published "Stanzas from the Grande Chartreuse," his most elaborate evocation of the medieval past, the Middle Ages had finally disappeared into the dim recesses of history and become a ghost town, peopled by half-alive monks and not the "flesh and blood" (48) brothers of St. Edmundsbury. Caught between past and future, trapped in a present that he consistently defines as an absence, Arnold can neither retreat into the

historical past nor confidently march forward towards a New Jerusalem. So like Moses, the prophetic poet of "Stanzas" lingers in the
"desert" (line 210) and points his wandering nation, the Hebraicized
Britons, in the direction of the promised land.

But while the past itself, represented in "Stanzas" by the
monks of the Grande Chartreuse, lingers only in a spectral afterlife
and cannot be resurrected, the ideology of the past can be. In its
institutionalized form, this ideology is culture, the predominantly
all-male (and manmade) arena that Arnold popularized as "the best
that has been thought and known in the world." By maintaining the
living link between past and future through culture—embodied in
the great books that, in a postbelief age, supersede the one Good
Book—Arnold hopes to enact England's "intellectual deliverance"
("Modern Element in Literature" 5). But this link is extraordinarily
fragile. Culture needs the security of new institutional forms to preserve and mete out the precious knowledge of the past, and so Arnold
finds himself constantly arguing for vessels and containers—the state,
academies, school curricula, men of culture—in which to pour this
liquid, shapeless thing called culture that is always in danger of
draining away.

Despite its fragility, culture plays the same role after 1850
that medievalism played before midcentury. It opposes industrial
capitalism by establishing a system of values other than those of the
marketplace; it positions itself as a transcendent authority to counteract the anarchy of modern life; and it looks back to the past in
order to "embalm a dead wisdom" (Miller 263) of a dead past that
can now be reconstructed only through its ideology. Arnold, culture's
most influential promoter, inherits the medievalists' critique of infant
industrialism and transforms it. The repudiation of cotton mills and
Chartist insurrections, rooted in the social dislocations of the Hungry
Forties, loses its historical specificity in Arnold, who unfolds and
amplifies that repudiation into a powerful condemnation of modernity
itself. While still an open question for Carlyle in the early 1840s,
the true nature of the Victorian "strange new Today" receives from
Arnold a definitive answer when he exhorts the Scholar Gypsy to flee
"this strange disease of modern life," as if modernity were a cholera
epidemic.

If the male critics' repudiation of modern life reaches it apogee in Arnold, so does its dematerialization: Arnoldian culture, the Arnoldian man of culture, and Arnold's conception of class all rest somewhat precariously upon an absent material base. The confusion that has historically surrounded culture arises out of the fact that culture is both a critic of institutions and the product of those selfsame institutions. As Raymond Williams notes in his well-known critique of Arnoldian culture, by not "extending his criticism of ideas to criticism of the social and economic system from which they proceeded," Arnold fails to secure his idea of culture to a specific social or economic mooring (*Culture and Society* 146). In this detached state, culture all too frequently becomes what Arnold in *Culture and Anarchy* claims to despise—an "engine of social and class distinctions" (408). And guarding over this dematerialized culture is the Arnoldian man of culture, an individual unhitched from the social world around him. According to Arnold, the man of culture's chief attribute is disinterestedness; but given the difficulties of being truly disinterested, it is not surprising that the men of culture who followed Arnold frequently became engineers of class and social distinctions.

Not only does Arnold unhinge culture and the man of culture from their material base, but he also unhinges England's class culture. By emphasizing the disposition of England's citizens at the expense of their condition, Arnold removes class from its material context and translates it into a collection of psychological traits. Arnold explains the Hyde Park rioting, which prompted him to write *Culture and Anarchy* in the first place, as the eternal spirit of the Populace, a mixture of blindness, force, irrationality, and ignorance, showing its disposition to riot. As Williams tartly intoned, when Arnold saw the railings around Hyde Park fall, his best self did not rise to the occasion. But Arnold's anxiety over the recent agitation in Hyde Park cannot fully account for his uncharitable characterization of the Populace. Rather, the characterization belongs to the text's general dematerializing scheme. Transforming a sociological concept into a psychological one, Arnold turns the whole notion of class inside out: Barbarians, Philistines, and the Populace are not three great estates but three emotional states. He invokes stereotypical essences (the natural pride of the aristocracy, the inherent selfishness of the bourgeoisie, the innate brutality of the working class) to answer Carlyle's condition-of-England question: "Is the condition of the English working people so wrong; so wrong that rational working men cannot, will not, and even should not rest quiet under it?" As Dickens and Carlyle had before him, Arnold decides that, in the end, it is "their disposition, their own thoughts, beliefs and feelings that are wrong," although to his credit it is no longer just the disposition of the English working people that he assails, but the disposition of the English. Carlyle's insistence that the "spiritual always determines the material" becomes in *Culture and Anarchy* an elevation of class to the realm of pure spirit.[22]

Given Arnold's extraordinary dematerializing tendencies, it is scarcely surprising that J. Hillis Miller would characterize him as the poet of vacuity. By draining out the social world in his writings, Arnold can fill his poems with grand empty spaces—darkling plains and deserts—in order to evoke the absence that constitutes his present. But he cannot sustain this emptiness in the poetry that evokes it, so that, for example, the world he claims as "powerless to be born" remains alive (if in its infancy) in the poem in which he most famously proclaims its absence. While the poet of "Stanzas from the Grande Chartreuse" chooses to seek shelter by the medieval abbey wall, all around him the woods are full of people engaged in frenetic activities:

> Years hence, perhaps, may dawn an age,
> More fortunate, alas! than we,
> Which without hardness will be sage,
> And gay without frivolity.
> Sons of the world, oh, speed those years;
> But, while we wait, allows our tears.
>
> Allow them! We admire with awe
> The exulting thunder of your race;
> You give the universe your law,
> You triumph over time and space!
> Your pride of life, your tireless powers,
> We laud them, but they are not ours. (lines 157–68)

Through a kind of poetic shorthand, these lines summon up modernity, at least in its technological manifestation. Nevertheless, Arnold's insistence that modernity remains embryonic, "powerless to be born," reminds one of nothing so much as the refusal by the medievalists to embrace the permanency of industrialism. With its denial of and evocation of a ripening modernity, "Stanzas from the Grande Chartreuse" underscores Arnold's problematic relationship to the social and material world he wishes to critique. This double move of Arnold's, in which he both engages the material world and disengages himself from it, results in a paralysis as the practical outcome of his social thinking. It leaves him idling by the abbey wall in "Stanzas," even though he knows the medieval world it represents is a wasteland; and it leaves him arguing for the status quo in *Culture and Anarchy,* where he upholds the "occupants of the executive power, whoever they may be" (444), even though he knows those occupants are motivated by self-interest.

Displayed in its fullest flowering, what one sees in Arnold are the two sides of the male dematerialization of the material world. By devaluing the material world they aim to condemn, the male critics destabilize their own critiques, a destabilization that produces the pronounced contradictions found in Ruskin, Carlyle, Dickens, and Arnold. But this dematerialization also permits these men to repudiate modernity, and thus it licenses a kind of transcendence that endows them with the visionary capacity to overleap—but not overlook—the inchoateness of the present and project a social shape onto the Victorian future. Rather than rendering the male critics irrelevant, as one might expect, this dematerialization gave their works formidable imaginative strength that perhaps in part accounts for their lasting influence. Even if the focus on the disposition of the working class may have destabilized their critiques of industrialism, they nevertheless made a serious impression on the disposition of the middle class, who adopted many of the conservative, aristocratic values embedded in both medievalism and culture, so that one finds woven into the fabric of modern English society certain premodern elements.[23]

In *All That Is Solid Melts into Air,* Marshall Berman concludes that "we might even say that to be fully modern is to be anti-modern: from Marx's and Dostoevsky's time to our own, it has been impossible to grasp and embrace the modern world's potentialities without loathing and fighting against some of its most palpable realities" (14). If we stopped our investigation of the Victorians' response to modernity, localized in their concerns about infant industrialism, after having read only the impassioned reactions of Carlyle, Disraeli, Ruskin, Dickens, and Arnold we could only agree with him. But as subsequent chapters will show, this modern antimodernism is the province of the male critics of industrialism. Victorian women writers have a different tale to tell.

# CHAPTER TWO

# The Fortunate Fall

## *Charlotte Brontë, Elizabeth Gaskell, and Female Myths of Progress*

> Better have pain than paralysis! A hundred struggle and drown
> in the breakers. One discovers the new world. But rather, ten
> times rather, die in the surf, heralding the way to that new world,
> than stand idly on the shore!
>
> Florence Nightingale, "Cassandra"

SO ACCUSTOMED are we as readers to accessing the industrial revolution through the condemnations of the male critics that we have
failed to see that the challenges industrialism posed to the social
order, and particularly to the gender relations underpinning that
order, did not move middle-class feminists like Charlotte Brontë or
Elizabeth Gaskell to similar denunciations.[1] A qualified acceptance
of the changes taking place throughout Victorian society distinguishes
the industrial texts written by Brontë and Gaskell, the two most
important and talented women novelists to respond to Carlyle's condition-of-England question, from those written by the male critics.
Quite simply, while the male literary tradition engages in a complicated rejection of modernity, both Gaskell and Brontë repudiate
the male repudiation and embrace Victorian industrialism. For these
women writers, history offers no golden age, no counterpart to the
male fantasy of the fourteenth century. Unappealing and unmourned,
the past in *Mary Barton, Shirley,* and *North and South* is represented
as brutal and barbaric, a time of mind-numbing labor and painful
social inequalities. With the same pioneering spirit that characterizes
Florence Nightingale's "Cassandra," Gaskell and Brontë turn their
backs on the old world and set out to seek the new.

Their rejection of the nostalgia that dominates the male

discourse is impelled not only by their desire to escape the oppressive social order they associate with the past but also by a sanguine belief that industrial capitalism promises women a brighter future. The factory woman enjoying a pint while her husband tended the "bairns" may have signaled to Lord Ashley a perversion of the natural order. Yet for middle-class feminists, who equated money with independence (a logical connection in a culture that deployed the term "independence" as a synonym for financial competency) and confronted daily the scarcity of employment opportunities for women of their own class, the wage-earning factory woman was less a cause for concern than for celebration. Having grown up in the genteel poverty of the parsonage, Charlotte Brontë told her publisher that she considered financial dependency "the one great curse of single female life" (Wise and Symington 3: 5). In her letters and in her fiction, Brontë bitterly laments what Virginia Woolf would decades later refer to as "the reprehensible poverty of our sex." When Woolf ascribes women's oppression to the womanly ignorance of "the great art of making money" (21) in *A Room of One's Own*, it is because for middle-class feminists like Brontë and Woolf, lack of money has traditionally been the root of all evil.

And more than anything else, the nineteenth century was a time for making money. The Victorian social critics designated the single-minded pursuit of wealth as one of the defining—and damning—characteristics of their age. Examples of it punctuate their works. They range from Carlyle's gospel of mammonism, in which the Hell of the English is "not making money" (*Past and Present* 270), to Engels's chilling encounter with a particularly hard specimen of Manchester businessman who met the young German's impassioned account of the appalling conditions of worker housing with the calm reply, "And yet there is a great deal of money made here; good morning, sir" (302). But while Engels and Carlyle as well as Ruskin, Dickens, and Arnold railed against greed—a sin the Victorians did not invent but to which industrial capitalism opened up new and hitherto unimagined prospects—the women writers, alive to the poverty of their sex, evidence an attitude towards money and money-making that is, on the whole, less censorious.[2] The incalculable human cost of reducing all social relationships to a bottom line never escapes either Gaskell or Brontë, but the almost magical ability of money to efface and transcend gender suggested the possibility of money as the great equalizer: money could endow a woman with power to do as she liked. Geraldine Jewsbury, a Manchester novelist who celebrated the entrepreneurial spirit of her hometown in *Marian Withers* (1851), proclaimed in an 1847 article entitled "Civilisation of 'The Lower Orders' " that "the practical republicanism of trade has for ever emancipated the lower orders from a condition of *permanent* inferiority. . . . Wealth is a great unlimited undefined *possibility*—there is hardly anything it *cannot* do for its possessor" (448). The "unlimited undefined possibility" of the unprecedented wealth generated by industrial capitalism intoxicated writers governed by the limited, defined possibilities of Victorian womanhood.

Jewsbury's belief in the equalizing instincts of the marketplace—the practical republicanism of trade—was widespread among mid-Victorian middle-class feminists. They wished to secure for themselves "non-manual work far removed from the grime and noise and physicality of the manual labour that was commonly the lot of working-class women" (Levine 127); and in their efforts to expand their own job opportunities, these equal rights feminists upheld the tenets of classic economic liberalism. One need only glance at the essays comprising Josephine Butler's *Woman's Work and Woman's Culture* (1869), a landmark text of equal rights feminism, to find the language of Adam Smith appropriated and turned to the advantage of middle-class women: Sophia Jex-Blake insists on the "demand for female physicians" (106) as reason enough for providing a supply, while Jessie Boucherett envisions a deregulated marketplace—where men and women can compete freely—as the solution to the problem of superfluous women. If one strand of Victorian thought abandoned the marketplace and embraced culture as the final arbiter of value (a strand of Victorian thought that Raymond Williams made so clearly visible in *Culture and Society*), then another strand looked to the marketplace as a site where rational economic choices unadulterated by the prejudices of gender could be made. For the women who contributed to Butler's *Woman's Work,* industrial capitalism and feminism were not mutually exclusive but mutually reinforcing.

Feminists like Butler, most famous for her crusade against

the Contagious Diseases Act, were not alone in descrying in the emergence of a wage economy women's liberation from the constraints of Victorian patriarchy. Even capitalism's greatest enemy, Karl Marx, believed in the liberating effects of the industrial revolution: "However terrible and disgusting the dissolution of the old family ties within the capitalist system may appear, large-scale industry, by assigning an important part in socially organized processes of production, outside the sphere of the domestic economy, to women, young persons and children of both sexes, does nevertheless create a new economic foundation for a higher form of the family and of relations between the sexes" (*Capital* 620-21). For his part, Engels overcame the initial, vehement objections to female employment he voiced in *The Condition of the Working Class in England* to seize upon and insist on the progressive tendencies of capitalism nearly forty years later in *The Origins of the Family, Private Property and the State.*

If we are to understand the industrial fiction produced by Elizabeth Gaskell and Charlotte Brontë, we must first accept that for them, industrial capitalism seemed to point the way to a better future for women.[3] In this regard, one cannot overemphasize the eminently bourgeois nature of their novels. For despite the strategic connections they make between middle-class and working-class women, neither Gaskell nor Brontë imagines a genuinely revolutionary alliance between bourgeois heroines and mill girls that would overthrow the forces of patriarchy and capitalism that oppress them both: the novelists want to mitigate patriarchal powers, and they see capitalism as the best weapon in their arsenal. Within the confines of their fictional worlds, Gaskell and Brontë ignore the class differences that might lead a working-class woman to be less positive about the overall progress of industrial capitalism, largely by silencing their texts' representative mill girls.

Later in the century, when the public opposition of equal rights feminists to protective legislation for women collided with laboring women activists' support for it, the middle-class orientation of equal rights feminism became inescapable. Fearing that regulations such as the Nine Hours Bill and the Shop Hours Bill, both introduced in the 1870s, would further institutionalize women's secondary position in the labor force, the equal rights feminists opposed them. In the struggle to promote female employment, middle-class feminists were willing to support any employer who hired women because, as Rosemary Feurer notes, "unregulated access to employment meant greater freedom to middle-class women," although it often "condemned working women to intolerable conditions" (258). What resulted in the last few decades of the century was a nasty split between feminists and laboring women activists, who did not see state intervention as oppressive but, rather, believed that the state could protect women from harmful working conditions. However, both Gaskell and Brontë, writing decades before this split, assume an alliance of interests between themselves and the working-class women for whom they claim to speak.

All three novels discussed at length in this chapter link women's liberation to the liberating effects of industrial capitalism. But they are not the only novels of the period to do so. Geraldine Jewsbury, the woman who proclaimed the "practical republicanism of trade" and was as deeply invested as Brontë and Gaskell in defining opportunities for middle-class women, uses her novel *Marian Withers* to link the triumphant progress of capitalism to the advancement of women. In outline form, *Marian Withers* resembles both *Shirley* and *North and South*. It too scripts a young girl's search for meaning in her life and finds it in a symbolic marriage that weds her to a mill owner and, by extension, the manufacturing interests. Yet here the similarities end because *Marian Withers*—written by a feminist who was also the protégée of Thomas Carlyle—stands astride two competing discourses. For this reason Jewsbury's novel is a rich place to begin identifying some of the core distinctions between Brontë's and Gaskell's novels and the male disposition-of-England discourse. *Marian Withers* retains the imprint of Thomas Carlyle, who was Jewsbury's intellectual mentor and sometime rival for the affections of Jane Carlyle. Altogether, it is much more imitative of the male tradition than *Mary Barton, Shirley*, or *North and South*.[4]

Taking imitation as its theme, *Marian Withers* offers its eponymous heroine three choices: she can model herself after a school chum who sacrifices herself on the altar of gentility and unhappily marries an old roué; she can mimic her industrialist father, a self-made man with a genius for invention, although being a daughter, she is limited to copying out his business correspondences; or she can pattern herself after the text's heroic captain of industry, Mr. Cunningham, by heeding his Carlylean challenge to stop fretting over her own trifling dissatisfactions and "live worthily *now*" (3: 132). Deciding between a wasted, willful life among the idle classes, clerical drudgery in the mill, or Cunningham's call for self-fulfillment through self-denying labor, Marian chooses the last option. Following Mr. Cunningham's lead, she locates this worthy work in the post of village schoolmistress, introducing ignorant factory lasses to the secrets of plain sewing and pot roasting. In the end, Jewsbury's heroine resembles the Lady Bountifuls that occupy so much Victorian thinking about female social action: Marian is a pale imitation of a Carlylean hero—the obliging handmaiden to Cunningham's captain of industry—and undistinguished when compared to the initiating (rather than imitating) heroines of *North and South* and *Shirley*. In these two novels, Margaret Hale and Shirley Keeldar, as businesswomen endowed (if only fleetingly) with mills of their own, need no prophet to point them towards the promised land, but turn prophet themselves and instruct unregenerate industrialists like John Thornton and Robert Moore in the duties of one class to another. Like their heroines, Brontë and Gaskell try to instruct rather than to copy, and one must read their novels as offering something strikingly original (women entrepreneurs, for example) rather than imitations of the Carlyle-inflected male discourse.[5] Even if they never succeed in fully entering the new world that Florence Nightingale invokes in "Cassandra," at the very least they wade out into the surf.

Perhaps Brontë and Gaskell depart most radically from the Carlylean disposition-of-England discourse when they insist on the materiality of the industrial revolution, although it is important to note that they insist on a particular set of material conditions, those arising from unemployment. But then, given the preoccupation of mid-Victorian feminists with the lack of employment opportunities available to middle-class women, this emphasis is to be expected. Certainly the unmarried, economically insecure Brontë made the problem of middle-class female employment a central concern in all her novels. And while none of Gaskell's heroines offers as direct a challenge to Victorian society as Brontë's Jane Eyre, who famously declaims from the Thornfield battlements that "women need exercise for their faculties, and a field for their effort as much as their brothers do" (141), Gaskell nonetheless remained alive to the single woman's plight. This mother of four daughters, friend of Charlotte Brontë and Florence Nightingale, and active sponsor of philanthropic schemes for single women was, as Pauline Nestor argues, "keenly aware of the problems facing the 'superabundant' woman" (36). Thus, it is the debilitating consequences of *unemployment* that threaten the workers' well-being in *Mary Barton, Shirley,* and *North and South.* So while Carlyle demands that his captains of industry address the bad disposition of the working classes, Gaskell and Brontë demand that their fictional industrialists acknowledge the awful conditions of the working classes *when they are not working*: the women novelists underscore the material sufferings engendered by unemployment and educate their industrialists in those sufferings as a precondition for their redemption.

Gaskell's and Brontë's focus on the material consequences of unemployment, rather than on the injuries of machine labor, allows them to embrace the industrial revolution and critique its more pernicious aspects. Their novels address the wrongs of women and workers without seeing industrialism itself as an unmitigated wrong. Indeed, all three texts go to great lengths to vindicate factory work, dismissing either through sheer evasion or mitigation its physical dangers. For example, in *Mary Barton,* the character one might point to as most likely to die before the novel concludes is Mrs. Wilson, a sickly woman injured years before in an industrial accident and introduced to the reader as a "delicate fragile-looking woman" (4). But the narrative thwarts our expectations when Mrs. Wilson's husband, by all accounts a perfectly healthy man, falls dead in a Manchester street while his wife outlives him and indeed survives the end of the novel. In fact, the only fatality in either of Gaskell's two factory novels that could be directly attributed to the occupational risks of mill work is Bessy Higgins's death in *North and South.* Yet for all the pathos of Bessy's end, Gaskell underscores the preventable nature of the lung disease Bessy contracts, which could have been easily avoided through proper ventilation.

Similarly, the narrator of *Shirley* refuses to represent the factory as a gothic house of horrors: "Child-torturers, slave masters and drivers, I consign to the hands of jailers; the novelist may be excused from sullying his page with the record of their deeds. . . . I am happy to be able to inform [the reader] that neither Mr Moore nor his overlooker ever struck a child in their mill" (90). *Shirley* defends Robert Moore's business practices from the charges made against the factory system in Frances Trollope's *Michael Armstrong,* a novel featuring a sadistic, child-abusing industrialist which Brontë dismissed as a "ridiculous mess" (Wise and Symington 2: 184) in a letter to her publisher. When one compares the relatively benign nature of factory work in *Mary Barton, Shirley,* and *North and South* to Engels's epic catalogue of injuries in *Condition of the Working Class,* it becomes apparent just how defensive of the factory system Brontë and Gaskell are.[6]

To be sure, they underplay the perils of factory work, but they never devalue the material realm after the fashion of the male critics. While their novels may celebrate the world "turned upside downwards" that so appalled the male critics, it would be wrong-headed to accuse them, in some single-minded pursuit of a feminist agenda, of simply ignoring the baleful effects of Victorian industrialism. On the contrary, Gaskell's and Brontë's focus on unemployment leads them to materialize and dramatize its bodily harms and deadly impact. The most direct and dire consequence of unemployment—hunger—emerges as one of the dominant tropes in *Shirley,* where Brontë reinscribes the body's privations onto the history of political insurrections: "misery generates hate" (62), in Brontë's complex investigation of the unbreakable bond between unemployment, starvation, and rebellion. In *Mary Barton,* Gaskell boldly thematizes the dismissal of the workers' physical condition—their corporeal suffering—and presents it as one of the most hateful aspects of the upper-class response to industrialism.[7] Above all else, the operatives in *Mary Barton* chafe at the fact that the destitution they experience during economic slumps is disowned by the government and the "very existence of their distress" (97) publicly discounted: "They could not believe that government knew of their misery: they rather chose to think it possible that men could voluntarily assume the office of legislators for a nation who were ignorant of its real state; as who

should make domestic rules for the pretty behaviour of children without caring to know that those children had been kept for days without
food" (97). With a certain ladylike indirection, Gaskell accuses the
national leadership of turning a blind eye toward the workers' material
conditions. Given Gaskell's emphasis on the physical hardships of
unemployment, it is not surprising that *Mary Barton* has been praised
since its publication for its bracingly honest portrayal of working-
class misery. "We defy any one to read *Mary Barton* without a more
thoughtful sense of what is due to the poor" (68), John Forster opined
in 1848, and few have disagreed in the intervening century and a
half. So in answer to Carlyle's question "Is the condition of the English
working people so wrong . . . [or] their disposition, their own
thoughts, beliefs and feelings that are wrong," both Gaskell and
Brontë reply that the condition of the English working people (when
they are not working) is terribly wrong.

   *Mary Barton, North and South,* and *Shirley* all acknowledge
the significance of the material conditions of working-class life in
their analyses and thereby challenge the ideology of an unhindered
free will that subtends the male dematerialization. While Carlyle
could declare with relative assurance that "the spiritual always determines the material," the strict gender system of Victorian Britain
led middle-class women like Gaskell and Brontë to suspect the opposite to be true. We may choose to remember the proper Victorian
lady as the angel in the house (the bodiless and selfless icon of domesticity), but we should not forget that her angelic status depended
upon her physical form. Paradoxically, Victorian domestic ideology
denied the female body while it simultaneously decreed that the body
was the determining factor in any woman's life. "Our bodies are the
only things of any consequence," Florence Nightingale complained
in "Cassandra" (408) because gender determined what she could and
should do. As a result of this paradox, the Victorian woman suffered
as much from being embodied as from being disembodied, in that
her material body "determined" her moral and intellectual nature as
well as her social role.

   Without absolutely repudiating free will, which Brontë and
Gaskell need to retain in some form to ensure the moral agency of
middle-class women like themselves, the female texts reveal its lim-

ited appeal within the industrial world. In fact, both authors force their representative mill owners to reconsider their blind faith in free will as the precondition for their moral reformations, so that it is the agency of middle-class men—as much as that of middle-class women—that these texts ultimately scrutinize.

Suffering under the weight of material conditions beyond their control, John Carson, John Thornton, and Robert Moore all come to understand how various contingencies can inhibit the exercise of free will. Carson submits "to be taught by suffering" (*Mary Barton* 458) and to accept that he possesses no special immunity from the material world around him when his son falls victim to the same industrial conditions—the deadly alienation between men and masters—that has deprived John Barton of his only son. John Thornton also submits to be taught by suffering, but he suffers by falling in love with *North and South*'s strong-willed heroine. Like Carson's bereavement, Thornton's uninvited passion for Margaret Hale forces him to acknowledge the limitations of free will, for just the thought of her can "melt away every resolution, all power of self-control, as if it were wax before a fire" (251). In Thornton's case, his physical passion and the mastery it exerts over him is the lesson that transforms him into a pattern industrialist. It makes him understand in a visceral way (by becoming dependent himself) what Margaret's many sermons on the interdependence of the human community cannot.

Even the stiff-necked Robert Moore submits to be taught by suffering. Adopting the approach favored by Henry Mayhew in *London Labour and London Poor* and Engels in *The Condition of the Working Class,* Moore launches an expedition into the poor man's country that brings about his conversion from an apostle of self-help to a proponent of social welfare:

> While I was in Birmingham, I looked a little into reality, considered closely, and at their source, the cause of the present troubles of this country; I did the same in London. Unknown, I could go where I pleased, mix with whom I would. I went where there was want of food, of fuel, of clothing; where there was no occupation and no hope. I saw some, with naturally elevated tendencies and good feelings, kept down amongst sordid privations and harassing griefs. I saw many originally low, and to whom lack of education had left

scarcely anything but animal wants, disappointed in those wants, ahungered, athirst, and desperate as famished animals: I saw what taught my brain a new lesson, and filled my breast with fresh feelings. . . . To respect himself, a man must believe he renders justice to his fellow-men. Unless I am more considerate to ignorance, more forbearing to suffering, than I have hitherto been, I shall scorn myself as grossly unjust. (*Shirley* 505-6)

Chastened and somewhat humbled by his newfound understanding of poverty's debilitating effects on the lives of the destitute, the reformed Moore goes on to become a model mill owner. To ensure his conversion, Brontë's narrative punctuates this speech with a well-aimed gunshot, so that Moore's vicarious experiences with human suffering becomes quite personal and palpable. One might even identify a punitive spirit at work in Moore's brush with mortality and his long convalescence in the hands of the redoubtable Mrs. Horsfall, similar both to Rochester's maiming and, more to the point, to John Thornton's literal bankruptcy (the analog to his initial moral bankruptcy) at the end of *North and South*. Both *Shirley* and *North and South* insist on diminishing their industrial heroes before allowing them to reemerge reformed and prosperous, perhaps to mark these men indelibly with a sense of their own contingency in order that they may understand the contingencies of others.

While Carson, Moore, and Thornton each undergoes a conversion experience, not one is translated into a Carlylean captain of industry ready to march his regimented masses forward into an industrial utopia: the martial and masculine spirit of Carlyle's captaincy is foreign to the new men Gaskell and Brontë imagine. In fact, the reeducated industrialists are less captains of industry than mothers of England in male garb: the sea change Carson, Moore, and Thornton each endures is in some sense a sex change. Drawing on the potent ideology of domesticity, Brontë and Gaskell domesticate the industrialist and replace their heroes' Hobbesian worldviews of ruthless individualism and fierce economic competitiveness with a vision of the family's tangled web of interdependent relations. Carson comes to understand that "the interests of one were the interests of all" (457) before he initiates a series of unspecified reforms, and Thornton abandons his dream of becoming the founding father of a great patriarchal trading firm—"the head of a firm that should be known for generations" (511)—in order to concentrate on nurturing the generation growing up around him. The liberal, dissenting Gaskell does not transform Thornton into a Tory paternalist, the good father who cares for his worker/children. Instead, she replaces the paternal metaphor for class relations with a hymeneal one: *North and South* ends with two betrothals, one between Thornton and Margaret and one between Thornton and his men. By allowing her industrialist hero to symbolically marry his men for the sake of "th' childer" (405)—real working-class children in this case—Gaskell transforms mill owners and workers into domestic partners who must rely on each other for the British family's greater good.

Emerging at the end of *Shirley* with plans to feed and clothe the multitude, Brontë's Robert Moore more closely resembles the classic paternalist than Gaskell's John Thornton. But the resemblance may be somewhat superficial because Moore embraces an ethics of interdependence and acknowledges his own dependence on the people who work his machinery. Robert Moore and his brother Louis, who becomes the local squire when he marries Shirley, promise to "divide Briarfield parish betwixt" them (597), a union of landed and industrial interests that bears out Terry Eagleton's reading of *Shirley* as a celebration of "the class-consolidation between squire and millowner, achieved as it was by the catalyst of working-class militancy" (*Myths of Power* 46). Nevertheless, Brontë's attenuated paternalism is less the rule of the good fathers than a family affair, for the Moore brothers' brides, Caroline and Shirley, have already shown themselves adept at charity work. One could even argue that Robert and Louis Moore merely take over the philanthropic activities that have all along been associated with the novel's women and make those actions part of their public role: Brontë replaces Tory paternalism with her own brand of Tory maternalism.

It is essential, however, that one read this final domestication of the male industrialist as only a partial triumph. Gaskell and Brontë ultimately discover that it is easier to domesticate the industrialist than to sustain their daring experiments in letting women learn the manly art of business: they can inject a dose of "womanly" values into the public sphere as an inoculation against misery and violence more readily than they can inject their heroines into the public world of work. That is because the ideology of domesticity made it possible to reform the industrialist—through the domesticated woman's moralizing influence—without directly challenging the patriarchal arrangements of Victorian society. In contrast to Victorian industrialism, which proved remarkably open to humanitarian reforms, stood Victorian patriarchal configurations, which proved remarkably resilient throughout most of the century. Marx and Engels, Brontë and Gaskell overestimated the liberating potential of capitalism by underestimating the reactionary force of patriarchy.[8] Although "the pure mechanisms of the process of valorization of capital, and the expansion of the commodity form, are gender-blind," Perry Anderson observes, "the early capitalist mode of production inherited and reworked this millennial inequality [between the sexes], with all its myriad oppressions, at once extensively utilizing and profoundly transforming it" (*Tracks* 90). Patriarchal structures, which resist being swept away by the rising tide of industrial capitalism, create endless difficulties and dissonances for the authors of *Mary Barton, Shirley,* and *North and South.* The challenge industrialism poses for these women novelists is not a cataclysmic dissolution of traditional authority but the refusal of that authority to dissolve.

To complicate matters, patriarchy is not something "out there," an impregnable fortress that Gaskell and Brontë hurl themselves against but cannot conquer. Both women remain enmeshed in the ideological structures they oppose, and the texts they produce are marked by ideological contradiction. Writing at the painful intersection of competing class and gender loyalties, they try to balance their desire for feminine autonomy against their wish to retain (or to obtain, in the case of *Mary Barton*) their heroines' middle-class respectability. This was a delicate balancing act performed by many nineteenth-century feminists. Because they wanted to ensure the middle-class woman's independence outside the family and her moral preeminence within it, Victorian feminists "only partially challenged the basic Victorian assumptions related to sex roles and women's 'separate spheres,'" as Judy Walkowitz notes (*Prostitution* 117). In the final analysis, tenacious patriarchal forms together with class and

gender assumptions embedded in the culture (and cultural frame-
works of both women) undermine Gaskell's and Brontë's attempts
to script the liberation of middle-class women through industrial
capitalism.

This chapter traces out the trajectory—from the celebration
of industrial modernity to the inevitable disappointment with it—
that characterizes *Mary Barton, Shirley,* and *North and South*. Possessing
an immediacy and urgency wanting in its successors, *Mary Barton*
connects the unemployment of working-class men with the idleness
of middle-class women in order to defend emergent industrialism
while still sympathizing with the struggles of Manchester's working
classes. But Gaskell's inability to disentangle her feminist inclinations
from the bourgeois norms of feminine conduct that she deploys to
defend her working-class heroine's sexual innocence leads her to condemn the independent and assertive Mary Barton to the idleness the
text deplores. Bravely, *North and South* tries to resolve the ideological
tensions in *Mary Barton*. To redeem Margaret Hale from Mary's sad
fate of inactivity and dependence, Gaskell replaces a working-class
heroine with a middle-class one and "maidenly modesty" with
"woman's work" as the reigning virtue. However, Gaskell soon discovers that the respectable occupations open to the middle-class
Margaret—domestic work and do-gooding—cannot deliver the autonomy that Gaskell admires in Manchester's mill girls. Nevertheless,
having been written in the more prosperous days of the 1850s, *North
and South* can rescript the male myth of the fall into modernity as a
fortunate fall and imagine its heroine "happier far" in Milton-
Northern's brave new world than in the quaint (and antiquated)
village of Helstone. Brontë stages the clash between industrialism's
revolutionary potential and patriarchy's tenacious power more starkly
than Gaskell, but the heroines of *Shirley* confront the same dearth of
opportunities for middle-class women as Margaret Hale. The old
patriarchal order remains largely intact, and the scrupulous realism
Brontë ties herself to in *Shirley* can record it but not undo it. Each
novel registers how fully imbricated patriarchy and industrial capitalism were becoming and thus bears witness to the impossibility of
dismantling one without dismantling the other.

# The Curse of Leisure: Unemployment in *Mary Barton*

In a letter sent to Lady Janet Kay-Shuttleworth during the summer of 1850, Elizabeth Gaskell once again found herself defending a novel she believed had been universally misunderstood: "I can not imagine a nobler scope for a thoughtful energetic man, desirous of doing good to his kind, than that presented to his powers as master of a factory. But I believe that there is much to be discovered yet as to the right position and mutual duties of employer and employed; and the utmost I hoped from Mary Barton has been that it would give a spur to inactive thought, and languid conscience a direction" (*Letters* 119). On the surface, the dual objectives of this letter—a defense of both the industrial system and a text Raymond Williams has called "the most moving response in literature to the industrial suffering of the 1840s" (*Culture and Society* 87)—seem at odds. Yet Gaskell defuses the tension she creates, and the resolution she ventures for these apparently contradictory impulses lies in her defense of the novel as a "spur to inactive thought." Throughout the writing of *Mary Barton,* Gaskell's chief enemy was inactivity, whether it was the moral laziness of the British public, seemingly indifferent to the tragedies of men like John Barton, or the destructive, indulgent, and idle speculations Gaskell herself engaged in after the death of her infant son, and to which *Mary Barton,* begun at the urging of her husband, was the remedial measure. So it is only fitting that a novel born out of Gaskell's own personal and political desire for action should be a text about the perils of inactivity. In *Mary Barton,* Gaskell writes a novel about unemployment, and in this way she meets the demands made by her dual objectives: she exposes to the public the pitiable circumstances under which Manchester's workers live without condemning the factory system as an inherent and unalterable evil. Gaskell saves Victorian industrialism by shifting the focus of her novel from the dangers of factory work to the dangers of being out of work: *Mary Barton* does not so much address the "crushing experience of industrialism" (Williams, *Culture and Society* 88) as it does the crushing experience of unemployment.

Or to be more precise, *Mary Barton* is a response to the crushing effects of the boom/bust cycle endemic to infant industrialism. For as Gaskell informs us in her preface, it was the "strange alternations between work and want" and the "lottery-like nature" (xxxv) of working-class existence that first aroused her sympathies for the mill hands. In *Capital,* Marx provides a brief summary of the "ebbs and flows" of those years, and it is a daunting chronicle of instability:

> White slave trade; 1835, great prosperity, simultaneous starvation of the hand-loom weavers; 1836, great prosperity; 1837 and 1838, depression and crisis; 1839, revival; 1840, great depression, riots, the military called out to intervene; 1841 and 1842, frightful suffering among the factory workers; 1842, the manufacturers lock their hands out of the factories in order to enforce the repeal of the Corn Laws. Workers stream in their thousands into the towns of Lancashire and Yorkshire, are driven back by the military, and their leaders brought to trial at Lancaster; 1842, great misery; 1844, revival; 1845, great prosperity; 1846, continued improvement at first, then reaction. (583)

Gaskell reproduces the fitful nature of the early industrial economy, with its periodic lurches from good times to hard times. When things are bad, they are very bad indeed, so that during the economic slumps, the workers "only wanted a Dante to record their sufferings" (96). Indeed, all the horrors Gaskell details, from the needless death of John Barton's son to the pathetic end of the cellar-dwelling Ben Davenport, come about during trade depressions and directly result from them. Significantly, the sole mill to surface in this tale of life in the nineteenth century's premier mill town makes a brief appearance when a blaze reduces it to a pile of ruins and thereby throws the mill hands out of work. In this telling detail we can read Gaskell's insistence that the mill's determining influence on the lives of her characters rests in its ability to provide employment. Thus the mill becomes visible—as a significant fact of Manchester life—only at the moment that it ceases to function.

Gaskell's Manchester is the urban equivalent of Dr. Jekyll

and Mr. Hyde. It is only by recognizing the duality of life in Manchester, its "lottery-like nature," that one can understand how Gaskell could produce a novel that has been praised by such an astute critic as Williams as capturing both "the characteristic response of a generation to the new and crushing experience of industrialization" and the "development of the sympathy and cooperative instinct which were already establishing a main working-class tradition" (*Culture and Society* 88). Somewhat paradoxically, Williams applauds Gaskell's text for revealing the factory system as hostile to working-class life, yet hospitable to working-class culture: for how can the experience of industrialization be inimical to human life when it is capable at the same time of sustaining strong family and community bonds as well as a sophisticated intellectual culture, all the apparatus and institutions of urban proletariat life that Gaskell records? Gaskell understands, however, that the emerging working-class culture depends on the high wages the mill workers earn combined with the stimulations of urban life. Indeed, when one juxtaposes Gaskell's Manchester with "The Great Towns" section of Engels's *Condition of the Working Class,* one might forget that the two accounts claim to represent the same city at the same historical moment. Engels sees nothing but squalor and shame, a populace completely crushed by its surroundings: "We must confess that in the working-men's dwellings of Manchester, no cleanliness, no convenience, and consequently no comfortable family life is possible; that in such dwellings only a physically degenerate race, robbed of all humanity, degraded, reduced morally and physically to bestiality, could feel comfortable at home" (96). But the Bartons, who are neither physically degenerate nor bestial, feel quite comfortable in their Manchester home, which Gaskell evokes precisely and lovingly as her novelistic eye for detail lingers over the material solidity of a household overflowing with furniture, crockery, and tea-trays. When work is plentiful, the factory workers enjoy high wages, live in relative comfort, and have the time, energy, and spare shillings for leisure pursuits, like Job Legh's amateur entomology. In *Mary Barton,* the significant accomplishments of the Manchester working class come about because of—not in spite of—the burgeoning factory system.[9]

Gaskell remains as invested in defending the industrial system as in condemning its local evils, and nowhere does this defense emerge more strikingly than in the play between past and present she keeps before the reader: the industrial present may be far from ideal, but the rural past is decidedly worse. An out-of-work mill hand who dies of starvation and disease in a damp cellar refuses to seek public assistance because, as his wife says, "my master is Buckinghamshire born; and he's feared the town would send him back to his parish" (72). Apparently, starving in a Manchester cellar with the hope that good times will soon return is preferable to the poverty of one's native village, where destitution and the workhouse are the only two options. Indeed, testifying to the sad logic of the man's decision are the memories of Alice Wilson, the Manchester washerwoman who retains strong links with the preindustrial past. Although Alice bathes the recollections of her country childhood in a nostalgic glow, Gaskell approaches them with an ironic detachment that gently but deftly subverts the old woman's fondness for the past. As Coral Lansbury reminds us, "The landscape Alice describes so rapturously is a barren waste. The Wilson farm was a shaded hillside, stone covered and eroded, where heather flourished but not crops or cattle. . . . It is a scene of bleak poverty, but in memory it can become a lost paradise" (34). Gaskell frames the intermittent sufferings of the workers not against a backdrop of pastoral contentment but against one of rural deprivation, so that the dying mill worker's refusal to return to Buckinghamshire and Alice's childhood of poverty serve to situate the lives of the factory operatives in a broadly progressive vision of rising working-class standards.

Gaskell also carefully frames the feast-or-famine existence of Manchester's industrial operatives against the living and working conditions of those employed in nonindustrial occupations, so that the true image of impoverishment can be found in Alice Wilson, a single woman who supports herself as a domestic servant and washerwoman. By juxtaposing the tea party thrown by the Bartons against one hosted by Alice, Gaskell neatly contrasts the Bartons' material prosperity with the material poverty endured by old Alice. No wonder Alice marvels at the "aspect of comfort" (16) she finds at the Barton tea party when, as a counter to the bounty of their table, she can barely afford the requisite bread, butter, and tea for her guests:

Half an ounce of tea and a quarter of a pound of butter went far to absorb her morning's wages; but this was an unusual occasion. In general, she used herb-tea for herself, when at home, unless some thoughtful mistress made a present of tea-leaves from her more abundant household. The two chairs drawn out for visitors, and duly swept and dusted; an old board arranged with some skill upon two old candle-boxes set on end (rather rickety, to be sure, but she knew the seat of old, and when to sit lightly; indeed the whole affair was more for apparent dignity of position than for any real ease); a little, very little round table, put just before the fire, which by this time was blazing merrily; her unlacquered, ancient, third-hand tea-tray arranged with a black tea-pot, two cups with a red and white pattern, and one with the old friendly willow pattern, and saucers, not to match. (30-31)

Through sheer accretion of detail, from the scant meal to the pathos of the unmatched china, Gaskell sketches a scene of poverty; and no matter how clean Alice's cellar dwelling may be, or how exhaustingly cheerful Alice is, it remains a portrait of economic distress. Nor does Gaskell try to argue that the social stability of Alice's life amply compensates for her poverty since, as a servant, Alice is as subject to frequent bouts of unemployment as Manchester's mill workers. Moreover, the occasional gift of tea-leaves only highlights her quasi-feudal dependence of the random kindnesses of her employers.

By deploying Manchester's seesawing economy as the organizing principle behind her representation of industrial life, Gaskell can defend the present from the nostalgic incursions of the past. But just as important, given Gaskell's larger design, Manchester's "strange alternations between work and want" permit her to raise the woman question without causing a radical disjunction between the text's industrial material and its feminist explorations because in *Mary Barton* both women and workers struggle against a common foe: unemployment. Feminist critics in recent years have refused to read Mary's plot as a distraction from the genuine and lasting interest generated by Gaskell's investigation of the condition of England through John Barton's narrative. On the contrary, they have insisted on the thematic connections between the father's industrial plot and the daughter's love plot because to ignore these connections is to reduce the novel's scope from an examination of industrialism's impact on men and women to its impact on men alone.[10]

If one does not recognize that the same economic and political issues inform and unite both father's and daughter's plot, one risks reproducing the sentimental reading of the heroine's plot that Gaskell disavows. In her nuanced interpretation of *Mary Barton* in *The Industrial Reformation of English Fiction,* Catherine Gallagher identifies a crazy quilt of narrative forms—melodrama, tragedy, domestic realism—that bespeak Gaskell's self-aware inability to represent working-class life adequately. Gallagher places particular emphasis on the dangers of melodrama, which can conceal the truth of class hatred behind a screen of romance by transforming political issues into personal matters. This concealment occurs most notably when Mary's relationship with Carson enters the public sphere after his murder as tragic tale of romantic jealousy: the murder becomes "some dispute about a factory girl" (*Mary Barton* 333), and in the eyes of the dead man's father, Mary is "the fatal Helen, the cause of all" (380), even though the reader knows that the genuine "cause of all" is the murderous alienation between the men and the masters, not the murderous resentment of a spurned lover. To read Mary's story melodramatically is to ignore Gaskell's warnings about the distortions of melodrama.

In particular, *Mary Barton* focuses on the way melodrama misrepresents women's lives by erasing their role within a political economy. The novel may, as Gallagher argues, hesitate to assign causality in John Barton's plot, but the text reinfuses economic causality into the women's stories by directly and uninhibitedly ascribing economic motives to the female characters' actions. For through Mary's entanglement with Harry Carson, Gaskell reveals that romance is the business of Victorian heroines. From the first, Gaskell makes clear that Mary regards her wealthy lover with the shrewd, appraising eye of a woman who understands the socioeconomic realities of the world. Lucre as much as love is a motivating force behind Mary's dangerous liaison with Carson, a fact the narrator openly admits: "Mary was ambitious, and did not favour Mr Carson the less because he was rich and a gentleman. . . . Mary dwelt upon and enjoyed the idea of some day becoming a lady" (91-92). Unlike Jem Wilson, her future husband, who by dint of hard work and talent fashions himself into that particular Victorian hero, the self-made man, and equally unlike Margaret Jennings, her best friend, who carves out a career as a singer, Mary possesses only one option—marriage—if she wants to fulfill her ambition and rise into the middle classes. So while Jem exploits his mechanical skills and Margaret her musical ability, Mary takes advantage of her special talents when she makes the rational economic choice that "her beauty should make her a lady" (27). Mary's flirtation with Harry Carson is not the act of a simple-minded girl but the conscious decision of an ambitious young woman pursuing one of the few avenues for advancement open to working-class women.

By unveiling the economic truths behind Mary's romantic cover story, Gaskell invites us to resituate the stories of the novel's other women, like Mrs. Carson and Aunt Esther, in an economic context as well. In the first half of the novel, Mary remains delicately poised between two possible futures: on the one side stands Mrs. Carson, the former factory girl who married well and is now luxuriously installed in the Carson villa, while on her other side stands the tragic counterpart to Mrs. Carson's success story, the novel's other ex-factory girl, Mary's Aunt Esther, now a prostitute. But as far apart as the suburban matron and the fallen woman may seem, Gaskell brings them together as two sides of the same coin: the triumphant and the failed capitalist. Simply, Esther is a speculator who went bust. Her elopement with an officer who subsequently abandoned her is a speculation on her capital (her beauty) that did not pay off. "As [Mary] is loving now, so did I love once, one above me far" (187), Esther tells Jem, but the comparison—knowing what we do about Mary's economic interest in Carson—nearly collapses under the weight of irony. Like her niece, Esther expected her beauty to be the making of her, and while she claims to have followed her army officer out of love, she also admits that "he promised me marriage" (188), and marriage to an army officer would have been her passport to gentility.

Moreover, through Esther, Gaskell exposes the ultimately deadly consequences of scripting one's life melodramatically. While Gaskell endows Esther with economic motives for her affairs of the heart, Esther revises her economic history into a self-defeating melodramatic narrative. So when Esther tells Jem the story of her life, she casts it as a tragic tale of how she risked all for love: "He was so handsome, so kind! Well, the regiment was ordered to Chester (did I tell you he was an officer?), and he could not bear to part from me, nor I from him, so he took me with him" (188). Esther's use of sentiment conceals the cold economic facts of her fall, for in Esther's rewriting of her life's story the economics of the elopement gets suppressed, and her lover's social class is derogated to a parenthetical inclusion: the most important element in Esther's history (her social ambition) is subordinated to the least (romance). Like the ragged finery that earns her the nickname "Butterfly," Esther's melodramatic narrative is a bad fit and full of holes because it prevents her from grasping the economic factors at work in her life, and thus it bars her from taking any remedial action. Instead of displaying anger at the officer who seduced and abandoned her, Esther turns her tale of abuse at the hands of an upper-class man into a story of her own moral lapse and wallows in guilt, self-pity, and alcohol, rejecting Jem Wilson's offer of redemption on the grounds that she needs drink to anesthetize herself against her fall into prostitution, to which she was driven by poverty and the cries of her dying child. In contrast, John Barton responds to the death of his son under similar dire circumstances by blaming the masters and channeling his anger into political activism. Although Gaskell ultimately recoils from Barton when his activism turns violent, she nevertheless acknowledges that his Chartist activities ennoble him, as she must in a book that is so heavily invested in the importance of action. So even if Gaskell has reservations about (male) working-class activism, she nevertheless attacks female inaction throughout the text and identifies melodrama, a dominant mode of narrating women's lives, as one source of female inertia.[11]

    *Mary Barton* evidences as much interest in women's work—and the lack of it—as it does for the poor "care-worn men" (xxxv) Gaskell regularly met on the streets of Manchester. For the "strange alternations between work and want" that Gaskell identifies as the central feature of Manchester life plays itself out in a modified form across class and gender lines, in both the idleness of wealthy ladies and the unemployment of poor men. Gaskell spins out a series of dialectical oppositions—between action and inaction, independence and dependence, proletariat and bourgeoisie—through which she organizes her exploration of women's work and women's want of work. Active and independent, Mary Barton becomes Gaskell's representative working woman, and it is her virtues, set off against the inactivity and dependency of middle-class women, that *Mary Barton* tries to uphold.

By paralleling the idleness of middle-class women with the unemployment of working-class men, Gaskell allows the emotional power of her analogy to affirm what explicitly goes unsaid: for both men and women, "leisure was a curse" (64). Out of boredom, Mrs. Carson turns hypochondriacal, a mental state the narrator insists could be remedied "if she might have taken the work of one of her own housemaids for a week; made beds, rubbed tables, shaken carpets" (237). Not surprisingly, presiding over a brood of somnambulant daughters who sleep through breakfast and yawn over tea does not provide enough stimulation. On the whole, the women in the Carson family bear an uncanny resemblance to John Barton's description of a "do-nothing lady, worrying shopmen all morning, and screeching at her pianny all afternoon, and going to bed without having done a good turn to any one of God's creatures but herself" (8). One might be willing to dismiss Barton's rancorous characterization of the middle-class woman as originating in his venomous hatred of the master class, but the novel confirms Barton's view. In *Mary Barton,* a lady is a woman who does nothing, so that when Mary daydreams of becoming a lady, she fittingly pictures herself "doing all the elegant nothings appertaining to ladyhood" (92).

Much to Mary's advantage, Gaskell contrasts the slugabeds of the Carson household with the bustling Mary, and although Mary's exertions may disqualify her for ladyhood, they do transform her into a heroine. In the dark days after Carson's murder, Mary's "mind unconsciously sought after some course or action in which she might engage. Any thing, any thing, rather than leisure for reflection" (312). This decision to take action not only preserves her sanity but it also saves the day, for if she had not discovered an alibi or pursued the *John Cropper* after it had set sail, Jem Wilson would surely have been convicted for a murder he did not commit. Although critics have been quick to dismiss Mary's adventurous rescue on the Mersey as a melodramatic set scene, it underscores the saving power of activity: in this particular case, Mary's leisure would certainly have been a curse because it would have cost Jem his life.

Unfortunately, Gaskell's inability to disentangle her incipient feminism from certain class-bound notions of femininity ultimately destabilizes the text: for the novelist's defense of Mary's sexual innocence will eventually undermine her excoriation of middle-class idleness. As a working woman, Mary was subject to the intense eroticization all working-class women underwent: Mary's prostitute aunt is not only the skeleton in the Barton family closet but the skeleton lurking in every working woman's closet.[12] In order to lift Mary above the sexual suspicions her working-class status might raise, Gaskell insists on the innate femininity of all women and posits (to take a liberty with Burns) that "a woman's a woman for a' that." Yet an irresolvable contradiction emerges out of Gaskell's championing of both middle-class femininity and woman's work. For the qualities that Gaskell most admires in Mary are those that stand in starkest contrast to Victorian notions of femininity. Mary's working-class virtues of self-reliance and assertiveness align her most dangerously with her prostitute aunt, the former factory girl whose fall John Barton attributes to an independent spirit derived from an independent income. Caught in an ideological bind and unable to imagine a possible third alternative for her heroine between the deadly inertia of the Carson women and the spiritual death of prostitution—between sleepwalking and streetwalking—Gaskell will in the end be forced to condemn Mary to the bourgeois idleness that the novel ostensibly rejects.

In spite of the high value Gaskell places on action, Mary's heroic acts come into direct conflict with her maidenly modesty, which requires passivity, inactivity, and uselessness. Quite appropriately, maidenly modesty begins exerting an influence on Mary's life immediately after she realizes she loves Jem Wilson, whose marriage proposal she has just rejected. At the moment she fulfills her destiny as a Victorian heroine by falling in love, she lapses into inertia: "Maidenly modesty (and true love is ever modest) seemed to oppose every plan she could think of, for showing Jem how much she repented her decision against him, and how dearly she had now discovered that she loved him. She came to the unusual wisdom of resolving to do nothing, but try and be patient, and improve circumstances as they might turn up. . . . she would try and do right, and have womanly patience, until he saw her changed and repentant mind in her natural actions" (153-54). Mary's decision to do nothing appears as "unusual wisdom" indeed in a book that usually counsels action. Moreover, in her case the decision proves to be a particularly unwise one because had Mary resolved on taking some course of action, like running after Jem, it might have circumvented his arrest for Carson's murder. By adopting maidenly modesty and its attendant virtue of patience, Mary moves precipitously close to her father's definition of a lady as someone who goes "to bed without having done a good turn to any one of God's creatures but herself."[13]

Independent female action of the sort that makes Mary a heroine proves incompatible with the values of Victorian femininity. Mary's final collapse into inertia occurs at the trial, and when she emerges after a long illness, it is as a childlike parody of her former self, a woman who looks into her fiancé's face with an "innocent, infantine gaze" (410). At the end of *Mary Barton,* Gaskell allows Victorian femininity to triumph over woman's work. The young woman who began the novel running errands for her mother and quickly graduated to running the Barton household is ultimately reduced to a state of infantile dependence. No wonder that when Jem tells her after the trial that "thou'rt not fit to be trusted home by thyself," he must do so "with fond exaggeration of her helplessness" (426). Only by exaggerating the helplessness of a woman who has just proven herself capable of saving his life can he possibly justify his "natural" role as Mary's protector. Like Jem, Gaskell too must exaggerate Mary's helplessness, even though it translates, in a different context, into the wasted lives of the Carson women.

Ironically, when Mary marries Jem she gets what she asks for—a life of "elegant nothings." Appointed "as instrument maker to the Agricultural College" in Toronto, a "comfortable appointment,—house,—land,—and a good percentage on the instruments made" (443), Jem may never become a wealthy industrialist like Mr. Carson. But the Wilson clan has evidently begun its climb into the respectable middle classes. Our last glimpse of Mary reveals her installed in the suburban paradise of the new world, patiently and passively waiting for her husband to return from work: Jem's old mother, long crippled by an industrial accident, now has "twice the spirit" of Mary (464). While Gaskell celebrates the active and useful lives led by Manchester's working-class women, she nevertheless dooms her heroine to life as a sleeping beauty in the Canadian wilderness, for in spirit if not in name, Mary becomes the second Mrs. Carson. Ensnared in an ideology that conflates independence and assertiveness with female sexuality, Gaskell resorts to conservative notions of femininity that enshrine dependence and inactivity in order to save her working-class heroine from the taint of immorality. But in the process, she destroys Mary because the values of work and the virtues of ladyhood are not reconcilable after all. Gaskell embraces what she had tried to repudiate and accepts for Mary the life of bourgeois "do-nothingism" in Canada that she had rejected in Manchester. In *Mary Barton* the brave new world looks remarkably like the old.[14]

## History, Luddism, and Medievalism in *Shirley*

Charlotte Brontë's second published novel, the much-anticipated successor to *Jane Eyre,* must have indeed seemed like a dish of "cold lentils and vinegar without oil" (39) to readers expecting the Sturm und Drang of the first. Despite Brontë's significant achievement, *Shirley* is not a novel calculated to keep readers on the edge of their chairs, turning pages until the small hours of the morning. As Brontë acknowledges in a letter to William Smith Williams, "Those who were most charmed with 'Jane Eyre' are the least pleased with 'Shirley'; they are disappointed at not finding the same excitement, interest, stimulus, while those who spoke disparagingly of 'Jane Eyre'—like 'Shirley' a little better than her predecessor. I suppose its dryer matter suits their dryer minds. . . . Mere novel-readers, it is evident, think 'Shirley' something of a failure" (Wise and Symington 3: 35). While admitting that *Shirley* failed to please the large Victorian population of novel readers, Brontë draws a distinction between those who read novels for pleasure and those who demand a more substantial meal from their fictions. Yet the "dryer matter" which disqualifies the average reader from appreciating *Shirley* is not, as one might expect, the industrial material that Brontë takes as her subject matter. After all, condition-of-England novels were in demand at midcentury. Gaskell's investigation of the industrial crisis a year earlier in *Mary Barton* did not prevent it from being a critical and popular success, and when Brontë sent her publisher the manuscript of her next novel, *Villette,* she apologized for its lack of topicality. Rather, the "dryer matter" for "dryer minds" that Brontë refers to in her letter is that dry-as-dust subject: history.

Brontë brings the subject of history, as the past remembered and dismembered, to the center of *Shirley*. Taking nostalgia as a starting point from which to launch an exploration of women in history and women's exclusion from history, Brontë writes in *Shirley* a woman's history of England. In doing so, she overturns the history of the nineteenth century popularized by the medievalists and scripts the fall into modernity as a fortunate one. But patriarchal structures and expectations subvert the novelist's attempts to envision the liberation of middle-class women through industrial capitalism. At the novel's conclusion, Brontë repudiates the past only to embrace a present that, for her heroines, proves to be a repetition of the past. Like *Mary Barton, Shirley* discovers a new world that all too closely resembles the old one.

Brontë understands that the volatile mixture of memory and desire creates a past that never was. In the opening lines of *Shirley,* the novelist forces the reader to acknowledge—so that she can quickly dismiss—the seductive power of nostalgia:

> But not of late years are we about to speak; we are going back to the beginning of this century: late years—present years are dusty, sun-burnt, hot, arid; we will evade the noon, forget it in siesta, pass the mid-day in slumber, and dream of dawn.
>     If you think, from this prelude, that anything like a romance is preparing for you, reader, you never were more mistaken. . . . Something real, cool, and solid, lies before you; something unromantic as a Monday morning. (39)

Brontë sets up an opposition between the "hot" and "arid" present and the romantic appeal of the past in order to arouse the reader's expectations for a Regency novel overflowing with belles in sprigged muslin and gallant officers. But she raises those hopes only to dash them, offering up instead a past replete with industrial riots, starving workers, and civil unrest on the home front. By writing about the Luddite riots of the 1810s rather than more recent outbreaks of industrial unrest, such as the Chartist agitations of the 1840s, Brontë serves her text's larger purpose: the past revealed in *Shirley* is indeed as "unromantic as a Monday morning."

*Shirley* investigates the "making of history," with all the ambiguities inherent in that expression. For as Brontë conceives it, history is twice made, first by the men and women who live through it and then by the historians who record, redefine, and reshape it. Like Disraeli's Young England novels, Brontë's *Shirley* explores the practice of recording history; however, writing as one of history's losers—as Milton's cook rather than Shirley's titanic Eve—Brontë grasps the essentially fictional and hence mythic nature of history. Disavowing what Hayden White identifies as the nineteenth-century faith in history as a factual discourse that can be distinguished from the fictional discourse of novels, Brontë conflates history and fiction, for neither is disinterested and both bear the political stamp of their authors. Consequently, she holds that there exists no one correct way to read past events because they are continuously being reevaluated in the light of present and personal contingencies. When Joe Scott, the mill's overseer, quotes St. Paul's maxims on female subjection, Shirley Keeldar, in good Protestant fashion, calls for the right to "private judgment," and Caroline Helstone offers a host of alternative readings: "It would be quite possible, I doubt not, with a little ingenuity, to give the passage quite a contrary turn; to make it say, 'Let the woman speak out whenever she sees fit to make an objection;' —'it is permitted to a woman to teach and to exercise authority as much as may be' " (323). By volunteering to reinterpret the historical context and the original text of St. Paul's epistle, Shirley and Caroline act as revisionist historians and rewrite history from a female perspective. Like her two heroines, Brontë denies the existence of absolute historical truths because all history—whether it be Shirley and Caroline's or Joe Scott's—is subject to "private judgment." It is this truth—and its ramifications for women's history—that engages Brontë in *Shirley*.

Brontë recognizes that history is a powerful political tool, particularly when the authority of the past is marshaled to justify present actions: witness Joe Scott's use of sacred history to defend the historical oppression of women. But by invoking "private judgment" and arguing for every individual's right to the past, Brontë opens history up and liberates it from exclusive claims of ownership. So, for example, when the Reverend Helstone, the Tory supporter of Wellington, and Robert Moore, the radical admirer of Napoleon, engage in a political dispute, both men invoke the past to legitimize the present. Each claims biblical history for his side and envisions his commander-in-chief as a second Moses. In Moore's account, Napoleon becomes the great liberator, leading the slavish peoples of Europe out of the darkness and decay of feudal traditions, while in Helstone's rendering, Wellington is metamorphosed into the leader of a "poor over-wrought band of bondsmen" (69), who will soon triumph over the superior military might of those latter-day Egyptians, the French. However apt the comparisons, neither man holds the patent on biblical history, and to complicate matters further, Brontë introduces into the text a "genuine" Moses, Moses Barraclough, the sometime tailor, sometime Methodist preacher and full-time Luddite. This Moses also asserts a right to the historical comparison, "I'm a very feeling man, and when I see my brethren oppressed like my great namesake of old, I stand up for 'em" (155). Speaking as he does for impoverished weavers who feel enslaved by their masters, Barraclough's historical analogy suits. Yet Brontë goes to such pains to discredit Barraclough (he is both a drunk and a liar) that it becomes impossible to claim that one group—the French, the English, or the weavers—rightfully owns the analogy, or by extension, history itself. By abolishing private ownership of the past, Brontë frees herself from the constraints of monolithic history and absolute historical truths, and in this way she gives women an access to history denied to them in a historical discourse that insists on its factual nature.

Having placed history in the public domain, Brontë then draws on its new availability to argue that what has been traditionally constituted as written history consigns women to the margins of the text. In the raid on the Hollow's End mill, Brontë offers a paradigm for the place of women in (male) history. The attack on Robert Moore's mill is itself a historical event writ large, the kind of grand dramatic incident guaranteed inclusion in any history book. Quite appropriately, it is also a re-creation of an actual historical occurrence, the Luddite raid on William Cartwright's mill at Rawfolds, that has, in fact, made its way into the history books. Of Brontë's reconstruction of the attack, Terry Eagleton contends that "the event is at once structurally central and curiously empty—empty because the major protagonist, the working class, is distinguished primarily by its absence" (*Myths of Power* 47). But while it is true that the workers are heard and not seen, it is equally true of the mill's defenders. Emblematic of women's participation in history, Caroline and Shirley are literally marginalized as they watch the events from a nearby ridge, and if they hear the weavers' shouts and the soldiers' shots, this is not Eagleton's "abstraction of action to sound" (48), but history from a female vantage point. For women like Caroline and Shirley, history is heard, or to be precise, heard about. Even their limited participation as ear-witnesses is a stolen pleasure: the mill's defenders go to great lengths to remove all the women from the site of the battle, keeping the approaching confrontation a well-guarded secret. In (male) history, women hear about events secondhand through mediating narratives that distort and falsify the experience, so that, true to form, the parsonage servants tell Shirley and Caroline that "twenty men were killed" (344), while Moore relates that "not a single man [was] hurt on our side" (350). Both accounts are exaggerations—one man was killed and Robert himself suffered a slight wound—but they underscore the unreliability of historical narratives and the traditional dependence of women on those unreliable narratives.

Although excluded from the history of public events both as participant and witness, women have nevertheless always possessed their own history, hidden from view, and it is the buried corpse—the unwritten corpus—of women's history that Brontë exhumes in *Shirley*. She does so by overturning the medievalist history that devalues the present and longs for the vanished, feudal past. When Caroline Helstone and her uncle pay a call at Fieldhead, a "gothic old barrack," Brontë offers this description:

> Mr and Miss Helstone were ushered into a parlour: of course, as was to be expected in such a gothic old barrack, this parlour was lined with oak: fine dark, glossy panels compassed the

walls gloomily and grandly. Very handsome, reader, these shining, brown panels are: very mellow in colouring and tasteful in effect, but—if you know what a 'Spring-clean' is—very execrable and inhuman. Whoever, having the bowels of humanity, has seen servants scrubbing at these polished wooden walls with bees-waxed cloths on a warm May day, must allow that they are 'tolerable [*sic*] and not to be endured;' and I cannot but secretly applaud the benevolent barbarian who had painted another and larger apartment of Fieldhead—the drawing-room to-wit, formerly also an oak-room—of a delicate pinky white; thereby earning for himself the character of a Hun, but mightily enhancing the cheerfulness of that portion of his abode, and saving future housemaids a world of toil. (208)

In this passage Brontë anticipates Ruskin's "The Nature of Gothic," which appeared a few years after *Shirley*. Like the great Victorian champion of the Gothic, she also judges a style of architecture (and the culture it represents) by examining the contribution of the worker, except that she focuses on the contribution of the working woman rather than the working man. So while Ruskin reads the facades of Gothic buildings, Brontë ventures inside looking for women's history; and if he discovers the principle of creative freedom for the individual workman embodied in the stones of Europe's Gothic cathedrals, Brontë finds, to her evident displeasure, long days of drudgery for the anonymous housemaids responsible for keeping the dust off the gargoyles.

By turning medievalist history inside out, she turns it upside down, so that Gothic architecture suddenly appears "execrable and inhuman" rather than as the noblest expression of the worker's individuality in art. Focusing on women in history, rather than on men, Brontë reverses the medievalists' judgment about the superiority of Gothic architecture and, by extension, the feudal past it embodies. For while history of the sort the Victorian medievalists were writing would label the interior redecorator of Fieldhead a "Hun" and a "barbarian," in Brontë's revision, the renovation of the old constitutes progress, at least for the housemaids of the world.

Brontë firmly rejects the concept of the medieval past as a paradise lost, or even as an era of greater human felicity, because she believes that for women the Middle Ages were the Dark Ages. At one point, *Shirley*'s two heroines propose to travel "back into the dim days of eld" when they project a visit to Nunnwood, "the sole remnant of antique British forest in a region whose lowlands were once all sylvan chase" (220). Whether the visit occurs or not we never find out, but it becomes increasingly clear that the journey, had it ever come off, would not have been a pleasure trip. To go back in time is to come face to face with a specifically female horror, for at the center of the forest stands the ruins of a nunnery. And in *Shirley,* as in *Villette,* the nun symbolizes the emotionally barren, sexually repressed, and socially useless lives led by so many women.[15] Certainly wherever Caroline Helstone turns, she is confronted with the nunlike existence of her female predecessors, from her aunt, a figure of silence and death, "living marble . . . a monumental angel" (81), to her mother, who suffered through the "sedentary, solitary, constrained, joyless, toilsome" life of a governess (363). For Caroline to wish a return to the past—whether to the nunneries of the medieval past or the modern nuns in her more immediate and personal past—would be to invite her own death, or more accurately, her own death-in-life. Brontë does not want women to turn back to the medieval past; she wants them to turn their backs on the medieval past.

Brontë even goes so far as to parody the medievalist fantasy of the fourteenth century through the figure of Shirley's erstwhile suitor, Sir Philip Nunnely, before she excludes him from the symbolic marriages with which the novel concludes. Sir Philip, the son of the late Sir Monckton, and the possessor of a Yorkshire estate known as the Priory, makes an appearance in *Shirley* so that the heroine can reject his marriage proposal along with the medieval world, to go by the family names alone, in which he is implicated. In fact, Sir Philip, whose two defining features are his "boyish" countenance (448) and his fondness for writing dreadful sonnets, appears to be nothing so much as a satiric sketch of one of the scribbling, aristocratic members of Young England, a skewed portrait of Lord John Manners, perhaps. With Shirley's rejection of Sir Philip, Brontë dismisses Victorian medievalism, and with it all nostalgic attempts to feudalize the nineteenth century.

She similarly disowns the working-class nostalgia of the Luddites. Like the medievalists, the Luddites are a reactionary force, and it is this nostalgia for a gilded past, which the machine-smashing weavers share with the practitioners of Victorian medievalism, that accounts for Brontë's ambivalent treatment of the Luddites.[16] On the one hand, Brontë celebrates the Luddites' bloody defeat at Hollow's End; but on the other hand, she openly sympathizes with the weavers' sufferings, exploiting the emotional power of an analogy between the hungry, out-of-work workers and the idleness and spiritual starvation of middle-class women. Like Gaskell before her, Brontë links middle-class women to working-class men through their common affliction: unemployment. The analogy that sustains *Mary Barton,* however, breaks down in *Shirley* because the interests of the male Luddites and those of the novel's women are not identical. When the frame-breaker Barraclough comes to debate the future of machinery with Moore, he informs the industrialist: "Or iver you set up the pole o' your tent amang us, Mr Moore, we lived i' peace and quietness; yea, I may say, in all loving-kindness. I am not myself an aged person as yet, but I can remember as far back as maybe some twenty year, when hand-labour were encouraged and respected, and no mischief-maker had ventured to introduce these here machines, which is so pernicious" (155). "Or iver"—before ever—Moore arrived, Barraclough argues, the weavers lived in a prelapsarian state of peace, love, and goodwill towards all. In one sense, Barraclough speaks the truth, for what *Shirley* captures, in all its painful process, is the gradual immiseration of the handloom weavers, the decimation of weaving communities and the disruption of a centuries-old way of life. Faced with their own extinction, the weavers responded by forging a collective memory of an idealized past, the "or iver" the factories came into Yorkshire: "The history of the weavers in the 19th century is haunted by the legend of better days," E. P. Thompson notes (269). Yet while Brontë can respond movingly to the weavers' distress, she professes nothing but hostility for the reversionary goals of the Luddites because she sees the technological changes so destructive to the weavers as benefiting the weavers' wives and daughters.

For what the modern reader of *Shirley* may forget is that the introduction of machinery occurred simultaneously with the opening up of employment opportunities for women and children in the mills.

"The two techniques that fuelled the classic Luddite attacks, the gig mill and the shearing frame, displaced six out of seven and three out of four men respectively," Berg notes ("Women's Work" 82). These machines, which Robert Moore imports into Hollow's End, would eventually destroy the old artisan traditions, but in the process they did make available waged labor to large numbers of women and children, who could be paid less than men and were considered more adaptable to the discipline of factory work. To be sure, women belonged to handloom weaving communities, and many took part in protests against the introduction of the machinery.[17] But by drawing on the cultural equation of industrialism with female employment and male unemployment so prevalent in the 1840s, Brontë ignores women's participation in the Luddite riots in order to heighten the opposition between the old technology, which she figures as the exclusive province of the male weavers, and the new technology, which opened up the labor market for women. We know the mill in Hollow's End employs women because Robert Moore's sister dismisses the independent "young coquines" (112) in his factory as unsuitable for domestic service. So it is not surprising that in a novel exhorting the "Men of Yorkshire" to seek for their daughters "scope and work" (379), and in which one of the heroines claims to wish for a profession "fifty times a-day" (235), Brontë defends the factory system as fiercely as Robert Moore defends his mill. If nothing else, the mill provides "scope and work" for some of Yorkshire's daughters. Like the historian Joan Kelly, Brontë recognizes that "one of the tasks of women's history is to call into question accepted schemes of periodization. To take the emancipation of women as a vantage point is to discover that events that further the historical development of men, liberating them from natural, social, or ideological constraints, have quite different, even opposite, effects upon women" (19). Conversely, events that further the historical development of women may have the opposite effect upon men. Brontë imagines that the industrial revolution might be one such historical development, one that works to the advantage of women, often at the expense of men.

But in the end, Brontë—like Gaskell in *Mary Barton*—finds herself betrayed by the progress of industrial capitalism. Although Shirley Keeldar is briefly empowered by a fortune linked to Robert

Moore's mill (she is his landlord), the text cannot legitimately claim that there exists a natural connection between Shirley's financial and personal independence and the industrial revolution. Shirley makes her money the old-fashioned way—she inherits it. In an 1839 letter sent to Emily from the home of a wealthy manufacturer where she was enduring life as a governess, Charlotte Brontë mused: "I could like to be at home. I could like to work in a mill. I could like to feel some mental liberty. I could like this weight of restraint to be taken off. But the holidays will come. *Corragio*" (Wise and Symington 1: 181). Yet what the elder sister knew, even if she knew nothing about factory work, was that industrial labor remained closed to the impoverished daughters of the middle classes. Moreover, Mrs. Gooch's Golden Rule for her upwardly mobile son that Matthew Arnold conjures up in *Culture and Anarchy*—"Ever remember . . . that you should look forward to being some day manager of that concern!" (433)—did not apply to the Gooch daughters. But in *Shirley,* Brontë evades the problem of Shirley's unearned and unearnable income to fantasize briefly about what it would be like if women could engage in the middle-class equivalent of factory work. It is just this scenario that she plays out through Shirley, only to find that if one is both a woman and an owner of the means of production, the iron will of patriarchy finds a way to prevail nonetheless.

Self-styled as Shirley Keeldar, Esquire, and Captain Keeldar, Shirley pretends to be a country squire and a captain of industry, but while she assumes the masculine titles, she can never assume masculine power: the sources of power remain mystified, even in the money-mad nineteenth century. Although Shirley's wealth gives her an extraordinary degree of autonomy over her own life, it does not lend her any political power to intervene in public events. Landlord or not, Shirley is treated like a girl and is expected to behave like one: "A chit like that would scarcely presume to give herself airs with the Rector of her parish, however rich she might be" (207), Helstone assures his niece, Caroline. The local elites even keep the impending confrontation at Hollow's End mill a secret from her, and if anyone has a right to that information, it is Shirley, who owns the mill property. Excluded from the world of public events, Shirley falls back onto women's traditional social role, transforming herself into Lady

Bountiful and dispensing the necessities of life to the starving families surrounding her. In the end, she more closely resembles that other bountiful provider, Milton's cook, than the titanic Eve of her fertile imagination. Despite her public standing, Shirley remains marginal in a man's world (her philanthropic activities fail to circumvent the violent conflict at the mill) and unable to escape, in her own life, the patriarchal model of mother Eve she so feverishly rejects. In Shirley's impotence to enact a new history for women, we must read Brontë's own recognition that modernity has not lived up to its promise, a failure which condemns the women of the present to relive the lives of their mothers. The tragedy in *Shirley* is not change but the inability of things to change.

Like Mary Barton, Shirley finds herself constrained by a variety of entrenched social configurations that refuse to yield automatically to advancing capitalist structures. The freedom with which Shirley's wealth endows her is a chimera, for it turns out to be nothing more than the freedom to choose her own captivity, which she promptly does by marrying Louis Moore. Modern readers find the master-slave imagery of their courtship embarrassing, and it is hard not to cringe when Shirley tells Louis Moore, in lieu of a declaration of love: "I am glad I know my keeper, and am used to him. Only his voice will I follow; only his hand shall manage me; only at his feet will I repose" (579). But perhaps we should instead applaud Shirley's honesty for refusing to cover over the legal bondage marriage will entail by resorting to the language of romantic love. If Shirley's personal independence depends upon her financial independence, she will lose her freedom on her wedding day, for according to Victorian property law, Louis will then become her keeper.[18]

Divided between what she hopes the consequences of industrial capitalism will be and her uneasy sense that the persistence of patriarchy may starve those hopes, Brontë concludes *Shirley* with an oddly incongruous vision that simultaneously embraces hope and anticipates disappointment. The ending ultimately subverts both the conventions of medievalist history and the novelistic conventions of the day. To much confusion, Brontë places her "private judgment," her sense of what a happy ending is (the progress of industrial capitalism), in a nostalgic narrative that laments change while at the same time she embeds the text's real tragedy (the lack of progress for middle-class women) in a traditional happy ending of love and marriage.

Brontë undermines the conventions of novelistic closure by being unable to assure the reader that her heroines will live happily ever after, for the marriages confirm a continuity with the past that Brontë repudiates: Shirley openly acknowledges her marriage to be a form of imprisonment, and Caroline stands on the verge of a future that threatens to replay her mother's and her aunt's cloistering. As Gilbert and Gubar observe, "Robert Moore starts perceiving Caroline's resemblance to the Virgin Mary. . . . for readers who remember Mary Cave the echo is ominous" (397). While Caroline confides to Shirley that "if we listened to the wisdom of experience" we would "make up our minds to remain single" (224), the two heroines ignore that wisdom nonetheless. Shirley and Caroline may know the past, but they are still doomed to repeat it.

Simultaneously, Brontë undermines the conventions of (male) history, Luddite or medievalist, that read change in tragic terms, by undercutting the lamentation for the past with which the novel closes. When Caroline complains that Robert's mill will "change our blue hill-country air into the Stilbro' smoke atmosphere" (598), Robert rebukes her and reminds her that "the houseless, the starving, the unemployed, shall come to Hollow's mill from far and near" (598). Given that *Shirley* records the terrible starvation and unemployment in Caroline's hill-country, one must consider that perhaps, within the moral economy of the novel, Robert offers a fair trade. The narrative then shifts suddenly to the future Moore and Caroline had just been envisioning and relates a conversation between the narrator and the narrator's housekeeper over the loss of Caroline's beautiful landscape, which has apparently now taken place. Indulging in nostalgia—the housekeeper tells her employer that "there is no such ladies" like Caroline and Shirley "now-a-days"—she proceeds to give a description of Hollow's End before the factories arrived in Yorkshire: "I can tell of it clean different again: when there was neither mill, nor cot, nor hall, except Fieldhead, within two miles of it. I can tell, one summer-evening, fifty years syne, my mother coming running in just at the edge of dark, almost fleyed out of her wits, saying, she had seen a fairish (fairy) in Fieldhead Hollow; and that was the last fairish that ever was seen on this country side. . . . A lonesome spot it was—and a bonnie spot—full of oak trees and nut trees. It is altered now" (599). Traditional readings of *Shirley* have seen the housekeeper's memorial for the "bonnie spot" as evidence of Brontë's own regret for a rural world vanishing in the wake of industrial progress. But if we pause to consider precisely what the housekeeper laments—the fact that fifty years ago her mother was driven to the point of madness because of superstitious fears—Brontë's irony at the housekeeper's expense becomes manifest. The passing of this country superstition is best left unmourned. The housekeeper's regret for the "bonnie spot," like Caroline's regret for her hill-country, is a nostalgic longing for the picturesqueness of a landscape emptied of people, and when one repeoples the landscape with the houseless, the unemployed, the starving, and the ignorant, the image loses some of its picturesque qualities.

*Shirley*'s double endings both literalize and amplify the duality that lies at the center of Brontë's response to the industrial world: her text heralds the world-transforming changes and laments the slow speed with which those changes are occurring. Industrial capitalism has not yet kept its revolutionary promise of a shining new world. Instead, the old patriarchal order remains intact, manifesting itself in the various patriarchal configurations, from the legal system to novelistic conventions, over which even the transfiguring imagination of Brontë cannot leap. Having promised its readers "something real, cool, and solid," *Shirley* gives us reality, with all its inherent disappointments and disillusionments.

## *North and South,* Nostalgia and Dissent: Gaskell's Double Bildungsroman

Improving economic conditions after midcentury allow Elizabeth Gaskell to distance herself from the immediate perils of industrial life (starvation, disease, unemployment) that occupy *Mary Barton* and *Shirley* in order to place the industrial experience represented in her next, and last, industrial novel into a wider historical framework that encompasses past, present, and future. Unlike the factory tales of the turbulent 1840s, *North and South* can openly embrace and celebrate cultural change, offering the reader an epithalamion in novel form, one that rejoices in the union of ethics and industry, workers and owners, women and men. The repaired industrial world that Gaskell imagines at novel's end is not, however, "a factory village in a tale," to paraphrase Margaret Hale's description of Helstone. Gaskell anticipates no Disraeliesque Millbank or Trafford but rather a decidedly prosaic Marlborough Mills. But then, given the thematics of *North and South,* it is unlikely Gaskell would conclude with any paradisiacal visions when so much of the novel's energies go into deconstructing the very notion of paradise lost.

Elizabeth Gaskell subtitled *Mary Barton* "A Tale of Manchester Life," but when she returns to the same subject matter six years later in *North and South,* she transforms Manchester into Milton-Northern, and by doing so, she signals to her readers the mythic intent of her text. Critics of *North and South* have long noted its connection to *Paradise Lost,* but they fail to appreciate Gaskell's use of Milton's epic poem to structure her own mythic text, where she deploys the notion of a fortunate fall to counteract the popular male literary myths that configure modernity as a fall from grace. Thus, *North and South*'s readers invariably, if incorrectly, connect Milton's Hell with Milton-Northern instead of with the aptly named Helstone, the heroine's rural home.[19] With its rose-covered cottages and rosy-cheeked inhabitants, Helstone may at first seem Edenic, but Gaskell's reading of *Paradise Lost* is closer to Blake's than to Milton's. Gaskell too is of the devil's party, or at least she takes the part of the dark, Satanic mill owners, whose angry response to *Mary Barton* led to her sympathetic portrait of an industrialist in the figure of John Thornton. The expulsion from paradise is a lucky break in *North and South,* for the narrative reenvisions the Edenic Helstone as hellish, a place associated by the novel's end with "the powers of darkness" (477) that an old woman calls upon when she roasts a neighbor's cat in an act of such brutality that even the "soft green influence" of the forest "could not charm away the shock and the pain in Margaret's heart, caused by the recital of such cruelty" (478).

For Margaret Hale, Gaskell's Victorian Eve, the trajectory

from England's rural past (Helstone) to its industrial present (Milton) is particularly fortunate, quite literally so when she inherits a factory-made fortune. Tennyson's sublime injunction, "Move upward, working out the beast," functions as the unacknowledged subtext for this novel committed to cultural and personal evolution.[20] By expanding the form of the bildungsroman to include cultures as well as characters, Gaskell finds an elegant solution to the problem of introducing feminist concerns into an industrial novel. She uses the structure of her text to connect women, workers, and industrialism, so that *North and South* traces the growth from childhood to adulthood of Margaret Hale, the novel's heroine; Nicholas Higgins, the novel's representative worker; and Great Britain, the nation they both inhabit.

One of the first things Margaret Hale must learn is what the narrator of *Shirley* already understands: for women and workers, the past is a site of oppressive social relations, and nostalgia for it entails grave moral and political dangers. But while Brontë explores nostalgia through the creation of the historical record, Gaskell does so by focusing almost exclusively on the personal recollections of her heroine. To disrupt her heroine's nostalgic indulgences, Gaskell the Unitarian Dissenter introduces the concept of dissent into her novel, strategically deploying it to reveal the depleted moral legitimacy of such hoary British institutions as the Church, the Navy, and the aristocracy. Repudiating a past she associates with these oppressive and authoritarian bodies, Gaskell embraces the industrial present only to discover that she can no more secure the links between female emancipation and the industrial revolution than Brontë could. As a result, *North and South* (like *Shirley*) ends on an ambiguous note that celebrates the transformational energies of industrialism and laments the slow pace of change.

While the opening frames of the novel—the marriage in London and the removal from Helstone—can seem disconnected from its industrial heart, these early scenes are central to Gaskell's project of dismantling nostalgia. When *North and South*'s heroine prepares to leave the London home where she has spent a large part of her childhood, she grows nostalgic and tries to commiserate with the old nurserymaid: "I think we shall all be sorry to leave this dear old room." Much to Margaret's surprise, the nurserymaid, curiously identified only as "Newton," rejects Margaret's use of the all-inclusive "we": "Indeed, miss, I shan't for one. My eyes are not so good as they were, and the light here is so bad that I can't see to mend laces except just at the window, where there's always a shocking draught—enough to give one one' s death of cold" (39). Although it is buried in the opening chapter's deftly ironic account of a society wedding, the nurserymaid's unexpected corrective to the heroine's longing for the lost world of childhood captures and distills the essence of the political critique of nostalgia that Gaskell undertakes in *North and South.* For the nurserymaid's refusal to participate in the heroine's sentimentalizing gesture towards her childhood is reenacted by Gaskell who, throughout *North and South,* provides the necessary emendations to her culture's sentimental attachment to its past. Expanded a thousandfold, the "dear old room" Margaret laments in the first chapter becomes the dear old Helstone of the second chapter. The aristocratic, agrarian, and Anglican village of Helstone represents, in the novel's symbolic deployment of space, both Margaret's and England's childhood. Here, Gaskell parts company with Charlotte Brontë. Brontë's fierce anti-Catholicism leads her to conjure up and then reject an overwhelmingly Catholic, markedly medieval past, whereas the liberal, dissenting Gaskell invents and subsequently repudiates a decidedly Tory past. While each woman deromanticizes and distances herself from any nostalgic regard for the past, they disagree on exactly where to locate that past.

Nevertheless, just as Margaret's nostalgia blinds her to the working conditions in the nursery, it also prevents her from seeing the class realities of her father's rural parish, which she obscures in such a dense fog of romance that it becomes the fictional "village in a poem" (42) she suggests it resembles. In subjecting Helstone to the same nostalgic gaze she fixes on her London nursery, Margaret overlooks those who must work as opposed to play in either the Harley Street nursery or Helstone. When Margaret describes her beloved Helstone to Bessy Higgins, the dying cotton mill worker, she admits that "sometimes I used to hear a farmer speaking sharp and loud to his servants; but it was so far away that it only reminded me pleasantly that other people were hard at work in some distant place, while I just sat on the heather and did nothing" (145). By juxtaposing her leisure against the field hands' labor, Margaret's speech is full of dramatic irony, and it momentarily forces us to consider the past from a different point of view, that of the farm servants, whose subjectivity remains a mystery to Margaret. She will eventually learn something of a subaltern subjectivity from her give-and-take discussions with the fiercely independent Nicholas Higgins. But her interactions with the Helstone villagers, limited to those who depend on her charitable offices, preclude any such enlightenment because, unlike Higgins, the objects of Margaret's philanthropy are disabled from speaking out by their dependence and the "dulness" (382) of their lives. The erased subjectivity of the Helstone poor allows Margaret to transform their deprivation into her poetry: she can nurse their babies, feed their sick, and sketch their tumbledown cottages— housing the heroine perceives as picturesque rather than as substandard and unfit for human habitation—without ever being forced to consider the power dynamics at play. In effect, Margaret's self-indulgent nostalgia for her own childhood becomes a kind of myopia that prevents her from recognizing the brutality of peasant life, where most of the people are condemned "to soaking in the stagnant waters" (382) of unmediated privation.

As the narrative moves from Helstone to Milton and back to Helstone for the village's ultimate subjection to the heroine's revisionary appraisal, *North and South* captures Margaret Hale's consciousness gradually awakening to the fortunate nature of a fall that initially seemed so catastrophic. The narrative returns Margaret to Helstone before she engages herself to Thornton and Milton-Northern so that she can let go of her romantic dreams of an Edenic past and welcome the contentious and imperfect present. It is a testament to Gaskell's delicate handling of Margaret's homecoming that the reader sympathizes with the heroine's distaste for the bustling changes wrought by the earnest new vicar while still acknowledging the beneficial nature of his alterations. Gaskell's deep human understanding allows her to concede the emotional truth of nostalgia, but she still forces her heroine beyond it, a strategy which proves more effective than Brontë's ironic treatment of nostalgia in a parallel scene at the end of *Shirley*. Along with Margaret, the reader comes to realize that although the "all-pervading instability" of the world may give pain, "if the world stood still, it would retrograde and become corrupt" (488). While any change in objects hallowed by familiarity may be jarring, when the story of a cat roasted alive in accordance with local superstition comes to light, Margaret fully apprehends the desirability of change. Even Mr. Bell, the Oxford old boy who is the novel's most ardent defender of the old ways, finally admits that any measures capable of eradicating the "practical paganism" of Helstone would be welcome (478). By ranking social justice above sentimental attachment, Gaskell renders explicit what remains implicit in *Shirley*: the old woman's superstitious fear of fairies becomes *North and South*'s fear that superstitions (as well as local customs, folkways, and gypsy lore) mask lives circumscribed by ignorance. Both Gaskell and Brontë demand that their readers consider the politics behind romanticized appreciations of folk life and the high price paid by the people who are subjected to such appreciations.

Not only does Margaret's nostalgia conceal the circumscribed lives of Helstone's inhabitants, but—and this is significant for the novel's feminist concerns—it also prevents her from perceiving her own similarly circumscribed existence. The young lady who moves back to Helstone after her cousin's marriage is deeply ignorant, unaware of the oppressive nature of her culture's class and gender regimes. Margaret's proprietary interest in the Helstone inhabitants she considers to be "her people" (48) arises from a false sense of her power over them. As a daughter and a dependent, the self-deceived Margaret has little more control over her own destiny than the people to whom she condescends. Although blissfully unconscious of the fact, Margaret resembles the laboring classes she ministers to, a connection Gaskell reveals obliquely through Margaret's likeness to Dixon, Mrs. Hale's servant from her aristocratic girlhood. After a tense scene between the two, Dixon praises Margaret for a show of anger: "Bless you, child! I like to see you showing a bit of a spirit. It's the good old Beresford blood. Why, the last Sir John but two shot his steward down, there where he stood, for just telling him that he'd racked the tenants, and he'd racked the tenants till he could get no more money off them than he could get skin off a flint" (178). The servant's fond remembrance for an aristocratic household where any articulated discontent was silenced with a well-aimed shot can only be described as false consciousness: one cannot imagine any of the Milton operatives praising the masters for such egregious behavior. But Sir John's hasty exercise of aristocratic privilege is merely the dark side of Dixon's feudal loyalty to Mrs. Hale, occasioned by her kindness to Dixon after an accident. Dixon cannot see that she is ensnared in a system that makes her dependent upon the arbitrary actions, whether cruel or kind, of her "superiors." But then neither can Margaret. Although she claims Helstone as her own, she remains there only at the discretion of her father, whose decision to give up his living and move to a manufacturing town, formulated without consulting Margaret or her mother, recalls in a somewhat diminished form Sir John's high-handed response to his steward.

To be fair, Gaskell draws a portrait of a gentle, ineffective man in Mr. Hale, but Gaskell's vicar of Helstone is nonetheless a pale copy of Charlotte Brontë's overbearing patriarch the Reverend Helstone, with whom he shares a name and an occupation. By linking Mr. Hale with Brontë's tyrannical cleric, a man who believes a new frock is the panacea to all female trouble, Gaskell connects *North and South*'s village of Helstone with *Shirley*'s Reverend Helstone and thus the former with the oppression of women through an allusion to the latter. And just as Brontë's Reverend Helstone refuses to acknowledge the seriousness of female dissent and dissatisfaction in his silent wife or quiet niece, believing that "so long as a woman was silent, nothing ailed her, and she wanted nothing" (82), so does Gaskell's vicar politely ignore his wife's long-standing dissatisfaction with Helstone. Indeed, Gaskell draws out the connections between Brontë's Reverend Helstone and the aristocratic world represented by the village and vicar of *North and South*'s Helstone, where dissent is either brutally suppressed, as in the case of Sir John Beresford's steward, or trivialized as female querulousness, as in the case of Margaret's female relatives. Although Margaret's Aunt Shaw married a rich older man whom she did not love, and her mother married the poor country parson whom she did, both remain discontented with their choices. Mrs. Shaw comically laments her loveless marriage and Mrs. Hale her husband's lack of worldly ambition, but a strong feminist reading could recuperate their ladylike peevishness as a form of dissent—as their continuing, submerged objections to the narrow options that were available to them as "poor pretty" (46) Miss Beresfords.

What ultimately distinguishes the vicar of Helstone from the Reverend Helstone and redeems him as a character is his own capacity for dissent, one of the novel's dominant tropes and a quality it holds in the highest regard. Although Mr. Hale ignores his wife's desires for worldly advancement and enacts his patriarchal prerogative to decide his family's fate, he is motivated to become a Dissenter by his opposition to the authority of the Anglican Church. And like the dissenting steward, Mr. Hale must ultimately pay for his dissent with his living (if not his life). In the moral economy of *North and South,* nostalgia and dissent are oppositional terms because nostalgia depends upon an act of forgetting, and what invariably gets forgotten in nostalgic recollections of the good old days are dissenting voices. So, for example, Margaret's nostalgic memories of her visits to Helstone efface the unhappiness of her mother's life there: "There had been slight complaints and passing regrets on her mother's part, over some trifle connected with Helstone, and her father's position there, when Margaret had been spending her holidays at home before; but in the general happiness of the recollection of those times, she had forgotten the small details which were not so pleasant" (49-50). Even here, the heroine's dawning recognition that all is not (and always was not) right with her parents' marriage comes through only in the most tentative form, as a "trifle" of regret on her mother's part. Like *Shirley, North and South* tries to unearth the history of the disgruntled by dissecting the nostalgia that encourages an individual (or a culture) to forget dissenting opinions.

That Gaskell upholds the right to dissent may in part be attributed to her position as the wife of a Dissenting minister and in part to her own special liking for it, as evidenced by her letters. "I suppose we all *do* strengthen each other by clashing together, and earnestly talking our own thoughts, and ideas" (*Letters* 116), she informed Lady Kay-Shuttleworth in 1850. Writing to Charlotte Froude a few months later, Gaskell proved willing to read her earnest quarreling with Charlotte Brontë as a hopeful sign of friendship: "She and I quarrelled & differed about almost everything . . . but we like each other heartily\I think/& I hope we shall ripen into friends" (*Letters*

129). Throughout *North and South,* Gaskell champions dissent. She does not try to diffuse it so much as prevent it from erupting into violence, as it does aboard the *H.M.S. Russell* in the subplot that introduces another dissenter into the novel, Frederick Hale, whose dissent spurs a mutiny. Frederick's narrative functions as a cautionary tale detailing the dangers of dissenting opinions' not being listened to by those in authority. Frederick "would speak his mind to Captain Reid" (154), but this dissent leads to open rebellion because Captain Reid enjoyed "arbitrary power" (154), Frederick's response was "too passionate" (153), and both lacked the self-control that modulates the dispute between Thornton and Higgins. The subplot offers Gaskell's clearest defense of dissent, articulated best in Margaret's uneasy assessment of her brother's actions: "You disobeyed authority—that was bad; but to have stood by, without word or act, while that authority was brutally used, would have been infinitely worse" (326). By challenging the moral authority of such venerable British institutions as the Navy, the Church, and the aristocracy through Frederick's, Mr. Hale's, and Dixon's narratives, the text represents dissent—particularly against tradition—as an individual's moral obligation.[21]

If Gaskell throws her heroine's fate in with that of the factories, it is because she locates the heroic potential of the factory owners in their dissent from the status quo. In a phrase that recalls Jewsbury's celebration of wealth as "a great unlimited undefined possibility," Gaskell praises Milton's entrepreneurs as men who can "defy the old limits of possibility" (217). By harnessing industrial capitalism's transformational capacities, the factory owners can retool existing social relations, which will free women and workers from the oppressive and infantilizing social arrangements of the past. Or at least this is what Gaskell hopes will happen. To this end, she traces the progressive effects of industrialization on workers and middle-class women through the experiences of Margaret Hale in Milton: the novelist scripts a double bildungsroman, a coming-of-age story in which women and workers can only reach adult maturity in the factory world.

In the crucible of Milton, the paternalistic social order that condemns both Helstone peasants and London ladies to perpetual childhood is burned away. When Nicolas Higgins, a Milton operative the heroine befriends, considers removing to the South after a failed strike, Margaret counsels against his projected emigration by convincing him, in language that echoes Engels's critique of peasant life, of the stupefactions of rural labor: "You would not bear the dulness of the life; you don't know what it is; it would eat you away like rust. Those that have lived there all their lives, are used to soaking in the stagnant waters. . . . they don't care to meet to talk over thoughts and speculations, even of the weakest, wildest kind, after their work is done; they go home brutishly tired, poor creatures!" (382). The unemployed Higgins concludes that starving in Manchester is preferable to ten shillings a week "soaking in the stagnant waters" of the South. Given the distinctions Gaskell draws between North and South, his decision seems a wise one. It is difficult to imagine the intelligent, proud, and independent Higgins living off the charity of his betters in a parish like Helstone, where the upper classes' interactions with the poor are limited to offerings of broth, good flannel, and a kind word.

Similarly, when Margaret flees the Helstone-London axis at novel's end and moves back to Milton, she escapes the childish dependency and confinement that passes for the adult life of a woman in Harley Street circles. Her return to London after her stay in Milton is figured as a return to childhood itself. When she briefly retreats to the household of her genteel aunt, it is clearly a regression back into the safe, womblike existence of childhood: her new bedroom is, rather ominously, the old nursery. Margaret chooses living and struggling in Milton over dining and dancing in London because the idleness she associates with London results in the kind of mindless, infantile pleasures and useless lives the energetic Gaskell found personally distasteful and socially destructive. Moreover, the somnambulant existence—"deadened into forgetfulness" (458)—that Margaret fears if she settles into her old London ways bears a strong resemblance to life in Helstone, where workers are pictured as soaking in "stagnant waters" and exhibiting the mental lives of plants. Margaret could no more stay in London, marry the society lawyer Henry Lennox, and risk becoming a darker copy of her insipidly childish cousin Edith than Nicholas Higgins could find a measure of happiness in the South. Despite the luxury of one and the grinding poverty of the other, both the London lady and the agricultural laborer live debased lives of dependence and insensibility that the text figures as arrested development and repudiates by linking human progress to industrial progress through the form of the bildungsroman.

Following the conventions of the bildungsroman, both Margaret Hale's and Nicholas Higgins's trajectories through the novel end with symbolic marriages that signal the social maturity of their participants. Because its invocation of upper-class fathers and working-class sons runs counter to the spirit of the bildungsroman and her liberal instincts, Gaskell rejects social paternalism as the guiding metaphor for industrial relations. But she is unwilling to reject the family-society trope that was central to the industrial debate and its negotiation of the relationship between the public and private realms of experience. So she replaces the paternal metaphor of fathers and sons with a hymeneal one of husbands and wives that marries both Margaret and Higgins to John Thornton. The romantic plot achieves its closure with the engagement of the incessantly feuding John Thornton to Margaret Hale, uniting, in Williams's words, "the practical energy of the Northern manufacturer with the developed sensibility of the Southern girl" (*Culture and Society* 92). In the same way, the feuding in the industrial plot ceases only after Thornton "engages" Higgins as his employee, a term Gaskell exploits for its double meaning. When Mr. Hale volunteers to intervene with Thornton on Higgins's behalf, Higgins rejects the offer on the grounds that "meddling 'twixt master and man is liker meddling 'twixt husband and wife" (384). The marital nature of the Higgins-Thornton relationship comes even more clearly into focus during their reconciliation scene:

> "Yo've called me impudent, and a liar, and a mischief-maker, and yo' might ha' said wi' some truth, as I were now and then given to drink. An' I ha' called you a tyrant, and an oud bull-dog, and a hard, cruel master; that's where it stands. But for th' childer. Measter, do yo' think we can e'er get on together?"
>
> "Well!" said Mr Thornton, half-laughing, "it was not my proposal that we should go together. But there's one comfort, on

your own showing. We neither of us can think much worse of the
other than we do now." (405)

The "proposal" that the two men "go together" for the sake of "th'
childer" is simultaneously a marriage and an employment proposal,
one that figures men and masters as partners in the joint enterprise
of producing goods and reproducing healthy, working-class children.
Moreover, because the children are real in this case, the orphans left
by the death of Boucher and his wife, the scene literalizes the metaphor
of social paternalism and thus subverts it indirectly by calling attention to the "real" differences between children and workers. By substituting matrimony for patrimony, Gaskell escapes the inevitable
infantilization of working-class men, yet she can nevertheless constitute society in the image of the family, which is indispensable for
her humane social vision.

Even though Gaskell imagines marriage as a partnership
where the two parties can come to the (negotiating or dinner) table
to have their say—a vision which speaks volumes about her relationship with William Gaskell—this mother of four never idealizes
or sentimentalizes the family.[22] Family life in *North and South* over-
flows with petty annoyances, serious hurts, and heavy burdens of
responsibility, and marriage does not promise peaceful coexistence so
much as it contains conflict within a binding structure of mutual
recognition and support. When Higgins offers his labor to Thornton,
he offers his eternal vigilance as well: "I'd promise that when I seed
yo' going wrong, and acting unfair, I'd speak to yo' in private first;
and that would be a fair warning" (397).[23] In this, their relationship
mirrors Margaret and Thornton's, for although the two lovers have
stopped disagreeing long enough to affiance themselves, the final
words of the novel promise more conflict to come. In fact, Gaskell
suggests that family members, because of their bonds of love and
blood, are uniquely suited to wrangling with one another, a notion
best exemplified by Mrs. Thornton's combative relationship with her
beloved son, which is based on "unpalatable truths" (137) spoken
between mother and son. A great believer in the value of speaking
"unpalatable truths" herself, Gaskell finds in her disputatious families
and quarreling couples a model for society that encourages dissent

while discouraging violent antagonism. To be sure, this model is not a utopian one, but then there is very little that is utopian in Gaskell's thinking.

Yet in spite of the elegance and economy of the twin bildungsromans, the novel never convincingly cements the connection between industrial progress and Margaret's growth upon which its formal structure depends. Whereas Milton's working classes seem to achieve a degree of maturity among the smokestacks denied to them in the infantilizing, aristocratic world of the South, the same cannot be said for the text's heroine. Gaskell's preference for Milton over London and Helstone rests on her faith that the nascent industrial world makes possible Margaret's independence (and hence maturation), as this passage, which recounts the Hales' difficulties securing a good servant, suggests:

> Margaret accordingly went up and down to butchers and grocers, seeking for a nonpareil of a girl; and lowering her hopes and expectations every week, as she found the difficulty of meeting with anyone in a manufacturing town who did not prefer the better wages and greater independence of working in a mill. It was something of a trial to Margaret to go out by herself in this busy bustling place. Mrs Shaw's ideas of propriety and her own helpless dependence on others, had always made her insist that a footman should accompany Edith and Margaret, if they went beyond Harley Street or the immediate neighbourhood. The limits by which this rule of her aunt's had circumscribed Margaret's independence had been silently rebelled against at the time. (109)

The passage sets the London Margaret, secretly dissenting from her aunt's domestic regime, against the Milton mill girls, freed from the low wages and familial constraints of domestic service. At the same time, it connects the Milton Margaret and the mill girls through the space they now occupy in common (the paragraph, the streets, Milton) and the mobility they now share (Margaret moves through shops, the mill girls through jobs, but they both traverse the same streets). Nevertheless, in spite of the narrative's rhetorical attempt to tie Margaret's newfound freedom to that of the mill girls, the factories cannot liberate Margaret from domestic dependency because of the unavailability of waged work for middle-class women. To escape the debilitating strictures of Victorian femininity that condemned Mary Barton to a life of idleness in Canada, Gaskell creates the impeccably upper-class Margaret Hale. But the social elevation of her heroine does not resolve the tensions surrounding woman's work and working women. Mary's working-class status makes independence achieved through waged work possible if morally suspect; Margaret Hale's eminently more respectable background can defuse certain sexual anxieties, but it leaves open few employment options, and none that would guarantee her the independence that Gaskell takes as the hallmark of adult life.

*North and South* largely succeeds in unraveling the contradictions in *Mary Barton,* where maidenly modesty ultimately reduces Mary to a helpless child. To redeem Margaret from Mary's sad fate, Gaskell questions the paramount value of maidenly modesty in a woman's life and substitutes in its stead the social mission of the domestic woman (what the text labels "woman's work") as the *sine qua non* of feminine morality. She broadcasts this vital change in allegiances during *North and South's* climactic riot scene. While Margaret recognizes the shadow cast on her dazzlingly pure maidenhood by her impulsive actions during the riot, where she intervenes between the striking men and their angry master, she nevertheless defends those actions as heroic in terms that set woman's work against maidenly modesty: "If I saved one blow, one cruel, angry action that might otherwise have been committed, I did a woman's work. Let them insult my maiden pride as they will—I walk pure before God" (247).

Margaret's intervention between Thornton and the strikers reenacts the role of the little girl in *Mary Barton* whose forgiveness of a street rough, lisped out in Christ's "He did not know what he was doing" (434), leads to the final reconciliation between the two much sinning and sinned-against men, Carson and Barton. But because Gaskell bravely substitutes the fully grown and sexualized Margaret for the innocent "fairy-child" of *Mary Barton* (434), Margaret's similar Christlike injunction to the rioters, "You do not know what you are doing" (235), has a different effect on its auditors. Margaret is answered by a stoning, an act that immediately connects her with another, quite different figure in the Bible, the woman taken in adultery. Drawing strength from an ideology that figured women as social missionaries, Margaret tries to be Christlike, but she is invariably seen—and comes to see herself—as a fallen woman, declaring, "How low I am fallen" (247), even before Thornton's unwelcomed marriage proposal brings the whole mortifying episode to a close. While Gaskell recognizes the cruel irony that transforms a female Christ engaged in an act of Christian redemption into a Mary Magdalene, that recognition does not prevent her from rushing in where Brontë fears to tread and allowing Margaret to enact the noble rescue that *Shirley* denies Caroline. By excluding both Caroline and Shirley from participating in the defense of Robert Moore's mill, Brontë emblematizes women's traditional nonparticipation in male history. In contrast, Gaskell uses Margaret's participation in the riot to address and overcome objections to women's entry into the public realm where history is visibly made.[24]

In *North and South,* the possible dangers public life represents to female innocence and purity are not good excuses to deny women the right to take up their divinely sanctioned work. Indeed, Gaskell challenges the value Victorian culture attributes to female innocence and makes a rather daring argument for the moral superiority of maturity, experience, and self-knowledge. Margaret's self-described fall in the riot must be placed within the bildungsroman trajectory of the novel, where Gaskell redefines Margaret's radical innocence as the less appealing radical immaturity. As most readers recognize, Margaret's impulsive actions during the riot arise from her mixed motives—from her genuine desire to prevent violence and protect a man she does not fully realize she loves. The bruise she receives is simultaneously a love wound (a sign of her maturing sexuality) and a stigmata (a sign of her Christlike sacrifice). Together, they signal Margaret's initiation into the life of an adult woman, which for Gaskell entails both marriage and a social mission, or woman's work.

If it takes a blow to the head to inaugurate Margaret into her own grown-up sexuality, then Gaskell gladly inflicts it because, for her, sex (like work) are facts of adult life. The young woman who initially feels violated by Henry Lennox's marriage proposal has matured immeasurably by the time she acknowledges her own strong sexual feelings for Thornton. For only by coming to terms with her sexual coming of age can Margaret finally exert "self-control," particularly valued by Unitarians, whose educational theories emphasized "man's capacity to evolve by reason and by will" (Lansbury 12).[25] After her participation in the riot, Margaret laments her lack of self-control: "I, who hate scenes—I, who have despised people for showing emotion—who have thought them wanting in self-control—I went down and must needs throw myself into the melee, like a romantic fool!" (247). Here, Margaret deploys the expression in its most ordinary usage, to indicate the control of the rational over the emotional faculties. But "self-control" in the more literal sense entails the ability to control one's life based not on the simple repression of emotions but on the open recognition of them. Self-control leads to self-determination, and Margaret cannot take her life into her own hands until she knows her own mind and her own heart, or to put it another way, until she sheds the overrated innocence Victorian culture demanded of young ladies.[26]

Moreover, by exposing the shared dangers of private and public life—of love and work—Gaskell's excoriation of female innocence even extends to a critique of the public/private opposition through which Victorian culture tried to ensure that innocence. She never questions typical upper-class attitudes about the dangers of public life, such as Edith's warnings to her slum-visiting cousin that the poorer parts of London are "not fit for ladies" (520). If anything, her heroine's dramatic wounding during the riot reinforces the attendant physical perils of woman's work. But Gaskell does interrogate the assumption that the domestic sphere offers a safe retreat from those perils by reenacting in private the blow Margaret suffers in public. During the strike in Milton, Margaret is "stricken" on the forehead, and this proliferation of strikes is replicated in private to confirm that violence occurs with some regularity in both spheres. Violence in the private sphere occurs after Bessy's death, when an intoxicated Higgins "looked ready to strike Margaret" (282)—although he decides to assault his younger daughter instead—and it almost occurs again when Thornton, as Margaret's unsuccessful suitor, wishes he "could have struck her before he left, in order that by some strange overt act of rudeness, he might earn the privilege of telling her the remorse that gnawed at his heart" (416). While not exactly a full-fledged indictment of domestic violence, *North and South* quietly undermines Victorian notions regarding the sanctity and safety of the domestic sphere by collapsing the public/private distinction. For Gaskell, the domestic space is not the queen's garden. Because she understands the family to be a site of contestation and occasional violence and cherishes no illusions about its immunity from the struggles of life, Gaskell cannot allow her heroine to seek refuge in domestic tranquillity. For Gaskell, the sentimentalized Victorian home where childlike women were suppose to reign benignly is just another nostalgic attempt to reexperience childhood and recapture the innocence that the Romantics insisted was childhood's essence. She even gently parodies the naive belief in childhood innocence through her portrayal of the childish Edith Shaw, who will only acknowledge her son's angelic behavior. Whenever his "stormy" side appears, Margaret carries him off to where "they two alone battled it out" (495).

However central the riot scene is to Gaskell's defense of woman's work, there is another, equally important component to Gaskell's strategy of championing woman's work over maidenly modesty. *North and South* advances in two somewhat contradictory directions: it undermines the importance of female innocence for middle-class women and reconfirms its importance for working-class women. That is because as part of her effort to redeem woman's work, Gaskell needs to reclaim working-class women from their tainted associations by re-presenting them as purer and less corrupt than Victorian culture generally allowed. She does this through the text's representative working woman, Bessy Higgins. Even though Bessy resembles neither the "merry and somewhat loud-talking" mill girls in *Mary Barton* (3) nor the "loud spoken and boisterous" women of Milton's factories who prefer "the better wages and greater independence of working in a mill" to going into service (109-10), she remains the one Milton working woman the text foregrounds.[27] Bessy succeeds Mary Barton as Gaskell's "typical" working-class woman, but Gaskell drains her of Mary's energy, sexuality, and spirit. If Mary possesses the devalued femininity of the lethargic Mrs. Carson by novel's end, *North and South* begins where *Mary Barton* leaves off.

The logic of *North and South* might lead one to read the dying mill girl as Margaret's working-class double, when in fact she resembles Margaret's invalid mother more than the hale and healthy Miss Hale. Even though they lived active lives as, respectively, vicar's wife and mill worker before their illnesses, both Mrs. Hale and Bessy Higgins spend most of their time asleep or resting. Moreover, the resemblance between the two goes to the core of their beliefs, for not only do they share an enervated state of being but certain moribund political views as well, an unexpected connection that becomes evident during the preparations for a dinner party at the Thorntons. In spite of being the daughter of a union leader, Bessy subscribes to a brand of Methodism that includes a heavy strain of Calvinist predestination that justifies the status quo. She cannot even sympathize with Margaret's reservations about attending the lavish party while the striking workers starve, but instead resigns herself and her class to starvation: "Some's pre-elected to sumptuous feasts, and purple and fine linen,— may be yo're one on 'em. Others toil and moil all their lives long" (201-2). Margaret's aristocratic mother may not endorse Bessy's theology, but she shares her social vision and similarly refuses to engage Margaret in a discussion of the dinner's moral ramifications. And like Bessy, she too shows an extraordinary concern for the state of Margaret's wardrobe, as if in their dying moments both women's conservative social energies are focused on their desire to impress upon the Milton millocracy Margaret's undeniable status as a lady. If Gaskell creates an independent, working-class woman in *Mary Barton* only to disown that independence as too dangerous, she eliminates any hint of working-class impropriety in *North and South* through the creation of Bessy Higgins, whose inertia threatens no one and links her with the text's least subversive women: Mrs. Hale as well as Mrs. Shaw, Edith Shaw, and the vapid Fanny Thornton.[28]

In fact, Bessy displays so little self-regard that she emerges as a model of self-sacrificing femininity, an angel in the house of Higgins. She has almost no instinct for self-preservation, let alone for the self-advancement that characterizes Mary Barton. It is no wonder she martyrs herself for her family. Triply trapped by the rapacious greed of the mill owners (who will not install proper ventilation in the carding room), the predatory sexuality of working men (the reason her father gives for not sanctioning a move to another factory), and the all-consuming demands of her family (which needs her salary), Bessy and her own best interests are ignored. "I ha' none so many to care for me; if yo' care yo' may come" (132), she pointedly tells Margaret. Indeed, Bessy suffers from terminal neglect, which may be Gaskell's way of underscoring the fact that the needs of working-class women always take a back seat to those of men of all classes. But Bessy's extreme listlessness also allows Gaskell to figure the working-class woman as a negative model of femininity, not because she carries the taint of sexuality and female aggression within her, but because she does not even possess the vitality of Margaret Hale. In a striking gesture, Gaskell overturns her culture's stereotype of factory women as indecorous and indecent to present them as victims who deserve middle-class pity and philanthropy.

At the figurative level, Bessy and Margaret change places, and this helps Gaskell in her reconfiguration of work as "safe" for middle-class women. When Margaret declares, after a morning of ironing, "I am myself a born and bred lady through it all, even though it comes to scouring a floor or washing dishes" (116), she emerges as a Carson woman reformed and rejuvenated, given the housework that Gaskell proposed as a partial remedy for middle-class unemployment in *Mary Barton*. But it is Bessy's passive, idle presence in the text that allows Margaret to proclaim herself "Peg the laundry maid" without leaving the reader to draw any uncomfortable comparisons. Margaret can be a lady and a worker in *North and South*, a combination Gaskell found impossible to sustain in *Mary Barton*, without any damage to her status or her soul. Yet the price to be paid for this is, sadly enough, the elimination of the working-class woman as heroine or historical agent from the middle-class woman's text. Just as Gayatri Spivak argues that *Jane Eyre*'s Bertha Mason must be sacrificed for Jane's emergent feminist subjectivity as a social missionary, so must Bessy Higgins be sacrificed, rendered inert, and killed off for Margaret Hale's emergent feminist subjectivity. By erasing the subversive energies associated with the working-class woman, Gaskell bolsters her claims that woman's work ennobles, rather than degrades, the middle-class woman who takes it up.

Of course, Bessy Higgins's unhappy destiny is symptomatic of a larger problem both Gaskell and Brontë have with the factory girl. While Lord Ashley, Disraeli and Dickens read the mill girl as a figure of disorder, the embodiment of the subversive potential of industrialism, Gaskell and Brontë are both attracted to and wary of that potential for disruption. This ambivalence makes itself felt in *Mary Barton,* where Gaskell splits the working-class woman in two: *Mary Barton* distinguishes its spirited working-class heroine, whose relatively genteel occupation—seamstressing—portends her final transfiguration into a do-nothing lady, from the text's representative factory girl, Mary's fallen and outcast Aunt Esther, who is relegated to the shadowlands of the subplot and condemned to such a stereotyped narrative of seduction, prostitution, and death that even Lord Ashley might approve it as a cautionary tale. The novels with middle-class heroines project a similar ambivalence in that they desire the independence associated with the factory girl yet do not wish to forfeit the class privileges, such as respectability and moral authority, enjoyed by their bourgeois heroines. To solve this problem they distance their working heroines from their texts' working girls. Despite demanding "scope and work" for Yorkshire's women, *Shirley* reduces the women working in Robert Moore's mill to a passing reference, even though Brontë's Luddites are disgruntled male handloom weavers displaced by Moore's female mill hands. Meanwhile, in *North and South,* Gaskell undoes the stereotype of the factory girl she presents in *Mary Barton* to produce its antitype and antidote in the dying Bessy Higgins. Nevertheless, she continues the erasure, not by burying the mill girl in a subplot but by literally burying her. If the male tradition turns the subversive mill girl into the Victorian cover girl, the women writers try to put her back under the covers.

Ultimately, the elaborate effacement of the mill girl in *North and South* carried out in the defense of woman's work proves futile because toilsome domestic labor and philanthropic do-gooding remain the only occupations open to Margaret, and neither promises the "freedom in working" (508) she desires. Housekeeping certainly cannot afford Margaret the independence that paid labor offers to Milton's female factory workers. Indeed, their preference for the high wages of mill work causes the Hales' servant problem in the first place and forces Margaret to assume the role of "Peg the laundry maid" vacated by the real laundresses, who have signed on as cotton spinners. Nor can unpaid female philanthropy offer Margaret any greater measure of autonomy. Even if it could, the novel remains surprisingly unconvinced of its efficacy. Although Margaret seems certain that her intervention in the strike spared men's lives—"If I saved one blow, one cruel, angry action that might otherwise have been committed, I did a woman's work"—the narrative entertains a host of alternate interpretations: "But the retrograde movement towards the gate had begun—as unreasoningly, perhaps as blindly, as the simultaneous anger. Or, perhaps, the idea of the approach of the soldiers, and the sight of that pale, upturned face, with closed eyes, still and sad as marble, though the tears welled out of the long entanglement of eyelashes, and dropped down; and heavier, slower plash than even tears, came the drip of blood from her wound" (235). The narrative ventures Margaret's intervention as one possible reason, and not even the best reason, for the crowd's dispersal. When it tries to link Margaret's martyrdom in the mill yard to the rioters' exodus, it falls into tortured syntax, and the phrase that begins with "the sight of the pale, upturned face" trails off into description, failing to connect back with the movement of the crowd. Even grammatically, the narrative hesitates to attribute the averted tragedy to Margaret's heroics. The two opportunities offered Margaret Hale in Milton entail either the domestic labor that working-class women, given other options, will avoid or unrewarded (and possibly unrewarding) female philanthropy. Neither one seems likely to liberate Margaret from the childlike dependency of the South.

It is money Margaret does not earn that establishes her as a mature, independent agent who can accomplish her woman's work. In the end, Margaret enacts positive social change by lending Thornton the money to continue his experiments in labor-management cooperation. This second act of rescue, coming in the form of Margaret's financial intervention, must be set against the dramatic first rescue, where she physically intrudes onto the public stage and thus risks being reclassed (or declassed) as a working woman. By letting her money work for her during the second rescue, Margaret displays an entrepreneurial spirit. No longer a mere worker whose bodily actions (throwing herself in front of Thornton) constitute her labor, Margaret emerges as a capitalist in her own right, one who owns capital and invests it wisely.

But there is an air of fantasy about this second rescue. Unlike Thornton, who originally recovered his family's fortunes through hard work and self-help, Margaret can accumulate capital only by inheriting it. She remains dependent for her independence on the deus ex machina of the English novel, the unexpected inheritance. In this regard, *North and South* replays *Shirley*; Margaret Hale follows in Shirley Keeldar's footsteps when she inherits a mill (or at least the land underneath it) and an independence of spirit along with it. Margaret's decision to take "her life into her own hands" (508) comes immediately after her (fairy) godfather leaves her a substantial independent income. Before her Cinderella-like transformation from poor relation to heiress but after her return to London, Margaret is "as docile to her aunt's laws as if she were still the scared little stranger who cried herself to sleep that first night in the Harley Street nursery" (508), and no wonder, as she is still in a state of childlike dependence on the good graces of her aunt. Not until Margaret obtains a measure of financial independence can she exert her own will. Without it, she would have had to spend the rest of her life "docile to her aunt's laws" because even the seemingly innocuous charity work Margaret undertakes in London offends her aunt's oppressive gentility. In *North and South,* the right to independent action depends upon a certain pre-achieved (financial) independence. Gaskell may tie Margaret's financial independence to emergent industrialism—the fortune she inherits derives from the expansion of industrial activity in Milton— but it is one she acquires in a distinctly old-fashioned manner, inheriting it from a man who calls himself her "preux chevalier" (431). The dawn of a new era that Gaskell witnesses in Milton does not expand women's horizons. It merely expands the range of possible sources from which they can inherit money.

Despite the persistence of the old world's patriarchal ways in Milton, by concluding with a revolutionary image of the world turned upside down, *North and South* tries to confirm Lord Ashley's charge that a "perversion . . . of nature" was occurring in the manufacturing districts. The marriage between Margaret Hale and John

Thornton takes place between an independent woman and a dependent man. The final scene plays out a carnivalesque celebration of role reversal in which Margaret proposes to Thornton, oddly offering him the financial dependence (a loan to save his failing mill) that she can anticipate as a married woman. There is a strange mixture of shop talk and sweet talk in this scene, as befits a business proposal that is also a marriage proposal, but the mixture reinforces the text's basic strategy of reconciling economic relations and human ones. The language of finance that infects the marriage proposal—Margaret must "pay" for the dead Helstone roses and she "owe[s]" (530) her aunt an explanation—underscores the fact that Margaret and John's marriage is as much a financial arrangement as a love match, in that he marries an heiress and she makes a wise investment. (In this regard, their marriage mirrors the "marriage" between Thornton and Higgins that precedes it, which also personalizes an economic transaction.) The thoroughly reformed Thornton can mouth Carlyle's denunciation of the cash nexus, but his engagement to Margaret results in a curious blend of the cash nexus and personal sentiment, since she becomes both his landlord and his ladylove. But this mixture of love and money also reminds us, in a less happy vein, that Victorian marriages were economic unions as well as companionate ones, in which the husband offered financial support in return for all his wife's worldly goods. So the gender reversal Gaskell imagines is unsustainable. Margaret's independence (and conversely, Thornton's dependence) will not endure beyond the marriage vows, for the same property laws that rob Shirley of her fortune determine Margaret's future as well: the moment Margaret marries Thornton, she will lose control of her inheritance.[29] *North and South* rather wisely draws a veil over the future married life of Margaret Hale and John Thornton, for by ending abruptly, the narrative evades owning up to the doubtful nature of the gender revolution that Victorian industrialism has brought about.

All three novels—*Mary Barton, Shirley,* and *North and South*—begin with a measured, tentative embrace of the industrial revolution only to be disillusioned in the end when their narratives run up against various patriarchal configurations, from Victorian codes of feminine conduct to property laws, that refuse to yield to advancing industrialism. A minor exchange between Margaret Hale and her cousin Edith at the end of *North and South* best captures the irresolution with which these texts ultimately confront the industrial revolution. After inheriting Mr. Bell's Manchester fortune and taking up London slum visiting, Margaret must calm her cousin's fears that she might become a "strong-minded" woman, and not "keep one or two vanities, just by way of specimens of the old Adam." She promises she will "be just the same . . . if you and my aunt could but fancy so" (508-9). Margaret's initial assurance that she remains unchanged leaves open the possibility that her months in Milton did not profoundly affect her. Certainly, one could argue that the disappointment of *North and South* may be that Margaret retains too much of the old Adam—or, more appropriately, the Old Eve—about her, and that like Shirley, she too ends up resembling Milton's cook rather than a titanic Eve. But then there is Margaret's afterthought—"if you and my aunt could but fancy so"—which hints at an imaginative act that Edith and Aunt Shaw must perform to retain the Margaret of old, no longer there unless her relatives indulge in a little fantasy. At best, Margaret's response remains ambiguous. But it is precisely this ambiguity—the fervent desire for a new Eve that exists alongside the strong suspicion that the old Adam persists—that ultimately defines Gaskell's and Brontë's responses to industrialism. Envisioning emergent industrialism to be pregnant with possibilities, each novel in turn comes to the sad realization that the attendant revolution in gender relations has been forestalled.

# CHAPTER THREE

# Frances Trollope, Charlotte Elizabeth Tonna, and the Early Industrial Discourse

BEFORE Elizabeth Stone lays out the plot of *William Langshawe, the Cotton Lord,* her 1842 novel about the ladylike daughter of an unassuming but upstanding factory owner, she must first reclaim her industrial setting as suitable for sentimental fiction and for the refined sentiments of readers. Writing a few years before the industrial revolution became an acceptable subject for fiction, Stone contemplates a scene in which an imaginary reader, the Marchioness of X——, receives her "monthly importation of fashionable literatures" and immediately declares, "Here's a book about the Manufacturing Districts that may go into the returning box at once" (1: 13). To recognize the sea change in fashionable tastes brought about in the 1840s, one only need compare Stone's defensiveness about her project to Charlotte Brontë's a decade later, when she apologizes in some earnest to her publisher because, unlike *Shirley,* " 'Villette' touches on no matter of public interest" (Wise and Symington 4: 14).

For the novel reader around 1840, the industrial world was virgin soil, an undiscovered country. The enduring literary form of the industrial revolution had not yet solidified in the bourgeois imagination. It remained to be forged by the canonical writers of the industrial revolution—from Carlyle, Dickens, and Disraeli to Gaskell and Brontë—all producing their seminal responses to industrialism in the ten traumatic years between 1844 and 1854. But in the late 1830s and early 1840s, a group of largely forgotten but historically important women were busily charting the terra incognita of the factory world. These fiction writers became the first to extract form and meaning from the chaos of industrialism.

This chapter will focus on Frances Trollope and Charlotte Elizabeth Tonna, the two early women novelists who were the most overtly hostile to industrialism and hence undertook the fullest investigation of it.[1] Considering the main argument of this book, that nineteenth-century women writers were more willing to accept the factory world than their male counterparts, this focus may strike some readers as problematic, if not perverse. But unlike the male critics, who engaged in a complicated repudiation of the factories, the women writers held on tightly to the material world of Victorian industrialism, either to celebrate it (in the case of Elizabeth Gaskell and Charlotte Brontë) or to confront and repair it (in the case of Frances Trollope and Charlotte Elizabeth Tonna). So while Trollope and Tonna may condemn the conditions of early industrialism, they accept industrialization as a material fact, and accepting the material world is a prelude to reforming it. Given the weight of material reality in their works, it becomes impossible to ignore, deny, or wish away: the coal and iron world found in the female-authored texts resists any sudden, alchemical transmutation into a golden world. Holding as indisputable fact the permanency of the industrial revolution, these two writers of early industrial fiction can only hope for amelioration and the good sense of Parliament to prevail.

Trollope's *Michael Armstrong, the Factory Boy* (1840) and Tonna's *Helen Fleetwood* (1841) and *The Wrongs of Women* (1843) offer their readers sustained, powerful critiques of the emergent factory system. Written in support of Lord Ashley's factory reforms, these fictions must be read within the context of the reform agenda, which aimed to limit the hours women and children could work in the mills. To combat the laissez-faire doctrine of British manufacturers, reformers drew on the overheated rhetoric of domesticity and argued that factory women and children had been forced out of their proper sphere—the home—in order to add to the swollen coffers of England's industrialists. So in addition to the cultural representations of the mill girl that we have already documented, we must acknowledge another. Alongside the factory girl as a perversion of nature (Mrs. Blackpool, for example), and the factory girl as a model of liberated womanhood (the "young coquines" and laughing mill girls who fill the background of Gaskell's and Brontë's novels), we can place the factory girl as victim and passive agent of male oppression. Because the mill girl was a contested, unstable cultural figure in the first half of the century, all three versions frequently overlap, sometimes in the same text, as they do, for example, in *North and South*. But in the reformist fictions of Tonna and Trollope, the predominating image of factory women and children is that of an industrial victim who needs the protection of an interventionist state.

Women and children take center stage in the early industrial fictions. The trials of men like Walter Gerard, Stephen Blackpool, John Barton, and Nicholas Higgins that occupy the more famous novelists are of little concern here. Because the adult male worker exists outside the parameters of the early factory reforms, he is excluded from the sympathetic embrace of Trollope's and Tonna's texts. Indeed, gender rather than class emerges as the most significant social fracture for both novelists, and the working man is often pictured as one source of the working woman's troubles. By deploying domesticity's separate spheres to critique the conditions under which factory women and children worked and lived, Trollope and Tonna produce divisively gendered representations of the nascent industrial world. And to a large extent, this accounts for their estranged portrait of the industrial revolution. For in place of the opposing camps of capitalists and workers that occupy the more familiar industrial texts, we find a ruling class already divided into a male world of production and a female world of consumption. We also find a working class similarly riven, with lazy, exploitative men on one side of the gender divide, and overworked, exploited women and children on the other.

What ultimately sets the novels of Trollope and Tonna apart from the canonical fictions and nonfictions of the industrial revolution is their reliance on the domestic ideology. Domesticity influenced all the writers of the industrial revolution, and its influence is evident in the texts they produced, from Dickens's creation of the domestic Rachel as the antidote to working-class misery to Gaskell's use of the domestic ideology to transform woman's work into Margaret Hale's social mission. But none of these writers appropriates domesticity's two spheres as the organizing principle through which to carry out a critique of the industrial system after the fashion of Trollope and Tonna.

In their monumental study of the men and women in the Victorian middle classes, Leonore Davidoff and Catherine Hall note that the domestic ideology, with its faith in a woman's place and a woman's mission, increasingly became accepted as an "obvious" and "accurate" representation of reality by the 1830s and 1840s: "The belief in the natural differences and complementary roles of men and women which had originally been particularly linked to Evangelicalism, had become the common sense of the English middle class" (149). Charlotte Elizabeth Tonna, editor of the *Christian Lady's Magazine* and heir to Hannah More, inhabits the domestic ideology more seamlessly and assuredly than Frances Trollope. Tonna emerged out of the same Evangelical circles as did domesticity, and her works bear the traces of her faith in God and the woman's mission. Occupying the comfortable artistic and intellectual circles of Harrow before her husband's financial instability led her to pursue a writing career, Trollope has a more strained relationship to domesticity. But even if her life circumstances moved her to question patriarchy and celebrate female independence, the ideology of domesticity nevertheless animates her work. For Trollope as well as Tonna, one a Tory radical and the other an Evangelical Tory, domesticity is "common sense," an accurate depiction of the world they know and represent in their literary texts.

The centrality of domesticity to the formation of the English middle classes and its paradigmatic literary form, the novel, has become a critical commonplace in recent years. Still, the politics of domesticity remain subject to healthy debate between those who celebrate the power it afforded middle-class women and those who see it as bolstering bourgeois hegemony. On one side of the debate are critics like Nancy Armstrong: aiming to write "a history of female forms of power" (26), Armstrong localizes these forms in the texts of both male and female domestic fiction writers and lauds the ideology of domesticity for endowing eighteenth- and nineteenth-century bourgeois women with historical agency to make (and not merely be made by) history. But on the other side, critics like Mary Poovey focus on the domestic ideal's complicity with bourgeois structures of power, arguing that it was "a crucial component in a series of representations that supported both the middle class's economic power and its legitimation of this position" (*Uneven Developments* 10).[2] Wisely, Elizabeth Langland suggests we steer between these two positions in order to explore domesticity's "discursive instability as a site for social change" (5). It is just this kind of "discursive instability" that results when Trollope and Tonna filter the industrial revolution through the lens of domesticity. The ideology of domesticity, first marshaled to carry out a critique of industrial capitalism, turns back on itself and explodes into a radically destabilizing critique of domesticity. It does so because what begins as a domestic critique of industrialism quickly becomes a materialist critique of domesticity when the complicated *evasion* of materiality—the hallmark of the male industrial critics—is replaced in Trollope's and Tonna's works by an investigation of the domestic sphere's material base.

This chapter explores the early industrial discourse and Frances Trollope's and Charlotte Elizabeth Tonna's place in it. First, it focuses on the material critique of domesticity that emerges out of the domestic critique of industrialism. Because it is situated at the intersection of many competing beliefs about gender, class, political economy, and the state, domesticity proves to be an unstable and consequently destabilizing discourse that lays bare the contradictions in middle-class cultural formations. *Michael Armstrong, Helen Fleetwood,* and *The Wrongs of Women* not only link public and private through the mechanism of female influence (the power granted women by the domestic ideology) but also—in a more subversive move—disclose the penetration of the public sphere into the sanctum of the domestic space. And in the course of exposing the unacknowledged affiliations between the sites of production and consumption, they represent what usually went unrepresented and render visible what usually remained invisible: the world of the Victorian factory. The second half of this chapter explores the cultural forces that kept the factories out of sight and the separate spheres separate. For in disclosing the massive, sustained concealment of the conditions of production, Trollope and Tonna reveal the mechanism in place to license that concealment: the intense eroticization of the factory. The widespread repression of the factories emerges as suddenly and starkly logical once one considers the sexual volatility ascribed to the Victorian workshóp.

## Domesticating the Factory

The domestic ideology inherited by Trollope and Tonna in the 1830s was neither monolithic nor stable. Although the separate spheres delineated by the domestic ideology implied a clear division between the public world of men and the private world of women, the boundaries between the two spheres remained contested. Indeed, as Davidoff and Hall note, the conflict over a woman's proper role and her relationship to the two spheres animated the most influential domestic treatises, such as those written by Sarah Stickney Ellis:

> A tension between the notion of women as 'relative creatures' and a celebratory view of their potential power lies at the heart of Mrs. Ellis's writing and helps to explain her popularity. Like Hannah More her belief in the separate spheres of men and women went together with a conviction that women's influence could be felt far beyond her own limited circle. *Influence* was the secret of women's power and that influence, as wives and mothers, meant that they did not seek other kinds of legitimation. . . . The tension between subordination and influence, between moral power and political silence, was one which preoccupied all the protagonists of 'woman's mission.' (183)

While Ellis insisted that it was a woman's influence alone that traveled out into the larger world, the domestic ideologues who followed her employed the notion of a woman's moralizing influence to invent real opportunities for women beyond the home and homemaking. This is certainly a goal of Anna Jameson, who published a popular domestic treatise, *The Communion of Labour,* in 1856. Taking the family as her model for "all the more complicate [*sic*] social relations" (24)—and not the hierarchical family of god/king/father but the domestic family where the influential mother reigns supreme—Jameson extends women's lives beyond the front parlor. Jameson asks her readers if they wish to deny women "the power to carry into a wider sphere the duties of home—the wifely, motherly, sisterly instincts, which bind them to the other half of the human race" (119). The key word here is "bind" because the domestic ideology articulated in *The Communion of Labour* does not immure the middle-class woman in the home but conveys her into the world. In fact, Jameson finds the perfect illustration of her "communion of love and communion of labour" (24) in the example provided by Florence Nightingale and her nurses at Scutari.

But even while domestic ideologues transported the moralized domestic woman into the wider world—where, in Jameson's rendering of it, "filial, even childlike" (99) men bow before her maternal authority—they nevertheless insisted upon the sanctity of the domestic sphere. Nowhere is the isolation of the Victorian home from the workaday world more scrupulously defended than in Ruskin's formulation of the domestic ideal found in the "Of Queens' Gardens" section of *Sesame and Lilies.* Contending that "so far as the anxieties of the outer life penetrate into it, and the inconsistently-minded, unknown, unloved, or hostile society of the outer world is allowed by either husband or wife to cross the threshold, it ceases to be home" (59), Ruskin envisions the home as a separate, Edenic space, an anodyne to the pressures of an increasingly frenetic, competitive world. At the center of this Edenic space stands the domestic woman, whose innocence of mercantile considerations underwrites the moral power she possesses. Yet like the magical powers of fairy-tale characters, moral power comes with a catch: it risks diminishment by any contact with a tainted "outer world." For once the private sphere and the domestic woman in it acknowledge an affiliation with the public sphere, they both cease to perform their restorative function of healing the emotional wounds caused by daily contact with a "hostile society."

In the tension between the woman's mission to reform society and the family's isolation from it Gallagher locates one of the central paradoxes of domesticity. "Society can be made similar to the family only if the family is rigorously isolated from society," she observes (*Industrial Reformation* 120), and this paradox meant that, in practice, domestic ideologues built up the protective walls around the private sphere and simultaneously deployed the concept of female influence to legitimize women's entrance in the public sphere. But it is precisely this paradox at the heart of domesticity that Frances Trollope and

Charlotte Elizabeth Tonna dismantle. They too draw on the notion of separate spheres to redraw the gendered boundaries of the Victorian social map; however, they not only install women in the public sphere but they also perform the potentially more damaging act of revealing how the public forms (and forms a part of) the domestic arena. While Ellis, Jameson, and Ruskin try to seal off the home from the ravages of public life, Trollope and Tonna fling the doors wide open and bring the outside world into the home.

The explanation for this important shift lies in the specific polemics of the early industrial discourse. Both novelists desired to awaken in their female readers a sense of a moral obligation to help the women and children in the factory districts at a moment when many middle-class women felt themselves to be increasingly disconnected from the public world of work. To stimulate their readers' interest in the Manufacturing Districts, the first factory novelists herald the factory's silent invasion of the home. By creating a private world either littered with or sustained by objects manufactured in the public world, they lay bare the submerged connections between the factory and the family. In doing so, they deny the divorce of the private and public realms and disallow the sanctity of a separate domestic sphere. The middle-class British matron may not have worked in a factory, nor did she (most likely) own a factory, but the early industrial fiction revealed its middle-class female reader to be directly implicated in a system of economic exchange and hence economic exploitation through her role as a consumer.[3]

No woman addresses with more passion or eloquence the estrangement between the commodity and the site of its making than Charlotte Elizabeth Tonna in "The Little Pin-Headers," one of the four tales in *The Wrongs of Women*. The enormously popular Evangelical writer who, in *Helen Fleetwood*, wrote what is widely regarded as the first industrial novel with a working-class heroine, comes up with a remarkably economic symbol—the straight pin—to join (or pin) the public and private realms together.[4] Tonna chooses the straight pin because it is an item so essential to the Victorian toilette that no one from the queen to a maid-of-all-work could dispense with it. Moreover, as Philip Fisher notes, the pin is a model object. It "has no uniqueness, each pin resembles every other" (54), and thus it was singled out by Adam Smith to "define the realm of ordinary social work within the factory system" (49). In what amounts to a direct rebuke to Smith, Tonna admires the pin as an artifact, concluding that "it is really a marvelous piece of delicate workmanship," but one that is "overlooked only because it is proverbially worthless from the immense quantities perpetually tossed about" (449). The paradox surrounding the pin—it is an extraordinarily useful yet universally ignored object—leads Tonna to discover one of the central problems of mass production: it cheapens a product's nonmonetary value as a wrought object. Because the factory system guarantees an ample supply of high-quality, eminently affordable pins, the consumer can readily forget that pins result from human skill and handicraft.

Thus, the pin is overlooked, and more to the point for Tonna, its infant producers are overlooked. The child workers in "The Little Pin-Headers" resemble the pins themselves: the pin-headers are also pieces of (God's) "delicate workmanship" and similarly ignored because of the "immense quantities" of such pauper children in Great Britain. Setting out to expose the abuses of child labor, "The Little Pin-Headers" relates the sad history of two children forced by a cruel stepmother into a pin manufactory. Yet significantly, the story opens not in the factory but at a lady's dressing table, tracing a pin's progress back from the middle-class bedroom to the workroom where the children toil. And by taking the reader into the factory where the pins are made, Tonna hopes to ensure that the next time the middle-class reader of the *Christian Lady's Magazine* picks up a pin lying on her dressing table, it will tell a tale of toxic labor. Tonna's text endows the pin with a "tongue" (449) to speak its origins in a sweatshop where young children are routinely transformed into factory slaves. She gives the pin a body and thus embodies it, thereby reminding her reader that it has been produced through the labor of a vulnerable human body.

By resituating the Victorian woman in a political as well as domestic economy, Tonna breaches the protective walls of domesticity and denies the Victorian home its immunity from the competitive, exploitative world of capitalism. As a user of pins—as well as a wearer of cloth woven in Manchester and a purchaser of knives manufactured in Sheffield—Tonna's female reader benefitted from the industrial order, and Tonna refuses to grant her any special dispensation from the social evils generated by the rapid and overwhelming process of industrialization. On the contrary, Tonna maintains that the imaginary *cordon sanitaire* erected around the middle-class home proves singularly ineffective in halting the moral contagion spread by industrial capitalism. Because she focuses on the production and consumption of commodities, Tonna can argue (as she does in "Milliners and Dressmakers," another tale in *The Wrongs of Women*) that every consumer bathes "in the guilt of innocent blood" (417).[5] To wash away the guilt, Tonna recommends that women promote positive social change through their concrete economic power as consumers. She gives the abstract notion of female influence a concrete formulation by materializing it as the power of the female consumer.[6]

At this point, we must consider why the commodity proved so effective in overthrowing the domestic sphere's claims to a privileged moral status. The answer lies in the dematerializing tendencies shared by both domesticity and capitalism. In conceiving a private sphere detached from any larger social structures, domesticity separated the middle-class family from the political and economic order on which its material well-being rested. The same process of disengagement occurs in capitalist systems, where objects are removed from the site of their making, resulting in the effacement of any given society's productive apparatus. According to Marx, this effacement occurs at the point of intersection between production and consumption and through the mediating form of the commodity. In *Capital,* Marx attempts to demystify the fetishization of commodities, the process whereby the "definite social relation between men" assumes "the fantastic form of the relations between things" (165). As a result, commodities are seen to relate only to each other, with each commodity possessing an abstract, inherent value rather than a socially produced one. The vital ingredient forgotten in the act of turning the sensuous material object into a commodity is human labor. Searching for an analogy to illustrate this fetishization, Marx turns to the religious mind, where the "products of the human brain appear as autonomous figures endowed with a life of their own, which enter into relations both with each other and with the human race" (165). In essence, Marx argues that commodities, like the gods and saints produced in the ferment of the human imagination, take on an independent existence. Men and women create gods, worshipping them as if they were self-generated, and thus grant them autonomy, just as men and women fabricate commodities and then grant them autonomy by losing sight of their genesis in human skill and sweat. So by recasting a set of gendered social relations into a relationship between the male-owned world of production and the female-run world of consumption, Tonna reveals a double effacement that is, in effect, a single one. The erasure of the material origins of the family's prosperity is the erasure of the material origins of commodities. Domesticity is commodity fetishization on an epic scale.

If Charlotte Elizabeth Tonna can movingly address the relationship between domesticity and commodity fetishization in *The Wrongs of Women,* it is in part because Frances Trollope had already made it an issue in *Michael Armstrong.* Armed with Lord Ashley's letters of introduction to the prime movers in the factory reform movement, Trollope travelled to Manchester in 1839, and the result of this fact-finding mission was a novel that builds its entire plot around nineteenth-century England's effacement of the factories and factory conditions. This might seem curious, as the famous blue book reports on the factories had begun appearing in the early 1830s, and the abuses of the factory system were no longer completely unknown. But *Michael Armstrong* does not so much address official ignorance about industrial life as it does the organized conspiracy to conceal the material conditions of production from the upper-class women who reaped the benefits of the new wealth generated by the factories. "Little did the kind-tempered, warm-hearted girl guess," the narrator informs us of a mill owner's daughter, "that for hours before she raised her healthy and elastic frame from the couch where it had luxuriously reposed through the night, thousands of sickly, suffering, children were torn from their straw pallets, to commence a long unvaried day of painful toil, to fill the ever-craving purses, of which her own was one" (93). By exhuming the buried links between the middle-class daughter's luxury and the working-class child's suffering, *Michael Armstrong* forces middle-class women to confront their own complicity in the pernicious practices of Victorian industrialism.

The plot of *Michael Armstrong* has a Homeric density. It follows the peripatetic title character from his first entrance onto the novel's stage as a child laborer under the thumb of a despotic industrialist, Sir Matthew Dowling, through his harrowing trials under the murderous factory-apprentice system; and it continues to trace Michael's subsequent career moves, from his stint as a Wordsworthian shepherd in the Lake District to his final transformation into a gentleman, which occurs after his improbable reunion with his long-lost brother, who now resides in a German castle. The mechanism which starts the young Michael on the checkered path from Sir Matthew's factory to the romantic Rhine is the suppression of production: it fuels the plot's engine and keeps the story moving.

The novel opens by introducing us to Sir Matthew Dowling, an industrial knight who only recently climbed out of the commonalty. Walking in his garden one fine summer night with Lady Clarissa Shrimpton and wishing to impress favorably his genuinely aristocratic companion, Sir Matthew shrewdly judges that turning the next bend, at which point his large textile concern will come into view, would not be the best way to win the confidences of the lady. Fortunately for Sir Matthew, a half-starved cow wanders by, and in the heat of the moment, he imaginatively transforms it into the scourge of the neighborhood. He sounds the alarm: "Good heaven! . . . There is that horrid spotted cow! she is the worst beast in the whole parish. Turn back, dearest Lady Clarissa! turn back instantly" (14). The lady screams, and a somewhat perplexed Michael wanders by at this inopportune moment to "rescue" her from the machinations of the milk cow. Putting a melodramatic shine on the whole affair, Lady Clarissa demands on the spot that Sir Matthew adopt her savior into his family.

Trollope then proceeds to trace out the cultural reproduction of this initial act of suppression. Sir Matthew, a too-clever-by-half businessman who knows that the packaging of an event, and not the event itself, is what really matters, turns his grudging adoption of Michael into a public relations coup. So while Michael, ill-treated and unhappy in the Dowling household, pines for his own family, Sir Matthew circulates an embellished version of the story, one that not only reenacts and reinforces the original effacement of production (his desire to keep his mill out of Lady Clarissa's sight) but also conceals his exploitative economic practices by trumpeting his generous behavior towards the factory boy: the revision transforms Sir Matthew the greedy capitalist into Sir Matthew the philanthropist. To offer the final blow to the already injured truth, a visiting poet immortalizes the incident in an amateur theatrical, appropriately entitled "A Masque," which celebrates Michael's (mock) heroics and Sir Matthew's (mock) benevolence. Thus, in the first hundred pages of the novel, Trollope offers the reader a capsule history of the canonization of the suppression of production.

Her exploration of this suppression even extends to the production of the raw cotton used for the Dowling mill. By midcentury over 70% of the cotton imported into Great Britain came from the United States, but as Ronald Bailey observes, "Too many people treat the history of cotton textile industrialization as if the source of the cotton was the moon, and not mainly (though not exclusively) the system of slave labor using people of African descent in the southern United States" (35–36). While Victorian critics of the factory system routinely appropriated the rhetoric of the antislavery movement to rail against the wage slavery of the working class, they rarely traced the cotton woven in the mills back to its source in the American slave economy. But Trollope is a notable exception. Having spent three years in America and written one of the first antislavery novels, *Jonathan Jefferson Whitlaw* (1836), Trollope makes the readers of *Michael Armstrong* confront the origins of cotton in the New World's slave economy.

She draws out the affiliations between the Old and New Worlds along two main lines. First, she figuratively turns Michael into a black slave. Observing Michael's transformation into a member of the Dowling household after his "rescue" of Lady Clarissa, the mill's corrupt doctor declares to Sir Matthew: "You have dressed up the little scamp so superbly, that nothing but the vulgar dark complexion could make one know that he was not one of your own" (55). He then notes Michael's "slavish, terrified air" and proceeds to racialize him thoroughly. "'Tis Africa and Europe"(55), the doctor proclaims when he sees Michael standing next to the flaxen Dowling offspring. Having conflated the black slave and the wage slave, the novel amplifies this connection by reminding its readers that the textiles produced in Sir Matthew's mill derive from cotton grown in the American South. In private, Sir Matthew effuses that he would like to turn "glorious America . . . into a cotton plantation" (119), although in public he keeps quiet about the transatlantic connections between cotton plantations and cotton mills. Indeed, many of Sir Matthew's fellow mill owners publicly present themselves as abolitionists; one is even identified as "an anti-(black)-slavery man, who subscribed to the African society, and the missionary fund" (149). This is a level of hypocrisy that Trollope cannot abide, so she exposes the mill owners' deceit in regard to both white and black slavery and holds them accountable for the homegrown slavery of the factory child as well as the slavery of the American blacks whom they officially wish to free.

Ultimately, the concealment of production (of raw cotton and cotton textiles) carried out by the mill owners in *Michael Armstrong* reveals itself to be Frances Trollope's figure in the carpet, the perceptual scheme around which she organizes her response to industrialism. Sir Matthew's desire to keep the mill out of Lady Clarissa's line of vision is not an impulsively romantic gesture on his part. Rather, it is fully in accord with the systematic effacement of production in both the Dowling household and in the home of the novel's heroine, Mary Brotherton, herself a cotton heiress.[7] Both the Dowling children and Mary Brotherton are shielded from the source of their prosperity: "No one speaks of the factory in the house of the manufacturer. Be this as it may, the fact is certain, and Mary Brotherton, like perhaps a hundred other rich young ladies, of the same class, grew up in total ignorance of the moans and misery that lurked beneath the unsightly edifices, which she just knew were called factories, but which were much too ugly in her picturesque eyes for her ever to look at them, when she could help it" (93). But when Mary opens her "picturesque eyes" and begins to search for Michael, who has been exiled by Sir Matthew to a hellish, out-of-the-way mill called Deep Valley for being insufficiently grateful, it quickly becomes a quest for the material base of her own wealth: the lost Michael embodies the forgotten origins of her own fortune. Trollope insists that the failure of middle-class women to seek out and acknowledge the material base of their own affluence is, not to put too fine a point on it, scandalous. For at the same time that the strong-minded Mary Brotherton begins on the road to enlightenment, the weak-willed daughter of Sir Matthew, Martha Dowling, unaware of the exploitative practices supporting her featherdown lifestyle, ignorantly helps to secure Michael's eventual banishment to Deep Valley, thus making her an unwitting accessory to what the narrator calls "as hateful a crime, as the black heart of long-hardened depravity could devise" (147). Trollope offers her female reader a clear choice: she can either strive to be a Mary Brotherton or a Martha Dowling, a heroine or a coward, a rescuer of factory children or an (albeit unwilling) agent in their destruction.

To be sure, while *Michael Armstrong* exposes the illegitimate source of Mary Brotherton's fortune, it never demands that Mary return it in a direct transfer. But it does script that return in an indirect, surprisingly radical way. At the end of the novel, Mary Brotherton retreats to a German castle with the two children she has rescued (Michael's brother Edward and a young girl) and the one who rescues himself (Michael). Rosemarie Bodenheimer rightly characterizes Frances Trollope as a female paternalist whose social vision is marked by contradiction, in that "her heroines are at once social paternalists and critics of male control, both socially active and innocent of the taint of power" (26). While acknowledging these enlivening contradictions, Bodenheimer nevertheless flattens out the conclusion of *Michael Armstrong* by labeling it paternalistic, conventional, and domestic, when it may in fact be genuinely utopian. For by the end of the novel, the aptly named Mary Brotherton, the text's female paternalist, metamorphoses into the spiritual "brother" of the texts two other brothers. Educating and elevating them (and thereby compensating for Sir Matthew's false philanthropy by practicing the real thing), she makes them her social equals and thus subtly defuses her own paternalism. In fact, since the text coyly hints that at some future date she marries Edward, it holds out the possibility that Michael Armstrong literally becomes her brother-in-law.

If anything, the domestic retreat Trollope imagines on German soil resembles Nashoba, the doomed utopian community founded in western Tennessee by Trollope's great friend Fanny Wright, and to which Trollope, much deceived by Wright's enthusiasm, traveled to America in the early 1830s to join. Wright purchased twenty slaves and several hundred acres, hoping to use the profits from farming to improve the slaves' condition by educating them and making them "enlightened citizens" before resettling them as freed men and women in another country (Heineman 41). When Trollope arrived at Nashoba to find nothing but a few fever-racked inhabitants and a straggling row of cabins, she immediately decamped to Cincinnati. But she returns to Nashoba imaginatively in *Michael Armstrong,* transforming Mary's German castle into a Continental Nashoba, a "Rhingau paradise" (396), where the former factory children she raises as "enlightened citizens" replace—but also recall— the black slaves of Nashoba. Mary Brotherton's Pygmalion-like scheme, funded through the profits from her father's mill, is a utopian solution to the abuses of child labor, but one that, like Nashoba, oddly mixes Old World paternalism with New World egalitarianism in its desire to make ladies and gentleman out of mill children.

Despite the political ambiguities of its ending, *Michael Armstrong* draws the same uncomfortable conclusion as "The Little Pin-Headers." It leaves the reader secure in the knowledge that divorcing artifacts from the factories in which they are produced is soul-wracking work. Nevertheless, even though both Tonna and Trollope grasp the moral dangers inherent in the twin dematerializing strategies of industrial capitalism and domesticity, it does not necessarily follow that, when faced with Carlyle's great question about the disposition and condition of the English working class, they had to choose the condition over the disposition as the causal explanation for the workers' discontent. After all, they could lament the effacement of the material conditions of production at the site of the commodity and still deny the consequentiality of those material conditions for individual workers. But like Charlotte Brontë and Elizabeth Gaskell, they remain steadfastly loyal to the weight of the material realm they have opened up and exposed. Their texts perform a double duty: first they lay bare the hidden world of production, and then they insist upon the inescapability of the material world revealed there. Life-threatening and consequential, the industrial worlds conjured up by Frances Trollope and Charlotte Elizabeth Tonna shape—and frequently break—their inhabitants.

While the early novelists lived within the same paradoxical configurations of femininity that may have pushed Brontë and Gaskell to question free will and embrace a materialist reading of the industrial realm, Trollope's and Tonna's materialism can also be traced back to their participation in the early reform discourses, which emphasized the deterministic and harmful effects of industrial labor. To be sure, causal contradictions abound in *Michael Armstrong* and *Helen Fleetwood* because, as Gallagher notes, "most industrial reformers were torn between the conflicting elements in their own propaganda: on one hand they wished to assert their belief in human free will and a benign Providence, and on the other to illustrate the helplessness of individuals caught in the industrial system" (*Industrial Reformation* 34). But by deploying Victorian England's uneven and contested notions of human agency in respect to women and children, Trollope and Tonna reconcile these contradictions, thereby accommodating their determinist factory worlds with, in Tonna's case, an Evangelical faith in free will and, in Trollope's case, a romantic faith in free will.

The debates about causality at the center of the reform discourse broke down along age and gender lines, with children and (more problematically) women singled out by reformers for protective legislation. On one side of the political divide stood the manufacturers, whose laissez-faire principles led them to reject state regulation of working hours on the grounds that their workers, free men and women all, should be left unmolested to sell their labor in the marketplace. Opposing them was a reformist coalition of working men, trade unionists, radicals, and Tories who maintained that women were "unfree agents" forced by economic necessity to leave their proper sphere and enter the factory.[8] Because the conscription of women and children into the mills ran counter to the mill owners' middle-class allegiance to domesticity, which the owners themselves saw as the key to social happiness and stability for men and masters alike, the reformers could use the rhetoric of domesticity to their political advantage. And this is precisely what they did when they highlighted woman's "natural" role within the home and continually pointed out the "contradictions between middle-class morality and the theories of political economy" (Clark 215). After much public wrangling, manufacturers and reformers found a way to reconcile domesticity and laissez-faire capitalism, and they enshrined their compromise in an 1844 factory act. It limited the daily work hours of women and children to twelve and thereby officially proclaimed their unfree status, but at the same time it "supported the myth that the state would be uninvolved in the economy" (Rose 55) by leaving adult men free to negotiate with bosses over wages and working conditions.

No one exploited the tension between laissez-faire economics and the domestic ideology more than Charlotte Elizabeth Tonna, who played a substantial role in shaping the reformers' domestic critique of political economy through her novels and her anonymously published pamphlet *The Perils of the Nation* (1843). In his reminiscences of her, Tonna's husband claimed that *Perils* had a "marked and decided influence, not only on the tone of public feeling, but directly on the Legislature. . . . It was quoted on platforms and discussed in private circles" (qtd. in Kestner 91). *Perils* puts in pamphlet form the argument in favor of government intervention on behalf of women and children that Tonna worked through two years earlier in *Helen Fleetwood*. The novel evidences no doubts about the consequential nature of the factory world, at least where the text's women and children are concerned. "The wickedness of the factories is not to be charged on the poor labourers, so much as on the vile system that makes slaves not servants of them," one worker declares (597), and the plot bears out this observation. Following the misfortunes of a rural family that immigrates to the industrial town of M., *Helen Fleetwood* details the decline and fall of various family members and their ward, the title character. Helen Fleetwood, a saintly young woman, quickly proves herself too good for this world by dying, while the other children in the family begin a moral backsliding that is halted only by their return to the countryside.

Tonna's belief that the women and children of M. lack agency allows her to reconcile the causal contradictions her text embodies. Reading *Helen Fleetwood* in terms of these contradictions, Gallagher contends that Tonna accommodates the determining environment of M. with her Evangelical faith in free will and a benign providential order by establishing M. as a separate, antiprovidential zone. But Tonna does not completely release the inhabitants of the factory world from the laws governing the rest of her moral universe. She releases only the female and underaged inhabitants and vouches, however tenuously, for the free agency of working men. Instead of dividing *Helen Fleetwood* into providential and antiprovidential zones, as Gallagher does, it is more accurate to speak of the gendered nature of consequentiality in the novel. For while M. destroys women and children, the unfree agents who inhabit its foul courts and staff its factories, men remain relatively unharmed.

The test case offered up by the novel is the Wright family, relatives of Helen Fleetwood's adopted family who had migrated to M. years before the novel begins. The move to M. transforms Mrs. Wright into a cruel, vindictive woman and kills, maims, or morally ruins the various Wright children, most dramatically turning the eldest daughter Phoebe into a vampire who feeds off the moral decline of others. Like most M. husbands, however, Mr. Wright remains an ineffectual but morally intact presence in the family. Tonna uses his impotence to telegraph the breakdown in paternalistic authority that has occurred at all levels of society, a breakdown that leads to the frustrating situation whereby the working-class father lays the destruction of his family at the feet of the manufacturer ("If he overwork them the blame is his"), while the manufacturer, in turn, lays responsibility on the father's shoulders ("It is not for me to judge what other people's children are competent to do") (620). On occasion, Tonna shows glimpses of sympathy for the working man, whom she acknowledges may be involuntarily selling his wife and children into wage slavery. But the domestic critique of laissez-faire economics forces her to repress such insights, and in the end she argues that working men should exercise their capacity for self-determination and avoid revolutionary working-class politics. According to Tonna, it is the responsibility of working men to support Lord Ashley's parliamentary actions because they possess the free will to choose between radicalism and reform, between the Chartism that will lead to their ruination and the factory reforms that will lead to their rehabilitation. By gendering agency in her novel, Tonna stays true to her faith in free will and the deterministic factory environment. She holds men of all classes accountable for their actions while excusing working-class women and children, whom she pictures as passive participants in their own moral degradation.

The unfree status of the novel's women, however, raises another problem for Tonna, because she cannot abandon completely all claims to female agency in a novel that charges middle-class women with the moral responsibility to take up the woman's mission and "use their influence over their own husbands, fathers, brothers and friends" (610) to ensure the passage of Lord Ashley's reforms. Judy Lown argues that the factory debates were essentially between manufacturers and landowners, with some input from working-class men, over "who should control women and what form this control should take" (*Women* 214). But Tonna's is one female voice that did enter the debate. And in entering it, she makes sure to distinguish between the unfree factory woman and her self-determining counterpart in the middle classes. By figuring Helen Fleetwood as an exception to the rule that women lack agency and licensing that exception through Helen's ambiguous class status, Tonna clears a space for middle-class female agency. As "the very beau ideal of an English village maiden" (635) and a "modest, right-minded female" who is mortally wounded by the immorality of the mill (628), Helen embodies middle-class femininity despite her humble origins. Indeed, other characters remark that the country-bred Greens and their ward, Helen, possess a "respectability" that distinguishes them from the "ragamuffin" factory people (547). This ambiguous class status allows us to see Helen's martyrdom in a new light. When Helen "turn[s] preacher" (534) and begins instructing the "savages" (625) in the mill, she takes up the (bourgeois) woman's mission. By stifling self "where self craves spiritual privileges and separation from the wicked," she becomes "instrumental in leading the poorest, the vilest, the most despised of her class" to see the "light that may conduct them into ways of holiness and peace" (629–30). Here, Tonna deploys the paradoxical language of the woman's mission, which demands a negation of self while legitimizing a woman's self-assertion: Helen passively resigns herself to God's will and simultaneously exercises her newly acquired "independent self-possession" (547) in the cause of the benighted factory folk. As the stand-in for the novel's ideal reader, Helen Fleetwood possesses the middle-class woman's moral agency and her obligations, which she undertakes on behalf of her unfree sisters in the factory. In this way, Tonna can reaffirm the social determinism of the factory world without forfeiting her belief that the factories can be repaired through human (and specifically female) intervention.

The absent figure of the female philanthropist, for whom Helen Fleetwood understudies, is present at the center of Trollope's novel, and thus middle-class female agency is never brought into question. Despite the controversy surrounding the agency of factory women, and the strategic use of it by factory reformers to destabilize the manufacturers' appeals to laissez-faire principles, Trollope studiously avoids all references to women's industrial labor in *Michael Armstrong*. It is a striking omission, and one that suggests that Trollope was made uneasy by the figuration of women as passive and childlike victims. Indeed, Trollope's championing of independent female action, evidenced in the heroism of Mary Brotherton and Mrs. Armstrong, a widowed needlewoman who struggles mightily to keep her fatherless boys out of the workhouse, would more likely than not lead her to sidestep any discourse that undermined female agency. So to preserve the autonomy of middle-class women like herself, which was implicitly challenged by the reform discourses she participated in, Trollope excludes factory women altogether from her analysis.

Given *Michael Armstrong*'s exclusive focus on factory children, whose status as unfree agents did not offer much of a challenge to the doctrine of free will, one would think there are no causal contradictions to attend to in Trollope's text. But her novel scripts the struggle between determinism and the romantic trajectory of the novel form, resolving it through an eminently novelistic device: she splits the novel's protagonists in two and allows the novel's eponymous factory boy to rescue himself and has her heroine rescue Michael's brother Edward, the text's other factory boy. But tellingly, Michael begins exerting himself only when he approaches manhood, and in this way, Trollope (like Tonna) retains and accentuates the moral agency of adult working men.

In Edward Armstrong's plot, Trollope privileges the condition of the working class over its disposition by having her heroine, Mary Brotherton, rescue Edward and transform him into a gentleman. The heroine's experiment in social engineering disproves the theory that working-class children are the unlucky heirs to degraded characteristics, and it provides empirical evidence on how the factory system is disposed towards "degrading the moral nature of the helpless slaves engaged in it" (203). So concretely does Trollope wish to underscore the consequentiality of the factory environment that the crippled Edward even outgrows his physical disability after his removal from the mill. His miraculous rehabilitation may seem improbable, but its very improbability serves Trollope's larger purpose: his recovery affirms the degree to which the factory system determines the factory child. Removed from the morally enervating and physically enfeebling industrial realm, Edward can be molded (through education) into any shape, even that of a gentleman. As a kindly, compassionate vicar tells the heroine, "The habits and character of all human beings depend upon education, and the circumstances in which they are placed" (203).

While Trollope wishes to remain faithful to the minister's words, her romantic impulses send the hero of the novel traveling on a different course. Because Michael Armstrong must possess heroic qualities that will allow him to triumph over the circumstances in which he is placed, he must overcome (and not be overcome by) the factory world. But those qualities which make him the hero also threaten to upset the central thesis of Trollope's text. This predicament no doubt accounts for the double plot line, which defuses the danger by allowing Michael to enact his own rescue while his brother, his "dearer second self" (297), must be rescued. Of course, Michael cannot take his fate into his own hands until he reaches the age of fifteen, when his "more than boyish judgment" (285) suddenly counsels flight from Deep Valley. But at the point of Michael's self-rescue, Trollope must confront the fact that an abused factory boy should not grow up into healthy, glowing manhood, and thus she must explain why, after years in the Deep Valley Mill, Michael is not an intellectual and physical cripple. In lieu of an explanation, she gathers together a variety of mitigating factors to account for Michael's ability to grow tall and sturdy despite his tenure as a factory apprentice. For example, in order to justify the adult Michael's good health (a salutary state his long years in the mill should have rendered impossible), the narrator informs us that an old woman secretly procured nourishing food for him. But since these awkward justifications only partially account for Michael's sound body and mind, the heroine rhetorically asks at the end of the novel, "Is not every event connected with a hero of romance, of necessity and by immutable prescription, singular?" (377). In effect, Trollope offers her readers a hero who is at once both typical and exceptional—the type of all tormented factory children, yet the singular hero of her novel. Trollope quite literally makes excuses for Michael, excuses that underline her insistence on the determining nature of the industrial environment but that come at the expense of her hero's heroic stature. Nevertheless, the contortions of Trollope's narrative, like those in *Helen Fleetwood,* testify to both novelists' profound commitment to a deterministic account of the industrial world.

It is their allegiance to the material realm they wish to reform that distinguishes the female from the male critics of the factories. Trollope and Tonna may share with Carlyle, Disraeli, Dickens, and Ruskin a dislike of the burgeoning industrial world, but their domestic critique of the industrial realm takes them in an opposite direction, away from the male critics' dismissal of the material conditions of industrial life. This is not to say that the male writers blithely evade the problems of industrialism, or of the huge and disturbing inequalities between the rich and the poor. Carlyle's and Ruskin's essays, Disraeli's and Dickens's novels, all helped to galvanize a nation into acknowledging a seemingly impassable gulf between the haves and the have-nots, what Disraeli famously identified as the "two nations" that were "as ignorant of each other's habits, thoughts, and feelings, as if they were dwellers in different zones, or inhabitants of different planets" (*Sybil* 65–66). Still, even in *Sybil,* where Disraeli calls on a wealthy nation to recognize its kinship with the poorer one living in its midst, the work that sustains the poor is not represented but actively effaced, in part because the idealizing male critics do not wish to represent industrial production as a determining force in Victorian society and thus hesitate to represent it at all. So even though they engage in a critique of industrial capitalism, the male critics reproduce many of its basic structures through their participation in the fetishizing strategies of capitalism. They focus on the disposition rather than the condition of England and thus engage in the very processes of effacement that Trollope's and Tonna's texts uncover in the course of making visible the secret world of Victorian production.

## Eroticizing the Factory

By rematerializing the dematerialized industrial realm, these female factory fictions rescue the contemporary context of early industrial England and return us to the original landscape in which the factories were transformed into a discursive subject and simultaneously suppressed as a subject of polite discourse. For in the process of disclosing the organized conspiracy to conceal the conditions of production, the early industrial novelists reveal the eroticization that legitimized that concealment. Drenched in a damning, illicit sexuality, the factory world offered up in the female texts has already been transformed into an erogenous zone.

If, as Thomas Laqueur argues, "everything in the new social order was heated up, changeable, morally shaky, and sex was the prism through which its dangers were imagined" (210), then it is no surprise that industrialization, the engine driving this new social order, should be conceived of in specifically sexual terms. In *William Langshawe,* Elizabeth Stone conjures up—so she can subsequently dismiss it—the stereotypical image of a manufacturing town in 1842:

> Odious factories, vulgar proprietors, and their still more vulgar wives, and their superlatively-vulgar pretensions; dense population, filthy streets, drunken men, reckless women, immoral girls, and squalid children; dirt, filth, misery, and crime;—such are the interesting images which rise, 'a busy throng to crowd the brain,' at the bare mention of the 'manufacturing districts:' vulgarity and vice walk side by side; ostentatious extravagance on the one hand, battening on the miseries of degraded and suffering humanity on the other. (1: 1–2)

"Filthy," "drunken," "degraded," "squalid," "immoral": the paragraph reads like a compendium of best-loved Victorian adjectives for describing the factory system. Certainly these adjectives are liberally scattered throughout the reports issued by the parliamentary commissions studying factory conditions in the 1830s and 1840s, and in the landmark pieces of social investigation published contemporaneously by Peter Gaskell and James Kay (later Kay-Shuttleworth). While the oft-repeated, exaggerated charges of moral delinquency hurled at the factory workers were probably the result of middle-class ignorance and squeamishness, the representation of the working classes as immoral served an important ideological function.[9] As Jeffrey Weeks notes, it displaced "the acute social crises from the area of exploitation and class conflict, where it could not be coped with, into the framework of a more amenable and discussible area of 'morality' " (20).

Charlotte Elizabeth Tonna and Frances Trollope never really contest these dominant cultural representations of the manufacturing districts and their inhabitants. But to stay true to their materialist insights, they must quarrel with the notion that working-class women and children are inherently and irrevocably immoral. Thus, their acceptance of the common view that "vulgarity and vice walk side by side" in factory towns engenders a dilemma of attribution as both novelists struggle to locate the source of the vice that adheres to—but does not inhere in—the factory workers. Turning to the Malthus-inflected economic theories of the day, Trollope and Tonna solve this dilemma by proposing that working-class women and children are not naturally vicious but made so by their conscription into the factory, now figured as a dangerous territory where production and reproduction converge and collapse into each other.

Under attack by middle-class and working-class men throughout the 1830s and 1840s, the Victorian mill girl had a bad reputation and needed all the good publicity Trollope and Tonna could muster. As we have seen, she was a potent emblem for the nascent industrial world and played a leading role in the early Victorian social imagination, out of all proportion to the actual number of women engaged in industrial labor. Ideologically she functioned as the domestic woman's Other, the monitory image of what English womanhood should not be. As the middle-class woman withdrew from active engagement in the public world of work and was increasingly defined as domestic, demure, refined, sober, and chaste, the mill girl emerged in middle-class discourses as a "problem," Deborah Valenze notes, "notorious for her promiscuity, coarse language, drinking, smoking and sexual misbehavior" (86). At the same time, working-class men found the construction of the factory girl as a "problem" just as useful to promote their own patriarchal goals.

Capitalizing on the rhetorical power of domesticity in the public arena, they also promoted the domestic woman as an ideal which the mill girl violated. So, for example, cotton operatives in the 1830s tried to neutralize the threat of female competition in the mills by arguing before parliamentary commissioners that factory work made women "immoral and undomestic" (Clark 212).

For middle-class observers in particular, the mill girl's violation of domesticity's separate spheres seemed to beget an extraordinary amount of anxiety. The public nature of her work made her a creature one had to keep an eye on. "Women and children were simply doing in the factory, under different conditions, the work they had always done in their homes," Ivy Pinchbeck observes (197); but one of the inevitable consequences of the factory system was that those tasks formerly executed in private were now performed under the public glare of the factory's gaslights. Hence, the factory girl came under intense scrutiny, a scrutiny that sexualized her in the act of surveying her. For the Victorian middle classes, who associated female publicity with impropriety, the high visibility of factory work rendered it a morally suspect activity. Governesses, seamstresses, and maidservants all worked at home (even if it was not in their own homes), but by laboring under the gaze of the public eye, the factory woman was on display and thus for sale—like the prostitute, the actress, and wares in a shop window.

The erotic thrill of looking is unmistakably present in Charles Dickens's description of his visit to a London lead mill under the guise of the Uncommercial Traveller. He cannot resist remarking that the female mill hands remind him of a "faithful seraglio" belonging to some "immensely rich old Turk" ("On an Amateur Beat" 351), an imaginative translation of the industrial laborer into an exotic harem girl that bespeaks her Otherness.[10] Similarly, when the narrator of *Coningsby* turns his male gaze on the weaving-room, "where a thousand or fifteen hundred girls may be observed in their coral necklaces, working like Penelope in the daytime; some pretty, some pert, some graceful and jocund" (136–37), he also exoticizes the female mill hands, so much so that one could easily forget he is depicting an industrial scene from the 1840s. Even the allusion to Penelope, the archetypal chaste wife, cannot diffuse the suggestiveness of the description. Indeed, Dickens's and Disraeli's descriptions, and ones similar to it in blue book reports, led Frank Mort to conclude that the male observers of the factories were exercising their erotic imaginations in print and that such "detailed descriptions of the girls' physical appearance . . . tell us much about the sexual desire of these professional men" (48).

If the representation of the independent and prosperous factory girl finally blurs into that of the fallen woman, it is because early factory critics connected the two, often implying a logical progression from the power loom to prostitution. Those thousand or fifteen hundred coral necklaces conjured up by Disraeli are no mere novelistic detail. They will reappear on the factory girls he describes in *Sybil,* girls who were "gaily dressed, a light handkerchief tied under the chin, their hair scrupulously arranged; they wore coral necklaces and earrings of gold" (88). In both cases, they serve as a red flag, warning Disraeli's upper-class reader of the perilous moral state of the industrial woman. The Victorian middle classes were frequently shocked and dismayed not by the poverty of the factory woman but by her relative prosperity. And since love of finery rather than economic necessity served the Victorians as an all-purpose explanation for a woman's descent into prostitution, any remark on the fashionable appearance of the female factory worker was less likely to be a compliment than a condemnation.[11] Elizabeth Gaskell's John Barton instantly recognizes the profession of his streetwalking sister-in-law Esther by her "faded finery" (143), a fall foretold by Esther's partiality for "fly-away veils" (6) years before, when she was still a decent mill girl. So when not accusing the mill girl of slatternliness, middle-class observers turned her outward signs of affluence against her, so that what could have been celebrated as the factory woman's increasing purchasing power and autonomy gets read as a sign of moral laxness. Of course, such a reading makes sense in a moral system that problematized desire and an economic system that demanded it. "Working-class women were thought to bear the dangers of uncontrolled desire that seemed to flow freely from one domain to another, from legitimate consumption to illegitimate sex" (208), Laqueur notes, and thus we can see that the mill girl and the prostitute are the nexus where the anxiety about desire (for sex and commodities) meet.

Remarkably, neither Trollope nor Tonna participates in this widespread sexualization of the mill girl. Figuring it to be a pretext for erasing the factories (and their wretched working conditions) from social visibility, they attempt to redeem the factory woman by giving her reputation a makeover. In *Michael Armstrong,* Trollope begins the factory girl's renovation by representing her reported immorality as mere rumor. While disclaiming any firsthand knowledge of the factory folk, Mary Brotherton's governess tries to dissuade her charge from taking an interest in them on the grounds that they are the undeserving poor. As the governess (mis)informs her charge, they are "the worst set of creatures that burden God's earth. The men are vicious, and the women dissolute, taking drams often, and often when they ought to buy food; and so horridly dirty and unthrifty that it is a common saying, you may know a factory-girl as far as you can see her" (96). Even though the governess has apparently never seen a factory girl, she passes along her culture's stereotype to her pupil in a misguided attempt to preserve and protect Mary's innocence.

Of course, the ignorance of governesses (and the young ladies in their care) mainly serves the manufacturers' self-interest, and this becomes apparent in *Helen Fleetwood.* "We are not . . . to suppose that what would wound the delicacy of a young lady causes any trouble to a bobbin-filler," one cotton baron proclaims in the novel (641). But then, it is to his advantage to trumpet abroad the assumed indelicacies of bobbin-fillers because their suspected moral glitches make the factories an unsuitable topic for his family's drawing-room conversation. When Helen Fleetwood's guardian complains about working conditions in Helen's factory to the owner, the unsympathetic industrialist first orders his daughter out of the room and then reprimands Helen's guardian "for introducing such improper subjects in the presence of a young lady, whose ears ought not to have been assailed by discourse so unfit for a delicate mind" (560). Like the wealthy daughters in *Michael Armstrong,* this young lady has grown up in closely guarded ignorance about conditions in her father's factory. But as Tonna's novel makes abundantly clear, factory girls like Helen pose no real threat to the bourgeois daughter's well-being. Helen's nightmarish experiences in the mill threaten the father's fraudulent claims to respectability, however, and therein lies the need to preserve the daughter's naiveté. As both Trollope and Tonna understand it, the industrialist benefitted from the factory workers' bad reputation because the factory became a thing that not only could be suppressed but also one that *had* to be suppressed. To rehabilitate the factories and make them the suitable subjects of concern for middle-class daughters, Trollope and Tonna re-present the mills and the much-maligned mill girl. They substitute one stereotype for another, replacing the aggressive, independent, and fallen factory girl of the popular imagination with one borrowed from the factory reform discourse, which figures her as the unwitting victim of a brutal industrial regime.

What authorizes both novelists to extricate the factory girl from this entanglement of accusation and innuendo is the domestic ideology. The mill owners who inhabit *Helen Fleetwood* and *Michael Armstrong* justify their employment practices by distinguishing between their domesticated daughters and the debauched mill girls, as if the two groups belonged to altogether different species of beings. Yet by extending the attributes of domestic femininity to their daughters and not to the women who work in their factories, they clearly violate the domestic ideology they invoke. In contrast, Trollope and Tonna appeal to domesticity's insistence on an innate femininity, and through it they transform the upper-class and working-class woman into "sisters" and thereby replace a set of inherited class characteristics with a set of inherited gender characteristics. This, in turn, enables them to remain loyal to their consequential social analyses and reformist impulses through a relatively simple line of argument: the material conditions of production in the mills destroy the natural femininity all women share. Helen Fleetwood, Tonna's living embodiment of feminine virtue who withers and dies in the fetid moral atmosphere of the factory, exemplifies the perils and possibilities of every working woman. So does Fanny Fletcher, Trollope's sweet-natured factory girl. Fanny's young age allows the author to skirt the issue of adult female agency, but when she blossoms into a flower of domesticity after Mary Brotherton rescues her from the Deep Valley Mill, she confirms Trollope's faith in a femininity that transcends class boundaries.

In both *Michael Armstrong* and *Helen Fleetwood,* the mill girl is not corrupt but corrupted by the conditions under which she labors, and the source of that corruption lies in the process of industrial creation itself. This strategy is unlike that taken by Elizabeth Stone, for example, who writes with a similar objective in mind, in that she too wishes to reclaim her novel's industrial setting as suitable for middle-class tastes. Yet while Stone heaps every scabrous charge she can imagine on the heads of her master-manufacturers and their workers, she subsequently dismisses them all as untrue. But Trollope and Tonna never challenge the negative representations of the manufacturing regions. Left to locate the source of the factories' seemingly irrefutable moral corruption somewhere, they place it in the work itself: to save the worker, they damn the work. The factory women and children in both *Michael Armstrong* and *Helen Fleetwood* may not possess fallen natures, but factory work is represented as fallen by nature.

With its masses of male and female bodies laboring together in dangerous proximity, the Victorian factory gets configured by both novelists as an arena of human reproduction as well as human production. "The confinement severe, and the numbers crowded into a given space . . . impregnate both the physical and moral atmosphere with poisonous qualities," Tonna complains to her countrymen in *The Perils of the Nation* (18). Of course, *Perils* merely repeats the main objections to industrial labor spelled out in *Helen Fleetwood*. When one of the country dwellers in Tonna's novel observes during his tour of a factory "the mixing of young people of different sexes, and the sort of conversation that seemed to be passing among them," he concludes that "there was a great deal going on, in an under-tone, that would not have borne publishing" (617). Nor are the impregnating qualities of the factory lost on Trollope. Sir Matthew Dowling wants reenacted, if only in pantomime, the act of human procreation on the site of human creation. When he takes the recently adopted Michael on a tour of his former workroom in the mill, he orders Michael, out of a grotesque sense of fun, to "take scavenger, No. 3, there round the neck; now—now—now—as she lies sprawling, and let us see you give her a hearty kiss." In a scene that perfectly captures the way middle-class men frequently projected their own sexual fantasies onto the factory population, here Sir Matthew first scripts and then enjoys his self-made spectacle of the two workers "sprawling together" on the factory floor (80–81).

Although Trollope's and Tonna's fictions dramatize the conflation of production and reproduction for readers in a particularly graphic and memorable way, this conflation occurs throughout the industrial debates. The idea of men and women working together in the mills occasioned an extraordinary amount of anxiety among the Victorians. At one point in a parliamentary debate over the Ten Hours Bill, Lord Ashley threatened to detain the House "by enumerating the evils which result from the long working of males and females together in the same room" (*Hansard* 1095).[12] The 1844 Factory Act finally banned night work for women, long a subject of dispute. Factory reformers claimed the rate of illegitimate births was higher among night workers, for if the factories were seen as breeding grounds of vice and misery during the day, after dark they simply turned into breeding grounds. Even Marx and Engels seem to have accepted this conflation as commonsensical. Engels insists in *Condition of the Working Class* that night work led to "unbridled sexual indulgence," citing a manufacturer who claims that "during the two years in which night work was carried on in his factory, the number of illegitimate children born was doubled" (180). The specter of night work also haunts *Capital*. While condemning the shift work that kept factories running twenty-four hours a day, Marx footnotes a parliamentary commission's findings that attest to the "great and notorious evils" (368) that followed from men and women working together throughout the night.

This sexualization is evident as well in the investigations carried out by James Kay and Peter Gaskell, two doctors who also "discover" in the course of their inquiries a troubling affiliation between human reproduction and industrial production. Peter Gaskell's *Artisans and Machinery* (1836) locates the cause of the mill workers' moral decline in the overheated atmosphere of the mill:

> The bringing together numbers of the young of both sexes in factories, has been a prolific source of moral delinquency. The stimulus of a heated atmosphere, the contact of opposite sexes, the example of license upon the animal passions—all have conspired to produce a very early development of sexual appetencies. Indeed,

in this respect, the female population engaged in mill labour, approximates very closely to that found in tropical climates; puberty, or at least sexual propensities, being attained almost coeval with girlhood. (103)

Turning to a climatic theory of human development, Gaskell insists that because the heat from the machinery overstimulates the senses, factory work signals a "triumph of sense over morals" (111). In *The Moral and Physical Condition of the Working Classes* (1832), Kay also notes the workers' moral decline but attributes it to overworking rather than overheating:

> Prolonged and exhausting labour, continued from day to day, and from year to year, is not calculated to develop the intellectual or moral faculties of man. The dull routine of ceaseless drudgery, in which the mechanical process is incessantly repeated, resembles the torment of Sisyphus. . . . The mind gathers neither stores nor strength from the constant extension and retraction of the same muscles. The intellect slumbers in supine inertness, but the grosser parts of our nature attain a rank development. To condemn man to such severity of toil is, in some measure, to cultivate in him the habits of an animal. (22)

The two physicians-cum-social investigators identify something intrinsically dehumanizing in the nature of factory labor that goes beyond the usual Pandora's box of social evils attributed to industrialization. In both men's accounts, factory labor transforms the worker into shoddy goods, embruting rather than ennobling in its tendency to exercise the sensual faculties alone.[13]

If Victorian critics eroticized industrial production, it is because contemporary economic theory made it available for this treatment. Embedded in much nineteenth-century economic thought is a subtle conflation of production and reproduction that emerges out of Malthusian writings. By way of an example, let us turn to Harriet Martineau's "A Manchester Strike" (1832), one of the more fully developed tales in her *Illustrations of Political Economy*. Believing that economic law was natural law, Martineau mixed together "Bentham's greatest happiness principle, Smith's laissez faire doctrine, Malthus's *Essay on Population,* and Ricardo's attack on the Corn Laws" (Pichanik

55) to invent a "lite" version of classical economic theory that tried to justify the ways of political economy to man, doing for Smith and Ricardo what Milton did for God.[14] Martineau was deeply committed to the emergent industrial world, a commitment evident in the Malthusian "A Manchester Strike," which seeks to illustrate the principle that population must be adjusted to capital and therefore strikes are counterproductive because they only depress wages. In a tale that reminds readers of the perils of overpopulation from its opening moments, where "several hundred work-people . . . [pour] out from the gates of a factory" (225) and head straight to their overcrowded dwellings, Martineau warns against early and improvident marriages. Since in Martineau's universe the only way to increase wages is to decrease the supply of labor, she counsels England's workers to live by the principle of supply and demand. If the workers would have smaller families and bring less labor to market, demand would exceed supply and wages would rise; but conversely, as one master informs them, if they "choose to bring up large families who will in turn rear large families to the same occupation, it is a necessary consequence that wages will fall to the very lowest point" (257). And not only does overreproductivity lead to lower wages, it also leads to overproductivity, which further reduces wages. In a market soon glutted with the huge quantities of goods produced by an ever-increasing army of workers, supply outstrips demand, and this exerts an additional downward pressure on wages. Acting together, overreproductivity and overproductivity conspire to impoverish the worker.

A fear of abundance, whether it be of the workers' sexual or commercial output, lies at the heart of Martineau's Malthusian interpretation of the marketplace. The reproductive and productive fecundity of the workers threatens to condemn them to lives of insufficiency. In the centuries before the industrial revolution a man calculated his wealth in terms of abundance—how much grain his land produced, how much milk his cows yielded, how many sons his wife bore him—but for the Malthusian nineteenth century, bounty suddenly and painfully took on the dimensions of a curse rather than a blessing. With a huge surplus population (the population of Britain doubled in the first half of the century), early industrial capitalism preached to its working class the minimalist value of less is more because, given the paradoxes of Malthusian doctrine, more led to less.[15] Working men and women heard repeatedly from middle-class reformers how later marriages and smaller families were the keys to the kingdom of capitalist success. Instead of blaming the capitalist means of production for the immiseration of the workers, as Marx did, Victorian capitalist culture blamed the workers' immiseration on their reproductive excesses. If the industrial workers would only control their sexual expenditure (in other words, practice restraint) they would be wealthier for it. In this Victorian frame of mind, poverty became the sign of—because it was seen as the result of—sexuality; and this is how one's lower-class status came to be understood as self-determined, or more precisely, determined by the uncontrolled urges of one's undisciplined working-class body. Given the logic of Malthusian economics and Martineau's tale, the massive dislocations of the Victorian economy could be seen as the fault of the workers because at the heart of these dislocations is not the machine, which remains invisible, but the uncontrollable, sexually active body of the worker. Instead of Marx's material dialectic, Malthusian interpreters like Martineau offer the sexed body of the worker as the engine of history.

Taking the Victorian conflation of production and reproduction to its logical end, *Helen Fleetwood* and *Michael Armstrong* configure factory labor as a bodily function and then transfer the same disgust and distaste the Victorians publicly evinced for their own bodily functions to the processes of industrial production. As Leonore Davidoff points out in her important essay on Arthur Munby and Hannah Cullwick:

> Middle-class Victorians shrank from naming their own bodily functions. Indeed bodily functions in general and sexuality in particular were separated from the public gaze, an example of the privatization we have come to associate with the development of industrial capitalism and part of a changing view of men's and women's positions in the cosmos and of their relations to Nature. Still, Victorians visualized the "Nether Regions" of society which, by their definition, were inhabited by the criminal classes, paupers, beggars and the work-shy as "the stagnant pools of moral filth" comprised of the "effluvia of our wretched cities." ("Class and Gender" 89)

The factory emerges in the novels of Frances Trollope and Charlotte Elizabeth Tonna as one of these "Nether Regions." Like the "workshop of filthy creation" in which Dr. Frankenstein gives birth to his child/artifact, the Victorian factory, where the erotic and the unclean converge, becomes a place where *only* filth is produced: industrial wastes, the by-product of the crude machinery and ventilation systems characteristic of the first factories, are presented in both novels as the factory's end-product.

Filth is certainly both the by-product and end-product of Sir Matthew Dowling's mill. When Frances Trollope guides her reader through an inspection tour of Sir Matthew's mill, she tries to capture the felt experience of entering a mill for the first time by focusing on its most visceral qualities, the sound and the smell:

> The ceaseless whirring of a million hissing wheels, seizes on the tortured ear; and while threatening to destroy the delicate sense, seems bent on proving first, with a sort of mocking mercy, of how much suffering it can be the cause. The scents that reek around, from oil, tainted water, and human filth, with that last worst nausea, arising from the hot refuse of atmospheric air, left by some hundred pair of labouring lungs, render the act of breathing a process of difficulty, disgust and pain. . . . the whole monstrous chamber, [is] redolent of all the various impurities that "by the perfection of our manufacturing system," are converted into "gales of Araby" for the rich, after passing in the shape of certain poison, through the lungs of the poor. (80)

That Trollope should be moved to outrage by the air quality is not in itself remarkable. Ignorant of germ theory, the Victorians thought bad air caused disease, a belief which prompted the sanitation reformer Edwin Chadwick to issue his famous proclamation, "All smell is disease." But Trollope's representation of the interior of the factory, with the "hundred pair of laboring lungs" producing "human filth," also serves as her representation of the manufacturing process. In this passage from *Michael Armstrong,* the perfection of the manufacturing process lies in its ability to take "various impurities" and convert them into "gales of Araby." Trollope's turn to the hyper-poetic phrase "gales of Araby" is an ironic gesture, coming as it does in the midst of her prosaic account of textile production. And while "gales of Araby" serves Trollope as a metaphor for monumental wealth, the sentence structure itself underscores the meteorological rather than monetary meaning of "gale" by figuring production as a system in which "various impurities" pass through the workers' lungs to produce these "gales." In other words, Trollope abstracts her already abstracted image of what the factory produces (profit) and presents it as nothing but a strong breeze. So in place of the weaving, spinning, and carding that formed the routine of any textile factory, Trollope displays a process whereby air becomes more air. The end-product of Dowling's mill, the "gales of Araby," is—at least figuratively—a scarcely transformed version of its by-product, the "hot refuse of atmospheric air."

"Polluted by clouds of fetid breath, all the sickening exhalations of a crowded human mass, whose unwashed, overworked bodies were also in many cases diseased, and by the suffocating dust that rose on every side" (554), the workroom in *Helen Fleetwood* is also an abode of filthy creation. Or more accurately, it is an abode of filthy destruction. When Tonna leads her readers on an inspection tour of a textile manufactory, she takes them through backwards, thus representing industrial production as a process of destruction rather than creation, a process that destroys both the made object and the maker's body. Instead of seeing cotton spun into thread, we see thread transformed back into cotton, "rent to pieces by the cylinders" and reduced to "beautiful flakes," which form the "fine particles of cotton wool" that the workers swallow at great risk to their own health (617). By focusing on the digested bits of cotton, along with the "fetid breath," "sickening exhalations," and "suffocating dust," Tonna fashions an image of production remarkably similar to Trollope's, in that both women see the final product of the factories as filth, disease, and death.[16] In both novels, the factories happen to make goods, but what gets represented is the way they unmake men and women.

In its inability to transcend the physical, factory work remains in both *Helen Fleetwood* and *Michael Armstrong* a debased and debasing form of human labor that degrades laborers rather than elevates them to the level of a godlike creator. While bourgeois culture imagined a body politic in which "middle-class men did brain work while the hands did menial work" (Davidoff, "Class and Gender" 89), the Hands in *Helen Fleetwood* and *Michael Armstrong* labor without hands, for they neither engage in handicrafts nor do they handcraft any object. Picturing textile production as the extrusion of bodily wastes rather than as the creation of artifacts, Trollope and Tonna fashion an industrial workforce that secretes, excretes, and exhales for a living. Their representation of factory work does not resemble Carlyle's panegyric in *Past and Present*—"All work, even cotton-spinning, is noble; work is alone noble: be that here said and asserted once more" (153)—because they see nothing noble in cotton-spinning. It belongs to a category of labor below even the most menial of manual chores. Representing factory labor as an extension of the natural functions of the worker's body, Trollope and Tonna despise it not because it is unnatural, but because it is too natural—a natural bodily function.

## Repairing the Factory

In spite of their extreme hostility towards industrial production, which they figure as the decomposition of the worker's body into its constituent fluids, neither Charlotte Elizabeth Tonna nor Frances Trollope renounces it, advocating parliamentary intervention of the kind forwarded by Lord Ashley instead. Trollope undertook the research for *Michael Armstrong* with letters of introduction from Lord Ashley himself, and Tonna charges her female readers in *Helen Fleetwood* to put pressure on their male relatives to elect to Parliament men who will back Ashley, whom she labels the "noble champion" of the factory folk (610). Nevertheless, their fictional factories remain largely immune to legislative interference. In the final analysis, their attempts to defuse the mill girl's notoriety by shifting the blame onto industrial production proves self-defeating and engenders a contradiction as destabilizing as that found in the male depreciation of the industrial realm. For in seeking out the material conditions that account for the factory worker's debased state, Tonna and Trollope disclose the eroticized nature of the manufacturing process, which pushes their consequential factory worlds beyond the cure of the parliamentary remedies their texts recommend. If the male dematerialization of the industrial world allows the male critics to transcend the material conditions of production, the rematerialization of the material world by these early women novelists has the opposite effect, rendering those conditions more intractable, less willing to be re-shaped and repaired by human intervention.

Her support of the Ten Hours Bill notwithstanding, Tonna acknowledges that restricting hours will do little to counteract the inalienable destructiveness of factory work. "Mr. Z., I know, has daughters growing up: would he send them among us for an hour every day?" the heroine of *Helen Fleetwood* asks, and then answers her own question: "Not he. He knows too well that their health would be destroyed by staying even so long in the heat, the steam, the stench and the dust of rooms where we are pent up from early morning to late night" (552). If one hour in the factory can undermine a woman's health, limiting her hours to ten a day will do nothing. Indeed, one perceptive worker in *Helen Fleetwood* remarks that the factory system "fattens [the rich] and melts the flesh off our bones" (626). Such insights into the exploitative, even cannibalistic nature of Victorian capitalism make Ashley's reforms seem ludicrously inadequate.

Frances Trollope finds herself in a similar bind in *Michael Armstrong*. Even the text's spokesman for parliamentary reform, a clergyman named Bell, acknowledges, "There is a great disproportion between my strong sense of the vice and suffering produced by the factory system, and the measure for its mitigation to which I now limit almost my wishes" (205). Nonetheless, he proceeds to detail the miraculous changes that will come about with the passage of the Ten Hours Bill, although Mary Brotherton remains openly skeptical. Mary declares that she would rather overhaul than overthrow the factory system, but she questions "whether, by the nature of things, it is impossible to manufacture worsted and cotton wool into articles useful to man, without rendering those employed upon it unfit to associate with the rest of their fellow-creatures?" (114–15). Through the official pronouncements of Mr. Bell, the text insists that the "magnificent power" of industrialism can one day "be made the friend of man" (205). Yet unofficially, the text sends back a resounding "yes" to Mary's question when its packs up and sends its protagonists off to live a leisurely life far from England. In the end, Mary's scheme to make ladies and gentlemen out of factory children is tenable only because she removes them altogether from the mills, leaving behind an intact and untransformed factory system. Perhaps one could read this conclusion as a dramatic enactment of Lord Ashley's parliamentary agenda, which hoped to legislate children out of the mills altogether, or as an extreme version of the reformists' beliefs in the importance of educating working-class children. But in either interpretation, *Michael Armstrong* still remains quite pessimistic about the possibility that legislative intervention can repair the factory world itself; and the novel's conclusion—with its protagonists resettled on the banks of the Rhine—testifies to that pessimism.

Faced with the inability of male political power to resolve the factory crisis, both novelists seek alternate solutions and find them, with varying degrees of success, in domesticity and the moral power it confers on women. To bridge the gap that yawns between their diagnoses of the factory system (where one class gobbles up the other) and the seeming banality of their cure (the Ten Hours Bill), they deploy the ideology of a woman's mission. It dispels the immediate dangers these texts represent and also allows them to retreat from the genuinely radical social restructuring that their analyses demand. Moreover, by strengthening Britain's class hierarchy and the middle-class woman's position in it at the precise moment when the moral legitimacy of that hierarchy has been called into question, the woman's mission enables Trollope and Tonna to figure themselves (and women like them) as social heroines—*the* solution to the problems created by men.[17] In the end, the domestic heroines of *Michael Armstrong* and *Helen Fleetwood* retain their moral purity not by staying at home, which has been polluted by the factory-made goods that furnish it, but by engaging in the reform of the industrial world. Without forfeiting any of their own class privileges, they move into the public sphere as the guides and protectors of working-class women and children, whose need to be saved allows the middle-class woman to display her superior moral (and hence class) status.

To be sure, Trollope's relationship to the domestic ideology is both complicated and attenuated.[18] Mary Brotherton takes up the woman's mission when she begins a moral crusade against the factory system, but she confronts it through direct actions rather than through the indirections of female influence, which are surprisingly ineffective in the novel. Unable to bring about any revolution of feeling in the cold, stony hearts of the text's manufacturers, Trollope's female paternalist resigns herself to relieving "individual cases of distress" on the advice of Mr. Bell (208). Given the magnitude of the problem, the mill world in *Michael Armstrong* proves immune to both female influence and legislative intervention, and the best Mary can do is deliver two of the novel's factory children from wage slavery and provide a home for them abroad. Concluding that the factories are irreparably broken, Trollope turns her back on them. Flight is the only way that Trollope can elude the contradictions her analysis engenders, whereby she finds herself recoiling in disgust from the irredeemable materiality of the material world she hoped to modify.

On the whole, the Evangelical Tonna remains more optimistic about the possibilities for reform through female influence. Lost in the din of Tonna's cries for upper-class men and women to rally around Lord Ashley lies the novelist's real answer to the factory question. She proposes the formation of a moral constabulary made up of middle-class women who would then police the mill workers by

> devoting two hours of their vacant morning to the sweet and sacred task of superintending the instruction of their young servants in religious and useful knowledge; shaming vice, overawing insolence, encouraging modesty, industry and cleanliness, by the mere force of their frequent presence and occasional admonitions. A clean, airy room, regular arrangements, a few minutes allowed for thoroughly cleansing their soiled skin and brushing their clothes, with easy, but distinct tasks assigned, and suitable rewards for such as excelled—all under the personal direction of the employer's family. (576)

Less a pound of cure than an ounce of prevention, the "frequent presence" of middle-class women serves a prophylactic purpose by interrupting the intimate links between production and reproduction in the mills. Tonna here engages in a familiar Victorian confusion. She conflates the moral filth of the factories (the vice and insolence) with their physical dirt (soiled skin and clothes) and then imagines middle-class women as capable of combating both. Tonna offers the only conceivable solution to a crisis framed in sexual terms: a battalion of women working to loosen the factory from the web of sex, dirt, and contagion entangling it. By dousing the tainted atmosphere of the factories with a liberal amount of religion and a large quantity of soap, the middle-class woman will put the workplace in order. To complement the factory's presence in the home, Tonna recommends a turnabout that will carry the middle-class woman into the factories. If the factory forms a part of the home, Tonna wants the home to reform the factory by turning it into a home, with the middle-class woman, now imagined in a supervisory capacity, managing the factory workers much in the same way as she manages her domestic space and servants.[19]

Tonna provides a model for female participation in the factories that clearly influenced her famous successors. Brontë and Gaskell also try to invent a role for middle-class women in the management of the factories, although their feminism leads them to imagine more equal opportunities for Shirley Keeldar and Margaret Hale, who briefly become mill owners and try to exercise the power that comes with ownership. But both Shirley and Margaret are shadowed by the figure of Lady Bountiful: Shirley takes up more traditional (and Tonna-like) actions when denied direct intervention in public affairs, and one can speculate that Margaret will return to the female philanthropy that marked her earlier career once John Thornton resumes full control of Marlborough Mills. Because mid-Victorian feminism and the domestic ideology share certain class assumptions, it is relatively easy for Gaskell and Brontë to slide from one to the other. What Antoinette Burton contends about mid-Victorian feminism is also true of the domestic ideology in which it is so thoroughly enmeshed, in that both "virtually dictated the existence of dependent clients on whom to confer aid, comfort, and (hopefully) the status of having been saved" (296). All three novelists seek a place for the middle-class woman in the factory world that will preserve her class and gender privileges, but Brontë and Gaskell initially hope that place will guarantee their heroines the freedom of action they associate with the factory girl.

We should note one other significant difference between

Gaskell's and Brontë's use of the domestic ideology and the use of it by earlier women novelists. Gaskell and Brontë turn to the woman's mission to reduce the tensions between the classes, and thus readers witness Margaret Hale throwing herself into the middle of a strike and Shirley Keeldar feeding starving workers. So despite their focus on women's roles in the new industrial order, Brontë and Gaskell never hesitate to dramatize the class struggles at the heart of the industrial revolution. In contrast, Trollope and Tonna deploy the domestic ideology to *elude* the intractable problems of class conflict and exploitation that their analyses inevitably raise. The strictly gendered universes that Trollope and Tonna create lead them to represent gender, and not class, as the major axis of conflict in *Michael Armstrong, Helen Fleetwood,* and *The Wrongs of Women.* The separation of spheres was one of the most basic organizing principles in Victorian society, and we have already seen how this fundamental division profoundly structures Trollope's and Tonna's analyses of industrialism. So it should not surprise us that while they represent a world of murderous class and gender exploitation, they frame that exploitation in terms of gender alone. If traditional Marxist accounts of the industrial revolution emphasize the importance of class at the expense of gender, Trollope and Tonna can be said to reverse the imbalance by emphasizing gender almost to the exclusion of class.[20]

Charlotte Elizabeth Tonna blames both upper- and lower-class men for the depredations of early industrialism, characterizing the factory in *Helen Fleetwood* as a place where "thousands of delicate little girls are habitually oppressed, overworked, starved, beaten, and that by men, frequently by their own fathers, to swell the gains of their labour" (581). In this passage, Tonna underscores the free agency of the working-class man by holding him responsible for his wife's and daughter's traumas, although even here, Tonna implies that it is not just working-class men who materially benefit from women's labor. She much more directly reproaches the industrialist in "The Forsaken Home," one of the four stories comprising *The Wrongs of Women* and the prequel to "The Little Pin-Headers." "The Forsaken Home" relates the history of the two little pin-headers immediately after their move to the city, where, so it falls out, only the mother and children can find work in a local screw manufactory. As a consequence of his enforced idleness and the wife's constant attendance in the factory, the husband turns to the twin intoxications of alcohol and Malthusian doctrine, and the family falls apart. Although Tonna contends that the collapse of the family arises from the mother's entrance into the factory and hence her inability to provide a comfortable and welcoming home for her husband, Tonna lays the blame for this domestic tragedy squarely on the shoulders of the manufacturer and the working-class husband: "On the common ground of selfishness, the avaricious gentleman meets the debauched inmate of a hovel, and strikes a bargain with him, to increase the inordinate gain of the one, and to secure the lazy indulgences of the other by the sacrifice of the poor man's wife or daughter to this most inhuman, most unchristian system" (437). To be sure, Tonna's tirade against the "debauched inmate" of the "hovel" bespeaks her prejudices against the working-class man. Still, man and master alike are held responsible for the fate of the poor man's wife and daughter, who emerge as the victims of middle-class greed and working-class indolence in Tonna's Tory indictment of the factories.[21]

As suits her more radical take on patriarchy, Trollope openly scripts capitalist fathers and their do-gooding daughters as the central antagonists in the industrial drama. By contending that the interests of middle-class daughters are not identical to those of their fathers, Trollope subverts the Victorian assumption that men reflect and therefore should represent their female relatives' interests. In *Michael Armstrong,* where Trollope equates filial devotion with moral cowardice, a daughter's best interests are served by opposing those of her father. For Martha Dowling to have saved Michael from his imprisonment in Deep Valley Mill would have required an act of disloyalty to her mill-owning father that she cannot commit; however, by remaining faithful to her father, Martha proves faithless to the text's representative working-class family and the novel's own moral imperatives. Meanwhile, Mary Brotherton displays her moral superiority by rejecting her dead father's legacy, the ill-gotten gains of his years in the textile business, and she employs her "preposterous wealth in assisting the miserable race from whose labours it has been extracted"

(232) in order to undo her father's life work. No wonder the narrator remarks that the death of Mary's father "was a great advantage to her" (84).

Indeed, if one only read the texts of these early women writers, one might conclude that the Victorians saw gender—more than class—at the root of the industrial crises of the 1830s and 1840s. So while it is important not to devalue the significance of class in the social formations of Victorian Britain, is it just as important to balance Disraeli's vision of the two nations divided into the rich and the poor with Tonna's and Trollope's vision of a nation divided along gender lines. By mapping the ideology of the separate spheres onto the industrial realm, Trollope and Tonna do indeed fashion a brave new world, one in which the inhabitants of the domestic sphere (women of all classes, children) struggle against the men and masters who perform industrial labor in the public sphere. Their texts remind us of the saliency of gender in the early Victorian social imagination, so powerful that it could beget a vision of nineteenth-century industrialism radically different from the ones we have come to know through the canonical texts of the industrial revolution.

Trollope's and Tonna's domestic critique of the factories leads them to places and insights that none of their successors—male or female—visit. In a remarkable way, the early novelists make visible what is hidden by the more famous texts of the industrial revolution. By focusing on the disposition of the working classes, Carlyle, Disraeli, and Dickens reproduce the cultural logic of industrial capitalism and participate in the effacement of the factories that Tonna's and Trollope's texts expose. By focusing on the conditions of workers and middle-class women when unemployed, Gaskell and Brontë also largely ignore the conditions of production that Trollope and Tonna scrutinize in the course of rematerializing the world of nineteenth-century industrialism. With a simple object inhabiting the Victorian home, like the lowly pin on the dressing table in "The Little Pin-Headers," the early women writers can guide us back to the place where the pin is made. It is the humble commodity that strikes the mightiest blow against a dematerializing symbolic order that insists on separating private and public, production and consumption, factories and families.

Given the power of the pin, it is appropriate to end with another one, this one belonging to John Ruskin, who invokes it as his model object in "The Nature of Gothic": "All the little piece of intelligence that is left in a man is not enough to make a pin, or a nail, but exhausts itself in making the point of a pin or the head of a nail. Now it is a good and desirable thing, truly, to make many pins in a day; but if we could see with what crystal sand their points were polished,—sand of human soul, much to be magnified before it can be discerned for what it is—we should think there might be some loss in it also" (87). While Tonna's pin, endowed with a tongue to speak its origins in the factory, takes us back to the wounded body of the industrial worker, Ruskin's pin recalls us to the worker's imperiled soul. Representing two different responses to the industrial crisis, both writers offer deeply moral condemnations of the incalculable human loss and suffering arising from this emergent form of social organization. And if we value the power of Ruskin's critique of this new kind of labor—and hence the new kind of laborer—then surely we must value Tonna's as well, for it is Ruskin's complement. Of all the British fiction writers and essayists who investigated the condition and the disposition of England, it was the early women novelists who most directly confronted what was so wrong with the condition of England's industrial workers.

# CHAPTER FOUR

# Nostalgia and the
# Ideology of Domesticity in
# Working-Class Literature

I would not leave thee, dear beloved place,
A crown, a sceptre, or a throne to grace;
To be a queen—the nation's flag unfurl—
A thousand times I'd be a Factory Girl!
To live near thee, and hear thy anvils clink,
And with thy sons that hard-won pleasure drink.
That joy that springs from wealth of daily toil,
Than be a queen sprung forth from royal soil.

Ellen Johnston, "Address to Napiers'
Dockyard, Lancefield, Anderston"

PROCLAIMING "a thousand times I'd be a Factory Girl," Ellen Johnston, a mid-Victorian Scottish textile worker and the author of *Autobiography, Poems and Songs,* embraces industrial modernity with a fervor that might disarm even Elizabeth Gaskell and Charlotte Brontë. Indeed, in her repudiation of indulgent queenliness, one can read not only an assertion of working-class pride but also an assertion of a working-class woman's pride, which rejects the queenly virtues of passivity and self-renunciation laid out in such middle-class domestic treatises as Ruskin's "Of Queen's Gardens" in favor of "daily toil" and the pleasures of comradeship. If Johnston praises her life among mills and machinery in tones reminiscent of Gaskell's and Brontë's celebrations of woman's work, might she not then be read as a vindication of the feminist novelists who saw the mill girl as a portent of industrialism's bright promise for female liberation?[1]

Yet before we rush to congratulate Gaskell and Brontë for having gotten industrialism "right," we should note that Johnston's autobiography could just as easily be read as a cautionary tale written by the factories' greatest critics. This self-styled "factory girl" is also a fallen woman, having produced one illegitimate daughter while still a teenager and boldly refusing to repent the fact. Her pluck notwithstanding, Johnston was unable to escape the typical fate of fallen factory women in such cautionary tales, and she sadly ended her days in a Glasgow poorhouse, where she died in 1873 before reaching her fortieth birthday. To seize upon Johnston as a feminist heroine or as a symbol of sexual anarchy is to project our own hopes and fears for the meaning of the industrial revolution onto her. A poet, a factory worker, and a single mother, Johnston defies and transcends such categorization: her "real" experiences during the industrial revolution cannot simply be delimited by the feminists' celebration or the male repudiation of the factory girl and the modernity she portended. Nor does the factory reformers' vision of the mill girl as industrial victim suit the vibrant, intrepid Johnston.

Of course, Johnston's texts cannot offer the reader unmediated access to those "real" experiences either. Her experiences and the literature they engendered were registered in and mediated by the dominant social and literary discourses of the day, the most significant of these discourses being domesticity. Despite Johnston's brave dismissal of the domestic woman, domesticity was just as hegemonic within Victorian working-class culture as it was among the middle classes. The working class did not slavishly ape its "betters" so much as adopt and adapt domesticity to perform its own ideological work. For the working man, domesticity resecured the conventional patterns of patriarchal authority threatened by industrialism, and thus we should not be surprised to find that male working-class writers, who connected the factories with female ascendancy, denounced industrial modernity with the same passion as Carlyle, Disraeli, Ruskin, Dickens, and Arnold. No working-class female tradition exists to counterbalance this male rejection of modernity: Ellen Johnston is an exception, one of the few working-class women to publish a collection of poetry in the nineteenth century and perhaps the only one to make her experiences as a mill girl the chief subject of her poetry. But this absence speaks volumes about the domestic ideal, which effectively denied a voice to working-class women.

Historians of the Victorian working classes generally agree upon two things. First, they concur that with the waning of the Hungry Forties and the receding threat of Chartism around 1850, Great Britain entered an era of relative calm in which cooperation replaced conflict as the byword of class and industrial relations.[2] In this regard, they are following in the footsteps of the Victorians themselves, for as Robert Gray notes, "Contrasts between the prosperity and harmony of the third quarter of the century and the distress and unrest of the second quarter seem to originate in the retrospective constructs of contemporaries" (173). Second, historians of the period recognize that at approximately the same time the working class fully embraced the ideology of domesticity, so that a wife comfortably supported by her husband's labors became the dominant cultural ideal on all rungs of the social ladder. Recently, feminist historians have begun to tease out the complex relationship between these two facts: the dwindling of the radical working-class activities that characterized Chartism and the contiguous—and perhaps concomitant—triumph of the domestic ideology.[3]

The convergence of the deradicalization and domestication of the Victorian working classes emerges as impressively logical when one remembers the symbolic significance of the female factory worker, for she is the point of intersection for these two historical trends. While the independent mill girl served as a symbol of all unnatural social disruptions caused by industrialization for both the Victorian gentleman and for the working stiff, the threat she posed to the working man was real as well as symbolic. As women flooded into the early factories, marketplace competition between the sexes emerged as a major source of tension. Women had always been integral to the domestic economies of preindustrial communities, frequently spinning the thread (hence the term "spinster") for their fathers or husbands if they did not have their own loom. But by employing large numbers of women and offering them waged work independent of male relatives, the mills antagonized working men, who often found themselves out of work and in desperate straights. Contemporary observers of the factories perceived a gain in status for the woman worker and a corresponding loss for the working man, who was no longer his own master, self-sufficient on the land or at the loom; and as his wives and daughters went into the factory, he risked losing his traditional authority over the family as well.

Eventually these meat-and-potatoes concerns for economic survival, which were mixed with and exacerbated by dislocated domestic relations, led working men to agitate for some remediation, and they found it in the ideology of domesticity, with its demands for a family wage and a stay-at-home mother. No one contests the fact that the ideology of domesticity became a central component of working-class culture by midcentury, but over the years there have arisen a variety of complex, nuanced explanations for its appeal to the working class. While Heidi Hartmann argues in "Capitalism, Patriarchy, and Job Segregation by Sex" that the demand for a family wage and for the exclusion of women from the workplace was male gender privilege exerting itself, Jane Humphries sees the family wage as an attempt to protect the embattled working-class family from the insults of industrial capitalism. Sonya Rose splits the difference, arguing that "the family wage ideology was a vehicle meant to improve living conditions for working-class households and was constituted by gender and class simultaneously" (132). Most recently, Anna Clark explores the allure of domesticity to Chartist women and attributes it to the Chartist promise "to transform the old marital misery into happy domesticity" (224). What one can extract from all these explanations is that in the 1830s and 1840s, working-class identity was being forged through "a set of differentiations—inclusions and exclusions, comparisons and contrasts—that relied on sexual difference for their meaning" (Scott 60). So if, as the century progressed, the working-class husband began to speak the same language of domesticity as the middle-class paterfamilias, this change did not signal the ideological triumph of the bourgeoisie. After all, as E. P. Thompson noted, the working class was "present at its own making" (9), and it was made up of the competing interests of class and gender.

This final chapter shifts to the relatively unknown territory of working-class literature, which is one way the English working class participated in its own making. But in a tellingly circular fashion, this chapter returns to the ground covered in the first because the male-dominated traditions of Chartist and dialect writing taken up here replay the male repudiation of modernity. The texts spawned by the Chartist movement and those subsequently produced by the dialect figures of Lancashire and Yorkshire were self-conscious attempts to create a unique, working-class literature. That fact makes the similarities between the working-class texts and the canonical male writings all the more striking.

Born in the wake of the Reform Bill of 1832, which admitted middle-class men into the electorate but barred the working classes, Chartism was the largest laboring class movement of the early nineteenth century. Although Chartism addressed a series of injustices, from the Corn Laws to the Poor Laws, the Chartists' foremost demand was for political representation. Therefore, it is hardly surprising that issues of representation were at the core of the movement. Chartism was a " 'literate and sophisticated' mass movement," Ian Haywood notes, "invested in cultural production" (3). Believing that only guaranteed political rights (such as the vote) would ever empower the working class and redress numerous economic and social wrongs, Chartist men and women demonstrated, struck, petitioned, and supported a network of newspapers and journals, most with poetry and fiction pages. Coming to prominence after the demise of Chartism, dialect writing lacked the national appeal and radical origins of Chartist literature, but it was the popular, commercial literature of the industrial North in the decades after midcentury. Rooted in the traditions of oral and ballad literature, it affectionately celebrates the culture of labor and is, in Martha Vicinus's estimation, one of the working class's great successes in its century-long "struggle to create and sustain a distinctive literature in the face of bourgeois economic and cultural control" (*Industrial Muse* 2).

When read against each other, it readily becomes apparent that Chartist and dialect writings correspond to the two moments in the middle-class male canon: medievalism and culture.[4] Before midcentury, a Chartist dream of a preindustrial paradise of independent farmers and craftsmen, in the form of the Chartist Land Plan, emerged to rival the upper class's medieval ideal. Like the Victorian medievalists, the Chartist writers disowned the materiality of the industrial world and hence tried to replace factories with farms in an effort to replant rural England. After midcentury, when the industrial revolution took on a permanent air, the dialect writers, like the cultural critics, tried to resurrect the golden past by locating it elsewhere. They did not, however, place it within a container marked "culture"; instead, they resituated it inside the four walls of a worker's cottage. With its roots in the Chartist embrace of the domestic ideal, dialect domesticity rediscovered paradise around the workman's hearth, thus redeeming the promise of a golden age that Chartism failed to keep.

Unfortunately, too many blank pages in the historical record disallow the kind of symmetry sought after by those accustomed to the architecture of a well-constructed plot. It is impossible to claim that the paradigm of male rejection and female acceptance of modernity is reenacted within the canons of Victorian working-class literature because there are too few working-class women writers to posit a well-developed female countertradition. In *The Industrial Muse,* a pioneering study of British working-class literature, Vicinus notes with some exasperation that she could find "only some half-dozen volumes" written by working-class women in the nineteenth century (5).[5] To explain this disparity—between the stacks full of poetry and prose published by working-class men in the nineteenth century and the pitifully few volumes produced by working women, which if ranged together would scarcely fill up a single shelf—one perhaps has only to consider the conditions under which most Victorian working-class women lived. Underfed, undereducated, and overworked, the Victorian working-class woman did not have the requisite room of her own, nor the time and energy to pursue what must have seemed like the leisurely self-indulgence of literary creation. But then, in this regard, she resembles no one so much as the working-class man, who was marginally better fed and educated than his female counterpart, yet suffered from a material condition of life that seems on the face of it just as hostile to the production of literature. Thus, if working-class men and women shared, both metaphorically and literally, the same room in the last century, we must look beyond material explanations for the disparity that exists, and this search will lead us back to the ideology of domesticity. For one factor, usually ignored, that may have contributed to the paucity of working-class women's texts was the prevailing intellectual and literary conditions among the working classes themselves.[6] In the second half of the century, working-class women were silenced by their class's adherence to the discourse of domesticity, which made it difficult for them to write of their own experiences as women who worked.

What few texts are available by individual laboring women indicate that they were weighed down by a prevailing ideology that could not recognize the complications of a life that included work and family. In the last section of this chapter, I will focus on two factory women/poets: Fanny Forrester, a young Manchester operative who actively published under this pseudonym throughout the 1870s in *Ben Brierley's Journal,* a popular periodical edited by the famous dialect storyteller; and Ellen Johnston, the Scottish textile worker with whom this chapter began. Both wrote within and around the hegemonic discourse of domesticity, and together they reveal the contrasting cultural scripts available to working-class women. Indeed, they rearticulate the multivalent and contradictory views of factory women established in the early industrial discourse, wherein the factory girl was either—for good or ill—the unwomanly woman (fallen, brazen, and independent) or else its opposite, the innocent victim of industrialization (passive, pure, and pining away in her improper sphere). Forrester insists on the innate domesticity and femininity all women share, and she laments her tragic position as a woman worker for whom the domestic ideal is inaccessible. In contrast, Johnston glories in her identity as an outcast from the world of Victorian domesticity, a fallen woman who panegyrizes her status as a single mother and takes delight in her life in the mills. By reading Forrester's and Johnston's texts against dialect poetry, that pure distillation of working-class domesticity, we can begin to gauge the formative (and deforming) pressures domesticity exerted on working-class women's writings.[7]

This chapter first examines the nostalgic impulse in Chartist literature and then takes a short detour through the history of the Ten Hours Bill because by the mid-1840s, "even Chartist stalwarts found their interest deflected toward the campaign for the Ten Hours' Bill" (Gareth Stedman Jones 166). In fact, the Chartists' nostalgic recollections of a golden past collide and merge with the domestic ideal in the discourse surrounding the Ten Hours Movement, so that by the time dialect writers are happily spinning out domestic fantasies in the 1860s and 1870s, domesticity has itself become a nostalgic enterprise. Only by first recreating the context out of which domesticity emerged as both a weapon against the social disruptions of the day and the means of recapturing the lost paradise of a vanished past can we then understand the complicated, multilayered response to the modern world found in working-class texts.

## The Lost Paradise of the Chartists

In "Eighteen Hundred and Forty-Eight," a poem that both rejoices in the revolutionary uprisings on the Continent and laments the absence of similar upheavals in England, the Chartist poet and former silk weaver Gerald Massey (1828–1907) asks: "Where is the spirit of our ancient Sires, / Who, bleeding, wrung their Rights from tyrannies olden?" (lines 46–47). True to the Chartist spirit, the revolution Massey anticipated and hoped his poetry would advance was one that looked forward to restoring lost freedoms. For the Chartist poets, liberty, equality, and fraternity were not new rights to be won but an old inheritance that had over the years passed out of the family. It is "the martyr days of old" when "the brave and heroic-souled— / Gave Freedom baptism of their best blood" ("Our Land" lines 2–4) that Massey's poetry recalls, a poetry that crystallizes what E. P. Thompson calls the political myth of English freedom before the "Norman bastard and his armed banditti," a concomitant to "the social myth of the golden age of the village community before enclosure and before the Wars" (230). Taken together, Thompson argues, these two form the foundation of the Chartists' political and social vision. With its demands for universal manhood suffrage, secret ballots, annual parliaments, equal electoral districts, salaries for MPs, and an abolition of the MPs' property qualifications, the Charter pointed toward a modern parliamentary democracy. But the world the Chartists hoped to legislate into existence was one their grandfathers rather than their grandsons would recognize.

Like any mass protest movement inspired by a heady mix of economic, social, and political discontents, Chartism embraced and contained a multitude of contradictions. Yet at the center of the Chartist agitations that galvanized the English working classes and convulsed the nation in the 1830s and 1840s stands the image of a lost paradise, an image to which the Chartists writers strove to give form and substance. Because of the polemical nature of Chartist writings, it is difficult to separate the politics of the Chartist movement from the literature it produced.[8] The poems and novels Chartism inspired were an attempt to create a class-based literature, one that would forward specific Chartist goals. In fact, Chartist leaders were frequently leading Chartist writers. Both Ernest Jones (1819–68), the upper-class lawyer turned radical whom Vicinus considers the preeminent Chartist novelist, and Thomas Cooper (1805–92)—the bootmaker, journalist, and teacher—endured prison sentences for their Chartist activities, while Thomas Wheeler (1811–62), responsible for one of the more popular Chartist fictions, *Sunshine and Shadows,* served as the secretary of the Chartist Land Company. By insisting on the spiritual and material prosperity of the working classes in the preindustrial past, these men (and other lesser-known writers dedicated to the Charter) fostered the controlling Chartist myth of a golden age before the coming of the factories.

In the Chartist worldview, the development of industrial capitalism was simply a "terrible calamity," as the Scottish *Chartist Circular* of 12 February 1842 summed it up in an aptly entitled article, "Man versus Machine." Running throughout Chartist writings one discovers the same distaste for modernity that pervades the canonical male literary tradition, distilled into a sharper, more bitter essence, perhaps because so many of the Chartist writers had begun life as craftsmen and thus had experienced firsthand the economic and social chaos of early industrialism. To garner a sense of how the loss of artisan status could devastate the individual worker, one has only to read the autobiographical introduction to William Thom's 1847 work, *Rhymes and Recollections of a Handloom Weaver.* A Scottish weaver, Thom offers the characteristic (male) artisan response to the factory, one full of intense loathing: "Virtue perished within its walls—utterly perished, and was dreamed of no more; or if remembered at all, only in a deep and woeful sense of self-debasement—a struggle to forget, where it was hopeless to obtain" (8).[9]

Chartist fictions articulate the same loathing for modernity found in Chartist life stories. For example, Thomas Cooper begins his 1845 collection of tales, *Wise Saws and Modern Instances,* with an almost pro forma condemnation of the industrial world: "The '*Old* Lincolnshire,' so often mentioned in these simple pieces, and endeared to the writer of them by the associations of thirty years of his life, is likely soon to disappear before the social changes of that *New* Lincolnshire which railway 'civilization' will summon into existence:— would that the manufacturing-misery of the modern Leicestershire, outlined in two or three uncoloured and painfully-veritable pictures, might, as speedily, evanish!" (1: viii). Both in the preface and in the tales that follow, Cooper evidences a deep skepticism about modernity, and he dismisses the notion of progress altogether. Outlining in bold, simple strokes how change is not always for the better, Cooper's "Davy Lidgitt, the Carrier," one of the tales in *Wise Saws,* tells the story of an ambitious and inventive man, known as the "young 'Reformer,' " who inherits his family's transportation business (1: 60) He tries to expand and diversify, but his entrepreneurial venture fails, and he finishes his days as a pauper, breaking stones for the parish. Moreover, his downfall stands in sharp contrast to the earlier success of his unimaginative, rather plodding father, who followed the pattern laid down by his ancestors and lived a happy, modest life. Subverting the rags-to-riches plot embedded in all Victorian self-help narratives, "Davy Lidgitt" suggests that change inevitably leads to unhappiness and innovation invariably disturbs the peace. Throughout *Wise Saws,* Cooper challenges the belief that progress enhances the quality of life, and in doing so he reinforces his readers' unease with the tremors of recent history.

If the Chartists recoiled from modernity in favor of a golden-hued past, they did not embrace the same past as the Victorian medievalists, who wanted to turn back to a feudal hierarchy that reaffirmed a rigid class structure and reasserted the paternalistic authority of the upper classes. As befits their radical politics, the Chartists conjured up a cooperative world of independent farmers and craftsmen that challenged the Victorian class system through its fundamental egalitarianism. No poem more fully gives shape to the Chartist dream of the English yeomanry's better days than W. J. Linton's "Bob Thin, or the Poorhouse Fugitive" (1845), a text which refracts the unfortunate tale of an impoverished handloom weaver through the lens of English history.[10] In essence, "Bob Thin" rehearses a poor man's history of England. It rails against the illegitimacy of Norman rule, laments the demise of the medieval church, and generally insists on the superiority of the past over the present:

> Time was when every man was free
> To manage his own cookery:
> Whether he got it in the chase,
> Or grew and eat it in same place.
> This was old time, long ere the days
> When 'merrie England' bask'd in the blaze.          (lines 3–8)

The vaguely recalled "merrie England" of "Bob Thin" bears little resemblance to the feudal age reconstructed in Carlyle's *Past and Present* or Disraeli's Young England novels. Linton (1812–97), one of the great Chartist poets and a wood engraver by trade, does not resurrect a world of forelock-tugging serfs and chivalrous landlords. To the contrary, he recreates the past as "the days of Natural Equal— / Ity and property for all" (lines 67–68), although this natural equality excludes women, who are "naturally" figured in Chartist discourses as existing outside the realm of history and politics.

Although the Chartists and the medievalists resurrected different versions of England's past, both offered deeply romantic historical tableaux, which more explicitly in Chartist fiction than in the historicized, avowedly unromantic romances of Disraeli and Carlyle excised the unpleasantries from history to present readers with an uncomplicated portrait of a golden age. Chartist fiction drew on and reinforced its readers' recollections of their childhoods (or their parents' childhoods), those misty memories of the village community that remained so central to the urban working-class imagination. Unlike the canonical male writers, who had to claim, in writing for an educated audience, a certain historical verisimilitude for their medieval idylls, the Chartist writers depended upon folk memories to transform their historical romances into historical "truths."

Ironically, those memories seem to have persisted most strongly among workers who had never known anything but industrial work, like the anonymous factory operative who published "The Factory Child" in the *Chartist Circular* (2 April 1842). Brought up in the mills, the poet compares the life of a "weari't fact'ry child" to the "shepherd tripping on the hill" and the "ploughman whistling at his plough" (lines 8, 25, 27). There exists a long-standing tradition in English country verse, particularly georgic verse, of obscuring "the functions of labor, to naturalize the productivity of the soil as magical plenitude" (Landry 23). But this effacement is typically found in poetry written by privileged members of society, whose status allows them the aesthetic detachment from farm work required for pastoral, and not in poetry written by the working class. To discover an instance of it in "The Factory Child" is a poignant reminder of just how cut off from the countryside the first generations of urban industrial workers were. Clearly the worker-poet who submitted this pastoral lament to the *Chartist Circular* had never herded sheep or ploughed a field. Nevertheless, memories of farm life passed down from his parents or grandparents remained an animating force in his imagination and in that of thousands of factory workers like him. Those memories mixed with desire to create among the working-class readership a readiness to accept as true what a more skeptical audience, lacking the recollections of a cottage weaver or small farmer, might have dismissed as mere nostalgia.[11]

To compensate for the industrial present, the world before the factories came to be seen as the sepia-tinted antithesis to the grainy, black-and-white reality of modern times. No where is this more striking than in Chartist representations of preindustrial labor, which tend to characterize the hard work of farm life as play. The whistling ploughmen and dancing shepherds of "The Factory Child" are one example. Samuel Bamford (1788–1872), the famous Peterloo radical, provides another. Bamford ventures a completely fanciful interpretation of preindustrial labor in "Farewell to My Cottage," where he imagines a prelapsarian world in which God's curse had yet to fall on Adam. Opening with an old man displaced from his rural home, "Farewell to My Cottage" recalls a rose-covered cottage blooming in the eternal springtime of the English countryside. But if this alone does not register as paradisiacal enough, Bamford represents labor, the scourge of modern life, as effortless in the agrarian world. The inhabitants of Eden were overworked when compared to Bamford's old cottager:

> And oft at my gate happy children would play,
> Or sent on an errand well pleased were they;
> A pitcher of water to fetch from the spring,
> Or wind-broken wood from my garden to bring;
> On any commission they'd hasten with glee.        (lines 33–36)

Not only does this image of frolicking children turn work into play, but nature in the form of an obliging breeze conspires to help ease man's burden in Bamford's vanished past. Bamford's idle idyll evades the economic realities of country living, and it effaces the economic reasons for the old man's expulsion from his rural retreat. The poem barely acknowledges that the threat of starvation forced the old man to migrate to the city, thereby dismissing hunger as one (possible) aspect of agrarian life just as it dismisses hard labor as another aspect.[12]

Anne Janowitz claims that the landscape poetic, borrowed by Chartist poets from the Romantics, frequently mystifies "the relationship between a rural past and a proletarianized present," and in such instances, it proves to be a "hindrance" to the political consciousness of Chartist poetry (261). By ignoring the fact that the English countryside had been capitalized and rural laborers turned into deracinated proletarians by the eighteenth century, "A Farewell to My Cottage" clearly participates in this mystification, which disables any rigorous critique that would tie the shared proletarianization of agricultural and urban workers to capitalist imperatives.[13] Bamford's past exists in a twilight time before the invention of political economy, when the laws of causation linking supply and demand, earning and spending, hunger and starvation, were in abeyance. It is important to note, especially in a poem as popular as "Farewell to My Cottage," the degree to which readers were willing to suspend realistic expectations. Even such inconsistencies as those found in Bamford's verses were apparently overlooked by workers in need of a myth satisfying to the soul in the way that, one expects, the cut-and-dried stuff of universal suffrage and secret ballots was not.

The points of the Charter were only the political means to a utopian end that the Chartist poets helped to define, an end that would turn modern Britain back into merry old England. Underlying this vision of a resurrected past was a belief in the impermanence of the industrial present because the Chartists, like the Victorian medievalists, did not view industrialization as an inevitable or irreversible process, the necessary next step in the march of human history. Gareth Stedman Jones notes that "the end of Chartism as a mass political force was . . . the end of an epoch—an epoch above all in which the existence of industrial capitalism itself had hung in the balance" (61). But before the demise of Chartism, before the inevitability of industrial capitalism became self-evident, the Chartists had mapped out a return route to the past through the National Land Plan, a well-received scheme to ensure every man a few acres and a cow.[14]

For example, Ernest Jones's "The Factory Town" (1847), a Chartist favorite written in support of Feargus O'Conner's Land Plan, envisioned the devolution of the industrial system, one easily dismantled by the will of the working class:

> Up in factory! Up in mill!
>   Freedom's mighty phalanx swell!
> You have God and Nature still.
>   What have they, but Gold and Hell.
>
> Fear ye not your masters' power;
>   Men are strong when men unite;
> Fear ye not one stormy hour:
>   *Banded millions need not fight.*
>
> Then, how many a happy village
>   Shall be smiling o'er the plain,
> Amid the corn-field's pleasant tillage,
>   And the orchard's rich domain!
>
> While, with rotting roof and rafter,
>   Drops the factory, stone by stone,
> Echoing loud with childhood's laughter,
>   Where it rung with manhood's groan!          (lines 93–108)

For Jones, the journey back to the past begins with a working class unified behind the Land Plan. Simply put, working-class solidarity (like that among the banded million who joined the Chartist movement) becomes itself the means to reverse and "correct" history.

Although it appears ill-conceived in retrospect, the Land Plan had a certain internal logic to it, given that the Chartists had no faith in the permanence of the industrial revolution and, contra Engels, did not believe that the modern working class came into being on the shop floor. The Chartists could seriously propose replanting Manchester mill hands in a Wiltshire wheat field with minimal disruptions because they disavowed the transformative impact of urbanization and industrialization. The assumption that industrialization had *not* indelibly remade the working class was widespread. For example, it surfaced in an 1849 article entitled "Social Effects of Peasant Proprietorship," which appeared in the *Northern Star,* the most influential of the Chartist newspapers. "Social Effects" contends that the move from industry to agriculture would improve the workers' quality of life: "The English peasantry of the middle ages ate off wooden platters, never knew the luxury of a cotton shirt, or of a cup of tea, and slept on straw pallets within walls of wattled plaster, and . . . in some counties, they used barley instead of wheaten bread. But it is absurd to imagine that, because they had to put up with these inconveniences, their situation, in more important respects, was not immeasurably superior to that of their living descendants" (14 April 1849). Considering the Chartist fondness for a mythologized past, this passage itself is not remarkable unless one registers its underlying argument: that the peasant living in a wattled hut did not differ intellectually, morally, or socially from the modern industrial laborer. The *Northern Star* evades the significance of cotton shirts, cups of tea, and wheat bread by dismissing such items as mere conveniences, when they are in fact broad indications of the transformational power of the industrial revolution. Arguing that material objects enable the individual "to enter a larger realm of self-extension" (144), Elaine Scarry writes: "It is only when the body is comfortable, when it has ceased to be an obsessive object of perception and concern, that consciousness develops other objects, that for any individual the external world (in part already existing and in part about to be formed) comes into being and begins to grow" (39). So in its hurry to decry the benefits of industrialization as window-dressing—compensatory diversions thrown up by modernity—the article's author reveals an inability to comprehend the epistemological and psychological changes embedded in simple material objects. The comfort of a cotton shirt and a feather bed, the luxury of tea and wheat bread, the very existence of the *Northern Star* itself, all signify the shift away from subsistence and account for the gap between what Engels saw as the vegetable-like state of the peasant and the developing consciousness of the modern proletariat. Ultimately, in order to dissolve the space between the peasant and the factory worker, the *Northern Star* divorces the worker's physical condition (his soft shirts, soft beds, and soft bread) from his disposition, and in the process it undermines the material weight of the industrial realm.

Throughout Chartist writings, there exists a generally divided mind over the consequentiality of the material realm. Both materialist and idealist positions are staked out, sometimes cheek-by-jowl in the same text, as in Ernest Jones's 1855 novel, *Women's Wrongs*. Jones declares with some assurance that in the poorest corners of English society, "the characters are just what society makes them" (2: 913), but only a few paragraphs later he reverses himself: "It is folly to say 'we can't help it,' 'we are the creatures of circumstances'— 'we are what society makes us.' We *can* help it—we can *create circumstances*—we can *make society*—or whence the efforts at redress and reform—moral, social, political, religious?" (2: 913–14). Perhaps this confusion inheres in any social movement that believes it can change the world because the world so desperately needs changing.[15] On the one hand, the Chartists mobilized in response to the tragic conditions of early Victorian industrialism, which they believed were slowly destroying the bodies and souls of the working class. On the other hand, because of the Charter's demand for electoral reform, the Chartists had to contend that the workers had heroically risen above their debilitating material conditions and thus were a disciplined, educated body prepared for self-government. Out of this shifting ideological landscape, with the simultaneous insistence on and denial of the consequentiality of the factory environment, sprouted the Chartist Land Plan, which emphasized Chartism's optimistic strain—Jones's "we can *create circumstances*" strain. By breaking, or at least intermittently disrupting, the connection between the condition of the working class and its disposition, Chartist writers (like the Victorian medievalists) refuse to acknowledge that the industrial revolution had already profoundly transformed the individual worker, and this is how they can imagine transporting him back to the eleventh century.

The bond between the dematerialization of the industrial realm and the dismissal of modernity is an intimate one in the male literary traditions of both classes.

The bond between imperiled masculine authority and the dismissal of modernity is also an intimate one in both traditions. One reason the Chartist writers wished to travel back to the eleventh century is that they located in the past a model of patriarchal domestic relations that they believed modernity had overthrown. Most feminist historians agree with Joan Scott's assessment that Chartism possessed a decidedly masculine tone (63). Unlike Owenism, an early brand of socialist utopianism with a strong feminist consciousness that just predated the Chartist movement, Chartism "could not reconcile its egalitarian ideals with its commitment to working-class patriarchy" (Clark 246).[16] But while the masculine orientation of Chartism has been amply documented, the important nexus of Chartism's patriarchal bent and its nostalgic core has not. By looking at two texts—Wheeler's *Sunshine and Shadows* and the anonymously published "The Charter and the Land," an 1847 short story that appeared in the *Labourer*—the remainder of this section shows how the conservative gender politics of the Chartists becomes inscribed in the language of nostalgia. This discussion also sets up the next section, which explores the controversy surrounding the Ten Hours Bill. For what *Sunshine and Shadows,* "The Charter and the Land," and the Ten Hours debates ultimately reveal is the development of a pastoral nostalgia in which the gender troubles of the present can be resolved only by returning to the domesticity of the past.

To begin with, it is important to establish the degree to which the rhetoric of domesticity that pervades the middle-class discourses characterizes Chartist writings as well. At least in their presentation of women's roles, Chartist fictions like Wheeler's *Sunshine and Shadows* are almost indistinguishable from bourgeois novels of the same period. Serialized at midcentury in the *Northern Star,* Wheeler's text follows the convoluted fortunes of a young Chartist whose various adventures lead him through the blighted landscape of early industrial England. The picaresque form serves the author's purposes well, as it allows Wheeler to provide a running social commentary on the condition of England. Of all the horrors and injustices that enrage the narrator, the evils of female employment call forth his most choleric outbreak. "Observe yon group of haggard females," the narrator exhorts, "compelled to desert their infant offspring, and sacrifice the joys of maternity at the Factory Moloch. Glance at that crowd of women-men inverting the order of Nature, and performing a mother's duties" (30 June 1849). Although Wheeler may clothe his anger in the hyperbolic language of stage melodrama, his naked antipathy for the perversely "unnatural" gender relations of the Victorian factory echoes the loud condemnations of female employment found in middle-class writings.

In contrast to the mill women sacrificed to the Factory Moloch, the model working-class woman in *Sunshine and Shadows* bears a close resemblance to the proper young miss of countless Victorian novels. "Early initiated into the secrets of domestic economy," and devoting her "whole time to the comforts and attentions of home," this feminine paragon's sole leisure activity is "her attendance on public meetings, whither she was generally accompanied by her parents" (15 October 1849). Perhaps the only difference between the working- and middle-class daughter as depicted in *Sunshine and Shadows* is that the solicitous parents of Wheeler's ideal woman chaperone her to Chartist gatherings, the "public meetings" to which the narrative alludes, rather than the teas and church services preferred by British burghers.

Wheeler's domesticated working-class heroine is hardly unique in Chartist writings of the late 1840s. As Dorothy Thompson points out, the domestic model of femininity proliferated in Chartist journals toward midcentury: "It is perhaps significant that when articles appear in Ernest Jones's *Labourer* or Bronterre's new *National Reformer* on the subject of women in the late forties, either they take the form of revelations from enquiries into women's labour . . . or they are written in a thoroughly middle-class manner, complaining that women are taught only to embroider and sing and not to exercise their minds, or even that a lack of female education lowers the quality of domestic servants" (131). Indeed, such inappropriately bourgeois images of working-class life lead Thompson to wonder "how the woolcombers' and shoemakers' wives of the Chartist areas received such addresses" (131).[17]

One solution to the disordered gender relations that Wheeler identifies in the manufacturing districts, where "haggard females" and "women-men" blot the landscape, is offered in "The Charter and the Land." Addressed to women who are fed up with their husbands' Chartist activities and skeptical about the Chartist Land Plan, "The Charter and the Land" relates the story of a typical working-class couple, William and Betsy Wright. The story opens with the same "perverse" status quo found in *Sunshine and Shadows*: after serving a brief stint in jail for his allegiance to the Charter, the unemployed and unemployable Will spends his days at the local pub, drowning his sorrows with the shillings his wife earns at the factory. The unhappy couple carry on a "cat-and-dog" (191) existence until the formation of the Chartist Land Plan, when Will becomes a born-again Chartist, renounces drink and begins investing his weekly beer money in the Chartist Land Company. Predictably, he wins a place in O'Connorsville, and his wife rejoices, "If [the Charter] does nout else, it has made thee a better man, and a better husband" (192), a remark that calls to mind Clark's contention that Chartist domesticity appealed to working-class women by promising to transform "marital misery into happy domesticity." Certainly, the Chartist Land Plan as represented in "The Charter and the Land" seems to offer working-class wives a respite from the "cat-and-dog" lives they shared with their husbands.

But as the time approaches for the Wrights' move to O'Connorsville, local women begin to make trouble for the lucky couple: "The women of Betsy's acquaintance, who were enamoured of the splendid misery of a town life, and the gin shop, constantly haunted her with evil forebodings of Will's unfitness for agricultural labour, and had actually turned her dreams of future joy into evil anticipations" (192). Legitimate concerns about a former factory worker taking up rustic labors are first put into the mouths of the townswomen (no doubt Betsy's fellow workers at the mill) and then dismissed through an ad hominem attack. These gin-soused mill women, who fulfill the negative stereotype of the independent factory girl, stand in opposition to the noble Chartist plans of Betsy's husband. Caught in the middle, Betsy is challenged by her husband to forgo her "parasol, fan and necklace" (once again, love of finery serves as a metonym for the factory woman's fall from grace) in favor of seeing her "children growing up well and getting good schooling" (192). The story presents Betsy's choices in clearly dichotomized terms. The town is a place of "splendid misery" where "unnatural" women work and enjoy the fruits of their labor in the form of commodities, while children wither away and husbands sink into surly debauchery. By contrast, the countryside is the realm of nature, where natural gender relationships and natural femininity, in the form of Betsy's maternal nature, can flourish. At the end of the story, Betsy does the right thing, and the Wrights, figured as "emancipated slaves" and pilgrims entering the "Holy Land" (193), move to O'Connorsville. There, the overworked Betsy, long accustomed to the early ringing of the factory bell, gets to sleep in late on her first morning and enjoy a hearty farm breakfast with the whole family. Of course, it is never made clear who cooks this substantial meal, but the promise of leisure and abundance with which the story concludes recalls other idle idylls of the Chartist tradition that nostalgically recreate the people's past as paradise lost. But then, recreating paradise is what the Chartist Land Plan aimed to do, and as "The Charter and the Land" makes plain, that recreation entailed the reordering of working-class domestic arrangements.

However, when industrial modernity began to appear as an inoperable fact of life, Chartism and the Chartist Land Plan's regressive goals ceased to be a viable alternative for the working class. The next generation of working-class writers found it impossible to ignore the industrial revolution altogether, but the heirs to the Chartist tradition did find a way to displace industrialism from the center of working-class life: in lieu of the pastoral nostalgia of the Chartist poets, the dialect writers take comfort in a nostalgic domesticity.[18] To draw out more fully how the pastoral nostalgia of the Chartist movement evolved into dialect's nostalgic domesticity, we must first turn to the debate over the Ten Hours Bill, the focus of much Chartist energy in the 1840s, because nowhere more insistently so than during the Ten Hours controversy do gender roles become the central issue, emerging as a highly contested element of modern working-class identity.

# The Ten Hours Bill and the Gendering
# of Nostalgia

When the Chartist parent in J. M'Owen's 1844 poem, "Father! Who Are the Chartists?" answers his inquisitive child's question, he frames his response in the abstract language of rights and wrongs that has characterized political radicalism in the West for over two hundred years:

> Millions who labour with skill, my child,
> On the land—at the loom—in the mill, my child.
>> Whom the bigots and knaves
>> Would keep as their slaves;
> Whom tyrants would punish and kill, my child.
>
> Millions whom suffering draws, my child,
> To unite in a glorious cause, my child.
>> Their object, their end
>> Is mankind to befriend,
> By gaining for all equal laws, my child.
>
> Millions who ever hath sought, my child,
> For freedom of speech and of thought, my child,
>> Though stripp'd of each right
>> By the strong hand of might,
> They ne'er can be vanquish'd or bought, my child.
>
> Millions who *earnestly* call, my child,
> For freedom to each and to all, my child;
>> They have truth for their shield,
>> And never will yield
> Till they triumph in tyranny's fall, my child.
>
> And they've sworn at a Holberry's grave, my child
> (That martyr so noble and brave, my child)
>> That come weal or come woe,
>> Still *onward* they'll go
> Till Freedom be won for the slave, my child!    (lines 1–25)

M'Owen's poem beautifully illustrates Gareth Stedman Jones's contention that the Chartists identified political, rather than social or economic, oppression as the root cause of their suffering and could maintain their radical stance only as long as the wretched conditions of early Victorian Britain could be blamed on the intransigence of an exclusionary political system. Once "the evidence suggested that real reform was possible within the unreformed system," Stedman Jones observes, "then radical ideology could be expected to lose purchase over large parts of [the Charter's] mass following" (106). The reforms Stedman Jones obliquely refers to are a series of measures passed into law in the 1840s—the Mines Act of 1842, the Bank Charter Act, the repeal of the Corn Laws, and most significantly, the Factory Act of 1847—which instituted the ten-hour day for mill women.[19] By making the Ten Hours Bill the law of the land, the government indicated to working men that the ruling classes were willing to ensure, and to socially engineer if necessary, traditional patterns of patriarchal authority in the working-class household. If large numbers of working men came to accept, or at least tolerate, the factory system after midcentury, it was in part on the belief that the government would enact legislation to preserve their traditional patriarchal privileges in the face of the disintegration of the preindustrial family structure.

Thus, the significance of the Ten Hours Bill went far beyond the immediate question of regulating women's working hours. It was a milestone piece of legislation precisely because it helped to map out the social and sexual geography of the emergent industrialized nation. All during the Ten Hours debate, the real issue under contention was not just women's working hours but their proper sphere. Like the discourse surrounding the Chartist Land Plan, the Ten Hours debates were framed in the political language of nostalgia. By reordering the working-class household, the bill promised to restore the working man to the "earthly Eden of English yeomanry," to borrow the evocative language of the great Ten Hours agitator, the Reverend Joseph Rayner Stephens. In this way, the Ten Hours Bill revises by reversing the strategy of the Chartist Land Plan. The Land Plan offered the working class a ticket back to merry old England, where "natural" domestic relations reign. The Ten Hours Bill took a more direct approach. By reestablishing "natural" domestic relations—the bill's primary aim in the mind of many of its supporters—it guaranteed the return of the good old days to the here and now.

In 1842, the West Riding Short Time Committee, a workers' organization set up to agitate for the passage of the Ten Hours Bill, hand-delivered to the prime minister, Sir Robert Peel, a series of proposals for improving the condition of England. Near the top of the list stood a request for "the gradual withdrawal of all females from the factories" (*The Ten Hours' Factory Question* 5). When Sir Robert reminded the workers that excluding all women from the factories would be unfair to those who were unmarried or widowed, the operatives wisely sidestepped the prime minister's volley by launching an attack on working women. Women in factories, they charged, "grow up in total ignorance of all the true duties of woman. Home, its cares, and its employments, is woman's true sphere; but these poor things are totally unfitted for attending to the one, or participating in the other. They neither learn, in the great majority of cases, to make a shirt, darn a stocking, cook a dinner, or clean a house. In short, both in mind and manners, they are altogether unfitted for the occupancy of the domestic position" (5). The operatives here cleverly co-opt the language of the masters so that their demands for an end to women's industrial labor cannot easily be denied without forcing the men in power to repudiate their own cherished ideological constructs. Whether the prime minister was at that moment delighted or dismayed to hear the discourse of domesticity turned back on the class that spawned it remains unrecorded. But in the hands of working-class men, the ideology of a woman's sphere proved a nearly invincible—because irreproachable—line of argument when extended to working-class women.

Moreover, when the operatives on the West Riding Short Time Committee invoked the domestic ideology to insist that women's industrial labor was "an inversion of the order of nature and of Providence—a return to a state of barbarism, in which woman does the work, while man looks idly on" (*Ten Hours' Factory Question* 6), they fashioned a new identity for themselves in the rapidly altering world of Victorian Britain, one rooted in the man's role as the family breadwinner. The operatives' appeal to natural law is hardly surprising, but the curiously ahistorical quality of their remarks is. By inverting the Short Time Committee's formula, one could conclude that, in the eyes of these operatives, working men and idle women followed both the laws of nature and tradition. Yet the norm of the non-earning, non-laboring wife had itself only gained currency among the upper reaches of society in the eighteenth century, and it was completely alien to working-class life, where women had traditionally engaged in an array of productive occupations. But as the Short Time Committee's remarks evidence, when Victorian working men struggled to secure the working-class woman in the domestic sphere, they situated her there not as an eighteenth-century homeworker (a weaver, a spinner, a lacemaker) but as the somewhat more familiar homemaker. Thus, it is important to read in the complaints of the West Riding Short Time Committee not only the transplantation of the domestic ideal into the working-class home, but also the ideological reconfiguration of the working woman as, ironically, a woman of leisure. In other words, to restrain female competition in the workplace, the working-class male adopted a representation of waged work that excluded women. Working-class husbands recouped some of the authority lost in the process of being proletarianized by reinventing themselves as the family's sole economic support; and as a consequence, "the wage-earning wife, once seen as the norm in every working-class household," became by the middle decades of the nineteenth century "a symptom and symbol of masculine degradation" (Taylor 111).

In delivering its blueprint for a better world to Prime Minister Peel, the working men from the West Riding made clear that patriarchal insecurities subtended their current rejection of factory life and that their future acceptance of it hinged on those insecurities being allayed. When they called on the government to suspend machinery's march of progress, they did so because of female factory labor. It was not the technology itself that the members of the committee opposed but the way it had been implemented. "Unregulated use and extensive introduction of machinery . . . has either superceded adult labour entirely, or replaced it by the cheaper labour of women and children," the committee members noted (*Ten Hours' Factory*

*Question* 8). For this reason, they demanded that the prime minister halt the advancing forces of the industrial revolution: "The dictates of sound political wisdom coincide with the dictates of humanity, morality, and religion, in calling upon us to retrace our steps, and arrest the progress of a system which is spreading disease, disorganization, and disaffection, in the factory districts" (9). The Short Time Committee retreated from modernity as pestilential, chaotic, and alienating for some of the same reasons that motivated the canonical male critics. Both feared that industrialism had turned the world upside down; and in the eyes of the West Riding Short Time Committee, restricting women's hours and legislating female domesticity seemed the logical first step in turning it right side up again.

Throughout the meeting with Sir Robert Peel, the West Riding men insisted that the working-class woman was a roughly hewn domestic angel forced out of her proper sphere by the factory system, and they did so in the sober tones befitting the occasion. The ideology of domesticity and its relationship to the politics of nostalgia is more dramatically represented in a fiery speech given by the Reverend Joseph Rayner Stephens before a friendly crowd of Oldham operatives who favored the Ten Hours legislation. Freed from the constraints of a prime ministerial audience, Stephens presents the domestic woman to his audience as the way things always were. The notion of an idle working-class wife did not restore the old order of things; it engendered a new one to fit the altered conditions of nineteenth-century life. Yet in his speech, Stephens incorrectly associated it with the misty, receding days before the coming of the factories. When he informed his receptive audience that husbands ought to be paid enough to maintain their families, he claimed the family wage not as a new right, which it was, but as one lost: "Bring back the good old times, I do not say when we were without Machinery, but when the full grown Man by his own labour could maintain his family in comfort" (*A Report of Important Proceedings* 25). The past that Stephens recalled was pure fabrication. Still, his appealing fiction of the golden age of independent producers—of the yeoman farmer or handloom weaver single-handedly supporting himself and his family—became for many working-class males an ideal pawned during the recent hard times that the ideology of domesticity promised to redeem.

For Stephens, God aboriginally placed woman in the domestic sphere to tend the earthbound trinity of father, husband, and child. In imagery that recalls the romances of Disraeli and Carlyle, Stephens informed the Oldham operatives that the "earthly Eden of yeomanry England" has been transformed "into a waste and howling wilderness" by the introduction of demon steam. That is because machinery removed employment from "the hands of MAN, the only proper operative, and placed it in those of the WOMAN, whose province according to God's original institution, is neither the Field, nor the Mill, but the House, the Home of the Father, her Husband, and her child" (*A Report* 24–25). Using the tropes of romance, Stephens articulates his own version of contemporary history, one that predictably reads the nineteenth century as an unfortunate fall into modernity. To keep his imagery consistent, Stephens should argue that the Satanic steam engines must be vanquished in order for paradise to be regained; but he instead turns his invective on woman's work, the real villain in his piece and the one that must be vanquished for the earthly Eden to be restored.

While Stephens fired up his audience with passionate denunciations of the factory system, and the members of the West Riding Short Time Committee appealed to Sir Robert Peel in dispassionate tones, both Stephens and the West Riding operatives delivered the same message: the only way to reconcile the working man to the modern wasteland of machinery was to reassert male dominance in the workplace. And this is precisely what did eventually happen. Victorian women lost their primary identity as workers and their status in the labor market, leading Judy Lown to conclude that Victorian working women *"cushioned* the effects of industrialisation for men. The ways in which women experienced industrialisation *enabled* men to secure a better deal out of the social and economic changes taking place" ("Not So Much a Factory" 36). The compromise between men and masters that slowly materialized ensured that the new technology would be used to advance the economic and patriarchal interests of working men; and it took the form of the widespread acceptance that the proper role for the working-class man was as the family's breadwinner. By the mid-nineteenth century, the majority of working men ceased to oppose the industrial system in return for ostensible control over women's access to employment. As long as all future technological advances would uphold patriarchal arrangements, which is precisely what the Ten Hours Bill indicated, working men were willing to acquiesce to the factory system.

When the *Chartist Circular* published an account of the meeting between the West Riding Short Time Committee and Sir Robert Peel, the journal made explicit the connection between working-class rebellion and the restriction of women's labor that the committee members only implied. Without the restraint that the august presence of England's prime minister must have exerted over the committee's deputation, the *Chartist Circular* endorses the projected removal of women from the factories and adds vague threats of treasonable insurrection if such a withdrawal failed to occur:

> Machinery, in its progress, has doubtless been the origin of terrible calamity: it has made the strong man so much live lumber. But as we cannot go back, and must go on, it is for statesmen and philosophers to prepare, for the crisis is as surely coming as the morning light. How, when machinery is multiplied, as it will be, a thousandfold? . . . How, when comparatively speaking, there shall be *no* labour for man? Will the multitude lie down and, unrepining, die? We think not—we are sure not. ("Man versus Machine" 12 February 1842)

It was the multitude rising up (not lying down) that frightened the upper classes throughout the revolutionary decades before midcentury. If the passage of the Ten Hours Bill would help to reconcile the working man to the machines, as the workers themselves seemed to promise it would, then the government was willing to compromise. Faced with the choice of revolution or regulation, the British government ultimately chose the latter. Like many political compromises, the consequences were double-edged. From our vantage point, we can see that the Ten Hours legislation loosened the death grip that laissez-faire ideology had on the British government, and along with the 1844 Factory Act and the Mines Act, it marked the beginning of the state's willingness to protect adult workers from the raw and rapacious appetite of uncensored capitalism. The Ten Hours Bill paved the way for the government's later interventions to safeguard all workers and was, in this regard, a milestone of humanitarian legislation.

Yet the Ten Hours Bill purchased stability by institution-alizing the socially conservative outlook of the working man. This fact did not escape contemporary critics on the left. G. Julian Harney's *The Democratic Review of British and Foreign Politics, History and Literature,* located on the radical fringes of the Chartist press, warned in 1850 that because the Ten Hours Bill diminished the likelihood of a social revolution, it was a "false step . . . intended to screw back society to a state superseded, long ago, by the present system" ("Ten Hours' Question" 373–74). As *The Democratic Review* observed, the struggles for the Factory Act of 1847 were an indication that the British working classes were beginning to make accommodations to the inevitability of the industrial system. No doubt the bill's passage helped to defuse a tense political climate. But just as important, in the minds of many working men the Ten Hours Bill signaled a return to patriarchal politics as usual and pointed the way to the recovery of the earthly Eden of yeomanry England.

## Dialect's Nostalgic Domesticity

Nearly two decades after the demise of Chartism, Ben Brierley, one of the most successful figures in the dialect movement, rewrote the history of early Victorian radicalism in "A Strike Adventure, or the 'Revolution' of Daisy Nook" (1867). Briefly, "A Strike Adventure" relates the comic misadventures of three would-be village revolu-tionaries during the industrial unrest that followed Parliament's 1842 refusal to accept the Charter. Sent off to discover whether, as rumor has it, a general strike has escalated into a full-scale workers' rebellion in a neighboring town, the local yokel emissaries are, somewhere along the way, misinformed that the day of reckoning for the rich has indeed arrived. Being by nature cowardly, however, they do not know whether to press ahead and risk getting caught up in the apocalyptic violence of revolution, or to go home. As a compromise, they stop in a pub, finding "a good substitute for a blazing town in the shape of a group of frothy bottles" (170). Departing the ale house somewhat the worse for drink, they begin spreading news of the insurrection throughout the countryside, only to come upon a trustworthy soul from whom "they gleaned that Ashton was not in a state of 'insurrection,' as had been reported, but quiet, the people having returned to work. That some disturbance had taken place in the neighbourhood was quite true, but it was of a more insignificant character than some people gave credit for" (175). Mortified by their own gullibility, they return home, go back to work, and burn old issues of the *Northern Star* in a symbolic renunciation of revolutionary ardor. All in all, Brierley tells the tale to great comic effect, but he also cannily revises recent history by refashioning working-class radicals into bumblers on a country ramble. Brierley revisits the Chartist agitations which had left many contemporary observers fearing imminent revolution and transforms them into a comic interlude— something of "insignificant character." Brierley (1825–96) as well as fellow dialect writers John Hartley (1839–1915), Samuel Laycock (1826–93), and Edwin Waugh (1817–90) disowned the radical inheritance of the Chartists in order to embrace a cooperative, politically conservative vision of working-class life. If the Chartists were for the most part committed radicals, the dialect authors were, or strove to be, professional men of letters who earned their livings by publishing, editing, and public readings.

Dialect poets and storytellers tried to minimize all aspects of class conflict. Perhaps the best example of encoded working-class accommodation to the industrial order can be found in Brierley's 1871 story, "The Cotters of Mossburn." Clearly allegorical, Brierley's tale juxtaposes Mossburn, "the last place in the civilised world upon which the light of progress dawned" (5) with the "thoroughly go-a-head village" of Chatterthorpe (109). With Dickensian convolutions, the plot of "The Cotters of Mossburn" traces out a series of internecine struggles to reveal how a Chatterthorpian captain of industry misappropriated the inheritance of his cousin, a comic Mossburn weaver named Little Robin. If the story ended here, one could easily unravel the allegory to read in it a condemnation of capitalism's illegitimacy, since the capitalist in the text, the aptly named Mr. Biggs, stole his fortune from its rightful owner, Little Robin. Yet in the resolution of the story, Brierley backs away from an indictment of capitalism's theft of the worker's property (his labor) and concludes by justifying the status quo. Having no desire to forfeit his modest lifestyle in Mossburn, Little Robin instead cheerfully forfeits the inheritance, demanding in compensation only a modest old-age pension. In his refusal, Robin admirably asserts the superiority of his humble, working-class values over the greedy materialism of the Chatterthorpians. Nevertheless, it is clear that in "The Cotters of Mossburn" dialect's reformism has replaced Chartism's radicalism. In exchange for basic welfare legislation, Brierley seems willing to forgo all demands for more root-and-branch changes.

If the Chartists spoke to and for a radicalized proletariat, dialect literature reflects the accommodating spirit of the post-1850 working class.[20] Poems such as John Hartley's "Persevere" offer the dialect poet's standard advice of patience rather than protest:

> If we think awr lot is hard,
>   Niver let us mak a fuss;
> Lukkin raand, at ivery yard,
>   We'st find others war nor us;
> We have still noa cause to fear!
> Let's ha' faith, an' persevere.          (lines 13–18)

Repeated with numbing regularity in dialect literature, Hartley's message to bear up stoically under life's hardships signifies an acceptance of the industrial present that constitutes a clean break with the Chartist traditions of the working class.

Of the Victorian working class in the second half of the century, Gareth Stedman Jones notes:

> Working people ceased to believe that they could shape society in their own image. Capitalism had become an immovable horizon. Demands produced by the movements of the pre-1850 period—republicanism, secularism, popular self-education, co-operation, land reform, internationalism etc.—now shorn of the conviction which had given them point, eventually expired from sheer inanition, or else, in a diluted form, were appropriated by the left flank of Gladstonian liberalism. The main impetus of working-

class activity now lay elsewhere. It was concentrated into trade unions, co-ops, friendly societies, all indicating a *de facto* recognition of the existing social order as the inevitable framework of action. The same could be said of music-hall. It was a culture of consolation. (237)

Yet despite the dispersal of radical energies within the working class, dialect writers remain indebted to the Chartists. They too reject the transformational impact of the industrial revolution on the urban working class, even if they accept the inevitability and permanence of industrialization. By creating a literature that for the most part offers up either nostalgic sketches of the preindustrial worker or sentimentalized portraits of the contemporary working-class home, dialect writers present an image of working-class life as generally immune to the incursions of industrialism itself. "The inspiration of the industrial muse was a complex one," Brian Maidment observes, "as so little of the verse was directly about industrial culture" ("Prose" 31).

With the failure of Chartism and its projected transcendence of industrial England, the remaking of British society in the image of the earthly Eden of yeomanry England becomes unthinkable except in the most utopian moments. Yet the dialect writers do not so much abandon the basic Chartist ideals (and the Chartist idealization of the past) as resituate them in the home. By the 1850s, domesticity was functioning as the dominant ideology within working-class circles, where it remained for the rest of the century as a largely unattainable but nevertheless potent ideal. So after the collapse of the Chartist movement, working-class writers turn inward and indoors, rediscovering the rural dream of the Chartists in the domestic oasis of the worker's cottage. The earthly Eden of yeomanry England translates into the Eden of working-class domesticity, where the "natural" domestic relations between men and women can once again flourish. If working-class culture becomes after midcentury a "culture of consolation," as Stedman Jones contends, then the domestic sphere is the working man's chief consolation prize.

In the dialect tradition, the working-class home is seen as a place unaltered by and secure from the unaccountable changes occurring in the outside world. Fittingly, when the wife in Edwin

Waugh's 1857 "Come Whoam to thi Childer an' Me," the most famous dialect poem of the century, pleads with her husband to return home, she tempts him with homespun pleasures and the seemingly timeless domestic joys available to the working man around his own hearth:

> Aw've just mended th' fire wi' a cob;
> Owd Swaddle has brought thi new shoon;
> There's some nice bacon-collops o' th' hob,
> An' a quart o' ale-posset i' th' oon.                    (lines 1–4)

The key to the attraction lies not only in the promise of domestic comfort, but in the mythic quality of the moment, its historical indeterminateness: Waugh could be sketching a hearthside scene of nineteenth-century life or one of eleventh-century life, since nowhere does the poem acknowledge the existence of the urban, industrial scene outside the front door. In the closed world of dialect domesticity, the home became not only an antidote to modernity but the repository of working-class traditions, as if the lost village community, abandoned in the nascent moments of industrialization, had been resurrected inside the worker's cottage. The dialect writers' "yearning for 'community,' " which Maidment identifies in *The Poorhouse Fugitives* (231) as one of the strongest impulses in dialect literature, found fulfillment in the family circle, where the affection and good cheer of simple folks with simple hearts substituted for the sense of security, mastery, and belonging lost with the demise of village life.

   Given the alienating conditions of industrial England, it is not surprising that working men would wish to seek refuge from the workaday world of the factories, even if that refuge took the form of poetic fantasies. For in spite of its considerable surface charm, "Come Whoam to thi Childer an' Me" implicitly acknowledges the tensions inherent in the idealization of the working-class home, which lacked the amenities—the servants, the space, the creature comforts—of the prosperous bourgeois mansion. Presenting two irreconcilable points of view, the poem takes the form of a dialogue between a homebound wife and an errant husband. Lonely, fretful, and left at home to tend children and darn socks, the wife laments her absent husband:

When aw put little Sally to bed,
Hoo cried, 'cose her feyther weren't theer,
So aw kiss'd th' little thing, an' aw said
Thae'd bring her a ribbin fro' th' fair;
An' aw gav' her her doll, an' some rags,
An' a nice little white cotton-bo';
An' aw kiss'd her again; but hoo said
'At hoo wanted to kiss *thee* an' o.

An' Dick, too, aw'd sich wark wi' him,
Afore aw could get him upstairs;
Thae towd him thae'd bring him a drum,
He said, when he're sayin' his prayers;
Then he looked i' my face, an' he said,
"Has th' boggarts taen houd o' my dad?"
An' he cried whol his e'en were quite red;—
He likes thee some weel, does yon lad!          (lines 9–24)

When her wandering mate finally returns from pursuing his own pleasures, he proclaims both his right to a "bit of a spree" and his enduring affection for home:

"God bless tho' my lass; aw'll go whoam
An' aw'll kiss thee an' th' childer o' round;
Thae knows that wheerever aw roam,
Aw'm fain to get back to th' owd ground;
Aw can do wi' a crack o'er a glass;
Aw can do wi' a bit of a spree;
But aw've no gradely comfort, my lass,
Except wi' yon childer an' thee."          (lines 41–48)

With unabashed sentimentalism, the poem embraces a domesticity that it cannot quite endorse: the husband's wanderlust testifies to its limitations. The simple comforts offered in the opening stanza fail to satisfy him, and even though he insists there is no place like home, he also hints that it is no place he particularly wants to be, thus leaving his wife with the sad futurity of many more such silent, solitary evenings. Yet by letting the husband have the last word, Waugh effectively irons over the tensions his poem raises, and "Come Whoam" concludes on a note of domestic concord. In the end, the poem contains the contradictions embodied in working-class domesticity, and thus it contributes to the mythologizing impetus of dialect poetry by actively translating the working man's humble cottage into his castle.

However understandable this translation may be, it depends on the effacement of women's labor. The long-suffering wife in "Come Whoam to thi Childer an' Me" never complains about her unending domestic chores, nor does she mention any paid labor she might have undertaken to supplement the household's income. That is because the working-class ideal, which Waugh's poem memorably brings to life, envisaged every working-class wife supported by her husband, although the working-class reality usually fell short of this goal. Until the end of the century, only the most prosperous and skilled workers could afford to keep an unemployed wife at home in any degree of comfort, and a large percentage of working-class women continued to add to their families' incomes after marriage. So while Waugh's celebration of the home as a paradise for husbands in "Come Whoam to thi Childer an' Me" may have put "Lancashire dialect poetry on the map" (Hollingworth 138), it is his "Down Again!," a humorous account of childbirth in a working-class family, that best encapsulates the dialect tradition's problematic relationship with the women it enshrined.

"Down Again!" presents childbirth from the husband's vantage point and thus ignores the most important actor as well as the true laborer—the pregnant wife—in order to focus on the husband's activities during the delivery:

> "What's o' thi hurry, Jem?" said he,
> As I went runnin' by:
> "I connot stop to talk to thee;
> We'n someb'dy ill," said I.
> "Who is it this time?" cried owd Clem;
> "Is it Nan, or little Ben?"
> "Nawe, nawe," said I, "it's noan o' them;
> *Our Betty's down again!*"
> . . . . . . . . . . . . . . . .
> I never closed my e'en that neet,
> Till after break o' day;

For they keep me runnin' o' my feet,
Wi' gruel, an' wi' tay:
Like a scoppteril up an' down i' th' hole,
I're busy at th' owd job,
Warmin' flannels, an' mendin' th' fires
An' tentin' stuff o' th' hob.

It wur getten six or theerabout;
I're thrang wi' th' gruel-pon;
When I dropt mi spoon, an' shouted out,
"How are yo gettin' on?"
"We're doin weel," th' owd woman said;
"Thou'd better come an' see;
There's a fine young chap lies here i' bed;
An' he wants to look at thee!"

I ran up i' my stockin'-feet;
An' theer they lay! By th' mon;
I thought i' my heart a prattier seet
I ne'er clapt e'en upon!
I kissed our Betty; an' I said,—
Wi' th' wayter i' my e'en,—
"God bless yo both, my bonny lass,
For evermoore, Amen!

"But do tak care; if aught went wrang
I think my heart would break;
An' if there's aught i' th' world thou'd like
Thou's nought to do but speak:
But, oh, my lass, don't lie too long;
I'm lonesome by mysel';
I'm no use without thee, thou knows;
Be sharp, an' do get weel!"         (lines 41–48, 65–96)

The poem never exploits the irony whereby the husband complains of the burdensome toil of fetching doctors and making tea while his unseen and unheard wife labors in childbirth. Instead, it concludes with a sudden turn toward the sentimental, the father's welcome to his newborn son, and thus reaffirms the strong ties of love and affection that bind the working-class family together. With its unwillingness to make visible the invisible laboring wife, "Down Again!" embodies the controlling irony of the dialect tradition: it is a class-based literature that consistently denies working women their class identity by refusing to recognize them as laborers.

A glance at the few published autobiographies of Victorian and Edwardian working-class women immediately reveals that these individuals did not expect their wage-earning days to end with their marriage vows. Certainly Lucy Luck, whose autobiography is reprinted in John Burnett's *Useful Toil,* held no such illusions about married life. Born in 1848 and brought up in a workhouse, Luck eventually marries, bears seven children, and never stops adding to the family income. A straw-plaiter by trade, she confesses at the end of her life: "I always liked my work very much and although I had trouble with it when I first learnt, it has been a little fortune to me. I have been at work for forty-seven years, and have never missed one season, although I have a large family" (77). While justly proud of her achievements, Luck has no sense that working for five decades and raising a large family is an extraordinary accomplishment. But then, given what we know of the lives of Victorian working-class women, it most likely was not. Contrary to popular belief, women did not stop working when they got married; in fact, they frequently had to stay in the labor market until their children were old enough to earn for themselves.

Yet domesticity so dominated working-class culture that the ideal was for years accepted as fact, and only recently has scholarship begun to insist on the regularity with which working-class wives continued to earn money after marriage.[21] Of course, women's working patterns varied according to the specificities of regional economies, but in the cotton districts of Lancashire, one of the centers of dialect activity, a long tradition of married women's work existed. Yet this is a state of affairs that one would never grasp from reading dialect poetry.

Moreover, and perhaps even more problematically, dialect domesticity denied women credit for the unwaged work they performed. Whether earning a wage or not, most working-class women had the primary responsibility of housekeeping, frequently a daunting task in urban settings where, according to Robert Roberts's *The Classic Slum,* a firsthand account of life in turn-of-the-century Salford, housewives fought a constant battle with "ever-invading dirt" and "wore their lives away washing clothes in heavy, iron-hooped tubs, scrubbing wood and stone, polishing furniture and fire-irons" (37). Yet the dialect home, like the golden past of the Chartists, was configured as a scene of leisure because dialect's nostalgic domesticity consistently refused to elevate housework to the status of work requiring skill, organization, and intelligence. Rather, in its need to set off the domestic realm (the site of natural relationships between men and women, parents and children) from the industrial realm (the site of unnatural, alienated relationships between men and masters, workers and machines), dialect literature reconstituted housework not only as "not work," but as one of woman's duties, or more precisely, one of her natural functions, like breathing and childbearing.

This is certainly the unstated assumption in Edwin Waugh's "Dinner Time," a poem about failed domesticity. When the husband returns home for his midday meal only to discover the house in a state of disarray, he complains bitterly to his wife:

> "Thou's nought to do, fro' morn to neet,
> But keep things clean an' straight,
> An' see that th' bits o' cloas are reet,
> An' cook one's bit o' meight;
> But thou's never done it yet, owd lass:
> How is it? Conto tell?"                    (lines 43–48)

First the husband belittles the wife's labor, and then he devalues it completely, attributing the household's disorder solely to her laziness and weakness for gossip. Although the poem opens with the wife's frantic attempts to put supper on the table, it closes with the husband's threat to leave the home and dissolve the family:

> "No wonder that hard-wortchin' folk
> Should feel inclined to roam
> For comfort to an alehouse nook,
> When they han noan at whoam.
>
> "I'm fast: I don't know what to say;
> An' I don't know what to do;

An' when I'm tired, at th' end o' th' day,
I don't know where to goo.
It makes me weary o' my life
To live i' sich a den:
Here, gi's a bit o' cheese an' loaf,
An' I'll be off again!"

(lines 55–66)

Nowhere in the poem does Waugh undermine the husband's point of view, so that "Dinner Time" dangerously obscures the adversities of housekeeping in a working-class home lacking all modern amenities. The poem also ignores the talent required to feed, clothe, and care for a family, even though, as Lady Florence Bell remarks in *At the Works* (1907), an account of life in a Yorkshire iron town, it was frequently a woman's managerial abilities rather than her husband's industrial capabilities that determined the economic well-being of the family: "The key to the condition of the workman and his family, the clue, the reason for the possibilities and impossibilities of his existence, is the capacity, the temperament, and, above all, the health of the woman who manages his house; into her hands, sometimes strong and capable, often weak and uncertain, the future of her husband is committed, the burden of the family life is thrust" (171). Unlike Lady Bell, Waugh cannot acknowledge the wife's unpaid domestic duties as valuable, difficult labor because to do so would undermine the home as the antithesis of the factory, the opposition upon which dialect's nostalgic domesticity depended.

Ultimately, dialect poetry not only devalued women's contributions to the household economy, but it strove to deny their labor altogether by encouraging working-class women to engage in acts of self-effacement and to erase as much as possible all traces of their domestic exertions. Dialect poets usually made this suggestion in the form of an advice poem, a subgenre of dialect poetry in which a speaker, usually an old man or woman, offers household hints to the newly married. Invariably, the dispenser of wisdom informs a young bride that although the secret to a happy marriage lies in the spotless purity and perfect orderliness of her domestic arrangements, a well-run home also renders invisible the labor involved in its upkeep. Somewhat ironically, these working-class poets seem to be advocating a fetishized domestic space where only the "commodity" (the cooked food, the clean house), and not the labor required to produce it, would be disclosed to the homeward-bound worker.

It is this lesson in concealment that the superannuated uncle in Samuel Laycock's "Uncle Dick's Advoice to Wed Women" tries to impart to his newlywed niece:

> When it's weshin' day, get done as soon as yo' con;
> Aw'll assure yo' it's very unpleasant for John
> To come into th' heawse ov a nooin' or neet,
> An' foind th' dirty clooas spread abeawt his feet.
> . . . . . . . . . . . . . . . . . . . . . . . . . . . . . . . . . . . . . .
> Oh! It's grand when one enters th' inside o' the'r cot,
> An' foinds 'at th' woife's made it a *heaven* ov a spot;
> An' her stondin' theer, bless her, to welcome yo' in,
> Wi' o' 'at's abeawt her as clean as a pin!
> . . . . . . . . . . . . . . . . . . . . . . . . . . . . . . . .
> Let 'em feel—when the'r wark's done—'at th' loveliest spot
> 'At the'r is under heaven, is *the'r own humble cot.*
> Ah! ther's lots o' poor fellows aw've known i' mi loife,
> 'At's bin driven fro' whoam bi a slovenly woife:
> When they'n come in at neet, wearied eawt wi' th'er toil,
> I'th' stead o' bein' met wi' a sweet, lovin' smoile,
> Ther's nothin' but black-lookin' holes met the'r een,
> An' a woife an' some childer, a shawm to be seen.
>
> (lines 13–16, 37–40, 49–56)

As Laycock's last stanza reveals, it is from the body of the housewife that the effects of domestic labor must primarily be erased.

In this regard, Uncle Dick's friendly advice does not differ from the "toothsome advice" a young married woman receives in Edwin Waugh's poem of the same name. "Toothsome Advice" echoes "Uncle Dick's Advoice to Wed Women" in its insistence that the ornamental appearance of the wife will attract—like a sexual magnet:

> "Thou mun keep his whoam pleasant an' sweet;
>   An' everything fit to be seen;
> Thou mun keep thi hearth cheerful an' breet;

> Thou mun keep thisel' tidy an' clean;
> A good-temper't wife *will* entice
>     To a fireside that's cosy an' trim;
> Men liken to see their wives nice;
>     And I'm sure that it's so wi' yor Jem."          (lines 25–32)

By asserting the desirability of the working-class wife only when she conceals the marks of her class identity (the dirt, the fatigue), Waugh reverses the middle-class fascination with the sexuality of the working-class woman. Moreover, while neither Waugh nor Laycock would demand that the working man, exhausted from his labors, arrive home cheerful and tidy, both expect the working wife to transform herself at the end of each day into a decorative object more befitting a bourgeois matron with a staff of servants than the poor drudge that she frequently was. Evolving as it did out of the peculiar conditions of middle-class life, the domestic ideal never fit the economic realities of the working class, and the only way the dialect poets could make it fit was, oddly enough, by eroding the class differences between middle- and working-class women. The practical and pernicious effect of this erosion was that dialect literature, which claimed a certain authenticity as the voice of the industrial working class, came to define the working-class woman in terms that ignored her class conditions.

A yawning and unbridgeable gap existed between the domestic ideal—which overlooked women's waged work and devalued their unwaged work—and the necessities of survival for working-class families in Victorian Britain. The ideal demanded that working-class women reproduce, albeit in a less opulent form, the bourgeois world inside the worker's cottage, a demand that the working-class wife could rarely achieve, and then only through small acts of daily heroism. Drearier than the rosy pictures sketched by the dialect poets, working women's lives were filled with long days of overexertion, as Robert Roberts observes:

> Realists among the old working class today remember, and with sadness, not King Edward's 'lovely ladies' and tea on the lawn at Hurlingham, but the many women broken and aged with childbearing well before their own youth was done. They remember the

spoiled complexions, the mouths full of rotten teeth, the varicose veins, the ignorance of simple hygiene, the intelligence stifled and the endless battle merely to keep clean. Unlike many in the middle and upper classes, fondly looking back, they see no 'glory gleaming.' They weep no tears for the past. (41)

Dialect writers, however, were not realists. They were idealists, if somewhat pragmatic ones. Tied to the working-class communities they spoke to and for, they fully understood that every working-class home did not meet the impossible standards of the domestic ideal. Certainly Edwin Waugh, who abandoned his own wife and children in a workhouse and took up with a wealthy Irish widow before penning "Come Whoam to thi Childer an' Me," comprehended something of the ideal's tentative nature.[22] Still, the ideal seems to have held emotional and imaginative sway over the British working classes. "Home, however poor, was the focus of all . . . love and interests," Roberts recalls, "songs about its beauties were ever on people's lips. 'Home sweet home', first heard in the 1870s, had become 'almost a second national anthem' " (53). But whether it was honored more in the breach or in the observance, the ideology of domesticity neglected the diversity of working-class women's experience in nineteenth-century Britain, where there were few occupations—from coal mining to fishing—in which women did not actively engage. Ultimately, dialect literature's single-minded devotion to the domestic ideal robbed working-class women of one of their best subjects: their lives as workers.

## "A Thousand Times I'd Be a Factory Girl"

Although the domestic ideal gained currency among working men throughout their struggles of the 1830s and 1840s, its adoption was neither immediate nor absolute among working women. Admittedly, many working women saw in the ideal some possible relief from their twin burdens of waged work and housework, and no doubt some were attracted by Chartism's promise to amend marital relations through domesticity. But not all embraced it, and those who did dispute its imposition lacked a language with which to articulate their discontents. As historian Barbara Taylor has shown in her investigations of the women who wrote letters to the "Woman's Page" of the *Pioneer,* a popular Owenite trades union journal of the 1830s, working-class women in the early part of the nineteenth century could evoke the traditional language of radicalism—of the rights of man and woman—to fight their battles. They could, and frequently did, argue against all "artificial aristocracies" (29 March 1834), whether of class or of gender. But Chartism, the next great wave of working-class radicalism after Owenism, repudiated the revolutionary feminism of its predecessor by heralding the domestic ideal; and the ideology of domesticity left working-class women without a solid foundation on which to base a critique of their unequal position within Victorian society at the same historical moment when gender inequities were being reasserted and reinscribed into a system of separate spheres.

Mary Merryweather's *Experience of Factory Life,* a record of her fourteen years as a teacher at the Courtauld silk mills in Essex, provides a case study of the difficulties working women had in finding the appropriate language with which to challenge the domestic ideal. Worried that their female employees would have too much free time on their hands after the passage of the Ten Hours Bill, the paternalistic Courtaulds hired the middle-class Merryweather in 1847, hoping she would initiate their female employees into the rudiments of domesticity and proper "feminine" behavior. Indeed, Merryweather is the ladylike presence that Charlotte Elizabeth Tonna called for in *Helen Fleetwood,* who, once installed in the factory, would shame vice and encourage modesty by the sheer force of her irresistable femininity. Unfortunately for Merryweather, the mill women in her care did not wish to be remade in the domestic image that she offered them, and their refusal formed a constant source of frustration for her. She complains that the factory woman "will scarcely be persuaded when she marries that it is better for her husband and for herself to remain at home, even if he wishes her to do so. The wives have so often told me that their husbands' wages will not buy all that is necessary; that they would rather go into the factory; that they were more fit for that work than for the harder work most cottage wives have to do" (77–78). Merryweather dismisses the compelling motives to feed and clothe their families that drove women into the factories with the familiar accusation that at the bottom of it all lies a love of finery and a perverse (and morally suspect) desire for independence: "A constant endeavour to dress beyond what is at all necessary or becoming, is one great inducement to some women to continue earning money, that they may have a right, as they think, to spend it without asking their husbands" (78). Wishing factory women would behave more like middle-class ladies and live by the restraints of bourgeois propriety, she established with these goals in mind a Lowell-style dormitory for the unmarried mill girls and instituted a whole series of regulations to counteract what she saw as the girls' wrongheaded independence and fondness for "unrestricted liberty" (44). Not surprisingly, the mill hands chafed at Merryweather's restrictions, occasionally burning copies of the house rules. After seven years Merryweather's residential experiment failed.

The unenthusiastic response by the Courtauld women to Merryweather's interference resembles that of a group of Leeds factory women who were the subject of an 1847 article in the *People's Journal*, a magazine run by the reform-minded, middle-class Howitts. According to the report, "Leeds Factory Women's *Soiree*," a Leeds linen draper decided to invite over one thousand customers, mostly factory women, to a complimentary tea party. But he insisted that they listen to various speeches of the improving kind before they could collect their tea and buns. During one speech on good housekeeping, however, the audience grew restless, and here is how the *People's Journal* correspondent records the ensuing events:

> The intelligent advocate of this sentiment [domesticity] committed the error of speaking in a language far beyond the capacity of his auditory: it was florid, but without energy, and was protracted to improper length. Signs of impatience soon manifested themselves, and a low murmur of conversation gradually crept across the room: this was led off by the elderly females, until the gentle rill became a noisy torrent. The women, for the most part, used to speaking amid the sounds of revolving wheels, roaring straps, and flying spindles, elevated their tones to the accustomed pitch, and this Babel with its thousand tongues heeded little the reiterated demands for silence. The women audibly declared they wished the speaker would "hod his din." (39–40)

By blaming the speaker's lackluster performance for the women's refusal to listen, the *People's Journal* reporter ignores another possible interpretation—that the Leeds factory women responded with hostility to the content (and not the delivery) of the talk. Of course, to arrive at this conclusion, one must "brush history against the grain," history being in this case the written record preserved in the *People's Journal,* which can see only bad manners, unfeminine behavior, and chaos—"Babel with a thousand tongues"—in the women's response. But by initiating their own private communications during the speech, it is just possible that the women were articulating to each other their real concerns, hopes, and fears, while the speaker's attempts to inculcate in them the appropriate domestic virtues was in their opinion mere "din" impeding their own conversations.

The burning of Merryweather's conduct rules and the drowning out of a droning lecturer are such striking images of the working woman's rebellion against the imposition of the domestic ideal that one is tempted to forget that although these are dramatic forms of protest, both are inarticulate. As we have seen, the domestic ideal proved an excellent rhetorical tool in the hands of working-class men, who used it to great effect in the Ten Hours debates. But the domestic discourse divested women of an oppositional discourse when they stood in the greatest need of it and created myriad difficulties for working-class women writers like Fanny Forrester and Ellen Johnston, whose experiences fell outside of the narrow confines of Victorian domesticity. Neither Forrester, who worked in a Lancashire dye-mill and published scores of poems throughout the 1870s in *Ben Brierley's Journal,* nor Johnston, who worked in a number of mills in Scotland, England, and Ireland and published one volume of poetry before her early death in 1873, lived a life of uninterrupted domesticity. Producing more poetry (and poetry about factory life) than any other "factory girl" poets in the nineteenth century, Forrester and Johnston are a study in contrasts. Both were excluded from the cultural script of domesticity, but they registered that exclusion differently: Forrester laments her tragic position as a victim of industrialization, while Johnston eschews such victimology and figures herself as a Romantic rebel fleeing the constraints of domesticity.

To frame Forrester's and Johnston's collisions with domesticity, it might be useful to consider first the poetry of a woman who did not write within or against the domestic ideal. Active at the midcentury mark and publishing in the *People's and Howitt's Journal,* a successor to the *People's Journal* dedicated to finding a wider reading audience for working-class poets, is a Chorley factory worker who signed herself "Marie." Not yet fully enmeshed in the Victorian cult of domesticity, Marie could freely configure herself as a worker and a woman without lapsing into contradiction. For example, the subject matter of Marie's "Labour," a Carlylean paean to the creative powers of work, would not alone make it a remarkable poem. What distinguishes it from working-class poetry written later in the century, however, is the imagery Marie deploys to realize her vision of the better world that can be created through hard work. Unlike Edwin Waugh, who in "Down Again!" effaces women's childbirth labor, Marie turns to childbirth as a metaphor for all human labor:

> When great nature, in sore travail,
>     Bringeth forth her child—
> Some old nation in convulsion,
>     With new freedom wild!—
> Some long-borne and huge injustice
>     That in dumbness stood,
> Pouring out its new-born utt'rance
>     In a jargon flood!—
> Be thou calm and unaffrighted
>     'Tis but nature's heart
> Beating in her children's bosom,
>     Bidding wrong depart.
> Ages are her fleeting moments,—
>     World-times are her years—
> In immensity she singeth
>     'Mid the shining spheres—
>
> 'Hark, hark, to God's heart beating;
>     Time is on the wing,
> Labour is the only worship
>     Any soul can bring!'          (lines 61–80)

Syntactical irregularities aside, by heralding labor's infinite capacity to form worlds anew, the poem celebrates creativity as procreativity:

work is both natural and "naturally" feminine. Instead of envisioning women's work as a perversion of the natural order, Marie can represent woman as a natural worker because women and work were not divorced in her mind.

Marie embraces the larger political struggles of her fellow workers and produces poems full of class-conscious rhetoric, bearing such outsized heroic titles as "Idealize the Real and Realize the Ideal," "Fellow Workers," "The Indomitable Will," and "Encouragement." Like some latter-day figure of Liberty leading the people, Marie writes to advance the cause of the working classes:

> Though ignored our lowly lot,
> Scornful glances harm us not;
> We accept our homely fate:
> And a beauteous life create;—
> From earth's bosom, brown and bare,
> Flowerets draw their colours rare;
> And though *we* are seeming stinted
> All our days are rainbow-tinted
>          By our noble will!
>
> Come there failure or success,
> We march on in nobleness;
> Naught can come amiss or wrong,
> If the soul be true and strong,
> On, and up, courageously!
> And our banner's motto be
> "Hope and work, with heart and hand—
> Naught can finally withstand
>          Those of earnest will!"
>
>            ("The Indomitable Will" lines 37–54)

Significantly, Marie represents class struggle from the position of the first person plural and includes herself in the empowering "we" of class solidarity. By identifying herself as a worker without the qualifying adjectives of gender, Marie reveals an understanding of the word *worker* that encompasses both men and women.

In the two decades dividing Marie from Fanny Forrester, we can place the final triumph of the domestic ideal. By the mid-1870s, the confluence of woman and worker called up contradictory and self-defeating images in the poetry of Fanny Forrester. Forrester entered a Salford dye-works at the age of twelve, but by twenty she was regularly publishing in *Ben Brierley's Journal,* which Vicinus characterizes as a "Lancashire working man's *Punch*" (*The Industrial Muse* 202). Her poetry ranges from somewhat lugubrious narratives of urban living to vaguely Romantic invocations of the preindustrial past; however, when focused on Manchester life, her poetry reveals the impediments a working-class woman faced when attempting to write about factory girls in the golden age of domesticity.

To some degree, Forrester was aware of her dilemma because in "The Lowly Bard" (1873), a humble male poet who is the poem's speaker and Forrester's public persona "mourns the incompleteness of his lyre" (line 8), a dissatisfaction justified by the poem's inability to find the appropriate poetic language for its subject: working-class women in the industrial city. Although Forrester wishes to make heroines out of mill hands, she knows that they are not conventionally heroic, and the tension between the poetic language of Victorian femininity and the prosaic reality of her female operatives threatens the poem's intelligibility:

> And o'er great looms slight figures lowly stoop
> And weary shadows cross their girlish faces
>   That like frail flowers o'er stagnant waters droop.
>
> Toil, toil to-day, and toil again tomorrow;
>   Some weave their warp to reach a pauper grave!
> Naught of romance doth gild their *common* sorrow;
>   Yet ne'er were heroines more strong, more brave.
>
> (lines 22–28)

Forrester uses the clichéd comparison of drooping flowers and mill girls even though she understands the inadequacy of this simile to capture and record the lives of her weavers. Despite the willowy weakness and fey feminine charm Forrester attributes to her workers, in the end she destabilizes her own characterization of them by acknowledging their strength and bravery. Enmeshed in a representational system that could see factory women only as victims (frail flowers needing the shelter of the domestic nook), Forrester cannot articulate coherently the life of a laborer like herself, and if she stumbles into contradictions, it is because a working woman in the 1870s *was* a contradiction, at least ideologically.

Unable to translate her own experiences of survival and success into poetic form, Forrester invariably depicts the industrial milieu as anathema to female life. Her inaugural piece in *Ben Brierley's Journal,* the three-part "Strangers in the City," which appeared in the spring of 1870, recounts the woeful tale of a young Irish woman who migrates to the city and dies shortly thereafter, worn out by her daily contact with the mill.[23] Yet this tragic emplotment, which recalls Charlotte Elizabeth Tonna's *Helen Fleetwood,* runs counter to what we know of the outlines of Forrester's life. The daughter of Irish immigrants who fled potato-blighted Ireland for Manchester, Forrester experienced early hardships that seem to have colored her outlook. Still, she went on to modest success as a popular contributor to *Brierley's Journal,* arousing so much reader interest that in 1875 the magazine took the unusual step of printing a biographical notice. In it, Brierley highlights the disconnections between Forrester's poetry and the poet's life: "She writes of fields and flowers as of things with which her earlier years were unacquainted, as treasures only reflected in books, or dreamt of in her dreams, and with which her soul yearns for companionship. We are assured that beyond the range of Peel Park [in Manchester], outward nature has hitherto been a sealed book to her; and that her studies of human life and character have been confined to the experiences of the mill and the dye-house" ("Fanny Forrester" 37). Brierley alludes to the fact that poems with urban settings like "The Lowly Bard" and "Strangers in the City" stand out as exceptions because most of Forrester's poetry recalls, in a plangent and irreconcilable voice, a sanitized, picturesque Ireland that the poet could never possibly have known. No doubt correctly, he surmises that her inspiration comes from other books, most likely those written by Romantic poets or by expressive female poets such as Felicia Hemans; and none of these poetic predecessors could provide her with a language for representing the lives of modern mill women with anything other than self-pity or evasion.[24]

In the end, it might be easy to dismiss Forrester for reproducing middle-class cultural norms by accepting bourgeois standards of femininity and judging herself and other factory girls by them. But Pamela Fox urges us to resist what she calls the "reproduction-resistance circuit" (3), whereby we evaluate working-class texts according to the degree to which they reproduce or resist hegemonic discourses. While clearly conservative in its adherence to Victorian conventions of femininity, Forrester's poetry recalls Fox's caveat: "What we identify as a 'conformist' attitude or position may be rooted in another kind of transgressive logic that is equally (if not more) compelling than the need to challenge capitalist or patriarchal ideologies directly" (19). Fox argues that while working-class women "were hardly oblivious to their predicament *as* women, they also sought to convince themselves that they *were* women by writing themselves into a middle-class feminine script," and she demands that feminist scholars acknowledge that script's desirability to "those it excludes" (103). It is just this script that Forrester tries to write herself into, and while one would not wish to overplay the "transgressive logic" of Forrester's poetry, it does underscore the gap between the Victorian domestic ideal and its reality, thereby indirectly challenging the ideal's status as an accurate representation of working-class life.

If Forrester undermines the domestic ideal from within, Ellen Johnston attacks it from without, through a daring and perhaps reckless frontal assault. A self-professed "self-taught scholar" (7), Johnston tries to resolve the dilemma facing working-class women writers like Forrester by turning to the Romantic tradition of rebellion, a literary model that encourages the oppositional, confrontational stance Johnston adopts in her *Autobiography, Poems and Songs*.[25] Casting herself as a Romantic rebel, Johnston engages in Miltonic inversions, transforming the heaven of working-class domesticity into a hell and, in turn, Blake's "dark, Satanic mills" into a personal paradise. As a result, she breeches the walls of the working-class home and lets some light shine into the unexposed and unexplored corners of the domestic ideal.

In the autobiographical preface to her poems, Ellen Johnston flatly rejects domesticity and reinvents herself as a Romantic heroine. She proudly boasts, "Mine were not the common trials of every day life, but like those strange romantic ordeals attributed to the imaginary heroines of 'Inglewood Forest' " (5); and, in fact, her life story does resemble something out of Byron's poetry or an overplotted Victorian romance. When her father decides to emigrate to America, her mother refuses to go; shortly after hearing false reports of her husband's death, she remarries, only to die from the shock when he unexpectedly returns years later. Meanwhile, left fatherless in Scotland, Johnston undergoes the first of her uncommon trials, one she alludes to as "the mystery of my life" (9). Although she remains highly circumspect throughout, she manages to convey the fact that as a child she suffered at the hands of her abusive (and perhaps sexually abusive) stepfather, whose attentions forced her as a young girl to run away from her mother's house "for safety and protection" (9).

Given her early history, it is scarcely surprising that Johnston never sentimentalizes the domestic sphere. Indeed, when the home appears at all in her poetry, it does so as a den of terror, as in "The Drunkard's Wife," a harrowing account of her aunt's unhappy marriage to an alcoholic. Ellen Johnston could have scripted her life as a domestic tragedy—as a cautionary tale about failed domesticity—but since she sees herself not as a victim but as a bohemian free spirit, she chooses instead to celebrate herself and her life with Whitmanesque energy, exulting in her homelessness and embracing the open road as a symbol of her liberation. She compares herself to a wandering Jew and proudly recalls her life's travelogue: "I have mingled with the gay on the shores of France—I have feasted in the merry halls of England—I have danced on the shamrock soil of Erin's green isle" (5). Even more daringly, she openly proclaims her moral wanderings and then, true to form, refuses to repent the birth of an illegitimate daughter: "I did not, however, feel inclined to die when I could no longer conceal what the world falsely calls a woman's shame. No, on the other hand, I never loved life more dearly and longed for the hour when I would have something to love me—and my wish was realised by becoming the mother of a lovely daughter on the 14th of September, 1852" (11). Having read an abundance of nineteenth-century fiction, Johnston knows that a proper Victorian lady, on becoming a single mother, should engage in some self-destructive display, but she gamely declines to play the role of the shame-ridden woman.

Glorifying her outcast state, Johnston rejoices in the motherhood that brands her a fallen woman.[26]

Of course, as a woman who worked in a factory and wrote poetry, Johnston was already outside the categories of conventional representation, especially in the eyes of her upper-class readers, for whom the autobiographical preface was written. "Self-taught writers were regarded as much as social phenomena as writers of serious poetry" (85), Maidment reminds us in "Essayists and Artizans." Wealthy Victorians were as interested in the lives of working-class poets as they were in the poetry itself, and Johnston's awareness of the fact that her celebrity derived at least in part from the novelty of her situation prompted her to write "An Address to Nature on Its Cruelty":

> Learned critics who have seen them [her verses]
> Says origin dwells within them;
> But when myself perchance they see,
> They laugh and say, 'O is it she?
> Well, I think the little boaster
> Is nothing but a fair impostor;
> She looks so poor-like and so small,
> She's next unto a nought-at-all;
> Such wit and words quite out-furl
> The learning of "A Factory Girl." '                    (lines 11–20)

Factory girls were not supposed to write poetry, nor were they supposed to be the subject of poetry. Surely for the aristocratic readers of Johnston's autobiography, like the duke of Buccleuch and the earl of Enniskillen, both of whom appear on the subscriber list, the factory girl would have been beyond the pale of respectable representation, which situated pure women in the domestic space. Perhaps trumpeting herself as a (sexually) fallen woman in the autobiography allowed her to be comfortable with what she ideologically already was: a woman who had fallen out of her proper sphere. In fact, one senses that, at least imaginatively, Johnston relishes her status as a fallen woman, finding power and a transformational energy in her emancipation from the constraints of Victorian womanhood.

By reversing the social and moral hierarchy of working-class domesticity, Johnston's factory poems sustain the rebellious posture that she assumes in the autobiographical preface. "Kennedy's Dear Mill," which Johnston probably wrote as an occasional piece to commemorate a factory outing or social event, upends the tropes of dialect poetry:

> And freedom's glorious shrine
> Is center'd in thy walls;
> No tyrant knave to bind,
> No slavish chain enthrals.
> The workers are as free
> As the sunshine on the hill;
> Thy breath is liberty
> Oh! Kennedy's dear mill.                    (lines 41–48)

While dialect domesticity usually figures the working-class home as an escape from the regimentation and regulations of factory life, in "Kennedy's Dear Mill" Johnston locates her freedom in a weaving shed; and then, to complete her break with the domestic discourse, she claims to find a home in Kennedy's mill and a family among her fellow mill workers. The mill rather than the home emerges as the emotional center of her life, so that all the affection and familial loyalty (and even the air of sanctification) that the dialect poets ascribe to the domestic sphere, she transfers to the factory:

> Thou hast a secret spell
> For all as well as me;
> Each girl loves thee well
> That ever wrought in thee.
> They may leave thy blessed toil;
> But, find work they will,
> They return back in a while
> To Kennedy's dear mill.                    (lines 17–24)

In fact, to be out of work for Johnston is to be removed from her spiritual home and to become an expatriate from paradise, a "factory exile" who writes love poems full of passionate longing for the mill she left behind: "Thou lovely verdant Factory! What binds my heart to thee? / Why art thou centered in my soul, twined round my memory?" ("The Factory Exile" lines 1–2).

An extraordinary poem, "The Factory Exile" relates a love affair gone wrong in the pastoral "verdant Factory" of the poem's opening stanza:[27]

> With tear-dimm'd eyes through fancy's veil I gaze upon thy walls;
> Their bright enamelled golden tinge my bleeding heart enthrals,
> I deem I am what once I was, still bending o'er my loom,
> And musing on a lovely form of beauty's sweetest bloom.
>
> (lines 5–8)

Deceived by the "lovely form" of line 8, she leaves the factory "disgraced, degraded, never more within thy walls to toil" (line 30). Yet Johnston narrates her "exile" not as a fall but as a betrayal:

> But God alone can only tell the base and cold reward
> That he gave me in return for such a true regard;
> He scattered thorns across my path, calumny o'er my name,
> And crushed the blossoms of my hope—the laurels of my fame.
>
> (lines 21–24).

Duped and (in Johnston's account) slandered by her lover, Johnston is exiled from the factory, transgressively configured in the poem as the site of genuine human emotions (her "true regard") and of respectability, since his "calumny," probably of the kiss-and-tell variety, gets her fired from the "verdant" factory where, so it would seem, even the merest hint of sexual scandal is not tolerated. Strikingly, Johnston's factory more closely resembles the privatized domestic sphere of dialect poetry than it does the dangerous and polluting place evident in blue book, parliamentary, and novelistic accounts from the 1830s and 1840s.

One could explain Johnston's factory effusions as a subtle parody of domesticity's oversentimentalization of the home, but her attachment to the factories seems sincere, grounded both in the treasured freedom she associates with mill life and in the sense of self-worth, perhaps not otherwise available to an unwed mother in

Victorian Scotland, that it affords her. If one considers the generally low status of the Victorian working-class woman, and the even lower status of domestic labor, factory work provided Johnston with one of the few areas in which she could achieve a certain standing and dignity. Frequently boasting of her prowess at the loom and relating all the praises her various employers have heaped upon her, Johnston seems to be as proud of her weaving skills as she is of her poetic ones. Her self-confidence is bolstered by the knowledge that she is a sound craftsman, a skilled worker with words and with wool.

While Johnston may have found in the radical strain of Romantic thought a paradigm that allowed her to validate her identity as a factory girl, she was also liberated by having no specific models from "high" art on which to pattern her industrial verses, since the Romantic poets left behind no body of factory poetry with which she needed to contend.[28] However, when she appropriates the subject matter of the Romantics as well as their subversive posture, the pressures exerted by male literary models and the ideology of femininity enclosed within them transform her sexual politics; and at these moments Johnston and Forrester most closely resemble one another. Johnston's few nonindustrial poems, mixed cocktails of Scott and early Wordsworth, reaffirm certain conservative notions of femininity that her autobiographical material repudiates. In one particularly Wordsworthian effort, the heroine of an ersatz lyrical ballad entitled "The Maniac of the Green Wood" is rejected by her lover and confirms her maiden modesty and innate femininity by going mad. Yet at the same time and in the same volume, Johnston's autobiography recounts a life that contains considerably more trying events than an unhappy love affair. Johnston survives child abuse, periods of unemployment, bouts of illness, and the experience of single motherhood; and through it all she retains a remarkable degree of optimism and emerges from the text as a resilient individual, the spiritual kin of the stalwart Lucy Luck. When Johnston imitates male literary models that embody conventional Victorian notions of femininity, her poetry loses any sense of fidelity to her own experience. Johnston's text, which juxtaposes autobiography and a scattering of poems straining to emulate canonical forms, opens up and lays bare the divide between male literary traditions and the working-class woman's realities.

In spite of her achievements, Johnston may have shattered one hall of mirrors only to have moved to another room in the patriarchal fun house. For while she can exuberantly proclaim, "A thousand times I'd be a Factory Girl," the epic celebration of herself throughout the *Autobiography, Poems and Songs* comes at a price. She may find a liberating voice in the rhetoric of Romantic rebellion, but that voice traps her into reinforcing the governing cultural assumptions about the immorality of working girls. Johnston presents herself to the reader as a fallen woman—a single mother, a sexual being, and a troublemaker. So in spite of her avowed enthusiasm for mill life, she implicitly acknowledges that to be a female factory worker is to have fallen out of one's proper sphere: she upends the domestic ideal only to reaffirm its hegemony within working-class culture.

But even if, in the final analysis, she fails to escape the dominance of the domestic ideal, Johnston succeeds in articulating experiences that could not be reconciled with the dictates of domesticity. By recounting her own private life—one filled with abandonment, abuse, and alcoholism—Johnston painfully reveals the essentially fictional nature of the working-class domestic ideal. But who knows how many women, lacking Johnston's daring, confrontational zeal, were dissuaded from writing about their own lives as women, wives, and workers? While the discourse of domesticity cannot alone account for the silence of working-class women in the Victorian period, clearly domesticity reinforced it. Domesticity may have embodied the dreams and desires of the Victorian working man, but by refusing to grant the working-class woman her class identity, it muted her voice.

And this leaves us with a conspicuous irony. The Victorian mill girl was ultimately silenced by a culture that initially embraced her as its emblem of what modernity portended. But then, given that the mill girl was so frequently conjured up as an apocalyptic figure of revolution, perhaps it should not surprise us that the threat of chaos she embodied was exorcised by a divide-and-conquer strategy, a discursive dismemberment into her constituent parts: "woman" and "worker."

# CONCLUSION

# Past and Present

## *The Industrial Revolution in a (Victorian) Post-Industrial World*

THIS BOOK began with Disraeli's young hero effortlessly dismissing the "wonderful city" of Manchester and the brave new world of industrialism it represented. As we have seen, Coningsby was not the only British man in the early nineteenth century wishing that industrialism would simply go away, like a bad cold. In reaction to the social dislocations of infant industrialism, the canonical male critics turned to the past to restore order to their disordered universe, frequently represented by the figure of a factory girl. Responding to the same set of social disruptions (and similarly figuring a working woman at the center of them), laboring-class men also looked to the past, first to the vanishing pastoral world of rural England and then to the earthly Eden of yeomanry England the dialect poets hoped to resurrect inside the worker's cottage.

No moment exists among the works of nineteenth-century women writers that corresponds to Coningsby's vanishing act. They did not dismiss the industrial revolution, nor did they see its upheavals in such cosmic, ill-boding terms. Indeed, they embraced the industrial present, either to celebrate it (in the manner of Gaskell, Brontë, and Johnston) or to critique and repair it (in the manner of Trollope, Tonna, and Forrester), just as they embraced the mill girl, either as a model of feminist liberation or as a victim of man's greed for industrial gains.

It is important to note, however, that most of the major figures in this study—Carlyle, Disraeli, Dickens, Gaskell, Brontë, Tonna, Trollope, and the Chartist writers—belong to the period before midcentury, when the meaning of Carlyle's strange new today was an open question. The exceptions—Arnold, the dialect poets, Forrester, and Johnston—belong to a later discourse, one that has accepted the permanency of the industrial revolution and actively engages in its containment and domestication. And once the industrial revolution became something that could be contained, the condition-of-England (as well as the disposition-of-England) debate was over. In the second half of the nineteenth century, the industrial revolution got absorbed into the fabric of British life. But it did so on terms that checked the more radical social disruptions it promised, in part by breaking the link between industrialism and sexual anarchy that was so central to the early factory debates. The great Victorian fear of the "perverse" gender arrangements emerging in the textile districts was to a large extent allayed by the passage of the Ten Hours Bill, which signaled to laboring men that the state was willing to promote their patriarchal dominance by guaranteeing women's subordinate position in the job market. At roughly the same time, industrial labor began to shed its initial association with male unemployment and female employment as male-dominated trades like engineering and metal work came to eclipse textile production as representatively modern. So after several decades as the focal point for the nation's apprehensions about the future and the nature of cultural change, the industrial revolution ceased to be the laboratory of modernity. That locus of shifting anxieties took up residence in London, and to gauge responses to modernity after 1850 the Victorians looked to the great southern metropolis, not Manchester, which gradually lost its cachet as a shock city.[1]

One need only turn to George Eliot's *Felix Holt, the Radical* (1866) to measure the distance between the industrial novels of the 1830s and 1840s and those produced later in the century. Written on the eve of the Second Reform Bill and set immediately after the passage of the First Reform Bill, *Felix Holt* is frequently read as a belated and unsatisfying industrial novel.[2] Yet it might be more fitting to read it as a postindustrial novel. Eliot's novelistic license and her own deep interest in history push her beyond the containment strategies that mark texts from the same decade, such as *Culture and Anarchy* and dialect poetry, to write a fictionalized history of the early nineteenth century. Eliot's history of England re-presents the industrial revolution as a past historical event and conveniently "forgets" the central role gender played in early industrial discourses. For these reasons, it is useful to pause and consider briefly Eliot's novel, which exemplifies how later Victorian culture mythologized the industrial revolution in order both to excise it from an emerging definition of Englishness and to naturalize the restabilized gender relations of the post-1850 world.

Made up of the arms and limbs of the condition-of-England texts that precede it, *Felix Holt* is a Frankenstein's monster: *Past and Present, Sybil, Marian Withers, and Mary Barton* all seem to have gone into its writing.[3] Yet in spite of the novel's overwhelming indebtedness to the literature of industrialism, very little industrial material is evident. The working conditions and grievances of the text's representative industrial workers, the rioting Sproxton miners, are so thoroughly effaced that one must turn to the Arnoldian "eternal Spirit of the Populace" to account for the men's violence. Of course, given Carlyle's influence on both Arnold and Eliot (and on all the "active and superior" minds of their generation), we should not be surprised at this dematerialization. The novel's eponymous working-class hero, who rejects his father's quack medicines as well as his own career in medicine, has walked out of the pages of *Past and Present*. No Morrison's Pills, no parliamentary solutions for Felix Holt, who—as the Carlylean hero should—believes that the disposition of the English working classes is wrong and only education can right it.

But while *Felix Holt* dematerializes the world of Victorian industrialism in the great tradition of the male critics, it also performs a more elaborate disappearing trick: it erases the industrial revolution by actively sealing it off from the text's multiple present tenses, which are engendered by the thirty-year gap between the novel's writing and its setting. To begin with, Eliot marginalizes the industrial revolution so that it only exists, in barely perceptive form, on the text's margins. It appears briefly during the famous coach ride through the Midlands that begins the narrative and reappears at the end as the elliptically invoked "ugly, wicked, miserable" (224) factory town where Felix will begin his life's work of educating the badly disposed working classes. Given the novel's conclusion, industrial modernity becomes something that is part of Felix's future but is exorcised from the novel's here-and-now (the early 1830s) and the reader's experience of it.

Moreover, the device of the coach ride, with its deceptive topographical account of the Midlands in the early 1830s, allows Eliot to exorcise the industrial revolution from the reader's present (the mid-1860s) and place it back into the reader's past:

> There were trim cheerful villages too, with a neat or handsome parsonage and grey church set in the midst; there was the pleasant tinkle of the blacksmith's anvil, the patient cart-horses waiting at his door; the basket-maker peeling his willow wands in the sunshine; the wheelwright putting the last touch to a blue cart with red wheels. . . . The passenger on the box could see that this was the district of protuberant optimists, sure that old England was the best of all possible countries, and that if there were any facts which had not fallen under their own observation, they were facts not worth observing: the district of clean little market-towns without manufacturers, of fat livings, an aristocratic clergy, and low poor-rates. But as the day wore on the scene would change: the land would begin to be blackened with coal-pits, the rattle of handlooms to be heard in hamlets and villages. . . . The breath of the manufacturing town, which made a cloudy day and a red gloom by night on the horizon, diffused itself over all the surrounding country, filling the air with eager unrest. Here was a population not convinced that old England was as good as possible. (7–8)

Certainly, this passage could be read as offering the familiar juxtaposition of past and present. Weighing an uncompromising vision of the present against an idealized, partial vision of the past, Eliot imposes on the countryside what Raymond Williams in *The Country and the City* identifies as a "willing illusion" (179) of peace and prosperity. By stacking the deck against the present in such a way, Eliot shows her hand: the woman who berated Victorian medievalism as an "aristocratic dilettantism which attempts to restore the 'good old times' by a sort of idyllic masquerading" ("Natural History" 178) is not above engaging in her own pleasant masquerade about the good old days.

Yet the passage also allows another interpretation—that there is no present here to be adjudged against a superior past. If one takes into account Eliot's repetition of "old England" and the historical perspective of the reader (the 1860s looking back on the 1830s), Eliot does not seem to be contrasting past and present so much as asking the reader to compare two starkly differentiated versions of old England: the sunshine world of contented village craftsmen (blacksmiths, basket-makers, and wheelwrights) and its shadowy counterpart, the world of discontented, dissenting industrial laborers. Disraeli's notion of the two nations, the rich and the poor, has been modified by Eliot, who imagines two national pasts, one rich in human contentment and one poor in it. In *Felix Holt*, the England of "dark, Satanic mills" emerges as one version of the national past, to be set along side its idealized Other (the preindustrial, prelapsarian, and mostly mythic world of the English countryside), so that the novel's hero can choose which England—merry old England or miserable old England—he wishes to claim as his inheritance.

However, Eliot's attempt to contain the industrial revolution by historicizing it proves difficult to sustain, and these difficulties nearly overwhelm the text when Felix tries to defend his choice of one inheritance over the other. Within the novel, Eliot localizes the two national inheritances as Felix's competing family inheritances: his parents' legacy of bourgeois professionalism versus his uncle's legacy of handicraft production. By deciding to follow the career path of his weaver uncle, Felix chooses the sunshine world of village craftsmen as the inheritance that will promise greater happiness and ensure a genuine continuity with the past. "My father was a weaver first of all," Felix explains. "It would have been better for him if he had remained a weaver still. I came home through Lancashire and saw an uncle of mine who is a weaver still. I mean to stick to the class I belong to—people who don't follow the fashions" (57). Felix does remain loyal to his family's artisanal traditions, but by becoming a watchmaker rather than a weaver, and this is a subtle but nonetheless revealing change. For it uncovers the text's silent conspiracy to evade one fact—that industrialism has already disrupted and transformed the handicraft world Felix wishes to join. By switching Felix's career, Eliot can ignore the eventual extinction of England's handloom weavers and the obstacles Felix would have faced as a handloom weaver in the early 1830s because by that point in history England's handloom weavers were an endangered species. While Eliot's most famous weaver, Silas Marner, could make a respectable living at the turn of the century, three decades later price reductions and the introduction of powerloom weaving had forced handloom weavers to "the edge— and sometimes beyond the edge—of the borders of starvation" (E. P. Thompson 286). Felix's father wisely abandoned his trade, and Felix's offhand remark that "it would have been better" if his father had remained a weaver does violence to the tragic history of Britain's handloom weavers in the nineteenth century.

To have allowed Felix to become a handloom weaver would merely have highlighted the discontinuities between England's rural past and its industrial present that Eliot wishes to obscure. Indeed, the only way Felix could remain in the family trade is if he became a powerloom weaver. But for Eliot to represent industrialism in its most memorable form—Lancashire textile production—is to acknowledge that the industrial revolution is not a discrete past event but an ever-present reality that has permanently transformed the "traditional" English countryside, populated in 1866 by the ghostly remains of once-thriving weaving communities. So when Felix rejects the mobility of modernism and its transformational potential for artisanal rootedness—thereby rejecting change for continuity—that continuity is a sham that his conversion into a watchmaker obscures. In truth, Felix Holt belongs to the 1860s. He is a figure in tune with the arts and crafts movement, one who self-consciously repudiates modernity in favor of craft production and the golden age it metonymically recalls.[4] Yet by switching Felix's craft from weaving to watchmaking, Eliot (like her hero) tries to repair time and undo the industrial revolution. She acknowledges the industrial revolution's place in English history by placing it in the past so that the English past can be brought forward into the present *as the present*. In this way, Eliot retains her broadly progressive vision of history and at the same time represents the industrial revolution as the bad, old news.

When read as an early, fictionalized history of nineteenth-century industrialism, *Felix Holt* is remarkable not only for its depiction of the industrial revolution as a historical event, but for its curious dismissal of gender from the heart of England's industrial crises. Unlike the earlier industrial novels, *Felix Holt* is not set in the textile districts, and it displays miners (instead of mill workers) as the typical industrial laborers. Moreover, these miners do not seem to have any female relatives, since not one appears in the text, and Felix's scheme of educating the working classes extends only to working-class boys. Eliot's complete erasure of working-class women is all the more striking because in the early 1830s, women in mining communities still worked underground in the pits; and when the 1842 Mines Regulation Act legislated women out of the pits, they worked above ground as pit brow lasses. To be sure, the immediate concern behind *Felix Holt* is the Second Reform Bill and the enfranchisement of working-class men, which Eliot feared would hand political power over to people the novel labels "blind and foolish" (224). But that a middle-class woman like Eliot could take up the complex weave of issues surrounding the industrial working classes, political power, and social stability without addressing the "problem" of women's work testifies to the sea change that occurred in the industrial discourse after midcentury. What *Felix Holt* registers, in its erasure of the working-class woman from the industrial world, is that by the 1860s, the Victorian mill girl had shed her subversive aura and had lost her iconic power to shock, repel, or excite.

Although the mill girl functioned as the domestic woman's Other throughout the industrial debates in the 1830s and 1840s, working-class women became increasingly domesticated—both symbolically and socially—as the century advanced.[5] Demonized as dirty, promiscuous, and insufficiently feminine by critics inside and outside their own class, working-class women who had once struck, demonstrated, and rioted alongside their fathers and husbands retreated from public life in the second half of the century. A combination of forces, ranging from their desire for respectability to their enforced secondary position in the job market, from their hope for reformed marital relations to their exhaustion from working the double shift, made domesticity an attractive and, by the turn of the century, attainable goal for working-class women.[6] As Elizabeth Roberts observes in her oral history of working-class women from 1890 to 1940, "Their emancipation lay, in their estimation, in the move *away* from work and into the home" (137).

One index of just how thoroughly domesticated the working-class wife became in the late Victorian imagination can be discovered in this palpable irony: having been represented by contemporary observers in the first half of the century as a domestic failure (a bad cook, a lousy mother, and a slovenly housekeeper), the working-class woman emerged in the second half as a figure who needed to be protected from domesticity's failures (spousal abuse, desertion, extortion). In 1870, the first Married Women's Property Act gave working-class women control of their own earnings under the assumption "that women would be working because of their husband's fecklessness and would therefore need legal protection for their earnings." A few years later, in 1878, working-class women earned the right to sue for separation and maintenance from their husbands, a right granted in response to Frances Power Cobbe's campaign against spousal abuse, characterized by Cobbe as "wife-torture" (Lewis 47). If the image of the mill girl as transgressively independent vied with the image of her as helpless victim in the early industrial debates, then one could say that the less threatening image triumphed after mid-century, and the working-class woman came to be figured in the official discourses of the state as demanding and deserving legislative protection.[7]

In this cultural milieu, feminist novels that specifically connected the industrial revolution to female emancipation were no longer tenable. Both Charlotte Brontë and Elizabeth Gaskell had recruited the factory girl to be their standard-bearer for the liberatory possibilities of the industrial revolution: the independent factory girl set free from patriarchal control by her pay packet was the very model of the modern working woman. But this feminist vision of the industrial revolution, formulated in the 1830s and 1840s, could not survive those chaotic years. As working-class women adopted the domestic ideology after midcentury, the alliance of interests between women of all classes upon which the feminist novels depended visibly fractured. Working women came to see their liberation in the move out of the public sphere, at the same time that middle-class feminists defined their liberation in conspicuously opposite terms, in the move from the private to the public sphere. The rancorous split that occurred between "equal rights" feminists and laboring women activists over protective legislation in the second half of the century is an indication of just how divisive these different interpretations of "women's liberation" were.

Of course, Gaskell's and Brontë's feminist vision of the industrial revolution could not even survive their novels' conclusions, which end with the heroine safely and perhaps sadly married off. The two novelists cannot transcend either the patriarchal configurations that stubbornly refuse to fade away, or their own class assumptions, which, in the case of Mary Barton, make work morally suspect and, in the cases of Caroline Helstone, Shirley Keeldar, and Margaret Hale, make well-paid work nearly impossible to obtain. Unable to sustain the "masculine" traits of independence and assertiveness in their heroines, they settle for the reverse. They feminize their industrial heroes by making them realize the limitations of such masculine notions as free will: Carson, Thornton, and Moore are all punished for their hubris with a fall that allows them to emerge duly chastened and transformed from hardened entrepreneurs into benevolent masters, willing to acknowledge the human dimensions of the workplace. Given each novel's sober conclusion, which records the failure of industrialism to fashion the world anew for middle-class women, it is no wonder that Gaskell's and Brontë's feminist embrace of the industrial revolution has gone unnoticed.

Like the novels of Gaskell and Brontë, those written by Frances Trollope and Charlotte Elizabeth Tonna have an unpredictable trajectory: both *Michael Armstrong* and *Helen Fleetwood* start as conservative tracts supporting Lord Ashley's factory reforms only to end up as surprisingly subversive critiques of nascent industrialism. By projecting domesticity's separate spheres onto the industrial realm, they fashion a materialist critique of domesticity that reveals commodity fetishization to be integral to both capitalism and domesticity. In the course of undoing this fetishization, they generate a vision of industrial production as inimical to human life, although they ultimately retreat from this vision because it is a self-defeating one in the context of a reform movement. So while Brontë's and Gaskell's enthusiasm for industrialism's liberating potential can easily be over-looked because of the conservative note on which their novels con-clude, Trollope's and Tonna's truly radical critiques of industrialism at the center of their fictions can just as easily be overlooked because of the conservative note on which their texts commence and conclude.

But when it comes to carving out a space for middle-class women in the brave new world of the factories, all four women nov-elists arrive at very similar solutions, even if they take different routes to get there. To bridge the divide between their representation of the factory world as profoundly incurable and their explicit desire to cure it through the Ten Hours Bill, Tonna and Trollope turn their backs on male political power in order to insert middle-class women into the public sphere, whether it be as Trollope's oddly egalitarian female paternalist or Tonna's female philanthropist. Given the dynamics of Victorian culture and the sway the domestic ideology held over the nineteenth-century social imagination, it is not surprising that Gas-kell and Brontë ultimately transform their middle-class heroines into social missionaries as well: Margaret Hale, Shirley Keeldar, and Car-oline Helstone all end up as the helpmates of their public-minded husbands. What all four women novelists discover is that the surest way to guarantee middle-class women access to the public sphere is through the ideology of domesticity. But *Shirley* and *North and South* powerfully insist that this kind of female power is consolatory, the next best thing to the genuine article—direct political power and female independence through waged work—that the industrial world briefly seemed to promise Victorian women.

In spite of the impact these novels had on their contemporary readers by forwarding the Ten Hours Movement or reminding mid-dle-class women of their social mission, the vision of modernity that had the most lasting influence was the one that out-and-out repu-diated industrialism. Indeed, the anti-industrial writings of Carlyle, Disraeli, Dickens, and Ruskin even had a measurable impact on Vic-torian industrialists, and the factory world that took shape after mid-century resembled the one imagined by its severest critics. "Carlyle and Ruskin's elevation of the employer as the Captain of Industry was taken seriously by the big employers," Patrick Joyce notes in his study of the paternalist culture of the late Victorian factory (*Work,*

*Society, and Politics* 143). The great northern factory firms refashioned themselves as benignly paternalistic and built employee loyalty through attractive benefits that included workers' dinners, trips, libraries, canteens, and gymnasiums. So strongly did this paternalistic vision of the workplace influence a generation of industrialists that feudalized factory towns of the sort proposed by Disraeli even sprung up, the most famous being Titus Salt's Saltaire on the outskirts of Bradford. And while one might think that paternalism contradicted the millocracy's devotion to laissez-faire capitalism, Joyce convincingly argues that paternalism is its "inevitable consequence" (140) because voluntary paternalism advertised abroad that enlightened factory owners could protect employees without the meddling of the state. In the end, the British manufacturer adopted paternalism as part of his social duty and slowly forfeited the entrepreneurial ideal for the gentlemanly one. The late Victorian factory owner was a new dog taught old tricks.

Factory paternalism and working-class domesticity proved to be remarkably complementary in the second half of the century, and this no doubt helped to lessen class antagonisms. Upper-class paternalism (with its roots in Victorian medievalism) and working-class domesticity (with its roots in the Chartist movement) were central to the formation of masculine identity in the nineteenth century, which was reconstituted along lines that emphasized British men as caretakers. The factory paternalist shouldered the responsibility for the welfare of his employees, while the respectable working man shouldered the responsibility for the welfare of his family and—through co-ops, friendly societies, and trade unions—for the welfare of the community as well. Instead of impinging on the working man's fierce independence, factory paternalism upheld it by reconstructing the factory in the image of the patriarchal family through the "combined strategies of paternalism and a rigorously enforced vertical segregation of labour by sex" (Lown, *Women* 214). Factory paternalism ensured patriarchal dominance within the working class and thereby bolstered the working man's own definition of masculine respectability, which rested on his ability to maintain a family at home through his role as breadwinner. Although the nineteenth-century working man may no longer have been an independent producer of goods, the dependency of a wife and children went some way to compensate for his loss.[8]

In addition to their conjoint patriarchal interests, factory paternalism and working-class domesticity also shared a fundamental antimodern bias, since both had their roots (via medievalism and Chartism) in the male repudiations of early industrialism's social dislocations. They are interrelated manifestations of an unofficial social compact entered into by a wide array of Englishmen, ranging from factory workers and factory owners to more likely sources of opposition to industrial modernity, such as the clergy, the aristocracy, and the professional classes, which produced in the years after 1850 a definition of Englishness that "denied its chief characteristics—the rise of industry" (Wiener 41). Like Felix Holt, when faced with the choice of competing national inheritances, late Victorian culture chose the green and pleasant idyll of merry old England over the "six counties overhung with smoke" of modernity.

This antimodernism transcended Britain's political and class divisions to emerge as a truly national ideal, deeply embedded in the social perceptions of its people.[9] Its pervasiveness helps to explain a figure as seemingly paradoxical as William Morris, who was the intellectual inspiration for the modern Labour Party but was himself a disciple of Ruskin and Carlyle, from whom he early imbibed a distaste for modernity. In *News from Nowhere* (1891), the many strains of Victorian antimodernism—both working-class and upper-class—come together in the form of a dream vision with a Marxist twist. The medieval utopia that Morris designs in *News from Nowhere*, which springs to life after a genuine workers' revolution, combines Ruskinian craft production with the Chartists' egalitarian scheme to resurrect an earthly Eden of small farmers and independent producers. Moreover, when Morris's dreamer wakes up in the future, the industrial past has been consigned to the historical dust heap, and the only character who shows any real interest in such antiquarian topics is Boffin, named in homage of Dickens's Golden Dustman. In this way, Morris's utopian socialist classic unexpectedly shares a vision of England's future with Eliot's *Felix Holt*. Despite Eliot's gradualist faith in progress and Morris's Marxist faith in a workers' revolution, both writers historicize the industrial revolution and represent it as part of the dark days of yore. In late-nineteenth-century Britain, liberals, conservatives, and even radicals like Morris could project a future English state "free" from the stains of industrialism: *News from Nowhere* merely offers a more conspicuous dismissal of England's industrial past as well as a more intoxicating vision of its postindustrial future than that found in *Felix Holt*.

Of course, both Eliot's and Morris's dismissal of the industrial revolution *as a past event* directly descends from the complicated denial of the industrial *present* evident in the works of the early male critics of industrialism. But while the devaluation of England's industrial heritage became a common—one might even say canonical—cultural move in the second half of the century, the response to industrialism in the first half of the century was decidedly more mixed. Writers struggled for the meaning of Carlyle's strange new today, and that struggle occurred across class and gender lines because class and gender interests were often played off against each other. One could argue, as historians certainly have, that the radical social possibilities of English industrialism were curtailed by a resurgent patriarchy that transcended class lines to restabilize a gender hierarchy threatened by the rise of the factories. So to erase gender as one of the key terms in early Victorian England's understanding of emergent industrialism is to distort the historical and literary record. We are well acquainted with the epic play of class struggle in the nineteenth century, but by focusing too exclusively on Marx's grand historical pageant, we have forgotten the domestic drama enacted on that same stage. Gender is not merely a subplot in the history of the industrial revolution; it is part of the main story line.

# APPENDIX

# Working-Class Writings

Reprinted here are some of the working-class poems discussed in the last chapter of this book. I have arranged them in a rough chronological fashion, moving from Chartist to dialect poetry and concluding with selections from Johnston's and Forrester's works. Some of this material has been reprinted before, but much of it has not. The best modern sources for Victorian working-class poetry are Brian Hollingworth's *Songs of the People,* Brian Maidment's *The Poorhouse Fugitives,* and Peter Scheckner's *An Anthology of Chartist Poetry.* Unfortunately, Hollingworth's anthology, which includes an excellent selection of Lancashire dialect poetry, is now out of print.

In addition to the working-class poetry, I also reprint Ellen Johnston's short autobiography because the text—which negotiates Johnston's identity as a woman, a worker, a poet, and a single mother in late Victorian Britain—might be of interest to a wide audience. Victorian working-class writing generally deserves more attention from literary critics than it has gotten over the years, and I hope this appendix will encourage scholars to consider incorporating it into their research projects and their classroom teaching.

## Contents

SAMUEL BAMFORD    Farewell to My Cottage

Farewell to my cottage, that stands on the hill,
To valleys and fields where I wander'd at will,
And met early spring with her buskin of dew,
As o'er the wild heather a joyance she threw;
'Mid fitful sun beamings, with bosom snow-fair,
And showers in the gleamings, and wind-beaten hair,
She smil'd on my cottage, and buddings of green
On elder and hawthorn and woodbine were seen—
The crocus came forth with its lilac and gold,
And fair maiden snowdrop stood pale in the cold—
The primrose peep'd coyly from under the thorn,
And blithe look'd my cottage on that happy morn.
But spring pass'd away, and the pleasure was o'er,
And I left my cottage to claim it no more,
Farewell to my cottage—afar must I roam,
No longer a cottage, no longer a home.

For bread must be earned, though my cot I resign,
Since what I enjoy shall with honour be mine;
So up to the great city I must depart,
With boding of mind and a pang at my heart.
Here all seemeth strange, as if foreign the land,
A place and a people I don't understand;
And as from the latter I turn me away,

I think of old neighbours now lost, well-a-day,
I think of my cottage full many a time,
A nest among flowers at midsummer prime;
With sweet pink, and white rock, and bonny rose bower,
And honeybine garland o'er window and door;
As prim as a bride ere the revels begin,
And white as a lily without and within.
Could I but have tarried, contented I'd been,
Nor envied the palace of lady the queen.
And oft at my gate happy children would play,
Or sent on an errand well pleased were they;
A pitcher of water to fetch from the spring,
Or wind-broken wood from my garden to bring;
On any commission they'd hasten with glee,
Delighted when serving dear Ima or me—
For I was their 'uncle', and 'gronny' was she.
And then as a recompense sure if not soon,
They'd get a sweet posy on Sunday forenoon,
Or handful of fruit would their willing hearts cheer;
I miss the dear children—none like them are here,
Though offspring as lovely as mother e'er bore
At eve in the park I can count by the score.
But these are not ours—of a stranger they're shy,
So I can but bless them as passing them by;
When ceasing their play my emotion to scan,
I dare say they wonder 'what moves the old man.'

Of ours, some have gone in their white coffin shroud,
And some have been lost in the world and its crowd;
One only remains, the last bird in the nest,
Our own little grandchild, the dearest and best.
But vain to regret, though we cannot subdue
The feelings to nature and sympathy true,
Endurance with patience must bear the strong part—
Sustain when they cannot give peace to the heart;
Till life with its yearnings and struggles is o'er,
And I shall remember my cottage no more.

*The Poorhouse Fugitives: Self-Taught Poetry and Prose in Victorian Britain,* ed. Brian Maidment (Manchester: Carcanet, 1987), 240–41.

ERNEST JONES   The Factory Town

> The night had sunk along the city,
>   It was a bleak and cheerless hour;
> The wild-winds sung their solemn ditty
>   To cold, grey wall and blackened tower.
>
> The factories gave forth lurid fires
>   From pent-up hells within their breast;
> E'en Aetna's burning wrath expires,
>   But *man's* volcanoes never rest.
>
> Women, children, men were toiling,
>   Locked in dungeons close and black,
> Life's fast-failing thread uncoiling
>   Round the wheel, the *modern rack!*
>
> E'en the very stars seemed troubled
>   With the mingled fume and roar;
> The city like a cauldron bubbled,
>   With its poison boiling o'er.
>
> For the reeking walls environ
>   Mingled groups of death and life
> Fellow-workmen, flesh and iron,
>   Side by side in deadly strife.
>
> There, amid the wheel's dull droning
>   And the heavy, choking air,
> Strength's repining, labour's groaning,
>   And the throttling of despair,—
>
> With the dust around them whirling,
>   And the white, cracked, fevered lips,
> And the shuttle's ceaseless twirling,
>   And the short life's toil-eclipse:
>
> Stood half-naked infants shivering
>   With heart-frost amid the heat;
> Manhood's shrunken sinews quivering
>   To the engines' horrid beat!

Woman's aching heart was throbbing
  With her wasting children's pain,
While red Mammon's hand was robbing
  God's thought-treasure from their brain!

Yet the master proudly shows
  To foreign strangers factory scenes:
"These are men—and engines those—"
  "I see nothing but—*machines*!"

Hark! amid the bloodless slaughter
  Comes the wailing of despair:
"Oh! for but one drop of water!
  "Oh! for but one breath of air!

"One fresh touch of dewy grasses,
  "Just to cool this shrivelled hand!
"Just to catch one breeze that passes
  "From our blessed *promised* LAND!"

No! though 'twas night of summer
  With a scent of new mown hay
From where the moon, the fairies' mummer,
  On distant fields enchanted lay!

On the lealands slept the cattle,
  Slumber through the forest ran,
While, in Mammon's mighty battle
  Man was immolating man!

While the great, with power unstable,
  Crushed the pauper's heart of pain,
As though the rich were heirs of *Abel*
  And the poor the sons of *Cain*.

While the priest, from drowsy riot,
  Staggered past his church unknown,
Where his God in the great quiet,
  Preached the livelong night alone!

Still the bloated trader passes,
  Lord of loom and lord of mill;
On his pathway rush the masses,
  Crushed beneath his stubborn will.

Eager slaves, a willing heriot,
  O'er their brethren's living road
Drive him in his golden chariot,
  Quickened by his golden goad.

Young forms—with their pulses stifled,
  Young heads—with eldered brain,
Young hearts—of their spirit rifled,
  Young lives—sacrificed in vain:

There they lie—the withered corses,
  With not one regretful thought,
Trampled by thy fierce steam-horses,
  England's mighty *Juggernaut!*

Over all the solemn heaven
  Arches, like a God's reproof
At the offerings man has driven
  To Hell's altars, loom and woof!

And the winds with anthems ringing,
  Cleaving clouds, and splitting seas,
Seem unto the People singing:
  "Break your chains as we do these!"

And human voices too resound:
  Gallant hearts! take better cheer!
The strongest chains by which you're bound,
  Are but the chains of your own fear!

Weavers! 'Tis your shrouds you're weaving,
  Labourers! 'Tis your graves you ope;
Leave tyrants toil-deceiving!
  Rise to freedom! Wake to hope!

Still, the reign of guilt to further,
  Lord and slave the crime divide:
For the master's sin is *murder,*
  And the workman's—*suicide!*

Up in factory! Up in mill!
  Freedom's mighty phalanx swell!

You have God and Nature still.
   What have they, but Gold and Hell.

Fear ye not your masters' power;
   Men are strong when men unite;
Fear ye not one stormy hour:
   *Banded millions need not fight.*

Then, how many a happy village
   Shall be smiling o'er the plain,
Amid the corn-field's pleasant tillage,
   And the orchard's rich domain!

While, with rotting roof and rafter,
   Drops the factory, stone by stone,
Echoing loud with childhood's laughter,
   Where it rung with manhood's groan!

And flowers will grow in blooming-time,
   Where prison-doors their jarring cease:
For liberty will banish crime—
   *Contentment* is the best *Police.*

Then the palaces will moulder,
   With their labour-draining joys;
For the nations, growing older,
   Are too wise for *royal toys.*

And nobility will fleet,
   With robe, and spur, and scutcheon vain;
For Coronets were but a cheat,
   To *hide* the brand upon a *Cain!*

And cannon, bayonet, sword and shield,
   The implements of murder's trade,
Shall furrow deep the fertile field,
   Converted into hoe and spade!

While art may still its votaries call;
   Commerce claim and give its due;
Supplying still the wants of all,
   But not the wastings of the few.

Gathering fleets may still resort,
  With snowy canvass proudly bent,
For bearing wealth from port to port
  But not for war or banishment!

Then, up, in one united band,
  Both farming slave and factory-martyr!
Remember, that, *to keep the* LAND,
    The best way is—*to gain the* CHARTER!

*An Anthology of Chartist Poetry: Poetry of the British Working Classes,*
*1830s–1850s,* ed. Peter Scheckner (Rutherford, N.J.: Farleigh
Dickinson UP, 1989), 175–79.

## MARIE   Labour

Calm and solemn is the midnight!
  Nothing do I hear
But my heart's dull measur'd beating
  Throbbing in mine ear:
Beating! beating! still repeating—
  'Listen, wakeful soul,
For every beat but brings thy feet
  Onward to the goal!
Spend not, then, the starry midnight
  In a useless sorrow,
But go rest thee, and upnerve thee
  For the working morrow.'
Blessed warning! New religion!
  And if e'er again
To my idol-grief returning,
Utter, clear and plain—
    'Hark, hark, to the live heart beating;
      Life is on the wing;
    Labour is the truest worship
      Any soul can bring.'

Thou who toilest, bless thy toiling!
  Not all nature sings
Nobler anthem, than the music
  When the hammer rings!
Every stroke of spade or hatchet,

Crieth out aloud,—
'Man is valiant in labour,
   And may well be proud.'
Stroke by stroke, glad time he keepth
   To his leaping heart;
Who shall, scorning, call him '*poor* man',
   Having this rich part?
He can boldly look existence
   In the very eye;
Nor needs tremble when night whispers
   'Neath the starlit sky—
      'Hark, hark, to the live heart beating;
         Life is on the wing;
      Labour is the truest worship
         Any soul can bring.'


Thou who idlest, quit thy idling,
   'Tis not meet to be
Dumb and voiceless 'midst the chorus
   Of God's melody!
Wind and wave are join'd in labour,
   And the very flowers
Add a beauty to creation,
   Scenting all her bowers.
Do some act that waits the doing—
   Speak some living word—
Lead some soul to cleansing waters
   By good angels stirr'd;
And the morn shall smiling wake thee
   With the dawn's grey light,
And in softest, gentlest cadence
   Thus shall sing the night—
      'Hark, hark, to the live heart beating;
         Life is on the wing;
      Labour is the truest worship
         Any soul can bring.'


When great nature, in sore travail,
   Bringeth forth her child—
Some old nation in convulsion,

With new freedom wild!—
Some long-borne and huge injustice,
   That in dumbness stood,
Pouring out its new-born utt'rance
   In a jargon flood!—
Be thou calm and unaffrighted,
   'Tis but nature's heart
Beating in her children's bosom,
   Bidding wrong depart.
Ages are her fleeting moment,—
   World-times are her years—
In immensity she singeth
   'Mid the shining spheres—
    'Hark, hark, to God's heart beating;
     Time is on the wing,
    Labour is the only worship
     Any soul can bring!'

       *The Poorhouse Fugitives: Self-Taught Poetry and Prose in Victorian*
        *Britain,* ed. Brian Maidment (Manchester: Carcanet, 1987),
            221–23.

MARIE    The Indomitable Will

On the long chaotic night,
Came the words, "Let there be light!"
Light and beauty burst abroad
At the fiat of their God:
Day, with sunbeams on her breast—
Night, with stars and holy rest—
Solid land, in wild-flowers drest—
Ocean, in her sea-green vest,
        Answered to His will.

And on man, in that first hour,
God bestowed a god-like power;
Power to will, and power to do,
Power to form and to subdue;—
And across the curbless sea,
He doth pass triumphantly!
And beneath the mountains grey

He hath made a great highway,
   By his mighty will!

Oh! upon our common day,
Let this mighty will have way;—
Every soul hath, more or less,
Power to conquer and to bless;
Let each being use its right,
And command, "Let there be light!"
And the lights of love will rise
In all quarters of our skies,
   By our force of will.

Out of wild chaotic life,
With its under-stream of strife,
We can form a realm of peace—
Make unholy hatred cease;—
No misfortune can arise
'Neath our quiet-beaming eyes:—
The serene, unmoved soul,
Holdeth *all* things in controul,
   By its power of will!

Though ignored our lowly lot,
Scornful glances harm us not;
We accept our homely fate:
And a beauteous life create;—
From earth's bosom, brown and bare,
Flowerets draw their colours rare;
And, though *we* are seeming stinted,
All our days are rainbow-tinted
   By our noble will!

Come there failure or success,
We march on in nobleness;
Nought can come amiss or wrong,
If the soul be true and strong,
On, and up, courageously!
And our banner's motto be
"Hope and work, with heart and hand—

Nought can finally withstand
  Those of earnest will!"
     *The People's and Howitt's Journal* 4 (1851): 63.


EDWIN WAUGH  Come Whoam to thi Childer an' Me

Aw've just mended th' fire wi' a cob;
Owd Swaddle has brought thi new shoon;
There's some nice bacon-collops o' th' hob,
An' a quart o' ale-posset i' th' oon;  *oven*
Aw've brought thi top-cwot, doesta know,
For th' rain's comin' deawn very dree;  *drearily*
An' th' har-stone's as white as new snow;—
Come whoam to thi childer an' me.

When aw put little Sally to bed,
Hoo cried, 'cose her feyther weren't theer,
So aw kiss'd th' little thing, an' aw said
Thae'd bring her a ribbin fro' th' fair;
An' aw gav' her her doll, an' some rags,
An' a nice little white cotton-bo';
An' aw kiss'd her again; but hoo said
'At hoo wanted to kiss *thee* an' o.

An' Dick, too, aw'd sich wark wi' him,
Afore aw could get him upstairs;
Thae towd him thae'd bring him a drum,
He said, when he're sayin' his prayers;
Then he looked i' my face, an' he said,
"Has th' boggarts taen houd o' my dad?"
An' he cried whol his e'en were quite red;—
He likes thee some weel, does yon lad!

At th' lung-length, aw geet 'em laid still;
An' aw hearken't folks' feet that went by;
So aw iron't o' my clooas reet weel,
An' aw hang'd 'em o' th' maiden to dry;  *clothes horse*
When aw'd mended thi stockin's an' shirts,
Aw sit deawn to knit i' my cheer,
An' aw rayley did feel rayther hurt,—
Mon, aw'm *one-ly* when theaw artn't theer.

"Aw've a drum an' a trumpet for Dick;
Aw've a yard o' blue ribbin for Sal;
Aw've a book full o' babs; an' a stick,          *pictures*
An' some 'bacco an' pipes for mysel;
Aw've brought thee some coffee an' tay,—
Iv thae'll *feel* i' my pocket, thae'll *see;*
An' aw've bought tho a new cap to-day,—
For aw al'ays bring summat for *thee!*

"God bless tho' my lass; aw'll go whoam
An' aw'll kiss thee an' th' childer o' round;
Thae knows that wheerever aw roam,
Aw'm fain to get back to th' owd ground;
Aw can do wi' a crack o'er a glass;          *chat*
Aw can do wi' a bit of a spree;
But aw've no gradely comfort, my lass,
Except wi' yon childer an' thee."

> *Songs of the People: Lancashire Dialect Poetry of the Industrial Revolution,*
> ed. Brian Hollingworth (Manchester: Manchester UP, 1977), 64–65.

## EDWIN WAUGH   Dinner Time

*The wife comes running into the house*
Heigh, Mary; run for the fryin'-pon;
An reitch that bit o' steak;
I see thi faither comin', yon;
Be sharp; for goodness sake!
He's as hungry as a hunter;
An' there'll be a bonny din
If he finds o' out o' flunter          *everything at sixes and sevens*
An' nought cooked, when he comes in!

"Lord, bless my life; why, th' fire's gone out!
Whatever mun I do?
Here, bring a match, an' a greasy clout,          *rag*
An' a bit o' chip or two:          *firewood*
An' look for th' ballis: doesto yer?          *bellows*

They're upo' th' couch, I think;
Or else they're hanged a-back o' th' dur;
Or else they're under th' sink.

"An' tak' those dish-clouts off that cheer;
An' shift yon dirty shoon;
An' th' breakfast things are stonnin' theer;
Put 'em a-top o' th' oon;
Be sharp; an' sweep this floor a bit:
I connot turn my back,
To speighk to folk, but o' goes wrang,
An' th' house runs quite to wrack.

"These chips are damp: Oh, Lord o' me!
I'm sure they'n never brun:
There's no poor soul's warse luck than me
That's livin' under th' sun!
Now then; what keeps tho stonnin' theer;
Hangin' thy dirty thumbs?
Do stir thy shanks; an' wipe that cheer;
It's no use; here he comes!"

*The husband comes in from work*
"By th' mass; this is a bonny hole,
As ony i' this town!
No fire; no signs o' nought to height;          *eat*
Nowheer to sit one down!
I have to run whoam for a meal,
When th' bell rings at noontide,
An' I find th' house like a dog-kennel:
Owd lass, it's bad to bide!

"Thou's nought to do, fro' morn to neet,
But keep things clean an' straight,
An' see that th' bits o' cloas are reet,
An' cook one's bit o' meight;          *meat*
But thou's never done it yet, owd lass:
How is it? Conto tell?
Thou mends noan, noather; an', by th' mass,          *you don't get*
I doubt thou never will!          *any better either*

"It's quite enough to have to slave
Fro' soon i' th' day to dark;
An' nip, an' scrat, an' try to save,          *take small meals*
An' no thanks for one's wark:

No wonder that hard-wortchin' folk
Should feel inclined to roam
For comfort to an alehouse nook,
When they han noan at whoam.

"I'm fast: I don't know what to say;
An' I don't know what to do;
An' when I'm tired, at th' end o' th' day,
I don't know where to goo.
It makes me weary o' my life
To live i' sich a den:
Here, gi's a bit o' cheese an' loaf,
An' I'll be off again!"

*Songs of the People: Lancashire Dialect Poetry of the Industrial Revolution,*
ed. Brian Hollingworth (Manchester: Manchester UP, 1977), 68–69.

EDWIN WAUGH   Down Again!

'Twur on a bitter winter neet,
When th' north wind whistled cowd;
When stars i' th' frosty sky shone breet,
An' o' wur still i' th' fowd;
I'd getten curl't up snug i' bed,
An' sleepin' like a top,
When Betty nudged my ribs, an' said,
"Oh, Jamie; do get up!"

I yawned, an' rubbed my e'en, an' said,
"Well, lass, what's th' matter now?"
Then Betty rocked hersel' i' bed,
An' said, "Get up, lad; do!"
"It's woint that troubles tho," said I,        *wind*
"Thou'd better have a pill."
"Oh, Jem," said hoo; "don't be a foo;
Thou knows what makes me ill!"

"Howd on, my lass," said I; "howd on!"
An', bouncin' out o' bed,
I began to poo my stockin's on:
"Oh, do be sharp!" hoo said;
But, my things had gone astray i' th' dark;
An', as I groped about,

Hoo said, "Oh, this is weary wark;
Thou'll ha' to goo without!"

"Goo wheer? Wheer mun I goo?" said I,
As I rooted upo' th' floor:   *searched about*
"Goo wheer?" said hoo; "thou leather-yed;
For th' doctor, to be sure!"
"Eh, aye," said I: "thou'rt reet, by th' mass!
An' if thou'll make a shift   *effort*
To tak thi time a bit, owd lass,
Thou's have him in a snift!"   *jiffy*

I donned my things, an' off I went
Like shot, through th' frosty neet;
Wi' nought astir but th' wintry woint,   *wind*
An' nought but stars for leet:
An' as through th' dark an' silent fowd,
My clatterin' gate I took,
I spied owd Clem, crept out o' th' cowd,
With his lantron, in a nook.

"What's o' thi hurry, Jem?" said he,
As I went runnin' by:
"I cannot stop to talk to thee;
We'n someb'dy ill," said I.
"Who is it this time?" cried owd Clem;
"Is it Nan, or little Ben?"
"Nawe, nawe," said I, "it's noan o' them;
*Our Betty's down again!*"

"Well done," cried Clem, "well done, owd lad!
Why that makes hauve a score!"
"It does," said I; "that's what we'n had;
An' we's happen ha' some moore."
"Never thee mind, my lad," cried Clem;
"It's a rare good breed, owd mon;
An' if yo han a hundred moore,
God bless 'em every one!"

Th' doctor wur up in hauve a snift;
An' off I scutter't back,
Like a red-shank, through the wintry drift,   *bare-legged person*
Wi' th' owd lad i' my track.

Th' snow wur deep, an' th' woint wur cowd
An' I nobbut made one stop,
At th' little cot at th' end o' th' fowd,
To knock her mother up.

I never closed my e'en that neet,
Till after break o' day;
For they kept me runnin' o' my feet,
Wi' gruel, an' wi' tay:
Like a scopperil up an' down i' th' hole,          *spinning top*
I're busy at th' owd job,
Warmin' flannels, an' mendin' th' fires
An' tentin' stuff o' th' hob.          *looking after*

It wur getten six or theerabout;
I're thrang wi' th' gruel-pon;          *busy*
When I dropt mi spoon, an' shouted out,
"How are yo gettin' on?"
"We're doin' weel," th' owd woman said;
"Thou'd better come an' see;
There's a fine young chap lies here i' bed;
An' he wants to look at thee!"

I ran up i' my stockin'-feet;
An' theer they lay! By th' mon;
I thought i' my heart a prattier seet
I ne'er clapt e'en upon!
I kissed our Betty; an' I said,—
Wi' th' wayter i' my e'en,—
"God bless yo both, my bonny lass,
For evermoore, Amen!

"But do tak care; if aught went wrang
I think my heart would break;
An' if there's aught i' th' world thou'd like,
Thou's nought to do but speak:
But, oh, my lass, don't lie too long;
I'm lonesome by mysel';
I'm no use without thee, thou knows;
Be sharp, an' do get weel!"

*Songs of the People: Lancashire Dialect Poetry of the Industrial Revolution,*
ed. Brian Hollingworth (Manchester: Manchester UP, 1977), 70–71.

EDWIN WAUGH   Toothsome Advice

### I

"Eh, Nanny; thou'rt o' out o' gear;
　　Do, pray tho, go peep into th' glass;
Thou looks dirty, an' deawly, an' queer;
　　Whatever's to do witho, lass?"
"Bless yo, Mary; if folk nobbut knew
　　The trouble I have wi' yon lad!—
He's at th' alehouse again, wi' th' owd crew:
　　It's enough to drive ony mon mad!"

### II

"Eh, my wench; I'm mich owder than thee,
　　An' it grieves me to see tho like this;
So, pray tho, now, hearken to me;
　　An' don't go an' tak' it amiss:
Thou once wur nice-lookin', an' mild,
　　An' tidily donned, too, as well;
But, now, thou'rt quite sluttish an' wild
　　About both thi house, an' thisel'.

### III

"It's hard to keep things reet with aught
　　That a body can manage to do;
But, a mon's sure to stray when he's nought
　　But dirt an' feaw looks to come to:
If thou wants to keep Jamie i'th house,
　　Thou mun bait th' trap wi' comfort, my lass;
Or, there's lots o' nooks, canty an' crouse,
　　Where he'll creep with his pipe an' his glass.

### IV

"Thou mun keep his whoam pleasant an' sweet;
　　An' everything fit to be seen;
Thou mun keep thi hearth cheerful an' breet;
　　Thou mun keep thisel' tidy an' clean;
A good-temper't wife *will* entice
　　To a fireside that's cosy an' trim;

Men liken to see their wives nice;
  And I'm sure that it's so wi' yor Jem.

### V

Thou mun have his meals cooked to his mind,
  At th' reet time, an' daicently laid;
Tak' pains; an' thou'll very soon find
  How nice a plain dish can be made:
Good cookin' keeps likin' alive,
  With a woman that's noan short o' wit;
And there's never a craiter i'th hive
  But's fond of a toothsome tit bit!"

### VI

"Eh, Mary; I'm nought of a cook,
  But just rough an' ready, yo know;
As for roastin' an' boilin' bi' th' book,—
  I'm o' little more use than a stone!"
"Don thi bonnet; an' hie tho wi' me;
  I'll soon put tho reet, if thou'll come;
And I'll larn tho some cookin', thou'll see,
  That'll help to keep Jamie at whoam!"

*Poems and Songs,* ed. George Milner (Manchester, 1893), 135–37.

## SAMUEL LAYCOCK   Uncle Dick's Advoice to Wed Women

NEAW, women, God bless yo'! yo' know aw'm yo'r friend,
An' as lung as aw'm able to stur, aw intend
To do what aw con, booath wi' tongue an' wi' pen,
To praise yo', an' get yo' weel thowt on bi'th' men.
At th' same toime aw shall noan be for howdin' mi tongue,
Iv aw foind 'at yo're guilty o' doin' what's wrong.
Aw dar' say yo' know very weel what aw meon;
Aw want yo' t' keep th' heawses o tidy an' cleon;

An' be sure—when yo'r husbands come in ov a neet—
To ha' th' har'stone new mopp'd an' th' fender rubb'd breet;
See 'at everythin's noicely put by in its place,
An' welcome 'em whoam wi' a smile on yo'r face.
When it's weshin' day, get done as soon as yo' con;
Aw'll assure yo' it's very unpleasant for John

To come into th' heawse ov a noonin' or neet,
An' foind th' dirty clooas spread abeawt at his feet.

Aw'll be hanged iv aw've patience wi' th' slatternly hags,
Sich as som'toimes aw see when aw'm goin' deawn th' flags;
It's no wonder the'r husbands should set off an' drink;
Will they stop wi' sich slovens as thoose, do yo' think?
Nowe, aw'll warrant they winnot, fo *aw* never should;
Aw'd "hook it" as sharply as ever aw could.
Whoa could ever expect one to ceawer in a hole,
Wheer a woman sits smookin', as black as a coal?

Iv a fellow gets wed to a cratur' like this—
Unless he's some very queer notions o' bliss—
Aw think he'll prefer bein' off eawt o'th' dur
To ceawerin' o'th' har'stone wi' someb'dy loike her.
But oh! a chap's blest when he gets a *good* woife,
To help him thro' th' world, and to sweeten his loife;
An' one or two youngsters to romp on his knee;
Neaw, aw've tried it, an' know what it is, do yo' see.

It's noice when a little thing meets one on th' way,
An' sheawts, "Come on, daddy, come on to yo'r tay."
Eh, women, aw'll ventur to gi'e mi owd hat
Iv yo'll foind ony music 'at's sweeter nor that.
Oh! It's grand when one enters th' inside o' the'r cot,
An' foinds 'at th' woife's made it a *heaven* ov a spot;
An' her stondin' theer, bless her, to welcome yo' in,
Wi' o 'at's abeawt her as clean as a pin!

An' it does seawnd some sweet when hoo tells yo' hoo's fain,
To see yo' come whoam weel an' hearty again.
Iv one's wantin' a bit o' *real pleasure,* it's here,
Bein' welcomed an' cared for bi thoose yo' love dear.
Ther's nowt 'at's moor dear to a chap i' this loife,
Nor th' breet smilin' face ov a fond lovin' woife.
Well, women, what are yo' for doin', neaw, come?
Will yo' promise an' try to keep th' husbands awhoam?

Let 'em feel—when the'r wark's done—'at th' loveliest spot
'At the'r is under heaven, is *the'r own humble cot.*
Ah! ther's lots o' poor fellows aw've known i' mi loife,

'At's bin driven fro' whoam bi a slovenly woife:
When they'n come in at neet, wearied eawt wi' th'er toil,
I'th' stead o' bein' met wi' a sweet, lovin' smoile,
Ther's nothin' but black-lookin' holes met the'r een,
An' a woife an' some childer, a shawm to be seen.

Neaw, women, aw beg on yo', do what yo' con
To mak' things look summat loike reet for a mon;
Ther'll be less drunken husbands, aw'm sure, if yo' will;
An' less money spent across th' road, at th' "Quiet Gill."
Yo'll be paid for yo'r trouble wi' th' comfort it brings
An' havin' moor brass for foine bonnets an' things.
Iv yo' want to be happy, aw'd ha' yo' be quick,
An' practise th' advoice o' yo'r friend, Uncle Dick.

*The Collected Writings of Samuel Laycock* (Oldham: W. E. Clegg,
1900), 98–100.

## ELLEN JOHNSTON　Autobiography of Ellen Johnston, the 'Factory Girl'

GENTLE READER,—On the suggestion of a friend, and the expressed wishes of some subscribers, I now submit the following brief sketch of my eventful life as an introduction to this long expected and patiently waited for volume of my Poems and Songs.

Like every other autobiographer, I can only relate the events connected with my parentage and infancy from the communicated evidence of witnesses of those events, but upon whose veracity I have full reliance.

I beg also to remind my readers that whatever my actions may have been, whether good, bad, or indifferent,—they were the results of instincts derived from the Creator, through the medium of my parents, and the character formed for me by the unavoidable influence of the TIME and COUNTRY of my BIRTH, and also by the varied conditions of life impressing themselves on my highly susceptible and sympathetic natures—physical, intellectual, and moral.

According to the evidence referred to, my father was James Johnston, second eldest son of James Johnston, canvas-weaver, Lochee, Dundee, where he learned the trade of stone-mason. After which he removed to Glasgow, where he became acquainted with my mother, Mary Bilsland, second daughter of James Bilsland, residing in Muslin Street, and then well known as the Bridgeton Dyer.

I do not remember hearing my father's age, but my mother at the time of her marriage was only eighteen years old. I was the first and only child of their union, and was born in the Muir Wynd, Hamilton, in 183__, my father at the time being employed as a mason extending the northern wing of the Duke of Hamilton's Palace.

When the Duke was informed that my father was a poet, he familiarly used to call him Lord Byron, and, as I have been told, his Grace also used to take special notice of me when an infant in my mother's arms, as she almost daily walked around his domain.

When I was about seven months old my father's contract at Hamilton Palace was finished, and being of an active disposition, somewhat ambitious, proud, and independent, with some literary and scientific attainments, with a strong desire to become a teacher and publish a volume of his poetical works, he resolved to emigrate, engaged a passage to America for my mother and himself, and got all things ready for the voyage.

But when all the relatives and friends had assembled at the Broomielaw to give the farewell kiss and shake of the hand before going on board, my mother determined not to proceed, pressed me fondly to her bosom, exclaiming—'I cannot, will not go, my child would die on the way;' and taking an affectionate farewell with my father, he proceeded on the voyage, and my mother fled from the scene and returned to her father's house, where she remained for some years, and supported herself by dressmaking and millinery.

Having given the evidence of others in respect to my parentage and infancy, let me now, gentle reader, state some of my own childhood's recollections, experience, and reflections thereon.

In my childhood Bridgeton, now incorporated with the city of Glasgow, abounded with green fields and lovely gardens, which have since then been covered over with piles of buildings and tall chimneys. The ground on which the factory of Messrs Scott & Inglis stands was then a lovely garden, where I spent many, many happy hours with 'Black Bess,' my doll, and 'Dainty Davie,' my dog, with whom I climbed many a knowe and forded many a stream, till one day he left my side to follow a band of music, and we never met again; but for whose loss I deeply mourned, and for three successive nights wept myself asleep, for 'Dainty Davie' was the pride of my heart, for I could not live without something to love, and I loved before I knew the name of the nature or feeling which swelled my bosom.

Perhaps there are few who can take a retrospective view of their past lives, and through their mind's eye gaze on so many strange and mysterious incidents. Yes, gentle reader, I have suffered trials and wrongs that have but rarely fallen to the lot of woman. Mine were not the common trials of every day life, but like those strange romantic ordeals attributed to the imaginary heroines of 'Inglewood Forest.'

Like the Wandering Jew, I have mingled with the gay on the shores of France—I have feasted in the merry halls of England—I have danced on the shamrock soil of Erin's green isle—and I have sung the songs of the brave and the free in the woods and glens of dear old Scotland.

I have waited and watched the sun-set hour to meet my lover, and then with him wander by the banks of sweet winding Clutha, when my muse has often been inspired when viewing the proud waving thistle bending to the breeze, or when the calm twilight hour was casting a halo of glory around the enchanting scene; yet in all these wanderings I never enjoyed true happiness.

Like Rassellas, there was a dark history engraven on the tablet of my heart. Yes, dear reader, a dark shadow, as a pall, enshrouded my soul, shutting out life's gay sunshine from my bosom—a shadow which has haunted me like a vampire, but at least for the present must remain the mystery of my life.

Dear reader, I have wandered far away from my childhood's years. Yes, years that passed like a dream, unclouded and clear. Oh that I could recall them; but, alas! they are gone for ever. Still they linger in memory fresh and green as if they were yesterday. I can look back and see the opening chapters of my life—I can see the forms and faces, and hear their voices ringing in my ears—one sweet voice above the rest echoes like a seraph's song; but I dare not linger longer at present with those joyous hours and beloved forms that were then my guardian angels.

In the course of time my mother received some information of my father's death in America, and again married a power-loom tenter when I was about eight years of age, till which time I may truly say that the only heartfelt sorrow I experienced was the loss of 'Dainty Davie;' but, alas! shortly after my mother's second marriage I was dragged, against my own will and the earnest pleadings and remonstrance of my maternal grandfather, from his then happy home to my stepfather's abode, next land to the Cross Keys Tavern, London Road.

## How I Became the Factory Girl

About two months after my mother's marriage, my stepfather having got work in a factory in Bishop Street, Anderston, they removed to North Street, where I spent the two last years of young life's sweet liberty—as it was during that time I found my way to Kelvin Grove, and there spent many happy hours in innocent mirth and glee—but 'time changes a' things.' My stepfather could not bear to see me longer basking in the sunshine of freedom, and therefore took me into the factory where he worked, to learn power-loom weaving when about eleven years of age, from which time I became a factory girl; but no language can paint the suffering which I afterwards endured from my tormentor.

Before I was thirteen years of age I had read many of Sir Walter Scott's novels, and fancied I was a heroine of the modern style. I was a self-taught scholar, gifted with a considerable amount of natural knowledge for one of my years, for I had only been nine months at school when I could read the English language and Scottish dialect with almost any classic scholar; I had also read 'Wilson's Tales of the Border;' so that by reading so many love adventures my brain was fired with wild imaginations, and therefore resolved to bear with my own fate, and in the end gain a great victory.

I had also heard many say that I ought to have been an actress, as I had a flow of poetic language and a powerful voice, which was enough to inspire my young soul to follow the profession. In fact, I am one of those beings formed by nature for romance and mystery, and as such had many characters to imitate in the course of a day. In the residence of my stepfather I was a weeping willow, in the factory I was pensive and thoughtful, dreaming of the far off future when I would be hailed as a 'great star.' Then, when mixing with a merry company no one could be more cheerful, for I had learned to conceal my own cares and sorrows, knowing well that 'the mirth maker hath no sympathy with the grief weeper.'

By this time my mother had removed from Anderston to a shop in Tradeston, and my stepfather and myself worked in West Street Factory. When one morning early, in the month of June, I absconded from their house as the fox flies from the hunters' hounds, to the Paisley Canal, into which I was about submerging myself to end my sufferings and sorrow, when I thought I heard like the voice of him I had fixed my girlish love upon. I started and paused for a few moments, and the love of young life again prevailed over that of self-destruction, and I fled from the scene as the half-past five morning factory bells were ringing, towards the house of a poor woman in Rose Street, Hutchesontown, where, after giving her my beautiful earrings to pawn, I was made welcome, and on Monday morning following got work in Brown & M'Nee's factory, Commercial Road. I did not, however, remain long in my new lodgings, for on the Tuesday evening, while threading my way among the crowd at the shows, near the foot of Saltmarket, and busy dreaming of the time when I would be an actress, I was laid hold of by my mother's eldest brother, who, after questioning me as to where I had been, and what I was doing, without receiving any satisfaction to his interrogations, compelled me to go with him to my mother, who first questioned me as to the cause of absconding, and then beat me till I felt as if my brain were on fire; but still I kept the secret in my own bosom. But had I only foreseen the wretched misery I was heaping upon my own head—had I heard the dreadful constructions the world was putting on my movements—had I seen the shroud of shame and sorrow I was weaving around myself, I should then have disclosed the mystery of my life, but I remained silent and kept my mother and friends in ignorance of the cause which first disturbed my peace and made me run away from her house for safety and protection.

However, I consented to stay again with my mother for a time, and resolved to avoid my tormentor as much as possible.

Weeks and months thus passed away, but, alas! the sun never shed the golden dawn of peaceful morn again around my mother's hearth. Apart from my home sorrows I had other trials to encounter. Courted for my conversation and company by the most intelligent of the factory workers, who talked to me about poets and poetry, which the girls around me did not understand, consequently they wondered, became jealous, and told falsehoods of me. Yet I never fell out with them although I was a living martyr, and suffered all their insults. In fact, life had no charm for me but one, and that was my heart's first love. If a sunshine of pleasure ever fell upon me, it was in his company only for a few short moments, for nothing could efface from my memory the deep grief that pressed me to the earth. I often smiled when my heart was weeping—the gilded mask of false merriment made me often appear happy in company when I was only playing the dissembler.

Dear reader, as this is neither the time nor place to give farther details of my young eventful life, I will now bring you to my sixteenth year, when I was in the bloom of fair young maidenhood. Permit me, however, to state that during the three previous years of my life, over a part of which I am drawing a veil, I had run away five times from my tormentor, and during one of those elopements spent about six weeks in Airdrie, wandering often by Carron or Calder's beautiful winding banks. Oh! could I then have seen the glorious gems that have sprung up for me on those banks, and heard the poetic strains that have since been sung in my praise, what a balm they would have been to my bleeding heart, as I wandered around the old Priestrig Pit and listened to its engine thundering the water up from its lowest depth. For days I have wandered the fields between Moodiesburn and

Clifton Hill, wooing my sorry muse, then unknown to the world—except to a few, as a child of song—in silence looking forward to the day when the world would know my wrongs and prize my worth; and had it not been for the bright Star of Hope which lingered near me and encouraged me onward, beyond doubt I would have been a suicide. 'Tis, however, strange in all my weary wanderings that I have always met with kindhearted friends, and there were two who befriended me when I was a homeless wanderer in Airdrie. Fifteen years have passed since I saw their tears roll down the youthful cheeks and heard the heavy sigh that exploded from their sympathising hearts. But the best of friends must part, and I parted with them, perhaps never to meet again in this lovely world of sunshine and sorrow.

Dear reader, should your curiosity have been awakened to ask in what form fate had then so hardly dealt with the hapless 'Factory Girl,' this is my answer:—I was falsely accused by those who knew me as a fallen woman, while I was as innocent of the charge as the unborn babe. Oh! how hard to be blamed when the heart is spotless and the conscience clear. For years I submitted to this wrong, resolving to hold my false detractors at defiance.

While struggling under those misrepresentations, my first love also deserted me, but another soon after offered me his heart—without the form of legal protection—and in a thoughtless moment I accepted him as my friend and protector, but, to use the words of a departed poet—

'When lovely woman stoops to folly,
And finds too late that men betray,
What can sooth her melancholy,
What can wash her guilt away?

The only art her guilt to cover,
To hide her shame from every eye,
To wring repentance form her lover,
And sting his bosom, is to die.'

I did not, however, feel inclined to die when I could no longer conceal what the world falsely calls a woman's shame. No, on the other hand, I never loved life more dearly and longed for the hour when I would have something to love me—and my wish was realised by becoming the mother of a lovely daughter on the 14th of September, 1852.

No doubt every feeling mother thinks her own child lovely, but mine was surpassing so, and I felt as if I could begin all my past sorrows again if Heaven would only spare me my lovely babe to cheer my bleeding heart, for I never felt bound to earth till then; and as year succeeded year, 'My Mary Achin' grew like the wild daisy—fresh and fair—on the mountain side.

As my circumstances in life changed, I placed my daughter under my mother's care when duty called me forth to turn the poetic gift that nature had given me to a useful and profitable account, for which purpose I commenced with vigorous zeal to write my poetical pieces, and sent them to the weekly newspapers for insertion, until I became extensively known and popular. As an instance, in 1854 the Glasgow Examiner published a song of mine, entitled 'Lord Raglan's Address to the Allied Armies,' which made my name popular throughout Great Britain and Ireland; but as my fame spread my health began to fail, so that I could not work any longer in a factory.

My stepfather was unable longer to work, and my mother was also rendered a suffering object; my child was then but an infant under three years of age, and I, who had been the only support of the family, was informed by my medical adviser that, unless I took a change of air, I would not live three months.

Under these circumstances, what was to be done? I did not then want to die, although I had wished to do so a thousand times before, to relieve me from unmerited slander and oppression.

Many sleepless nights did I pass, thinking what to try to bring relief to the afflicted household—although I did not consider myself in duty bound to struggle against the stern realities of nature, and sacrifice my own young life for those whose sympathies for me had been long seared and withered. Yet I could not, unmoved, look on the pale face of poverty, for their means were entirely exhausted, without hope to lean upon. Neither could I longer continue in the factory without certain death to myself, and I had never learned anything else.

Under those conflicting conditions and feelings, one night as I lay in bed, almost in despair, I prayed fervently that some idea how to act would be revealed to me, when suddenly I remembered that I had a piece of poetry entitled 'An Address to Napier's Dockyard, Lancefield, Finnieston,' which a young man had written for me in imitation of copperplate engraving, and that piece I addressed to Robert Napier, Esq., Shandon, Garelochhead, who was then in Paris, where it was forwarded to him. Having written to my employer for my character, which was satisfactory, Mr. Napier sent me a note to call at a certain office in Oswald Street, Glasgow, and draw as much money as would set me up in some small business, to see if my health would revive. According to the good old gentleman's instructions, I went as directed, and sought £.10, which was freely given to me; and I believe had I asked double the amount I would have readily received it.

Dear reader, I need not tell you what a godsend those ten pounds were to my distressed family, and kept me out of the factory during five months; after which I resumed work in Messrs Galbraith's Mill, St Rollox, Glasgow, where I continued till July, 1857, when my health again sank; and for a change of air I went to Belfast, where I remained two years, during which time I became so notorious for my poetic exploits that the little boys and girls used to run after me to get a sight of 'the little Scotch girl' their fathers and mothers spoke so much about.

In 1859 I left Belfast and went to Manchester, where I worked three months, and then returned again to my native land, much improved in body and mind.

New scenes and systems made a great change in my natures. I became cheerful, and sought the society of mirthmakers, so that few would have taken me for the former moving monument of melancholy. I had again resumed work at Galbraith's factory, and all went on well. 'My bonnie Mary Auchinvole' was growing prettier every day and I was growing strong; peace and good-will reigned in our household, the past seemed forgiven and forgotten, and the 'Factory Girl' was a topic of the day for her poetical productions in the public press, but the shadow of death was hovering behind all this gladsome sunshine.

My mother had been an invalid for several years, and, to add to her sorrow, a letter had come from her supposed dead husband, my father, in America, after an absence of twenty years, inquiring for his wife and child; on learning their fate he became maddened with remorse, and, according to report, drank a death-draught from a cup in his own hand; and my mother, after becoming aware of the mystery of my life, closed her weary pilgrimage on earth on 25th May, 1861. Thus I was left without a friend, and disappointed of a future promised home and pleasure which I was not destined to enjoy, I therefore made up my mind to go to Dundee, where my father's sister resided, whose favourite I was when a child.

Dear reader, were I to give details of my trials, disappointments, joys, and sorrows, since I came to 'bonnie Dundee,' they would be, with a little embellishment, a romance of real life, sufficient to fill three ordinary volumes. Suffice here to say, that after myself and child had suffered neglect and destitution for some time, I got work in the Verdant Factory, where the cloth I wove was selected by my master as a sample for others to imitate, until, on the 5th of December, 1863, I was discharged by the foreman without any reason assigned or notice given, in accordance with the rules of the work. Smarting under this treatment, I summoned the foreman into Court for payment of a week's wages for not receiving notice, and I gained the case. But if I was envied by my sister sex in the Verdant Works for my talent before this affair happened, they hated me with a perfect hatred after I had struggled for and gained my rights. In fact, on account of that simple and just law-suit, I was persecuted beyond description—lies of the most vile and disgusting character were told upon me, till even my poor ignorant deluded sister sex went so far as to assault me on the streets, spit in my face, and even several times dragged the skirts from my dress. Anonymous letters were also sent to all the foremen and tenters not to employ me, so that for the period of four months after I wandered through Dundee a famished and persecuted factory exile.

From the foregoing statements some may think that I am rude, forward, and presumptuous, but permit me to say this much for myself, and those who know me best will confirm my statement, that I am naturally of a warm-hearted and affectionate disposition, always willing, to the extent of my power, to serve my fellow-creatures, and would rather endure an insult than retaliate on an enemy. All my wrongs have been suffered in silence and wept over in secret. It is the favour and fame of the poetic gift bestowed on me by nature's God that has brought on me the envy of the ignorant, for the enlightened classes of both sexes of factory workers love and admire me for my humble poetic effusions, so far as they have been placed before the public, but I merely mention this to clear away any doubt that may possibly arise in the mind of any of my readers.

In conclusion, I am glad to say that the persecution I was doomed to suffer in vindication not only of my own rights, but of the rights of such as might be similarly discharged, passed away, and peace and pleasure restored to my bosom again, by obtaining work at the Chapelshade Factory, at the east end of Dundee, where I have been working for the last three years and a-half to a true friend. I had not been long in my present situation when I fortunately became a reader of the 'Penny Post,' and shortly afterwards contributed some pieces to the 'Poet's Corner,' which seemed to cast a mystic spell over many of its readers whose numerous letters reached me from various districts, highly applauding my contributions, and offering me their sympathy, friendship, and love; while others, inspired by the muses, responded to me through the same popular medium some of whose productions will be found, along with my own in the present volume.

And now, gentle reader, let me conclude by offering my grateful thanks to the Rev. George Gilfillan for his testimony in respect to the merits of my poetic productions, to Mr Alex. Campbell, of the 'Penny Post,' for his services in promoting their publication, as well as to the subscribers who have so long patiently waited for this volume, which I hope may prove a means of social and intellectual enjoyment to many, and also help to relieve from the incessant toils of a factory life.

*Autobiography, Poems and Songs of Ellen Johnston, the 'Factory Girl'*
(Glasgow, 1867), 3–15.

ELLEN JOHNSTON    Kennedy's Dear Mill

Oh! Kennedy's dear mill!
    To you I'll sing a song
For winter dark and dull;
    For another season's gone,
And summer's bright sunshine
    Thy little shed doth fill.
Prosperity is thine,
    Oh, Kennedy's dear mill!


'Tis not alone o'er thee
    Adversity hath passed,
For all the kingdoms three
    Hath felt its withering blast,
I shared thy better days,
    I also shared thine ill;
Now I hail hope's rays
    In Kennedy's dear mill.


Thou hast a secret spell
    For all as well as me;
Each girl loves thee well
    That ever wrought in thee.
They may leave they blessed toil;
    But, find work they will,
They return back in a while
    To Kennedy's dear mill.

The girls so neat and fair,
  The boys so frank and free;
I see a charm that's rare
  In them as well as thee.
The sunlight of their smile
  Doth linger near me still,
And cheers me at my toil
  In Kennedy's dear mill.

And freedom's glorious shrine
  Is center'd in thy walls;
No tyrant knave to bind,
  No slavish chain enthrals.
The workers are as free
  As the sunshine on the hill;
Thy breath is liberty,
  Oh! Kennedy's dear mill.

We feel no coward fear
  When our dear master comes;
And when he's standing near,
  And gazing on our looms,
He hails us with a smile
  That is a brother's still,
No haughty lord of toil
  Owns Kennedy's dear mill.

Through Erin's vast commerce
  He bears a generous name;
And o'er the universe
  His praise I will proclaim.
When his workers are in grief,
  It is against his will;
He's the first to send relief
  From Kennedy's dear mill.

We will be happy yet,
  And bid all care adieu;
For we shall have a trip
  In another week or two.
And o'er in Bedford Street
  A happy band we will

In unity all meet
  At Kennedy's dear mill.

Now, Kennedy's dear mill,
  The best wish of my heart
Shall linger near you still,
  When from you I depart.
Whate'er my fate may be,
  Let me wander where I will,
Peace and prosperity
  To Kennedy's dear mill.

*Autobiography, Poems and Songs of Ellen Johnston, the 'Factory Girl'*
(Glasgow, 1867), 19–21.

ELLEN JOHNSTON    The Factory Exile

Thou lovely verdant Factory! What binds my heart to thee?
Why art thou centered in my soul, twined round my memory?
Why dost thou hover o'er my dreams my slumbers to beguile?
When falsehood of the deepest dye has doomed me an Exile.

With tear-dimm'd eyes through Fancy's veil I gaze upon thy
  walls;
Their bright enamelled golden tinge my bleeding heart enthrals,
I deem I am what once I was, still bending o'er my loom,
And musing on a lovely form of beauty's sweetest bloom.

The love-born joy that swells my soul, whilst I in fancy toil
Within thy much-loved walls again—where first I saw a smile
That I can never see again save with a sad regret;
Its sunny lustre now is lost in gloomy retrospect.

Ah, me! that one so beautiful should own so cruel a heart
As injure one who still to him did act a friendly part;
What have I done that he hath wrung my heart with bitter woe?
I was to him a faithful friend—Why has he grown my foe?

Language never can express how much I thought of him,
I prized his perseverance—so deep did I esteem
His active, energetic powers, his patience, and his worth:
Alas! I thought that he excell'd all other men on earth.

But God alone can only tell the base and cold reward
That he gave me in return for such a true regard;
He scattered thorns across my path, calumny o'er my name,
And crushed the blossoms of my hope—the laurels of my fame.

And God alone can only tell how I have been betrayed,
But vengeance unto Him belongs—then why am I dismayed?
Though I am tossing to and fro on sorrow's galling wave,
The persecuted findeth rest and peace beyond the grave.

Thou lovely, verdant Factory! though doom'd a poor exile—
Disgraced, degraded, never more within thy walls to toil,
I will forgive my enemies, though they have me belied,
And may the wrongs I bore in thee to me be sanctified.

*Autobiography, Poems and Songs of Ellen Johnston, the 'Factory Girl'*
(Glasgow, 1867), 25–26.

## FANNY FORRESTER    The Lowly Bard

He tunes his lyre within his lowly dwelling,
  He sings of hopes all rosy-hued but vain,
And, while the thrilling melody is swelling,
  His soul is burning for a loftier strain.
Ye mighty dead, that haunt the poet's slumber,
  His efforts cheer, his feeble muse inspire,
Who tells the world in many a mournful number
  He mourns the incompleteness of his lyre.

He tunes his lyre where busy wheels are grinding,
  And flying straps are never, never still;
Where rigid toil the buoyant limbs is binding
  That fain would wander from the dusty mill.
He hears the carol of the country maiden—
  Oh, welcome fancy! real-like and sweet!—
The children bound, with trailing grasses laden,
  And fling their treasures at the rhymester's feet!

And while their eyes grow round with baby wonder
  His toil-stained fingers 'mongst their tresses stray;
But, lo! the engine booms like angry thunder,
  And frights the sympathetic band away!

Spindle and bobbin fill their vacant places,
  And o'er great looms slight figures lowly stoop,
And weary shadows cross the girlish faces
  That like frail flowers o'er stagnant waters droop.

Toil, toil to-day, and toil again tomorrow;
  Some weave their warp to reach a pauper grave!
Naught of romance doth gild their *common* sorrow;
  Yet ne'er were heroines more strong, more brave.
Poor common herd! they never dream of glory!
  *This* is their work—to *live* is its reward.
Ah! when they end their sad but common story,
  Will the great God such *common souls regard?*

Yes, yes, however menial be the duty,
  He deems it noble, if 'tis nobly done;
The lowliest soul contains the highest beauty,
  In its resemblance to that humble one
Who came, not where the kings of earth assembled
  To pay their homage to the Royal Child,
But where the lowliest bent the knee and trembled
  As the blest Babe His sweet approval smiled.

He tunes his lyre in sickly court and alley,
  Where the caged lark, though captive, boldly sings,
As if, above some pleasant country valley,
  He bore the sunbeams on his buoyant wings:
The seamstress hears, and lo! the weary fingers,
  'Mid front and wristband, white and listless lie;
And though his glance upon the gusset lingers,
  No thought of scanty wage nor toil is nigh.

Long e'er she knows her crystal tears are dripping
  O'er the dead bouquet on her window sill—
Her loving lips among the grasses dripping,
  To show, though faded, they are precious still—
Her grateful heart is tenderly recalling
  The sweet, sweet, longing that their perfume made;
And hallowed tears, with withered leaves, are falling:
  She mourns their blight, even while herself does fade.

He tunes his lyre within the garret lonely,
    Where kindly priest in muffled whisper speaks
(Where weary, weary eyes are watching only
    The hectic flush upon the hollow cheeks
Of him who raves of labour long neglected,
    Of children starving and reproaching him).
Oh, God! hath he their piteous prayers rejected?
    The flush dies out, his haggard eyes grow dim.

'Mine, only mine, to toil for and to cherish!
    Lay your cool hand, sweet Mary, on my brow!
Children, plead more, they must not, shall not perish!
    There, do not hold me—I am stronger now!
I've much to do, and precious time is fleeting.'
    The priest bends lower o'er the ragged bed—
No banner waves, nor muffled drum is beating;
    Yet, 'tis a hero that lies still and dead.

He tunes his lyre, in humble chapel kneeling,
    And every note contains some pure desire—
Yea, angel forms, through floating incense stealing,
    Seem breathing benedictions on his lyre.
The great may flaunt their pampered bards above him,
    But when *their* laurels shall be sere and brown,
Kind heaven will grant, because the lowliest love him,
    To the poor rhymester an *eternal crown*.

*The Poorhouse Fugitives: Self-Taught Poetry and Prose in Victorian Britain,* ed. Brian Maidment (Manchester: Carcanet, 1987), 156–58.

# NOTES

## Introduction

1. For an etymological account of the term *industrial revolution*, see Raymond Williams's *Keywords*.

2. Perry Anderson began to trace out the antimodern spirit of the English in a series of articles he published during the sixties in the *New Left Review*. See his "Origins of the Present Crisis" and "Components of a National Culture." More recently, Martin J. Wiener frames the revulsion toward modernity as one of the central features of English culture, and in a controversial thesis, he attributes England's economic decline in the late nineteenth century to it.

3. Margaret Thatcher has always presented a problem for modern feminists. On the one hand, she was the first female prime minister of Britain, but on the other hand, many of her policies harmed women, particularly poor women. One recent account of Thatcher and feminism identifies in Thatcherism a "conservative feminism rooted in liberalism" (Jessop 51). Since liberal feminism, with its emphasis on equal rights, was characteristic of mid-Victorian feminists like Brontë and Gaskell, perhaps the connection between Thatcher and the two novelists is less surprising.

4. In *The Industrial Reformation of English Fiction*, Gallagher highlights the relationship between the debates over industrialism and the developing formal structures of the English novel, while in *The Politics of Story*, Bodenheimer explores the ways in which social ideology is embedded in narrative form. My work is greatly indebted to both studies. Yet neither Gallagher nor Bodenheimer places gender at the center of her work, so for a sustained analysis of the intimate connections between gender and Victorian industrialism, I turned to the work of feminist historians like Anna Clark, Leonore Davidoff, Judy Lown, Sonya Rose, Barbara Taylor, and Deborah Valenze.

## One: A "World Turned Upside Downwards"

1. Wolfgang Schivelbusch's *Disenchanted Night* offers a history of lighting technologies in the nineteenth century. Schivelbusch observes that gaslighting, associated with industrial production, met with fierce resistance from Victorian householders, who perceived it to be "out of place in domestic rooms used for relaxing and entertaining" (157).

2. Lumping together critics of such diverse political and class backgrounds may seem problematic, but Martin Wiener argues convincingly that "despite the immense sweep of personal idiosyncrasy among mid-Victorian social thinkers, their reponses to the advancing world of industrial capitalism tended to converge." He notes that they were primarily "professional men" who shared the "predilections of that class," and thus they moved "*with* more than against the tide of gentrification" (30–31). For an analysis of the professional middle class, see Perkin's discussion of what he calls the "forgotten middle class" in *The Origins of Modern English Society*.

3. Two of the most comprehensive historical studies of this conservativism are David Roberts's *Paternalism in Early Victorian England* and Wiener's *English Culture and the Decline of Capitalism*.

4. For example, Sonya Rose examines the way gender affected economic relations during the industrial revolution through the construction of masculine and feminine identities within the working class; Judy Lown supplies a case study of gender at work in the Courtauld silk mills in mid-Victorian Essex; and Barbara Taylor reconstructs the gender politics in early-nineteenth-century reform movements.

5. Berg even suggests that economic historians, who have recently begun to reject altogether the notion of an industrial revolution marked by "economic and technological transformation" ("What Difference" 22), may have underestimated growth during the late eighteenth and early nineteenth centuries by ignoring the importance of female labor in high-productivity industries. For a historiographic overview of the economic history of the industrial revolution, see David Cannadine's "The Present and the Past in the English Industrial Revolution." Even if contemporary historians now generally see the industrial revolution as a "limited, restricted, piecemeal phenomenon, in which various things did *not* happen" (Cannadine 162), Victorian men and women in the 1830s and '40s felt themselves to being living through a period in which unprecedented, unlimited change was occurring.

6. Like so much else about the industrial revolution, the status of the woman worker, in terms of whether her lot improved overall or not, is

a matter of much debate. Deborah Valenze addresses this issue by looking at the redefinition of women in the late eighteenth and early nineteenth century as nonproductive and concludes: "By the early decades of the nineteenth century, factory employment was one of a declining number of options, and compared to its foremost rival, domestic service, it offered considerable advantages" (103). In other words, given the diminished economic opportunities available for working-class women in the nineteenth century, factory labor was one of the better choices. Nevertheless, the factory girl's liberation from the family economy was probably overestimated by contemporary observers, and her "much vaunted independence may have been more widely discussed than experienced" (Valenze 104).

7. John Rosenberg points out that Carlyle organizes *Past and Present* around two bodies in order to contrast the "thriving community" that grows up around St. Edmund's corpse with the "trail of contagion and death" that follows the Irish widow (123).

8. His emphasis on personal achievement firmly situates Carlyle within the professional classes, for whom the "ideal society was a functional one based on expertise and merit" (Perkin 258). Like many other professional men in the nineteenth century, this son of a Scottish peasant made his way largely by dint of his own talent.

9. Carlyle's anxiety about an imperiled masculinity during the early stages of his career may have had a more personal dimension as well, one arising from his "feminine" occupation as a professional writer. See Norma Clarke's "Strenuous Idleness: Thomas Carlyle and the Man of Letters as Hero." For a wide-ranging account of the Victorian crisis of masculinity, see James Eli Adams's *Dandies and Desert Saints,* which begins with a discussion of Carlyle.

10. For elaborations of Williams's concept of culture, see Eagleton's *Function of Criticism* as well as the critical works of Parrinder and Baldick.

11. Parrinder argues that the "idea of the man of letters as hero was an attempt to assert the cultural authority of the intellectual class" (119), while Eagleton links this assertion of cultural authority to the critic's social marginalization: "The sage is no longer the co-discoursing equal of his readership, his perceptions tempered by a quick sense of their common opinion; the critic's stance in relation to his audience is now transcendental, his pronouncements dogmatic and self-validating, his posture toward social life chillingly negative" (*Function of Criticism* 40).

12. Stockton makes Carlyle the unlikely bedfellow of such feminist theorists as Jane Gallop and Donna Haraway by arguing that in Carlyle

the feminists, *"materialism has to do with concealment*: Carlyle's historical enigmas, akin to Gallop's bodily enigmas, reveal resistance to our linguistic and conceptual control, thus heightening their existence apart from us" (131).

13. My discussion here of the complicated history of Christian communion is indebted to Maggie Kilgour's *From Communion to Cannibalism*.

14. Of course, by labeling the emancipated slave an idle gentleman, Carlyle links him to those other targets of his outrage, the nonworking aristocrats of *Past and Present,* who also "made no use of their souls; and so have lost them" (153). One could argue that there is no real difference between *Past and Present* and "The Nigger Question" because in both idleness is the supreme, soul-destroying sin. But the connection between the ex-slave and the aristocrat is a somewhat disingenuous one on Carlyle's part, since the emancipated slaves worked to meet their own needs—as even Carlyle acknowledges—and British aristocrats depended on the hard labor of others to support their upholstered lifestyles.

15. Dickens's inability to grasp Coketown's paradoxes stands in contrast to his remarkable understanding of the paradoxical nature of Victorian London. See Williams's *The Country and the City.*

16. Although reformed in the end, Gradgrind also stands accused of committing the same crime against his children that Bounderby commits against his workers; he too focuses exclusively on the "what is" and ignores the "what might be" by filling his children up with Facts and not Fancy. After the breakdown of her marriage, Louisa Gradgrind charges her father with having "robbed me . . . of the immaterial part of my life . . . my refuge from what is sordid and bad in the real things around me" (216). In this, she echoes the narrator's earlier complaint that Gradgrind's utilitarian system had "chained her down to material realities" (168). As both thief and jailer, Gradgrind robs his daughter of her freedom to flee from the "material realities" of Coketown. Her escape from these hard realities lies in the "immaterial" Fancy that Dickens sets in opposition to "material" Fact.

17. Oddly enough, Dickens even associates the circus with the Gothic through the "ecclesiastical niche of early Gothic architecture" (20) in which Slearly collects the entrance charge.

18. Culler identifies three distinct kinds of medievalism: "the Whig view, which returned to the Anglo-Saxons; the conservative view, which returned to the feudal system of the Normans; and the radical socialist view, which returned to the brief interval between the decline of the feudal and the rise of the commercial system" (155). He acknowledges, however,

that the conservative view prevailed in the first half of the century, although, I would add, only in upper-class circles. This upper-class medievalism, and its fundamentally conservative outlook, is documented by Alice Chandler and Jeffrey Spear. For a sumptuously illustrated tour through the nineteenth century's fascination with all things medieval, see Mark Girouard's *Return to Camelot*.

19. Interestingly, when Disraeli steered the Second Reform Bill through Parliament in 1867, he linked railroads and democracy to suggest an inevitability about both that was absent from his thinking in the 1840s. Asa Briggs writes: "After the second Reform Bill of 1867 had been attacked by both the Whig *Edinburgh Review* and the Tory *Quarterly Review,* the two great organs of traditional English politics, Disraeli compared them to two old-fashioned rival posting-houses. They had each described his policy as dangerous, revolutionary, and precipitate. So, said he, 'you may behold the ostler at the Blue Lion and the chambermaid at the King's Arms, though bitter rivals in the bygone epoch of coaches and post-horses, making up their quarrels and condoling together in the street over their common enemy the railroad' " (*Victorian People* 265).

20. Rosenberg argues compellingly that in *Past and Present* "Carlyle's power of endowing the past with extraordinary 'presence' is enhanced by his complementary genius for undermining the actuality of the here and now. He is the poet of the insubstantiality of the 'real' and the reality of the phantasmagoric, the one always heightened by the other" (24). To a lesser degree, Disraeli deploys this strategy in his Young England novels as well, and thus it seems to be a central component of the medievalist critique of modernity.

21. Rosemarie Bodenheimer and Gary Handwerk also identify Baptist Hatton as the figure of the novelist in the text. Pairing Hatton with Stephen Morley, Sybil's other suitor, Bodenheimer contends that the two are "matched studies in the incompatibility of action and theory" (183), while Handwerk argues that by masterminding the riot to restore Sybil's patrimony, "Hatton emerges as a hero of conservatism who channels and controls those forces that might otherwise rend the fabric of society" (340). But neither critic focuses on the exegetical talents shared by both Hatton and Disraeli, who are able to distinguish the true medieval ideal (Sybil) from its pretenders.

22. In *"Culture and Anarchy* Today," Stephen Marcus argues that Arnold is not an essentialist but a social constructionist because *Culture and Anarchy* asserts "in every one of us, whether we be properly Barbarians,

Philistines, or Populace, there exists, sometimes only in germ and potentially, sometimes more or less developed, the same tendencies and passions which have made our fellow-citizens of other classes what they are" (450). While Arnold's slippery prose and unsystematic thinking allow such a reading, they also undermine it. To be sure, Arnold acknowledges his own Barbarian instincts: "I never take a gun or fishing-rod in my hands without feeling that I have in the ground of my nature the self-same seeds which, fostered by circumstances, do so much to make the Barbarian" (450). But he is more circumspect when it comes to acknowledging his relationship to the Populace, diminishing the connection between himself and the Populace by a strategic avoidance of the first person singular: "Every time that we are envious, every time that we are brutal . . . he has found in his own bosom the eternal spirit of the Populace" (451). More to the point, Arnold never links the brutality he associates with the working class to the material conditions of life that may foster it, and he certainly never mentions the occasion for the Hyde Park riots, which occurred during the debates over the Second Reform Bill and grew out of the workers' frustrations with a political system that excluded them from nonviolent political participation through the ballot box.

 23. Wiener explicitly links the antimodernism of modern Britain to the conservative politics of the male critics, whose influential critiques he believes contributed "to the containment of industrial values and the shaping of a new cultural tradition for twentieth-century Britain" (31).

## Two: The Fortunate Fall

 1. While Brontë's feminist credentials are not much disputed, Elizabeth Gaskell's occasionally are. See, for example, Deanna Davis's "Feminist Critics and Literary Mothers: Daughters Reading Elizabeth Gaskell." Using feminist psychoanalytic theory, Davis provides an intriguing account of recent feminist interactions with the "motherly" Gaskell and grounds both the "feminist neglect and feminist celebration of Elizabeth Gaskell" in the "equivocal status of the mother within feminism" (507). For me, Gaskell's emphasis on the maternal values of nurturing does not make her a care theorist feminist, as Patsy Stoneman argues in her *Elizabeth Gaskell,* but an eminently Victorian feminist who uses the contradictions within the ideology of domesticity to imagine a public role for women.

 2. This interest in moneymaking is in line with what Ellen Moers identifies as one of the central elements of female novelistic realism. "Money

and its making were characteristically female rather than male subjects in English fiction," she notes in *Literary Women* (67).

3. Whether or not industrialization improved the status of Victorian working-class women is taken up in the first chapter of this book. For a more general discussion that includes middle-class women, see Janet Thomas's "Women and Capitalism: Oppression or Emancipation?" Thompson positions optimistic idealists against pessimistic materialists to argue that "optimists regard the spread of bourgeois freedoms to women, and particularly legislative and political reforms subsequent to industrial capitalism, as sufficient index of their improved status. Pessimists regard these as a mockery in the face of continued discrimination against women in the workplace" (545).

4. In *Ambitious Heights,* Norma Clarke assesses *Marian Withers* as one of "literature's might-have-beens" because it is "the work of an unconventional and daring thinker who tried, and failed, to write a conventional book" (203–5), while Rosemarie Bodenheimer expects less and thus is pleasantly surprised to find the narrative "original, attractive, and psychologically acute" (84). The book is more competent than critics generally allow, but less "original" than Bodenheimer claims. Nevertheless, Bodenheimer offers an illuminating and compelling analysis of *Marian Withers* in *The Politics of Story,* where she examines Jewsbury's novel along with Elizabeth Stone's *William Langshawe, the Cotton Lord* and Eliot's *Felix Holt,* categorizing all three as novels "built on a dichotomy between the amenities of genteel life and the integrity of work" (69). Because all three are more concerned with middle-class gentility than the condition-of-England question, they remain on the margins of this study, although it is interesting to note that both Jewsbury and Stone, also a Manchester native, fiercely defend the industrial system in their novels.

5. Constance Harsh argues for "a mythic consistency" in condition-of-England novels by male and female writers. She locates "a covert feminism [that] would have offered an attractive resolution of their culture's social dilemma" (15) in these novels and thereby labels them fundamentally "feminocentric" in their orientation. To me, such a position is tenable only if one disregards the gendered nature of the industrial discourse.

6. It is possible to read *North and South* as a literal apology to (as well as for) Manchester's industrialists: Gaskell created John Thornton, her heroic industrialist, to make amends to the Manchester mill owners, many of them members of her husband's congregation, who felt she had unfairly represented them in *Mary Barton.*

7. Even though she foregrounds the material conditions of the working classes instead of their spiritual disposition, Gaskell is not a crude determinist. The relationship between the material and the spiritual in her works is especially complex because her Unitarian determinism comes into conflict with a new strain of Unitarianism that tried to make space for free will. See chapter 3 of Gallagher's *Industrial Reformation.*

8. The problematic relationship between capitalism and patriarchy is a central theme in feminist materialist criticism. See Hamilton, Sargent, and Hartsock.

9. In *The Literature of Change,* John Lucas sympathetically compares Gaskell's treatment of Manchester to Engels's, and he concludes that Gaskell, who spent all her adult life there, understood certain aspects of working-class culture and domestic life that eluded the German-born Engels.

10. The Marxist critics who first rehabilitated the critical reputation of *Mary Barton* did so at the expense of Mary's plot. Writing in *Culture and Society,* Raymond Williams found Mary's story "of little lasting interest," nothing but the "familiar and orthodox plot of the Victorian novel of sentiment" (89); and in "Mrs. Gaskell and Brotherhood," John Lucas declared Mary's love story extraneous to the novel. In recent years, feminists have abandoned this position. Gallagher's *Industrial Reformation* and Hilary Schor's *Scheherezade in the Marketplace* argue for a connection between the love plot and the industrial plot, identifying the problems that both women and workers have with language and representation, while Nancy Armstrong's *Desire and Domestic Fiction* and Ruth Bernard Yeazell's "Why Political Novels Have Heroines" contend that the romance plot is used to deflect or displace the anxieties raised in the political plot. At the other end of the spectrum from either the Marxist or the feminist approaches is Felicia Bonaparte's *The Gypsy-Bachelor of Manchester,* which wrongheadedly depoliticizes Gaskell, arguing that she "had no genuine interest in social, economic, and political questions" (135). For an excellent overview of Gaskell criticism, see Schor's "Elizabeth Gaskell: A Critical History and a Critical Revision."

11. Amanda Anderson takes up the problem of Esther in her rich discussion of the relationship between aesthetic form and social reform in *Mary Barton.* But while Anderson reads Esther as a character out of melodrama who dramatizes the "limits of sympathizing with a literary representation" (122), my reading of Esther focuses on the way "real" people deploy cultural narratives to give meaning to their lives. The dangers of the melodramatic narrative for women like Esther is not only that it will produce a hopeless response in readers but that it limits the agency of the subject.

12. Factory women in particular were assumed to possess few moral scruples. The promiscuity of the mill girl was such a common stereotype in Victorian England that one writer in the *Morning Chronicle* flatly declared that there was scarcely a thing as a "chaste factory girl" (qtd. in Rule 199). Of course, Mary is a seamstress, but as the daughter and niece of factory workers, she is closely aligned with them and subject to the same stereotyping.

13. Maidenly modesty also rears its unattractive head in the romance of Margaret and Will Wilson. While walking home from Old Alice's funeral, Jem asks Margaret to keep Will occupied for a few minutes while Jem talks to his mother, but, "No! that Margaret could not do. That was expecting too great a sacrifice of bashful feeling" (402). Here again Gaskell calls attention to how "bashful feeling," which is just another way of saying "maidenly modesty," actively prevents women from making themselves useful.

14. One could argue that by sending her heroine off to the splendors of Canada's open spaces, Gaskell beats a pastoral retreat from the problems of industrialism. But the novel's conclusion does not represent a flight from industrialism, even though emigration was frequently proposed (and acted upon) as a solution to both male and female unemployment throughout the nineteenth century. Rather, the Canada Gaskell chooses for Jem and Mary resembles the Green Heys Fields of the novel's first chapter. She does not send them off to the frontier but to a suburb of Toronto, and thus Gaskell restores the happy times that existed at the novel's opening, when both the Bartons and the Wilsons were fully employed and living in relative prosperity. Moreover, even though Jem becomes an agricultural instrument maker, one assumes this is still essentially industrial work, since his experience is in industrial engineering. Presumably, he will help manufacture the farm machinery needed for the vast tracts of Canadian wilderness that were being transformed into arable land.

15. I do not wish to argue that medieval nuns lived barren, sexually repressed, and socially useless lives. Rather, in *Shirley,* Brontë's native anti-Catholicism merges with her critique of the Victorian medievalists, so that the nun, representative of both a Catholic and a medieval world, becomes the ideal embodiment of the miserable lives women have led throughout history. For a rich discussion of the significance of *Shirley*'s nuns, see chapter 11 of Gilbert and Gubar's *Madwoman in the Attic.*

16. Brontë's treatment of the Luddites has been one of the more controversial aspects of *Shirley.* Terry Eagleton's *Myths of Power* condemns

Brontë for penning "a lurid travesty of the Luddites" (49); and his argument that Brontë merely echoes the middle-class myth of the Luddites is also found in Thompson's *Making of the English Working Class*. Patrick Brantlinger accuses Brontë of envisioning the Luddites as a mob in "The Case against Trade Unions in Early Victorian Fiction," while Igor Webb writes that Brontë simply misunderstood the Luddites' demands for their traditional rights. As they had in *Mary Barton,* feminist critics insist on the thematic connections between the industrial material and the women's plots. Gilbert and Gubar see Brontë working out the genesis of hunger, wherein workers and women are cultural outsiders condemned to starvation; and Helene Moglen argues that *Shirley* details the victimization of both women and workers by patriarchal power.

17. Anna Clark notes that "men and women participated together in riots against power looms because they threatened the familial, home-based textile workers' economy" (131).

18. According to Herbert N. Mozley's "The Property Disabilities of a Married Woman, and Other Legal Effects of Marriage," which appeared in Butler's *Woman's Work and Woman's Culture,* "the immediate effect of marriage is to place [a woman's] personal property at once absolutely in the power of her husband, and to give him a certain qualified interest in her real property. . . . In the ordinary case of a woman entitled to 'real' property, marriage would confer upon her husband a right to receive the rents and profits for the joint lives of husband and wife" (187). Of course, as Mary Shanley points out, "Under equity, any woman rich enough to have the legal documents drawn up could have her 'separate property' or 'separate estate' protected by a trust" (59), but even this arrangement limited a woman's financial freedom, since a trustee now had control over her wealth. In Shirley's case, the most logical trustee would be her narrow-minded uncle, with whom she clashes throughout the novel.

19. For example, in *Scheherezade in the Marketplace,* Schor contends that Milton is "both Mill-town and an invocation of Satan's Hell" (139), while Jenny Uglow sees Thornton, one of Milton's proudest civic boosters, as "caught in a Dantesque circle" (385).

20. Tennyson was Gaskell's favorite contemporary poet, and her letters record the pains she took to secure a copy of *In Memoriam* when it was first published in 1850. As pre-Darwinian accounts of evolution as progress, *North and South* and *In Memoriam* share certain thematic interests. For an elaboration of the connections between Gaskell, evolution, and Darwin (who was a cousin of Gaskell's), see Carol Martin's "Gaskell, Darwin, and *North and South.*"

21. In its investment in dissent, *North and South* echoes Florence Nightingale's attack on the domestic imprisonment of bourgeois women in "Cassandra." Gaskell wrote much of *North and South* at the Nightingale family home, and in an 1855 letter to Catherine Winkworth, Gaskell compared her heroine to Nightingale: "I did not think Margaret *was* so *over* good. What would Miss B[rontë] say to Florence Nightingale? I can't imagine!" (*Letters* 327). While there is no way to ascertain whether Gaskell saw the manuscript of "Cassandra," which Nightingale completed in draft form by 1852, "Cassandra" does share *North and South*'s faith in the value of dissent: "Was Christ called a complainer against the world? Yet all these great teachers and preachers have had a most deep and ingrained sense, a continual feeling of the miseries and wrongs of the world. Otherwise they would not have been impelled to devote life and death to redress them" (416). Like "Cassandra," *North and South* makes a virtue of a feminist necessity and upholds dissent as a moral principle.

22. My argument here is indebted to but diverges from Gallagher's analysis of family-society tropes in *North and South*. In *The Industrial Reformation of English Fiction,* Gallagher contends that Gaskell rejects the paternalist metaphor and replaces it with the metonymic domestic ideology. But I think Gaskell replaces the paternal metaphor with a domestic metaphor and tries to reconstitute the public world in the image of her loving, albeit imperfect families. In doing so, she ignores the patriarchal structure of her text's families, in which the men have ultimate authority and the women rely on their moral influence over the men.

23. Gaskell may not infantilize the workers, but her hymeneal metaphor feminizes them. As Higgins's promise here to speak his mind to Thornton suggests, Higgins acts very much like the bourgeois wife in his "marriage" to Thornton, using his influence to mend Thornton's erring ways.

24. My discussion of the riot scene is indebted to Barbara Leah Harman's "In Promiscuous Company: Female Public Appearance in Elizabeth Gaskell's *North and South,*" which beautifully details the complicated relationship between private and public realms in Gaskell's novel and concludes that Gaskell accepts the dangers inherent in women's entry into the public realm.

25. R. K. Webb's *Harriet Martineau, a Radical Victorian* offers a good introduction to nineteenth-century Unitarianism, while Valentine Cunningham's *Everywhere Spoken Against* provides an overview of Gaskell's own deep Unitarian roots.

26. Margaret's immature denial of the human passions is related to a similar denial of the passions on the part of both the men and the

masters in Milton. If Helstone belongs in a poem by Tennyson, so does Milton, except that the poem is *In Memoriam,* for the nature of Milton is "red in tooth and claw." The violence of the workers' riot is often remarked upon, but the physical rage beneath the civil surface of Milton society that transcends both class and gender is less generally discussed. Margaret occasionally resorts to "gentle violence" (310, 530), while Thornton, who sees life as a Darwinian struggle for existence, is not above wishing to do bodily harm to Margaret. But it is the animal nature of men and women, their irrational, often violent passions, that all the main characters deny. The riot occurs because the "workmen's calculations were based (like too many of their masters') on false premises. They reckoned on their fellow-men as if they possess the calculable powers of machines, no more, no less; no allowance for human passions getting the better of reason" (291). Thornton is certainly one of those short-sighted masters given to false premises, for he demands that human nature bend to the inexorable logic of political economy. When man or master fails, he expects them to "lie down and quietly die out of the world that needed them not" (204); and he can only berate the irrationality of the workers when they refuse to starve quietly. Both the men and the masters must, like Margaret, openly acknowledge human passions before they can exert genuine self-control.

27. Bessy Higgins has either been ignored by critics or dismissed as a simple reminder of the dangers of factory work. One exception can be found in Catherine Barnes Stevenson's " 'What Must Not Be Said': *North and South* and the Problem of Women's Work," which figures Higgins as a projection of Gaskell's own anxieties about being a woman working in the literary marketplace.

28. It is technically inaccurate to say that Bessy threatens no one because, after a long rambling passage in which she expresses doubt about there being a next world to compensate for the troubles in this one, she takes Margaret's hand and declares, "I could go mad and kill yo' " (145). But it is precisely Bessy's emphasis on the rewards of heaven—which allows her to accept passively the pains of this world—that Gaskell cannot abide. The profound differences between Gaskell's Unitarianism and Bessy's Evangelicalism is best captured in the following anecdote cited by Coral Lansbury: "In 1801 the Unitarian John Cartwright met William Wilberforce, the Evangelical, in Westminster, and the exchange between them summarised the fundamental difference in religion between the two. Cartwright recalled: 'Among other friendly expressions, [Wilberforce] said he hoped we should meet in a better world: I answered that *I hoped we should first mend the world we were in*' " (14–15).

Since Bessy's violent outburst occurs when she momentarily questions her evangelical faith in the rewards of the hereafter, one might read her threat, occasioned by her doubts, as a positive sign because it forces her to abandon her deadly inertia.

29. Margaret offers Thornton £18,000, or nearly half of the £40,000 estate she inherits. As Shanley points out, when wealthy families established trusts for their about-to-be-married daughters, "the rule in such cases was to settle half the property on the wife and children, and the remainder on the husband, although the amount could vary according to circumstances" (59). Fittingly, Margaret lends Thornton roughly the amount he would be entitled to by custom after their marriage; moreover, since the rest of her property is real estate, which remained a woman's property (except for the rents) after marriage, she keeps before marriage what will remain hers after it. The care with which Gaskell seems to have worked out the financial arrangements between Margaret and Thornton is not surprising, given that as a successful writer who earned a substantial income, Gaskell was keenly aware of the laws regulating married women's property. In 1856, along with Elizabeth Barrett Browning, George Eliot, Harriet Martineau, and other prominent women writers, she signed the Married Women's Property Committee's parliamentary petition asking for a revision of the law. Apparently, she was quite adept at maneuvering around the law and somehow squirreled away enough money to surprise her husband with a retirement home immediately before her death.

## Three: Trollope, Tonna, and the Early Industrial Discourse

1. In addition to the writings of Trollope, Tonna, and Stone, one must include Harriet Martineau's *Illustrations of Political Economy* (1832) in any list of early industrial writings by women. Like the Manchester-bred Stone, Martineau defended the burgeoning middle-class world of commerce out of which she emerged. The daughter of a failed bombazine manufacturer from Norwich, Martineau eventually became industrial capitalism's most ardent supporter and a tireless popularizer of classical economic theory.

2. To her credit, Armstrong strives to endow eighteenth- and nineteenth-century British women with agency, establishing them as makers of history and not merely its victims. Yet, the insistent, monologic narrative of domesticity that Armstrong constructs (her "political history of the novel") has the ironic effect of effacing the female agency it articulates, partly by conflating the feminized discourse of domesticity with women as actors in history. The modern individual, Armstrong provocatively declares, "was first

and foremost a woman" (8). But after helping to produce bourgeois culture (and taking honors as its first citizen), the middle-class woman in *Desire and Domestic Fiction* oddly disappears from history as an agent of change and presents no further dissent from the status quo. Thus, Armstrong flattens out both the complexities within the texts she explores as well as the complex workings of ideology itself. Poovey provides an important corrective to Armstrong by reminding us that the "middle-class ideology often associated with the Victorian period was both contested and always under construction; because it was always in the making, it was always open to revision, dispute, and the emergence of oppositional formulations" (3). And while I do not wish to deny that the domestic ideal bolstered the middle class, I do want to suggest that the improvisational nature of Victorian ideology that Poovey identifies meant that it could be used (and was by Tonna and Trollope) to critique as well as subtend middle-class power.

3. Given the divorce between production and consumption in capitalist culture, it is not surprising that Victorian advertisements reinforced the separateness of the domestic sphere. In *Consuming Angels,* Lori Anne Loeb notes that "the home as portrayed in the Victorian advertisement was a protective but attractive enclave, which was shaped by feminine hands and shielded its members from ugliness, but strengthened them to confront the world outside. This was an appealing vision. It constituted a significant backdrop for the elaboration of hedonistic themes, especially a commercial focus on superfluous variety" (26). Victorian ads ensured that the connection between the "ugliness" outside the home and the "superfluous variety" in it was never made.

4. Both *The Wrongs of Women* and *Helen Fleetwood* appeared serially in the *Christian Lady's Magazine,* a successful monthly magazine which, according to Monica Correa Fryckstedt, catered to bourgeois women's "demand for instructive as well as entertaining reading: while inculcating Christian principles in their mind, the magazine provided them with some basic knowledge of politics, religion, science, factory legislation and economics" (49). Tonna's influence on the early Victorian factory debates has been discussed by Kestner, Kovačević and Kanner, Kaplan, and Gallagher (*Industrial Reformation*). Apparently, her readership was large enough to merit an American edition of her complete works in the mid-1840s; Harriet Beecher Stowe wrote the introduction, in which she attests to Tonna's great fame.

5. The assertion that the purity of the middle-class home is stained by the shameful conditions under which commodities are produced most frequently appears in distressed seamstress tales, not factory fictions. Seam-

stressing attracted shabby-genteel or lower-middle-class as well as genuinely working-class women, and tales of ladylike young women forced to work long hours so that their wealthier sisters could shine in society's ballrooms formed a popular subgenre of Victorian fiction, where the perceived gentility of seamstresses made them attractive objects of pity. Tonna's "Milliners and Dress Makers" is one example of such fictions, as is Elizabeth Stone's *The Young Milliner* and the early chapters of Elizabeth Gaskell's *Ruth*. Of course, the most famous literary production about seamstresses is Thomas Hood's "The Song of the Shirt," which first appeared in 1843 in a struggling new publication called *Punch*. Interestingly, Hood appeals not to women as consumers but to men: "Oh, Men, with Sisters dear! / Oh, Men, with Mothers and Wives! / It is not linen you're wearing out, / But human creatures' lives!" (lines 25–28). Charles Kingsley's *Alton Locke*, a variation on the distressed seamstress tale, takes up the problem of the sweated tailoring trade in London. In it, Kingsley uses a cholera-infested coat that kills its owner to make the necessary connection between commodities and the sometimes wretched conditions under which they are produced; and in this way, he breaks new ground by emphasizing the physical as well as the moral dangers of ignoring the conditions of production.

6. In a fine essay, Kaplan argues that bourgeois femininity is threatened by consumption in Tonna's works because, as a consumer of tainted goods, the middle-class lady participates in the working-class woman's fall from domesticity.

7. Novels that extol the blessings of industrialism, such as *William Langshawe* and *Marian Withers*, highlight the mill owners' readiness to expose their mills (inside and out) to public view. Moreover, the model manufacturers in Stone's and Jewsbury's texts force their daughters to confront the source of their riches. William Langshawe's daughter remarks that her father "has insisted on my frequently visiting the mill with him, in order, as he said, that I might have a just idea of the value of wealth by seeing the toil to others by which it was obtained" (I: 108). Nor does her father's factory remain a mystery to Marian Withers. Informing her that "to my mind women had better come and work in a factory than do nothing but sit all day with their hands before them" (I: 238), Mr. Withers even makes Marian join a party that he is proudly escorting through his mill. The openness of both industrialists signals that they (and the factories they run) have nothing to hide.

8. Parliament adopted the term "unfree agents" from Leonard Horner, the factory inspector who reported in 1843 that working-class

women were "much less free agents" than men and consequently needed state protection. For an overview of the Ten Hours Bill and subsequent pieces of protective legislation aimed at women, see ch. 3 of Rose's *Limited Livelihoods*.

9. Contending that no hard evidence exists to support these widespread accusations of immorality, Michael Mason points to the middle-class investigators' inability to read the codes of working-class life: "they applied inappropriate standards of decorum in speech and personal address, to conclude, for example, that certain kinds of swearing, or conventions of behavior between young people, denoted sexual license" (157).

10. Unlike *Hard Times,* where factory work goes unrepresented, "On a Amateur Beat" describes the productive processes in the lead mill in some detail, although the fanciful description recalls the extreme metaphoricity of *Hard Times.* Significantly, at the end of his visit, Dickens remarks: "I parted from my two frank conductors over the mills, by telling them that they had nothing there to be concealed, and nothing to be blamed for" (352). Dickens's unstated assumption here is that most mills did have something to conceal.

11. Mariana Valverde traces out the Victorian connection between fashion and the fallen woman in "The Love of Finery."

12. During the same debate, Lord Ashley claimed that women were biologically incapable of working outside the home; and he marshaled a regiment of medical evidence—infertility rates, reports of difficult births, the problems of the nursing mother—to illustrate graphically the unsuitability of the "delicate constitutions and tender forms of the female sex" for industrial production (*Hansard* 1089). For Ashley, the factory was a site of illicit human reproduction, and it simultaneously interfered with natural, healthy reproductive processes.

13. Of course, it is only a short leap from Kay's and Gaskell's condemnations to John Ruskin's more famous critique of factory production. While Ruskin never speaks the medical language of Kay or Gaskell—the early onset of puberty or the retraction of muscles makes no appearance in Ruskin's "The Nature of Gothic"—his argument is essentially the same: factory labor makes workers "less than men" (86) because it exclusively exercises the physical, sensual side of the individual worker. It is only "by thought that labour can be made happy" (90), Ruskin told his Victorian readers. Appearing over a decade after the works of Trollope and Tonna, "The Nature of Gothic" also connects the realms of production and consumption through the form of the commodity. But as we have seen, while

Ruskin exposes the material conditions of industrial production, his primary interest remains the disposition of the English workers.

14. Elaine Freedgood contends that the popularity of Martineau's *Illustrations* rested on the "cosmological consolations" they offered readers, who were assured by Martineau's "tranquilizing tales" that things would work out for the best, despite the current topsy-turvy nature of the economy (34–35).

15. See Catherine Gallagher's "The Body versus the Social Body in the Works of Thomas Malthus and Henry Mayhew." She notes that "Malthus's theory destroyed the homological relationship between individual and social organisms by tracing social problems to human vitality itself. . . . Malthus's argument ruptures the healthy body / healthy society homology. Simultaneously, by making the body absolutely problematic, he helps place it in the very center of social discourse" (84–85). By challenging Enlightenment notions of human perfectibility, Malthus also undermined the nineteenth century's faith in unbounded economic growth. One wonders if Martineau, despite her investment in industrial modernity, found something reassuring in Malthus's insistence that there were limitations to society's capacity for radical transformation. For a solid introduction to Malthus's writings, see Donald Winch's *Malthus*.

16. Tonna reconsiders and tries to salvage the artifact when she writes *The Wrongs of Women* two years later. Still, even within a story like "The Little Pin-Headers," which calls on the reader to admire the straight pin, the pin becomes admirable only after it leaves the workshop, for in the "dirty-looking" place where the pin-headers labor, the pins are themselves dirty, "not yet whitened or polished" (451).

17. By acknowledging the hierarchical nature of the domestic ideology, we can see how it both endowed middle-class women with agency (as Armstrong argues) but also subtended bourgeois forms of power (as Poovey argues in *Uneven Developments*).

18. Bodenheimer provides the best analysis of Trollope's contradictory relationship to the domestic ideology. She argues that Trollope creates heroines who can act in the world of men by penetrating "the strategies of male power" and yet remain untainted by that knowledge because Trollope represents "woman's consciousness and activity as private, secret, or separate from the flow of public affairs known to male characters" (24).

19. For a discussion of the managerial role played by middle-class women within the Victorian home, see ch. 1 of Langland's *Nobody's Angels*.

20. The classic feminist indictment of the Marxist inattention to gender is Heidi Hartmann's "The Unhappy Marriage of Marxism and Feminism." For a more recent analysis of how untheorized notions of gender structure Marxist thinking, see Joan Wallach Scott's subtle analysis of E. P. Thompson's writings in *Gender and the Politics of History*.

21. Tonna's as well as Trollope's fierce attacks on mill owners should be seen as part and parcel of their Toryism. It was the strategy of Tory paternalists like Lord Ashley to figure the manufacturers as the exploiters of working-class women and children, and landowners like themselves as the natural protectors of the poor. But since Trollope's and Tonna's texts question the efficacy of parliamentary intervention, what gets represented is a situation in which middle-class women do battle with mill owners and male workers in order to rescue the women and children who labor in the factories.

## Four: Nostalgia and the Ideology of Domesticity

1. The Appendix to this book reprints Johnston's "Autobiography," as well as a number of the working-class poems discussed in this chapter.

2. Tholfsen, Perkin, Foster, Stedman Jones, Joyce, and Kirk all take as their starting point the existence of mid-Victorian stability and proceed to offer various and variously intriguing explanations for the mid-Victorian social consensus. Tholfsen contends that working-class culture became assimilated into that of the ruling bourgeoisie; Perkin argues for the triumph of middle-class ideology; Foster looks to the emergence of a labor aristocracy; Stedman Jones insists on the limited political aims of Chartism; Joyce in *Work, Society, and Politics* attributes stability to the paternalistic structure of the mid-Victorian factory; and Kirk grounds it in the ethnic tensions that split working-class communities apart in the wake of the massive Irish immigration during the postfamine years.

3. The working-class adoption of domesticity has been much discussed by feminist historians of Victorian Britain. See Taylor, Lown, Rose, Valenze, and Clark. Clark goes the farthest in positing a direct causal relationship between the decline of Chartism and the rise of a domesticated working class.

4. The intricate links between Victorian medievalism and Victorian cultural criticism are forged in the first chapter of this book.

5. In the eighteenth century, there was a thriving tradition of laboring-class women's verse by poets like Mary Collier and Ann Yearsley,

who, according to Landry, worked "within the ideology of natural poetic genius and the complex circuitry of patronage and marketplace" but still "managed some surprising innovations" (280). By the 1790s, however, this tradition had died out. Florence Boos contends that there were "hundreds, perhaps thousands of working-class women poets throughout Victorian Britain, whose verses have disappeared without a trace" (53). She claims to have located "roughly three dozen Scottish working-class poets who published at least a volume of poetry" (55), but it is not clear how many of these volumes were produced by women, other than the three female poets (Ellen Johnston, Janet Hamilton, and Jessie Russell) she discusses. Still, even Boos acknowledges that most Victorian working-class women poets worked on the obscure margins of the literary world, enjoying none of the fame of their male counterparts.

6. David Vincent first broke with purely materialist explanations to account for the scarcity of working-class women's writings when he considered the emotional and intellectual conditions of the working class and attributed the absence of working women's autobiographies to their low self-esteem and the lack of "the self-confidence required to undertake the unusual act of writing an autobiography" (8).

7. Neither Fanny Forrester nor Ellen Johnston is usually located within the dialect camp, and thus, reading them against the dialect tradition may seem random at best, misleading at worst. However, both women were active during the height of dialect's popularity, and they emerged from the same social and geographical milieu that spawned the major dialect figures. Moreover, the Scottish-born Johnston, heir to the tradition of Robert Burns, occasionally used the Scots dialect; and even though Forrester wrote exclusively in standard English, she published the majority of her poems in *Ben Brierley's Journal,* a magazine edited by one of the masters of dialect prose.

8. In the third chapter of *The Literature of Labour,* H. Gustav Klaus traces the connection between Chartist politics and literature. The best introduction to the works of the Chartists is found in Vicinus's *The Industrial Muse* and continued in her essay "Chartist Fiction and the Development of a Class-Based Literature" in Klaus's *The Socialist Novel in Britain.* Two recent anthologies, one edited by Peter Scheckner and the other by Ian Haywood, make Chartist fiction and poetry available to modern readers.

9. Thom goes on to complain about the disordering of nature as the most pernicious consequence of industrialism: "Man becomes less manly. Woman unlovely and rude" (12). This fear of sexual disorder, as this chapter will reveal, is central to the Chartists' repudiation of modernity.

10. Additional information on Linton, the London engraver and

poet whom Vicinus considers (along with Jones, Cooper, and Massey) one of the best and best-known Chartist writers, can be found in F. B. Smith's biography of Linton. Further biographical information on the Chartist poets is available in Vicinus's *The Industrial Muse* and Brian Maidment's *The Poorhouse Fugitives* as well as in Nigel Cross's chapter entitled "The Labouring Muse" in his *Common Writer.*

11. In *Distinction* Pierre Bourdieu argues that the difference between intellectual and popular aesthetics may be summed up in their relationships to the thing represented: "Intellectuals could be said to believe in the representation—literature, theater, painting—more than in the things represented, whereas the people chiefly expect representations and the conventions which govern them to allow them to believe 'naively' in the things represented" (5). Bourdieu's distinction illuminates the gap between Victorian medievalism, with its complex claims to historical accuracy, and the "naive" nostalgia of Chartist poetry. Nevertheless, the preconditions for nostalgia that Chase and Shaw articulate—it requires "a secular and linear sense of time, an apprehension of the failings of the present, and the availability of evidences of the past" (4)—apply equally to the nostalgic writings of the working class and the medieval texts of the upper class.

12. Bamford's erasure of hunger as a fact of preindustrial life resembles W. J. Linton's in "Bob Thin," where Linton declares that in the past "there were no Poor-Laws, for this good / Reason, that no man wanted food" (lines 69–70).

13. In her study of Romanticism's legacy to the Chartists, Janowitz contends that the landscape poetic could be both a hindrance and a help. It was a hindrance when it led to the mystification found in "Farewell to My Cottage," but it was "helpful to Chartist poets insofar as it, however marginally, linked the contemporary struggle to a communitarian past located in the countryside. It was helpful when it intersected with a vision of the future built on the premises of popular sovereignty, and when it was given poetic shape in images of the nation as belonging to a people defined as the universalizing of the working class" (261).

14. For more on the mass appeal of the Chartist back-to-nature scheme, see G. D. H. Cole's essay on Feargus O'Connor in his *Chartist Portraits.*

15. The causal contradictions within the Chartists' writings are similar to those found in the factory reform debates discussed in Chapter 3.

16. Barbara Taylor beautifully recovers the feminist consciousness of the Owenite movement and locates the breaking of the "link between

women's freedom and class emancipation" (263) in the shift from Owenism to Chartism, from radical egalitarianism to conservative domesticity.

17. Ian Haywood seems to be alone in finding "strong evidence of Chartist writers possessing a feminist consciousness" (17). He labels the Chartist concern over the social and sexual exploitation of women as feminist, but it is perhaps more accurately adjudged to be paternalistic.

18. One could characterize the Chartist Land Plan as utopian nostalgia and the privatized domestic vision of the dialect poets as just plain nostalgia. The difference is that utopian thinking possesses an "optimistic confidence that the childlike but not infantile can be restored to our public life," while nostalgic thinking resigns itself to the "irredeemability of our collective structures" (Chase and Shaw 6).

19. Clark notes that of all the reforms passed in the 1840s, only the Factory Act and the Mines Act had an immediately beneficial impact on working-class lives, and therefore she concludes that, more than anything, "the factory acts took the wind out of the Chartist sails" (244).

20. Most critics of dialect literature agree about its essentially conservative, backward-glancing orientation. Maidment argues that dialect poetry engages in "a search for a lost 'history' of ordinary people, most usually associated in their world with a rural/industrial village life which just predates urbanization and the factory system" (*Poorhouse Fugitives* 231). Vicinus points out that the choice of dialect itself was an attempt to forge a connection with the past, since "the spoken dialect belonged to the past and to the country in the minds of many city dwellers" (*Industrial Muse* 190). And in the preface to his anthology of dialect verse, Brian Hollingworth notes that after its golden age in the 1850s and 1860s, dialect poetry quickly degenerated into "an antiquarian and rather nostalgic attempt to conserve a dying culture and language" (5). Breaking with the pack, Patrick Joyce in *Visions of the People* contends that dialect writers embraced a political liberalism and its attendant faith in progress. But he also acknowledges that the "vision of a lost Eden" (284) persisted in dialect literature and that "golden-age notions served constantly to undercut facile ideas of progress" (288).

21. Moira Maconachie quotes the following figures for female employment from the 1851 census: out of a population of 7,043,701 adult women, 2,846,097 were in paid employ and 500,000 worked in family businesses. One assumes that these figures, which amount to roughly half the adult female population, do not include the part-time and irregular labor women engaged in. The prevalence of working wives in Victorian Britain and the economic consequences of the domestic ideal are discussed by Rose,

Lown, Alexander, and Osterund. Because the ideology of domesticity assumed that every woman had—or would soon have—a husband to support her, women were forced into the lowest-paid jobs. For visual confirmation of the extent and variety of nineteenth-century working women's experiences, see Michael Hiley's *Victorian Working Women*, which reproduces many of the pictures collected by Arthur Munby, who had a lifelong fascination with working-class women, most notably with Hannah Cullwick, the servant whom he secretly married. Perhaps the most interesting chapter in the book is the one on the Wigan pit brow girls, which juxtaposes portraits of the women in their pit trousers with studio shots of the same women in their Sunday dresses, looking very much like demure young ladies. At least in their visual self-representations, the Wigan pit girls seemed to have reconciled waged work and femininity, even if Victorian culture could not.

22. *The Ambiguities of Self-Help*, Vicinus's short biography of Edwin Waugh, details Waugh's irregular domestic arrangements. For a lengthy, sympathetic account of Waugh's life and his construction of a social identity, see Joyce's *Democratic Subjects*.

23. The three parts appeared successively in the March, April, and May issues of *Ben Brierley's Journal*, under the titles "Homeless in the City," "Toiling in the City," and "Dying in the City."

24. For a discussion of Forrester's identity as a working-class female poet and how she negotiates it through the powerful tradition of female expressivity, see my "Lowly Bards and Incomplete Lyres: Fanny Forrester and the Construction of a Working-Class Woman's Poetic Identity," forthcoming in *Victorian Poetry*.

25. Julia Swindells fleshes out the literary influences on Johnston's autobiography, particularly its indebtedness to such romantic figures as Sir Walter Scott.

26. Boos notes that Johnston excises any mention of her pregnancy and illegitimate daughter from the second edition of *Autobiography, Poems and Songs*. No doubt the nature and presentation of this aspect of her life proved too transgressive for the book's intended audience.

27. According to Johnston's autobiography, she was fired from the Verdant Factory in Dundee, so no doubt she is punning here. It is interesting to compare her account of her dealings with the Verdant Factory in this poem and in her autobiography, where she claims that she had to sue her employers to get her week's pay after summarily being fired. One gets a much better sense of Johnston's marginal economic position from the autobiography, in which she appears as a "famished and persecuted factory exile" (14) after losing her job. Johnston's autobiography, like the novels of

Elizabeth Gaskell and Charlotte Brontë, scripts unemployment as a woman's greatest enemy, and that fact may help explain the poet's celebration of factory work in many of her poems.

28. Johnston's high-spirited tributes to factory life owe an unacknowledged debt to the "low" tradition of the broadside, which as Vicinus notes, often praised the "liveliness and vitality of factory towns" (*Industrial Muse* 53). But by explicitly aligning herself with Byron, Scott, and Wordsworth, Johnston attempts to locate her work within the canonical tradition of English literature; and in this sense, she shares much in common with the working-class writers whom Vicinus identifies as seeing literature as their vocation.

## Conclusion: Past and Present

1. Judith Walkowitz notes in *City of Dreadful Delight* that by the end of the century London reclaimed "its status as the cultural and nerve center of the nation and empire, overshadowing Manchester and Liverpool as the embodiment of the 'modern city' " (24).

2. Although he praises Eliot not for what she observes but for the "quality of the witness" (103), Williams includes *Felix Holt* in his chapter on industrial novels in *Culture and Society,* and critics have followed his lead. Both Gallagher and Bodenheimer conclude their book-length studies with *Felix Holt.* For Gallagher, *Felix Holt* marks the end of the tradition of industrial fiction because once the natural or divine order of society is exposed as fiction, which *Felix Holt* accomplishes, writers no longer can criticize industrial society as unnatural or ungodly. Bodenheimer arrives at a somewhat similar conclusion at the end of her analysis of how social ideology is embedded in narrative form, and for her, *Felix Holt* is a metafiction of industrialism because it "present[s] politics as one of the many constructed fictions about society" (233).

3. Critics have long noted the connections between Eliot's novel and previous industrial texts. See Gallagher *(Industrial Revolution)*, Bodenheimer, and Yeazell.

4. Interestingly, Felix Holt's rejection of social mobility resembles William Morris's justification for not overpaying the workers at Morris and Company. Morris "feared that if he dramatically improved the lot of his own workers," Peter Stansky writes, "he would simply reinforce the great doctrine of 'getting on,' and make of them men content to belong to the bourgeoisie, rather than workers anxious to help transform the world" (47).

5. One of the major exceptions to this domestic rule was the Lan-

cashire mill girl, who remained fairly true to her pre-1850 work patterns. While domesticity was clearly the dominant ideal in mid- and late Victorian Manchester (witness both dialect poetry and Fanny Forrester's verse), Lancashire women nevertheless remained in the textile factories in large numbers, and family life adapted. Textile families were famous for their equitable distribution of domestic labor, and the husbands of textile workers were sometimes mocked by other laboring men for their "feminine" domestic skills. "Lancashire cotton workers were by far the highest paid and best organized of all working class women," Liddington and Norris note in their history of the women's suffrage movement, adding that "the pride they took in their work and their status as skilled workers led them to demand the vote for themselves" as early as the 1890s (262).

6. With more discretionary income to spend on housekeeping as the century progressed, working-class women transformed the home into their power base. Unlike middle-class housewives, they frequently took control of the family's finances, became domestic exchequers, and made all major decisions about the family's purchases. This was not the "nought to do" domesticity found in dialect poetry, where the home is figured as a male fantasy of fetishized labor, but a domesticity that underscored woman's household arts as a form of female accomplishment and pride. See Joanna Bourke's "Housewifery in Working-Class England."

7. One way to gauge the profound change in public representations of the working-class woman between the first and second halves of the century is to compare the fallen factory girl with her successor in the public imagination, the prostitute, who emerged in the 1850s and 1860s as "the great social evil." But she did so, according to Judy Walkowitz in *Prostitution and Victorian Society,* as a social nuisance and not as a threat to the social order as the factory girl had been. The Victorian anxiety about sexuality, women, and the public sphere characterizes the nineteenth century's response to both the fallen factory girl and the fallen woman. But by excluding industrial work from this erotic mix through an increasing focus on the prostitute, the Victorians began to extricate the factories from their tangled inscription as places of production and reproduction. If the prostitute functioned for the Victorians as "a highly visible symbol of social dislocation attendant upon the new industrial era" (Walkowitz 32), the dislocations she represents are those of mass urbanization, since the Victorians primarily saw prostitution as a problem of the urban streets. Thus, she signals the shift from the factory to the metropolis as the primary site of modernity.

8. See Keith McClelland's "Some Thoughts on Masculinity and

the 'Representative Artisan' " for a discussion of the importance of independence to the working man's definition of masculinity.

9. This modern antimodernism can be found buried deep in the structure of the Labour and Tory parties well into the twentieth century. One can set next to Harold Macmillan's remark, "The Victorian age was simply an interruption in British history," a similar statement made by George Lansbury, deputy secretary of the Labour Party, in 1934: "I just long to see a start made on this job of reclaiming, recreating rural England. I can see the village greens with the Maypoles once again erected and the boys and girls, young men and maidens, all joining in the mirth and foll of May Day" (qtd. in Wiener 122–23).

# REFERENCES

Adams, James Eli. *Dandies and Desert Saints: Styles of Victorian Masculinity.* Ithaca: Cornell UP, 1995.

Alexander, Sally. "Women's Work in Nineteenth-Century London: A Study of the Years 1820–1850." *The Rights and Wrongs of Women.* Ed. Juliet Mitchell and Ann Oakley. Harmondsworth: Penguin, 1976. 59–111.

Althusser, Louis, and Etienne Balibar. *Reading Capital.* Trans. Ben Brewster. London: Verso, 1979.

Anderson, Amanda. *Tainted Souls and Painted Faces: The Rhetoric of Fallenness in Victorian Culture.* Ithaca: Cornell UP, 1993.

Anderson, Perry. "Components of a National Culture." *New Left Review* 50 (1968): 3–57.

———. *In the Tracks of Historical Materialism.* Chicago: U of Chicago P, 1984.

———. "Origins of the Present Crisis." *New Left Review* 23 (1964): 26–54.

Armstrong, Nancy. *Desire and Domestic Fiction: A Political History of the Novel.* New York: Oxford UP, 1987.

Arnold, Matthew. *Culture and Anarchy.* 1869. *Poetry and Criticism of Matthew Arnold.* Ed. A. Dwight Culler. Boston: Houghton Mifflin, 1961. 407–75.

———. "The Function of Criticism at the Present Time." *Poetry and Criticism of Matthew Arnold.* Ed. A. Dwight Culler. Boston: Houghton Mifflin, 1961. 237–58.

———. *Letters of Matthew Arnold.* Vol. 1. Ed. George W. E. Russell. 2 vols. London: Macmillan, 1901.

———. "On the Modern Element in Literature." *Essays, Letters, and Reviews by Matthew Arnold.* Ed. Fraser Neiman. Cambridge: Harvard UP, 1960. 3–19.

————. "Stanzas from the Grande Chartreuse." *Poetry and Criticism of Matthew Arnold.* Ed. A. Dwight Culler. Boston: Houghton Mifflin, 1961. 185–90.

Bailey, Ronald. "The Other Side of Slavery: Black Labor, Cotton, and Textile Industrialization in Great Britain and the United States." *Agricultural History* 68 (1994): 35–50.

Baldick, Chris. *The Social Mission of English Criticism, 1848–1932.* Oxford: Clarendon, 1983.

Bamford, Samuel. "Farewell to My Cottage." *The Poorhouse Fugitives.* Ed. Brian Maidment. Manchester: Carcanet, 1987. 240–41.

Bell, Florence. *At the Works: A Study of a Manufacturing Town.* 1907. London: Virago, 1985.

Belsey, Catherine. *Critical Practice.* New York: Routledge, 1987.

Berg, Maxine. "What Difference Did Women's Work Make to the Industrial Revolution?" *History Workshop Journal* 35 (1993): 22–44.

————. "Women's Work, Mechanisation, and the Early Phases of Industrialisation in England." *The Historical Meanings of Work.* Ed. Patrick Joyce. Cambridge: Cambridge UP, 1987. 64–98.

Berman, Marshall. *All That Is Solid Melts into Air.* New York: Penguin, 1988.

Blake, Robert. *Disraeli.* London: Eyre and Spottiswoode, 1966.

Bodenheimer, Rosemarie. *The Politics of Story in Victorian Social Fiction.* Ithaca: Cornell UP, 1988.

Bonaparte, Felicia. *The Gypsy-Bachelor of Manchester: The Life of Elizabeth Gaskell's Demon.* Charlottesville: UP of Virginia, 1992.

Boos, Florence. "Cauld Engle-Cheek: Working-Class Women Poets in Victorian Scotland." *Victorian Poetry* 33 (1995): 53–74.

Bourdieu, Pierre. *Distinction: A Social Critique of the Judgement of Taste.* Trans. Richard Nice. London: Routledge and Kegan Paul, 1984.

Bourke, Joanna. "Housewifery in Working-Class England, 1860–1914." *Past and Present* 143 (1994): 167–97.

Brantlinger, Patrick. "The Case against Trade Unions in Early Victorian Fiction." *Victorian Studies* 13 (1969): 37–52.

————. *The Spirit of Reform: British Literature and Politics, 1832–1867.* Cambridge: Harvard UP, 1977.

Brierley, Ben. "The Cotters of Mossburn." *Tales and Sketches of Lancashire Life.* London, 1866.

————. "Fanny Forrester." *Ben Brierley's Journal.* 23 January 1875: 37–38.

————. "A Strike Adventure; or, The 'Revolution' of Daisy Nook." *Daisy Nook Sketches.* Vol. 3 of *Tales and Sketches of Lancashire Life.* 8 vols. Manchester, 1882.

Briggs, Asa. *Victorian People: A Reassessment of Persons and Themes, 1851–1867.* Chicago: U of Chicago P, 1955.

———. "Victorian Values." *In Search of Victorian Values: Aspects of Nineteenth-Century Thought and Society.* Ed. Eric Sigsworth. Manchester: Manchester UP, 1988. 10–26.

Brontë, Charlotte. *Jane Eyre.* 1847. Ed. Q. D. Leavis. New York: Penguin, 1966.

———. *Shirley.* 1849. Ed. Andrew Hook and Judith Hook. New York: Penguin, 1974.

Burnett, John, ed. *Useful Toil: Autobiographies of Working People from the 1820s to the 1920s.* London: Penguin, 1984.

Burton, Antoinette. "The White Woman's Burden: British Feminists and the Indian Woman, 1865–1915." *Women Studies International Forum* 13 (1990): 295–308.

Butler, Josephine, ed. *Woman's Work and Woman's Culture.* London, 1869.

Butwin, Joseph. "*Hard Times*: The News and the Novel." *Nineteenth-Century Fiction* 32 (1977): 166–87.

Cannadine, David. "The Present and the Past in the English Industrial Revolution 1880–1980." *Past and Present* 103 (1984): 131–72.

Carlyle, Thomas. "Chartism." 1839. *Critical and Miscellaneous Essays.* 5 vols. New York: AMS Press, 1969. 4: 118–204.

———. *Latter-Day Pamphlets.* 1850. *A Carlyle Reader: Selections from the Writings of Thomas Carlyle.* Ed. G. B. Tennyson. London: Cambridge UP, 1984. 420–59.

———. *Letters of Thomas Carlyle to John Stuart Mill, John Sterling, and Robert Browning.* Ed. Alexander Carlyle. 1923. New York: Haskell House Publishers, 1970.

———. "The Nigger Question." 1849. *Critical and Miscellaneous Essays.* 5 vols. New York: AMS Press, 1969. 4: 348–83.

———. *On Heroes, Hero Worship, and the Heroic in History.* 1841. Boston: Houghton Mifflin, 1907.

———. *Past and Present.* 1843. Vol. 10 of *The Centenary Edition of the Works of Thomas Carlyle.* 30 vols. New York: Scribner's, n.d.

Chandler, Alice. *A Dream of Order: The Medieval Ideal in Nineteenth-Century Literature.* Lincoln: U of Nebraska P, 1970.

"The Charter and the Land." 1847. *The Literature of Struggle: An Anthology of Chartist Fiction.* Ed. Ian Haywood. Aldershot: Scolar Press, 1995. 191–94.

*Chartist Circular.* 1839–42. New York: Greenwood Reprint Co., 1968.

Chase, Malcolm, and Christopher Shaw. "The Dimensions of Nostalgia."

*The Imagined Past: History and Nostalgia.* Ed. Malcolm Chase and Christopher Shaw. Manchester: Manchester UP, 1989. 1–17.

Clark, Anna. *The Struggle for the Breeches: Gender and the Making of the British Working Classes.* Berkeley: U of California P, 1995.

Clarke, Norma. *Ambitious Heights: Writing, Friendship, Love — The Jewsbury Sisters, Felicia Hemans, and Jane Welsh Carlyle.* New York: Routledge, 1990.

———. "Strenuous Idleness: Thomas Carlyle and the Man of Letters as Hero." *Manful Assertions: Masculinities in Britain since 1800.* Ed. Michael Roper and John Tosh. New York: Routledge, 1991. 25–43.

Cole, G. D. H. *Chartist Portraits.* London: Macmillan, 1965.

Cooper, Thomas. *Wise Saws and Modern Instances.* 2 vols. London, 1845.

Cross, Nigel. *The Common Writer: Life in Nineteenth-Century Grub Street.* Cambridge: Cambridge UP, 1985.

Cunningham, Valentine. *Everywhere Spoken Against: Dissent in the Victorian Novel.* Oxford: Clarendon, 1975.

Culler, A. Dwight. *The Victorian Mirror of History.* New Haven: Yale UP, 1985.

Davidoff, Leonore. "Class and Gender in Victorian England: The Diaries of Arthur J. Munby and Hannah Cullwick." *Feminist Studies* 5 (1979): 89–141.

Davidoff, Leonore, and Catherine Hall. *Family Fortunes: Men and Women of the English Middle Classes, 1780–1850.* Chicago: U of Chicago P, 1987.

Davis, Deanna. "Feminist Critics and Literary Mothers: Daughters Reading Elizabeth Gaskell." *Signs* 17 (1992): 507–32.

Dickens, Charles. *American Notes.* Greenwich, Conn.: Fawcett, 1961.

———. *Hard Times.* 1855. New York: New American Library, 1961.

———. *The Letters of Charles Dickens.* Vol. 7. Ed. Graham Storey et al. Oxford: Clarendon, 1993.

———. *Old Lamps for New Ones.* Vol. 35 of *The Gadshill Edition of the Works of Charles Dickens.* London: Chapman and Hall, 1908.

———. "On an Amateur Beat." *The Uncommercial Traveller and Reprinted Pieces.* New York: Oxford UP, 1958. 345–52.

Disraeli, Benjamin. *Coningsby.* 1844. Ed. Sheila Smith. New York: Oxford UP, 1981.

———. *Sybil.* 1845. Ed. Sheila Smith. New York: Oxford UP, 1982.

Eagleton, Terry. *The Function of Criticism: From "The Spectator" to Post-Structuralism.* London: Verso, 1984.

————. *Myths of Power: A Marxist Study of the Brontës.* London: Macmillan, 1975.

Eliot, George. *Felix Holt, the Radical.* 1866. Ed. Fred Thomson. Oxford: Clarendon, 1980.

————. "The Natural History of German Life: Riehl." *Prose by Victorian Women.* Ed. Andrea Broomfield and Sally Mitchell. New York: Garland, 1996. 173–206.

————. "Thomas Carlyle." *Essays of George Eliot.* Ed. Thomas Pinney. New York: Columbia UP, 1963. 212–15.

Engels, Frederick. *The Condition of the Working Class in England.* London: Panther Books, 1969.

*The Factory Lad; or, The Life of Simon Smike; Exemplifying the Horrors of White Slavery.* London, 1839.

Feurer, Rosemary. "The Meaning of 'Sisterhood': The British Women's Movement and Protective Labor Legislation, 1870–1900." *Victorian Studies* 31 (1988): 233–60.

Fisher, Philip. "Pins, A Table, Works of Art." *Representations* 1 (1983): 43–84.

Forrester, Fanny. "Strangers in the City." *Ben Brierley's Journal.* March 1870: 42; April 1870: 58–59; May 1870: 66.

————. "The Lowly Bard." 1873. *The Poorhouse Fugitives.* Ed. Brian Maidment. Manchester: Carcanet, 1987. 156–58.

Forster, John. "An Unsigned Review of *Mary Barton.*" *Elizabeth Gaskell: The Critical Heritage.* Ed. Angus Easson. London: Routledge, 1991. 67–70.

Foster, John. *Class Struggle and the Industrial Revolution: Early Industrial Capitalism in Three English Towns.* London: Weidenfeld and Nicolson, 1974.

Fox, Pamela. *Class Fictions: Shame and Resistance in the British Working-Class Novel.* Durham: Duke UP, 1994.

Freedgood, Elaine. "Banishing Panic: Harriet Martineau and the Popularization of Political Economy." *Victorian Studies* 39 (1995): 33–53.

Fryckstedt, Monica Correa. "Charlotte Elizabeth Tonna and *The Christian Lady's Magazine.*" *Victorian Periodicals Review* 14 (1981): 42–50.

Frye, Northrop. *Anatomy of Criticism: Four Essays.* Princeton: Princeton UP, 1957.

Gallagher, Catherine. "The Body versus the Social Body in the Works of Thomas Malthus and Henry Mayhew." *The Making of the Modern Body: Sexuality and Society in the Nineteenth Century.* Ed. Catherine

Gallagher and Thomas Laqueur. Berkeley: U of California P, 1987. 83–106.

———. *The Industrial Reformation of English Fiction: Social Discourse and Narrative Form, 1832–1867.* Chicago: U of Chicago P, 1985.

Gaskell, Elizabeth. *The Letters of Mrs. Gaskell.* Ed. J. A. V. Chapple and Arthur Pollard. Manchester: Manchester UP, 1966.

———. *Mary Barton.* 1848. Ed. Edgar Wright. New York: Oxford UP, 1987.

———. *North and South.* 1855. Ed. Dorothy Collin. New York: Penguin, 1970.

Gaskell, Peter. *Artisans and Machinery: The Moral and Physical Condition of the Manufacturing Population.* London, 1836.

Gilbert, Sandra M., and Susan Gubar. *The Madwoman in the Attic: The Woman Writer and the Nineteenth-Century Literary Imagination.* New Haven: Yale UP, 1979.

Girouard, Mark. *The Return to Camelot: Chivalry and the English Gentleman.* New Haven: Yale UP, 1981.

Gray, Robert. "The Languages of Factory Reform in Britain." *The Historical Meanings of Work.* Ed. Patrick Joyce. Cambridge: Cambridge UP, 1987. 143–79.

Hamilton, Roberta. *The Liberation of Women: A Study of Patriarchy and Capitalism.* London: George Allen and Unwin, 1978.

Handwerk, Gary. "Behind *Sybil*'s Veil: Disraeli's Mix of Ideological Messages." *Modern Language Quarterly* 49 (1988): 321–41.

Harman, Barbara Leah. "In Promiscuous Company: Female Public Appearance in Elizabeth Gaskell's *North and South.*" *Victorian Studies* 31 (1988): 351–74.

Harsh, Constance. *Subversive Heroines: Feminist Resolutions of Social Crisis in the Condition-of-England Novel.* Ann Arbor: U of Michigan P, 1994.

Hartley, John. "Persevere." *Yorkshire Ditties.* London, 1868. 69–70.

Hartmann, Heidi. "Capitalism, Patriarchy, and Job Segregation by Sex." *Signs* 1 (1976): 137–69.

———. "The Unhappy Marriage of Marxism and Feminism: Towards a More Progressive Union." *Women and Revolution: A Discussion of the Unhappy Marriage of Marxism and Feminism.* Ed. Lydia Sargent. Boston: South End Press, 1981. 1–41.

Hartsock, Nancy. *Money, Sex, and Power: Toward a Feminist Historical Materialism.* Boston: Northeastern UP, 1983.

Haywood, Ian, ed. *The Literature of Struggle: An Anthology of Chartist Fiction.* Aldershot: Scolar Press, 1995.

Heineman, Helen. *Mrs. Trollope: The Triumphant Feminine in the Nineteenth Century.* Athens, Ohio: Ohio UP, 1979.

Hewison, Robert. *The Heritage Industry: Britain in a Climate of Decline.* London: Methuen, 1987.

Hiley, Michael. *Victorian Working Women: Portraits from Life.* Boston: David R. Godine, 1979.

Hobsbawm, Eric. *Industry and Empire: From 1750 to the Present Day.* Harmondsworth: Penguin, 1969.

Hollingworth, Brian, ed. *Songs of the People: Lancashire Dialect Poetry of the Industrial Revolution.* Manchester: Manchester UP, 1977.

Hood, Thomas. "The Song of the Shirt." *The Poetical Works of Thomas Hood.* 5 vols. Boston, 1856. 1: 193–96.

Houghton, Walter. *The Victorian Frame of Mind.* New Haven: Yale UP, 1957.

Humphries, Jane. "Class Struggle and the Persistence of the Working-Class Family." *Cambridge Journal of Economics* 1 (1977): 241–58.

Jameson, Anna. *The Communion of Labour.* London, 1856.

Jameson, Fredric. *The Political Unconscious: Narrative as a Socially Symbolic Act.* Ithaca: Cornell UP, 1981.

Janowitz, Anne. "Class and Literature: The Case of Romantic Chartism." *Rethinking Class: Literary Studies and Social Formations.* Ed. Wai Chee Dimock and Michael T. Gilmore. New York: Columbia UP, 1994. 239–66.

Jessop, Bob, et al. *Thatcherism: A Tale of Two Nations.* Cambridge: Polity Press, 1989.

Jewsbury, Geraldine. "Civilisation of 'The Lower Orders.' " *Douglas Jerrold's Shilling Magazine* 6 (1847): 443–52.

———. *Marian Withers.* 3 vols. London, 1851.

Johnston, Ellen. *Autobiography, Poems and Songs of Ellen Johnston, the 'Factory Girl.'* Glasgow, 1867.

Jones, Ernest. "The Factory Town." *An Anthology of Chartist Poetry.* Ed. Peter Scheckner. Rutherford, N.J.: Fairleigh Dickinson UP, 1989. 175–79.

———. *Women's Wrongs.* Vol. 2 of *Notes to the People.* Ed. Ernest Jones. 2 vols. 1852. London: Merlin Press, 1967.

Jones, Gareth Stedman. *The Languages of Class: Studies in English Working-Class History, 1832–1982.* Cambridge: Cambridge UP, 1983.

Joyce, Patrick. *Democratic Subjects: The Self and the Social in Nineteenth-Century England.* Cambridge: Cambridge UP, 1994.

————. *Visions of the People: Industrial England and the Question of Class, 1848–1914.* Cambridge: Cambridge UP, 1991.

————. *Work, Society, and Politics: The Culture of the Factory in Later Victorian England.* Brighton: Harvester Press, 1980.

Kaplan, Deborah. "The Woman Worker in Charlotte Elizabeth Tonna's Fiction." *Mosaic* 18 (1985): 51–63.

Kay-Shuttleworth, James Phillip. *The Moral and Physical Condition of the Working Classes Employed in the Cotton Manufacture in Manchester.* London, 1832.

Kearns, Katherine. "A Tropology of Realism in *Hard Times.*" *ELH* 59 (1992): 857–81.

Kelly, Joan. *Women, History, and Theory: The Essays of Joan Kelly.* Chicago: U of Chicago P, 1984.

Kestner, Joseph. *Protest and Reform: The British Social Narrative by Women, 1827–1867.* Madison: U of Wisconsin P, 1985.

Kilgour, Maggie. *From Communion to Cannibalism: An Anatomy of Metaphors of Incorporation.* Princeton: Princeton UP, 1990.

Kingsley, Charles. *Alton Locke, Tailor and Poet.* 1849. New York: Dutton, 1923.

————. *Yeast: A Problem.* 1848. New York: Macmillan, 1888.

Kirk, Neville. *The Growth of Working-Class Reformism in Mid-Victorian England.* Urbana: U of Illinois P, 1985.

Klaus, H. Gustav. *The Literature of Labour: Two Hundred Years of Working-Class Writing.* Brighton: Harvester Press, 1985.

Kovačević, Ivanka, and S. Barbara Kanner. "Bluebook into Novel: The Forgotten Industrial Fiction of Charlotte Elizabeth Tonna." *Nineteenth-Century Fiction* 25 (1970): 152–73.

Landry, Donna. *The Muses of Resistance: Laboring-Class Women's Poetry in Britain, 1739–1796.* Cambridge: Cambridge UP, 1990.

Langland, Elizabeth. *Nobody's Angels: Middle-Class Women and Domestic Ideology in Victorian Culture.* Ithaca: Cornell UP, 1995.

Lansbury, Coral. *Elizabeth Gaskell, the Novel of Social Crisis.* New York: Barnes and Noble, 1975.

Laqueur, Thomas. "Sexual Desire and the Market Economy during the Industrial Revolution." *Discourses of Sexuality: From Aristotle to AIDS.* Ed. Domna Stanton. Ann Arbor: U of Michigan P, 1992. 185–215.

Laslett, Peter. *The World We Have Lost.* London: Methuen, 1965.

Laycock, Samuel. "Uncle Dick's Advoice to Wed Women." *The Collected Writings of Samuel Laycock.* Oldham: W. E. Clegg, 1900. 98–100.

"Leeds Factory Women's *Soiree.*" *The People's Journal* 3 (1847): 39–40 (appendix).

Levine, Philippa. *Feminist Lives in Victorian England: Private Roles and Public Commitment.* Oxford: Basil Blackwell, 1990.

Lewis, Jane. *Women in England, 1870–1950: Sexual Divisions and Social Change.* Bloomington: Indiana UP, 1984.

Liddington, Jill, and Jill Norris. *One Hand Tied behind Us: The Rise of the Women's Suffrage Movement.* London: Virago, 1978.

Linton, W. J. "Bob Thin, the Poorhouse Fugitive." 1845. *The Poorhouse Fugitives.* Ed. Brian Maidment. Manchester: Carcanet, 1987. 73–84.

Loeb, Lori Anne. *Consuming Angels: Advertising and Victorian Women.* New York: Oxford UP, 1994.

Lown, Judy. "Not So Much a Factory, More a Form of Patriarchy: Gender and Class during Industrialisation." *Gender, Class, and Work.* Ed. Eva Gamarnikow et al. London: Heinemann, 1983. 23–45.

———. *Women and Industrialization: Gender at Work in Nineteenth-Century England.* Minneapolis: U of Minnesota P, 1990.

Lucas, John. *The Literature of Change: Studies in the Nineteenth-Century Provincial Novel.* New York: Barnes and Noble, 1977.

———. "Mrs. Gaskell and Brotherhood." *Tradition and Tolerance in Nineteenth-Century Fiction.* Ed. David Howard, John Lucas, and John Goode. London: Routledge and Kegan Paul, 1966. 141–205.

Maconachie, Moira. "Women's Work and Domesticity in the *English Women's Journal.*" *Studies in the History of Feminism.* Ed. Sally Alexander. London: U of London Dept. of Extramural Studies, 1984.

Maidment, Brian. "Essayists and Artizans: The Making of Nineteenth-Century Self-Taught Poets." *Literature and History* 9 (1983): 74–91.

———. *The Poorhouse Fugitives: Self-Taught Poets and Poetry in Victorian Britain.* Manchester: Carcanet, 1987.

———. "Prose and Artisan Discourse in Early Victorian Britain." *Prose Studies* 10 (1987): 30–41.

Manners, Lord John. *A Plea for National Holy-Days.* London, 1843.

Marcus, Steven. "*Culture and Anarchy* Today." *Culture and Anarchy.* Ed. Samuel Lipton. New Haven: Yale UP, 1994. 165–85.

———. *Engels, Manchester, and the Working Class.* New York: Norton, 1974.

Marie. "The Indomitable Will." *The People's and Howitt's Journal* 4 (1851): 63.

————. "Labour." 1850. *The Poorhouse Fugitives.* Ed. Brian Maidment. Manchester: Carcanet, 1987. 221–23.

Martin, Carol. "Gaskell, Darwin, and *North and South.*" *Studies in the Novel* 15 (1983): 91–107.

Martineau, Harriet. *Illustrations of Political Economy.* London, 1834. 9 vols.

————. "A Manchester Strike." *Fact into Fiction: English Literature and the Industrial Scene, 1750–1850.* Ed. Ivanka Kovačević. Leicester: Leicester UP, 1975. 225–301.

Marx, Karl. *Capital. Vol. 1.* Trans. Ben Fowkes. New York: Vintage, 1977.

Marx, Karl, and Frederick Engels. *The Communist Manifesto.* Trans. Paul Sweezy. New York: Modern Reader Paperback, 1968.

Mason, Michael. *The Making of Victorian Sexuality.* New York: Oxford UP, 1994.

Massey, Gerald. "Eighteen Hundred and Forty-Eight." *The Poetical Works of Gerald Massey.* London, 1861. 315–18.

————. "Our Land." 1850. *An Anthology of Chartist Poetry.* Ed. Peter Scheckner. Rutherford, N.J.: Fairleigh Dickinson UP, 1989. 274–75.

McClelland, Keith. "Some Thoughts on Masculinity and the 'Representative Artisan' in Britain, 1850–1880." *Manful Assertions: Masculinities in Britain since 1800.* Ed. Michael Roper and John Tosh. New York: Routledge, 1991. 74–91.

Merryweather, Mary. *Experience of Factory Life.* London, 1862.

Miller, J. Hillis. *The Disappearance of God: Five Nineteenth-Century Writers.* Cambridge: Harvard UP, 1975.

Moers, Ellen. *Literary Women.* New York: Doubleday, 1976.

Moglen, Helene. *Charlotte Brontë: The Self Conceived.* New York: Norton, 1976.

Morris, William. *News from Nowhere.* 1891. Ed. James Redmond. London: Routledge and Kegan Paul, 1970.

Mort, Frank. *Dangerous Sexualities: Medico-Moral Politics in England since 1830.* London: Routledge, 1987.

M'Owen, J. "Father! Who Are the Chartists?" *An Anthology of Chartist Poetry.* Ed. Peter Scheckner. Rutherford, N.J.: Fairleigh Dickinson UP, 1989. 292–93.

Mozley, Herbert N. "The Property Disabilities of a Married Woman, and Other Legal Effects of Marriage." *Woman's Work and Woman's Culture.* Ed. Josephine Butler. London, 1869. 186–237.

Nestor, Pauline. *Female Friendships and Communities: Charlotte Brontë, George Eliot, and Elizabeth Gaskell.* Oxford: Clarendon, 1985.

Nightingale, Florence. "Cassandra." *The Cause: A Short History of the Women's*

*Movement in Great Britain.* 1928. By Ray Strachey. London: Virago, 1979. 395–418.

O'Kell, Robert. "Two Nations, or One? Disraeli's Allegorical Romance." *Victorian Studies* 30 (1987): 211–34.

Osterund, Nancy Grey. "Gender Divisions and the Organization of Work in the Leicester Hosiery Industry." *Unequal Opportunities: Women's Employment in England, 1800–1918.* Ed. Angela John. Oxford: Blackwood, 1986. 45–68.

Parrinder, Patrick. *Authors and Authority: A Study of English Literary Criticism and Its Relation to Culture, 1750–1900.* London: Routledge and Kegan Paul, 1977.

Perkin, Harold. *The Origins of Modern English Society, 1780–1880.* London: Routledge and Kegan Paul, 1969.

Pichanick, Valerie Kossew. *Harriet Martineau: The Woman and Her Work, 1802–1876.* Ann Arbor: U of Michigan P, 1980.

Pinchbeck, Ivy. *Women Workers and the Industrial Revolution.* 1930. London: Virago, 1981.

*The Pioneer; or, Grand National Consolidated Trades' Union Magazine.* 1833–34. New York: Greenwood Reprint Co., 1968.

Poovey, Mary. *Making a Social Body: British Cultural Formation, 1830–1864.* Chicago: U of Chicago P, 1995.

———. *Uneven Developments: The Ideological Work of Gender in Mid-Victorian Britain.* Chicago: U of Chicago Press, 1988.

*A Report of the Important Proceedings of a Public Meeting Held in the Chapel, Union Street, Oldham.* Oldham, 1836.

Richards, Jeffrey. "Victorian Values Revisited." *Encounter* 68 (March 1987): 73–76.

Roberts, David. *Paternalism in Early Victorian England.* London: Croom Helm, 1979.

Roberts, Elizabeth. *A Woman's Place: An Oral History of Working-Class Women, 1890–1940.* Oxford: Basil Blackwood, 1984.

Roberts, Robert. *The Classic Slum: Salford Life in the First Quarter of the Century.* 1971. Harmondsworth: Penguin, 1988.

Rose, Sonya O. *Limited Livelihoods: Gender and Class in Nineteenth-Century England.* Berkeley: U of California P, 1992.

Rosenberg, John. *Carlyle and the Burden of History.* Cambridge: Harvard UP, 1985.

Rule, John. *The Labouring Classes in Early Industrial England, 1750–1850.* London: Longman, 1986.

Ruskin, John. "The Nature of Gothic." 1853. *Unto This Last and Other*

*Writings.* Ed. Clive Wilmer. Harmondsworth: Penguin, 1985. 75–109.

———. *Sesame and Lilies.* 1865. New York: Dutton, 1960.

Sargent, Lydia, ed. *Women and Revolution: A Discussion of the Unhappy Marriage of Marxism and Feminism.* Boston: South End Press, 1981.

Scarry, Elaine. *The Body in Pain: The Making and Unmaking of the World.* New York: Oxford UP, 1985.

Scheckner, Peter, ed. *An Anthology of Chartist Poetry: Poetry of the British Working Class, 1830s–1850s.* Rutherford, N.J.: Fairleigh Dickinson UP, 1989.

Schivelbusch, Wolfgang. *Disenchanted Night: The Industrialization of Light.* Trans. Angela Davies. Berkeley: U of California P, 1988.

Schor, Hilary. "Elizabeth Gaskell: A Critical History and a Critical Revision." *Dickens Studies Annual* 19 (1990): 345–69.

———. *Scheherezade in the Marketplace: Elizabeth Gaskell and the Victorian Novel.* New York: Oxford UP, 1992.

Scott, Joan Wallach. *Gender and the Politics of History.* New York: Columbia UP, 1988.

Shanley, Mary Lyndon. *Feminism, Marriage, and the Law in Victorian England, 1850–1895.* Princeton: Princeton UP, 1989.

Smith, F. B. *Radical Artisan: William James Linton, 1812–1897.* Manchester: Manchester UP, 1973.

Smith, Sheila. Introduction. *Coningsby.* By Benjamin Disraeli. New York: Oxford UP, 1981. vii–xxii.

"Social Effects of Peasant Proprietorship." *The Northern Star.* 14 April 1849: 3.

Southey, Robert. "The Manufacturing System." *Selected Prose of Robert Southey.* Ed. Jacob Zeitlin. New York: Macmillan, 1916. 416–23.

Spear, Jeffrey. *Dreams of an English Eden: Ruskin and His Tradition in Social Criticism.* New York: Columbia UP, 1984.

Spector, Stephen. "Monsters of Metonymy: *Hard Times* and Knowing the Working Class." *Charles Dickens.* Ed. Harold Bloom. New York: Chelsea House, 1987. 229–44.

Spivak, Gayatri Chakravorty. "Three Women's Texts and a Critique of Imperialism." *Critical Inquiry* 12 (1985): 243–61.

Stansky, Peter. *Redesigning the World: William Morris, the 1880s, and the Arts and Crafts.* Princeton: Princeton UP, 1985.

Stevenson, Catherine Barnes. " 'What Must Not Be Said': *North and South* and the Problem of Women's Work." *Victorian Literature and Culture* 19 (1990): 67–84.

Stockton, Kathryn Bond. "Bodies and God: Poststructuralist Feminists Return to the Fold of Spiritual Materialism." *Boundary 2* 19 (1992): 113–49.

Stone, Elizabeth. *William Langshawe, the Cotton Lord.* 2 vols. London, 1842.

Stoneman, Patsy. *Elizabeth Gaskell.* Bloomington: Indiana UP, 1987.

Sussman, Herbert. *Victorians and the Machine: The Literary Response to Technology.* Cambridge: Harvard UP, 1968.

Swindells, Julia. *Victorian Writing and Working Women: The Other Side of Silence.* Minneapolis: U of Minnesota P, 1985.

Taylor, Barbara. *Eve and the New Jerusalem: Socialism and Feminism in the Nineteenth Century.* London: Virago, 1983.

*The Ten Hours' Factory Question: A Report Addressed to the Short Time Committees of the West Riding of Yorkshire.* London, 1842.

"The Ten Hours' Question." *The Democratic Review of British and Foreign Politics, History, and Literature* 1 (1850): 373–74.

Terdiman, Richard. *Present Past: Modernity and the Memory Crisis.* Ithaca: Cornell UP, 1993.

Tholfsen, Trygve. *Working Class Radicalism in Mid-Victorian England.* London: Croom Helm, 1976.

Thom, William. *Rhymes and Recollections of a Handloom Weaver.* London, 1847.

Thomas, Janet. "Women and Capitalism: Oppression or Emancipation?" *Comparative Studies in Society and History* 30 (1988): 534–49.

Thompson, Dorothy. *The Chartists.* New York: Pantheon, 1985.

Thompson, E. P. *The Making of the English Working Class.* New York: Viking, 1966.

Thompson, F. M. L. *The Rise of Respectable Society: A Social History of Victorian Britain, 1830–1900.* Cambridge: Harvard UP, 1988.

Tilly, Louise, and Joan W. Scott. *Women, Work, and Family.* New York: Holt Rinehart and Winston, 1978.

Tonna, Charlotte Elizabeth. *Helen Fleetwood.* 1841. Vol. 1 of *The Works of Charlotte Elizabeth.* 2 vols. New York, 1847.

———. *The Perils of the Nation: An Appeal to the Legislature, the Clergy, and the High and Middle Classes.* London, 1843.

———. *The Wrongs of Women.* 1843. Vol. 2 of *The Works of Charlotte Elizabeth.* 2 vols. New York, 1847.

Trollope, Frances. *The Adventures of Michael Armstrong, the Factory Boy.* 1840. London, 1888.

Uglow, Jenny. *Elizabeth Gaskell: A Habit of Stories.* London: Faber and Faber, 1993.

United Kingdom. *Hansard Parliamentary Debates.* 3d ser. 73 (1844).

Valenze, Deborah. *The First Industrial Woman.* New York: Oxford, 1995.

Valverde, Mariana. "The Love of Finery: Fashion and the Fallen Woman in Nineteenth-Century Social Discourse." *Victorian Studies* 32 (1989): 169–88.

Vanden Bossche, Christopher. *Carlyle and the Search for Authority.* Columbus: Ohio State UP, 1991.

Vicinus, Martha. *The Ambiguities of Self-Help: Concerning the Life and Works of the Lancashire Dialect Writer, Edwin Waugh.* Littleborough, Eng.: George Kelsall, 1984.

———. "Chartist Fiction and the Development of a Class-Based Literature." *The Socialist Novel in Britain: Towards the Recovery of a Tradition.* Ed. H. Gustav Klaus. New York: St. Martins Press, 1982. 7–25.

———. *The Industrial Muse: A Study of Nineteenth-Century British Working-Class Literature.* New York: Barnes and Noble, 1974.

Vincent, David. *Bread, Knowledge, and Freedom: A Study of Nineteenth-Century Working Class Autobiography.* London: Methuen, 1981.

Waugh, Edwin. "Come Whoam to thi Childer an' Me." *Songs of the People.* Ed. Brian Hollingworth. Manchester: Manchester UP, 1977. 64–65.

———. "Dinner Time." *Songs of the People.* Ed. Brian Hollingworth. Manchester: Manchester UP, 1977. 68–69.

———. "Down Again!" *Songs of the People.* Ed. Brian Hollingworth. Manchester: Manchester UP, 1977. 70–71.

———. "Toothsome Advice." *Poems and Songs.* Ed. George Milner. Manchester, 1893. 135–37.

Walkowitz, Judith. *City of Dreadful Delight: Narratives of Sexual Danger in Late-Victorian London.* Chicago: U of Chicago P, 1992.

———. *Prostitution and Victorian Society: Women, Class, and the State.* New York: Cambridge UP, 1980.

Webb, Igor. *From Custom to Capital: The English Novel and the Industrial Revolution.* Ithaca: Cornell UP, 1981.

Webb, R. K. *Harriet Martineau, a Radical Victorian.* London: Heinemann, 1960.

Weeks, Jeffrey. *Sex, Politics, and Society: The Regulation of Sexuality since 1800.* London: Longman, 1981.

Wheeler, Thomas. *Sunshine and Shadows: A Tale of the Nineteenth Century. The Northern Star.* 1849–50.

White, Hayden. *Tropics of Discourse: Essays in Cultural Criticism.* Baltimore: Johns Hopkins UP, 1978.

Wiener, Martin J. *English Culture and the Decline of the Industrial Spirit: 1850–1980.* Harmondsworth: Penguin, 1985.

Williams, Raymond. *The Country and the City.* New York: Oxford UP, 1973.

———. *Culture and Society, 1780–1950.* London: Chatto and Windus, 1958.

———. *Keywords: A Vocabulary of Culture and Society.* New York: Oxford UP, 1976.

Winch, Donald. *Malthus.* New York: Oxford UP, 1987.

Wise, T. J., and J. A. Symington. *The Brontës: Their Lives, Friendships and Correspondences.* 1933. 4 vols. Philadelphia: Porcupine Press, 1980.

Woolf, Virginia. *A Room of One's Own.* New York: Harcourt Brace Jovanovich, 1957.

Wright, Patrick. *On Living in an Old Country: The National Past in Contemporary Britain.* London: Verso, 1985.

Yeazell, Ruth Bernard. "Why Political Novels Have Heroines: *Sybil, Mary Barton,* and *Felix Holt.*" *Novel* 15 (1985): 126–44.

Zlotnick, Susan. "Lowly Bards and Incomplete Lyres: Fanny Forrester and the Construction of a Working-Class Woman's Poetic Identity." Forthcoming in *Victorian Poetry.*

# INDEX

antimodernism, 60–61, 171, 176, 273n. 2; in nineteenth century, 2, 14, 234; in twentieth century, 2–4, 278n. 23, 297n. 9

Arnold, Matthew, 2, 4, 7, 19, 56–61, 63, 169; on class, 58–59, 277n. 22; and culture, 22, 23, 44, 57–58; *Culture and Anarchy*, 14, 23, 58–59, 60, 96, 224, 225; "The Function of Criticism at the Present Time," 19; and Middle Ages, 56–57; "Modern Element in Literature," 57; and revolutions of 1848, 48; "Stanzas from the Grande Chartreuse," 56–57, 59–60

Arnold, Thomas, 14–15, 48

Ashley, Lord Anthony (later 7th Earl of Shaftsbury): and factory reform literature, 124, 133, 141, 142, 159, 160, 161, 162, 231; on women workers, 17–18, 19, 41, 63, 118, 120, 153, 288n. 12, 290n. 21. *See also* factory reform

Bamford, Samuel, "Farewell to My Cottage," 179–80, 292n. 13

Bell, Lady Florence, *At the Works,* 205

*Ben Brierley's Journal,* 174, 211, 214, 215, 291n. 7, 294n. 23

Bentham, Jeremy, 154

Berman, Marshall, 60–61

Bodenheimer, Rosemarie, 6, 137, 273n. 4, 277n. 21, 279n. 4, 289n. 18, 295nn. 2, 3

Brierley, Ben, 215; "The Cotters of Mossburn," 196–97; "A Strike Adventure," 195–96

Brontë, Charlotte, 2, 4, 8, 62–75, 122, 124, 223, 283n. 21; and causality, 70–72; and domestic ideology, 72–74, 163–64, 232; on factory women, 9, 63, 65, 117–18, 124–25, 168, 230; and feminism, 62–68, 163, 230–31, 273n. 3, 278n. 1; Gaskell's opinion of, 106; *Jane Eyre,* 67–68, 87, 117; materialism of, 67–70, 138–39 ; and money, 63–64; *Shirley,* 66–75, 87–99; on unemployment, 8–9, 67–70,

Library of Congress Cataloging-in-Publication Data

Zlotnick, Susan
    Women, writing, and the industrial revolution / Susan Zlotnick.
    p.   cm.
    Includes bibliographical references and index.
    ISBN 0-8018-5829-1
        1. English literature—Women authors—History and criticism.    2. Industrial
revolution in literature.    3. Women and literature—Great Britain—History—18th
century.    4. Women and literature—Great Britain—History—19th century.
5. English literature—18th century—History and criticism.    6. English literature—19th century—History and criticism.    7. Literature and technology—Great
Britain—History.    8. Industrial revolution—Great Britain—History.    9. Industrial revolution—Literary collections.    10. Industries—Literary collections.
I. Title.
    PR448.I54Z57    1998
    820'.9'9287—dc21        97-49985        CIP